DECODING WOMEN'S MAGAZINES

Decoding Women's Magazines

From *Mademoiselle* to *Ms.*

Ellen McCracken

Associate Professor of Comparative Literature
University of Massachusetts, Amherst, USA

First published 1993 by
THE MACMILLAN PRESS LTD
Houndmills, Basingstoke, Hampshire RG21 2XS
and London
Companies and representatives
throughout the world

ISBN 0–333–53589–8 hardcover
ISBN 0–333–53590–1 paperback

A catalogue record for this book is available
from the British Library.

Printed in Hong Kong

For my parents, Clare and William McCracken, whose generosity, support and encouragement are boundless

Contents

List of Illustrations

Acknowledgements

I wish to thank the National Endowment for the Humanities, under the Directorship of Joseph Duffey, for a year-long fellowship that enabled me to begin this study. I am grateful as well to the University of Massachusetts, Amherst, for granting me a sabbatical leave for the project.

Jean Franco, Gaye Tuchman, and Herbert Schiller offered important support for this study in its early stages. The staff and researchers at the Instituto Latinoamericano de Estudios Transnacionales (ILET) in Mexico City generously allowed me to research in their excellent library; Noreene Janus and Viviana Erazo discussed crucial aspects of the project with me during my stay at ILET.

I very much appreciate the encouragement of family and friends, especially Daphne Patai whose careful critical reading of the chapters and insightful discussion of the issues are an essential component of the book. Mario García's continued support, encouragement, and intellectual interchange were invaluable in completing this project.

Agradezco especialmente a Lucía Troncoso por haber cuidado a mis niños con tanto amor y cariño mientras yo escribía este libro. Giuliana and Giancarlo deserve special thanks for enduring my long absences while I wrote this book.

I wish to thank Belinda Holdsworth of Macmillan for her enthusiastic support for this project and Anne Rafique for copyediting the typescript. Carol Dobson of Bloomington and Lilla Burgess of Santa Barbara spent long hours wordprocessing the chapters with extreme care and professionalism.

A vital component of the ideas put forth in this book are the photographic reproductions of advertisements and magazine covers that appear here. Because a number of corporations refused to grant permission for their images to be reprinted, I am especially grateful to those that cooperated in this regard, thereby facilitating the free flow of information and interchange of ideas. The following have kindly given permission to reprint the covers and ads listed below:

Harper's Bazaar and the Hearst Corporation, January 1981 front cover; *Town & Country* and the Hearst Corporation, December 1981 front cover, Joel Baldwin, photographer;

Working Woman and Hal Publications, Inc., June 1981 front cover; *Savvy* and Family Media Inc., February 1981 front cover; Armstrong World Industries, ads for Solarian Supreme and Tiffany flooring; Lee Pharmaceuticals, ad for Zip Wax depilatory; Yungjohann Hillman Inc., ad for Mombasa mosquito netting; Revlon, Inc., ad for European Collagen Complex; Christian Dior Perfumes Inc., ad for Teint Dior; New Retail Concepts, two ads for Candie's footwear; Sara Lee Hosiery, two ads for Hanes hosiery; Maybelline Inc., ad for Maybelline cosmetics; Weight Watchers Food Company, ad for Weight Watchers Pizza; Alberto Culver USA Inc., ad for TCB hairdressing products; Cosmair Inc., ad for L'Oréal Crème Riche lipstick; The Quaker Oats Company, ad for Aunt Jemima Pancake Mix; Conde Nast Publications, Inc., ad for *Self*; and Quintessence, Inc., ad for Jovan products.

Introduction

Traditionally, critical textual analysis has focused on selected literary works that those trained in the academy have deemed worthy of exegesis. Delineating the special linguistic techniques that writers use to communicate unique perceptions about reality, critical analysis privileges a certain body of texts which has come to be termed high culture. The choices critics have made about the objects they study – justified ideologically as the attention due inherently great works – have frequently excluded from serious analysis the important artifacts of mass culture. In fact, however, the value judgments that privilege elite forms over the more widely consumed ones have constricted the understanding of culture and left vast areas of cultural production unexamined.

In contrast, a number of critics, among them Fredric Jameson and Roland Barthes, have argued in theory and in practice for a relaxing of the traditionally strict barriers between the study of high and mass culture, paralleling the changes in postmodern cultural production. Jameson views the elite and the popular as dialectical elements of a single cultural continuum, as "twin and inseparable forms of the fission of aesthetic production under late capitalism" with a profound structural interrelatedness.[1] Barthes' semiotic method expands the notion of the text to visual as well as verbal communicative systems; the critical tools previously reserved for the study of literature can increase one's understanding of the photographic food displays in a women's magazine, for example, or the verbal captions in a fashion feature.[2] These broader definitions are especially necessary in an age when technological advances and increased opportunities for financial gain through the production of commodified culture have greatly widened the scope and audience of mass culture. Critical techniques refined through years of literary analysis offer models for decoding the familiar, naturalized texts of mass culture.[3]

Magazines addressed to women are one such mass cultural form – a multi-million dollar business which presents pleasurable, value-laden semiotic systems to immense numbers of women. The largest of magazine categories, this group contains nearly fifty titles which compete specifically for women's attention each month. The texts analyzed here are those glossy publications easily available to women on US news-stands, in supermarkets and other retail outlets, or by subscription from 1981 to 1983. They include the widely disseminated women's service magazines, publications directed to employed women, those addressed to minorities, such as *Essence* and *Cosmopolitan en español*, and special-interest publications on such topics as home decorating, fitness, gourmet cooking, wedding preparation, and parenting. With paid circulations as large as eight million and as small as 16,000, and "pass-on" readerships that increase these figures, these magazines reach a broad spectrum of women with messages that conflate desire and consumerism. In most cases, the meaning systems are immensely successful in selling both copies of the magazines and the products advertised inside. Consequently, because of publishers' reluctance to deviate from techniques that have brought financial success and despite the appearance of change and innovation, there is a strong structural continuity in these magazines. Whether part of a large mass audience of magazine readers or a small select one, millions of women are likely to be addressed by these structurally similar messages well into the next century.[4]

Although the consumers of these texts are not passive and frequently may operate as what De Certeau has termed "poaching readers,"[5] this group of magazines functions in many ways as a master narrative which a materialist semiotic analysis will begin to decode here. The ostensibly authoritative grand narrative of reality developed month after month in these texts appears to be a women-centered articulation of the world. Rendering thousands of aspects of everyday life as knowable, controllable entities, women's magazines suggest, much as nineteenth century realist narrative did, that an apparently comprehensive and straightforward detailing of the everyday can capture reality discursively for readers. The smaller narrative segments that build the master tale here – from lessons in saving one's marriage to preparing meals, beautifying the self, and succeeding on the job – offer women multiple pleasures. One frequent technique of this narrative first allows the pleasure of the transgressive and the forbidden, and then attempts to contain these elements by invoking dominant moral values.

While in no sense is a text ever completely "decoded" – made neutral or devoid of codes – this book begins the process of decoding by analyzing the semiotic strategies with which women's magazines attempt to secure discursive closure over signification. Following Stuart Hall's neo-Gramscian model which understands ideology as a site of struggle for discursive power in which communicators try to establish preferred meanings in texts and "common-sense" views of reality,[6] I argue here that a varied yet structurally homogeneous constellation of negative tropes underlies the preferred meanings that women's magazines attempt to fix in order to sell commodities. The multiple mini-narrative segments that begin on the front cover and extend to the ads and features inside combine to foreground a pleasurable, appealing consensus about the feminine. Readers are not force-fed a constellation of negative images that naturalize male dominance; rather, women's magazines exert a cultural leadership to shape consensus in which highly pleasurable codes work to naturalize social relations of power. This ostensibly common agreement about what constitutes the feminine is only achieved through a discursive struggle in which words, photos, and sometimes olfactory signs wage a semiotic battle against the everyday world which, by its mere presence, often fights back as an existential corrective to the magazine's ideal images.

Under the broader schematizations of culture discussed above, the widely communicated messages of women's magazines merit the same care in analysis accorded literary texts. In the chapters that follow, close textual readings of the visual and verbal systems of magazines join an analysis of the infrastructure of the women's magazine industry. The signs an ad employs, for example, relate to such factors as the fiscal health of the magazine, the price of the advertising space, and the product's parent corporation. Textual analysis of editorial features must also delimit their connection to the magazine's paid advertisements, the links between the publishing and editorial divisions of the magazine, and the features' relation to the magazine's fiscal health.

Understanding women's magazines as business enterprises and as cultural texts reveals the crucial role of advertising in shaping the cultural content of these publications. Advertising and editorial material are, on a practical level, inseparable in women's magazines and in one sense refer to a spurious dichotomy. There are, of course, separate divisions in magazine production for ads and editorial features, and ads generate revenue more directly and visibly than do features. Repeatedly, however, one encounters the interconnectedness of the two even when focusing on them separately as occurs in the two main sections of this book. The front cover, for example, whose ostensible content is the editorial material one will find inside, is, in fact, the magazine's most important advertisement. The editorial content of *Ms.* in the 1980s, to cite another example, cannot be divorced from the consumption-based model of women's liberation that underlies its advertising and the publishing philosophy that its founders publicly articulated.

Because of advertising's crucial role in the fiscal survival of these magazines and in the shaping of their cultural content, this study begins with an analysis of the three principal kinds of advertisements in women's magazines: first, the front cover – the label or packaging without which readers might not be enticed to see the other ads inside; second, covert advertisements – the promotions of products, disguised as editorial material or hidden in some other form so that they appear to be non-advertising material; and third, purchased advertisements which occupy the majority of most magazine's pages, earning immense revenues for publishers.[7] Together the three forms constitute a complex structural whole whose primary message – that women should buy certain products – is encoded with numerous subtexts or secondary meaning systems that frequently induce insecurities while simultaneously creating pleasure. Understood as this tripartite system, advertising occupies up to 95 per cent of the space in some women's magazines, earning these publications the more appropriate title, "women's advertising magazines."[8]

The key role of women as the primary purchasers of goods and services in the consumer society is the material explanation for the continued existence of this genre of mass culture. Especially in the areas of food and cosmetics – the two largest advertising categories in women's magazines – but also in numerous other areas of consumer goods, women continue to be responsible for the time-consuming, repetitive task of shopping for themselves and others, even as less time is available to many of them because of employment outside the home. Magazines foster a reifying image of woman as shopper in order to attract advertisers. The publishers of *Seventeen*, for example, boast that the magazine's young teenage readers are "Born to Shop"; the reader of *Modern Bride* is, according to the magazine's promotional slogan, "determined to *spend* the rest of her life"; and *Parents*' publicity argues that its reader is "very special because she buys more for her family and herself."[9]

Although this study focuses on a critical decoding of magazine texts, the nature of women's continued attraction to this mass cultural form must be discussed at the outset. The interdependent cycle of magazine profit, advertising, and women's role as purchasers would, of course, break down were women not immensely attracted by the verbal and visual messages of magazines. How do these texts generate pleasure?

Critics have developed a number of theories about why mass culture attracts people. Michele Mattelart has suggested that the culture industry continually re-stimulates certain unconscious deep structures in audiences, thereby helping people to reinvest alienated psychic patterns. Key to the attractive powers of mass culture, she suggests, is its ability to join the real and the imaginary so that the boundary between the two becomes progressively vaguer. Fredric Jameson argues that there is a process of compensatory exchange at work in mass culture, whereby people are offered a series of gratifications in return for consenting to be passive. Precisely by awakening protopolitical and potentially dangerous impulses in audiences, the media attempt to contain these impulses. Tania Modleski, in a study of romance fiction and soap operas, suggests that these cultural forms both address and soothe over real problems and tensions in women's lives, allowing women to manage their oppression and invest it with a certain degree of dignity. Janice Radway, in one of the few studies that utilize extensive interviews with audiences about the nature of their attraction to mass culture, argues, for example, that habitual readers of romance fiction receive constant reassurance about their own value by repeatedly identifying with a female character in the process of sexual awakening who discovers as a result that she is a valuable person and worthy of love.[10]

The statements of one group of *Cosmopolitan* readers reveal much about the popularity of women's magazines. When asked to describe what attracted them to the December 1980 issue of *Cosmopolitan* and why they found it pleasurable, a group of university students offered several explanations.[11] On the material level, some pointed to the colorful layout and attractive pictures, the glossy texture, and even "the smell of the printed page." One respondent noted the key role of the front cover in attracting readers: "The cover usually gets my attention – more so than other covers of women's magazines." For this reader, the articles are a second source of attraction: "If they look interesting, I will usually buy the issue." Others expressed the belief that the ads help them to compare products and become informed about new ones, describing what can be termed a utilitarian or practical pleasure derived from advertising. Some readers experience a pseudo sense of community, noting, for example, that the advice columns aid them with their problems and help to assure them that other women experience similar difficulties.

Statements about the pleasure derived from reading the "naughty, openly sexual" articles on "a somewhat forbidden subject" corroborate Jameson's theories. Readers' comments also show that the pleasure derived from this temporary transgression of dominant values does not, in fact, endanger these values: "[*Cosmo*] also gives me a look at a world I really don't have any part in (and I really don't want one but I still enjoy looking)"; another reader notes: "Even though [the articles] contain values which I'm against [they] spark up interest, especially because some of them are so far out." The disclaimers that both of these respondents attach to the admission that they enjoy a transgressive pleasure from *Cosmopolitan* ("I really don't want one" and "values which I'm against") exemplify Jameson's ideas about the compensatory exchange at work in mass culture; readers are allowed the pleasure of temporary encounters with the forbidden in exchange for reaffirming their belief in dominant values and allowing these values to regulate their behavior.

A number of the comments show the utopian nature of the pleasure readers derive from *Cosmopolitan*: "I like to imagine that I can someday be like the women in the magazine – beautiful, successful, etc." Another reader notes: "Looking at [*Cosmo*] can be a definite incentive to lose weight." The distance between the imaginary world of *Cosmopolitan* and that of its readers helps to intensify the pleasure: "[The articles] are fun to laugh at because they are so far-fetched but it's also fun fantasizing that your lifestyle is like that (e.g., pick-up, ménage-à-trois). I also like to look at the fashions even though no one I know dresses like that and I know I never could. It's fun to escape and relax with the unreal world sometimes" or "The fashions are outrageous, either being too luxurious for me to buy or too expensive . . . [but] I'd love to be able to have the clothes and the figures the models have." Although the utopian vision seems to be out of reach to these readers, imagining that they participate in this world creates pleasure. At the same time, as is the case in other utopias, there is closeness to one's own world: "I simply enjoy looking at the clothes that are currently 'in style' . . . I am interested in how the provocative woman of the 1980s is supposed to behave according to Cosmo" or "People can get ideas of who [and how] they want to present themselves as by looking at the women."

One reader notes a disillusionment, however, when the magazine's ideal world does not correspond to real life: "The magazine is always disappointing to me because I rarely am left with what I have been promised by the ads, articles, etc." These remarks corroborate Mattelart's thesis that the ability to join the real and the imaginary are key to the attractiveness (or, it should be added, the failure to attract) of mass culture. If readers are constantly reassured about their own value when reading *Cosmopolitan*, as Radway suggests occurs when women read romance fiction, it is at the level of an imaginary investment of one's real world, according to the comments of several of these respondents. As one reader notes, "the very tenor of the magazine says we're superior just by virtue of reading it: we become the ever-popular, ever-beautiful, ever-open Cosmo girl."

An important factor that the respondents here do not mention is the pleasurable nature of the reading process itself. In what ways do the specificities of magazine reading help to generate pleasure? Reading patterns are conditioned by such factors as the amount of time available, one's physical environment, whether one is engaged in a first or subsequent reading of the magazine issue, and the specificities of the genre in hand. Within particular genres, as well, individual titles utilize different conventions that affect the reading process. Nonetheless, three general reading patterns can be isolated here in order to discuss the pleasure readers experience. In one practice, usually the first perusal of the magazine, one leafs through the pages, focusing briefly on the ads and the intervening editorial material. Here, by virtue of their predominance, the ads constitute the primary text. There often follows a second reading in which various articles are selected and engaged with more closely. A third level of reading occurs when one alternates between levels one and two, giving substantive attention at one moment to advertisements and at another to editorial material.

A process of delay and interruption is at work on all three reading levels that helps to heighten the reader's pleasure, as Dennis Porter has argued occurs in the reading of detective fiction.[12] Because reading I is primarily the experience of successive ads, the intervening editorial features are experienced as interruptions; pleasure is enhanced precisely by the delay of pleasure. Here, unlike the experience of viewing a television program at the time it is broadcast, one controls the length of the interruption by the speed chosen to turn each page; one may savor the delay from time to time by pausing to look more closely at an editorial feature and even, perhaps, to read it. When this occurs, one temporarily enters the reading II mode. What is important, however, is that the reader herself is actively controlling the retardation of reading I.

The ads and features are experienced differently in reading II. On this level, one focuses specifically on the editorial features and the intervening and surrounding ads interrupt the progression of plot or argument as distractions or hurdles to be passed quickly in locating the article's continuation. The interrupting ads often work in montage with the verbal text to create new meanings that may be pleasurable. (See "Internal and External Montage," Chapter 4.) Sometimes the reader is willingly distracted by the surrounding and intervening ads and temporarily shifts to the level of reading I. Here, pleasure is created not precisely as occurs in detective fiction, where elements of the narrative itself impede the narrative's progress, but by extra-narrative elements; in effect, the reader allows herself a pleasurable oscillation between the two modes of reading which constitutes another level – reading III. Key to the pleasure experienced at all three levels is a process of delay that is reader- rather than sender-controlled.

The numerous levels of women's attraction to this form of mass culture frequently disguise the fact that the attractive experiences are ideologically weighted and not simply innocent arenas of pleasure. The visual, verbal, and sometimes olfactory signifiers in these magazines offer women multiple layers of signifieds; along with the pleasure come messages that encourage insecurities, heighten gender stereotypes, and urge reifying definitions of the self through consumer goods.

Those who construct the master narratives in magazines often do not consciously intend to produce these negative signifieds. Ellen Levine, Editor of *Woman's Day* has argued, for example:

> quite frankly, . . . we do not believe that it is in the best interest of *Woman's Day* or in the interest of the millions of women to whom we write, to propagate any kind of stereotype or cultural distortion. Our goal as journalists and editors is to help the women who are loyal readers in whatever arena they need support, from something as simple as do-ahead recipes that are as nutritionally sound as possible to something as serious as significant illness or financial need or emotional support.[13]

Levine has correctly described part of the message that her magazine communicates; the assistance with meal preparation, illnesses, finances, and emotional problems greatly contributes to the pleasure readers derive from the magazine. Nonetheless, she fails to understand her professional work as hegemonic; whether editors are conscious of them or not, there exist strong ideological messages that attempt to anchor "common-sense" views of reality in these very signs of ostensible helpfulness and on most of the pages of women's magazines.

Virginia M. Mueller, Sales Manager of *Newsweek Woman*, offers a similar partial reading of her magazine's cultural messages: "*Newsweek Woman* is simply an advertising edition; a media [*sic*] through which marketers can target their advertising messages to a select group of female subscribers who want and need the in-depth reporting and commentary we provide weekly."[14] As Chapter 7 in this book shows, however, the ads in this special demographic edition of *Newsweek* exist in relations of montage with the adjacent editorial texts, foregrounding gender-segregated meaning systems that mediate certain women's understanding of contemporary world events.

The critical textual analysis begun in this book is an attempt to go beyond and through the pleasure that these magazines generate to decode the attempts to secure discursive closure that are at work. Whether they address young teenage readers or working mothers in their thirties and forties, mainstream or minority audiences, wealthy or working-class readers, the messages exhibit a remarkable continuity. The structural similarities between these ostensibly different publications result from a common material factor: all of these magazines base their continued existence on the cycle of publishing profit, advertising, and women's role as the primary purchasers of consumer goods. Whether the imaginary ideal reader is addressed as "Mademoiselle" or as "Ms.," it is ultimately because of her spending power and buying patterns that she is addressed at all by this attractive form of commercial culture.

Part One:
Advertising Texts

1 The Cover: Window to the Future Self

Waiting for her evening bus, the working woman quickly peruses the magazines on the news-stand. Brightly colored images and graphics compete for her attention as she is drawn to the largest single group of magazines – the women's publications. In contrast to the drab office surroundings that she has just left, the glamorous images are especially appealing: an executive woman typing at the beach on the cover of *Working Woman*; close-up shots of flawless, sophisticated faces on the covers of *Vogue* and *Glamour*; three-quarter, middle-distance shots of the *Cosmopolitan* and *New Woman* models in evening attire; the impeccably appointed family room beneath the logo of *House Beautiful*; and the perfectly prepared food on the cover of *Better Homes and Gardens*. What do these diverse images of perfection have in common?

Each functions as an idealized mirror image of the woman who gazes at them in which the everyday and the extraordinary are conjoined. While viewing the magazines, the woman herself participates in the construction of the idealized images; she performs a kind of pleasurable work by combining fantasy with elements of her everyday reality. As John Berger has noted with respect to advertisements,[1] the news-stand offers her a series of windows to her future self, hinting that she will attain these ideal visions by purchasing the appropriate magazines. Whether a perfect face, dress, meal, or furniture arrangement, these symbols appear all the more attainable because they urge the viewer to link the fantasy to her everyday life. The executive on the beach seems to be working, offering a more pleasurable version of the office worker's everyday tasks. Other covers transform basic needs such as food and furnishings into attractive, elaborate arrangements which for the tired worker who must prepare a meal and clean her house that evening, present goals to be attained by following the instructions in the magazines, or at least an arena of temporary vicarious pleasure. Together, the visual images and headlines on a magazine cover offer a complex semiotic system, communicating primary and secondary meanings through language, photographs, images, color, and placement.

These idealized mirror images or windows to the future self embody what Berger has termed "ways of seeing"; a photograph or an image is a selective view of reality, "a record of how x [has] seen y." Representing a judgment about what constitutes ideal femininity, cover images frequently contain an invisible yet implicit man who approves of and defines the feminine ideal. Thus, the "way of seeing" is often that of an implied male spectator.[2]

These windows to the future self, then, are selective frames that color both our perceptions of ideal femininity and what is to follow in the magazines. The systems of signification on covers do not arise autonomously but are closely connected to the commercial nature of women's magazines. Like many other forms of mass culture, the women's magazine is a commodity bought and sold on the market. The cover helps to establish the brand identity of the magazine-commodity; it is the label or packaging that will convince us to choose one magazine over the competitors. We are to buy the magazine, however, not simply to increase the publisher's sales, but so that we will also purchase the goods and services advertised inside. Thus, the intricate system of verbal and visual signs on a cover are not only glamorous messages about ideal femininity but an enticement for us to see the other ads in the issue. In effect, the front cover is the most important advertisement in any magazine.

THE COVER AS ADVERTISEMENT

More crucial than the labels of most products, covers must attract audiences not only in order to sell the magazine, but so that the latter can succeed in its important function of selling other commodities. In fact, it is often more lucrative to attract "quality" readers (those with high spending power) to the ads inside than to sell a given issue. Sales of the magazine represent only part of the publisher's income and are only one element in securing large revenues from advertisers who are also concerned with such factors as secondary or "pass-on" readership, the income levels and buying habits of readers, and specific target audiences for various products. Thus, the magazine markets itself through its cover primarily in order to secure advertising revenue.

In one important sense, the cover's goal is literally to sell us the ads inside the magazine which, in turn, will sell us products and habits of consumption. Many of us do, in fact, purchase the advertisements whether literally, through buying the magazine, the bulk of which is ads, or more indirectly, through the higher prices we pay for the advertised products. The cover is somewhat duplicitous, however, because it appears to be selling other things. Its verbal text lists the brand name, price, and title of the issue, and overtly advertises the features inside. The photographic text markets an idealized image of women for potential readers to desire, identify with, and expect to attain through consuming the magazine. The combined verbal and visual texts present an image that the magazine wishes to promote about itself – an identity that will cause it to be recognized, differentiated from its competitors, purchased, read, or at least leafed through. Thus, the cover openly sells us one group of things while its real goal is to sell us the advertisements that fill many of its pages.

Most covers of women's magazines are also ads more indirectly for specific cosmetics, jewelry, clothing, interior decorating items, or food. The cover photograph is often reproduced on an early page of the magazine, accompanied by a credit listing the specific brands and sometimes prices of the items shown on the cover. In combination with this covert advertisement disguised as a cover credit, the cover thus leads the reader into the consumerist ideology that permeates the magazine as a whole. Even more subtly, the cover directs readers to other covert ads in the magazine; as we will see in Chapter 2, many of the features advertised on the cover themselves contain hidden ads for products.

Sometimes the cover leads readers to the purchased and covert ads with fewer mediations. The enticing dish of pasta on the 8 February 1983 cover of *Woman's Day* (permission to reprint denied) is pictured from the line of vision of the prospective diner. The forkful which our right hand is potentially lifting to our mouth is suspended in a kind of freeze frame to await us as we turn to the "Pasta Lover's Cookbook," as the cover line directs us, to learn how to prepare (and subsequently consume) this symbol of successful womanhood. While the photo and caption ostensibly invite readers only to turn to the cookbook inside which contains many covert ads for pasta products, they also lead us to the unusually high number of purchased ads for pasta products in the issue: Chesebrough-Pond's Ragu (p. 9), American Home Foods' Chef Boyardee (pp. 108–9, 117), Norton Simon's Hunt-Wesson tomato paste (pp. 120–1), General Mills' Bisquick "Impossible Lasagna" (p. 161), H. J. Heinz's Weight Watchers' Lasagna (p. 170), and Contadina Spaghetti Sauce Concentrate (p. 64); and, although less directly, to two ads for Ogden Food Products Corporation's Progresso Italian products (pp. 179, 181). In a sense, the photo and headline on the cover sell us the ads for pasta inside the magazine, although they claim only to be offering us the "Pasta Lover's Cookbook."

The cover's role as primary advertisement for the magazine shapes the cover's cultural characteristics. As George Gerbner has noted with respect to romance magazines, the design and content of the cover reflect the distribution requirements and market relations of the magazine.[3] The competition engendered by the battle between magazines to deliver "quality" groups of women to advertisers surfaces in the cover's cultural form. The distinct cultural identities of the nearly fifty magazines for women on US news-stands today cannot be explained simply as cultural developments. Whether we see a healthy young woman with the look of the outdoors, a professionally dressed business woman, or ornately decorated food on a cover depends on current market conditions in the magazine industry.

A case in point is *Redbook*'s 1981 drive to find an appropriate cover image for the troubled market. The principal women's service magazines, the "seven sisters" as the industry calls them (*Family Circle*, *Woman's Day*, *Good Housekeeping*, *Ladies' Home Journal*, *McCall's*, *Redbook*, and *Better Homes and Gardens*), suffered a serious drop in advertising volume in 1981. With the exception of *Good Housekeeping*, whose ad pages were up slightly for the year, the service magazines received more and more last-minute advertising commitments and found their ad pages down in number almost every month compared to 1980 figures.[4] Although the publishers of the service magazines blamed the economy for the declines, they also recognized that the images previously projected to the public were no longer appropriate. Consequently, *Redbook* began a campaign to involve readers in the updating of the cover image, urging the submission of biographical letters and photos of "real people" who might appear on future covers (April 1981, p. 4) and soliciting readers' responses to two experimental covers used in a "split-test" of the market in May 1981. The subtext of *Redbook*'s expressed concern about which cover "readers like most" is the publisher's need to determine which cover will sell the most, and which will be, as one Editor termed it, the best "hook . . . to actually bring the reader into the magazine."[5]

Having received over 400 responses from its requests for input, *Redbook* ended 1981 with four covers showing "real people." All four women – a housewife who works part-time, a student who has undergone a beauty makeover, a woman in a non-traditional occupation, and a 4-year old who symbolizes an ideal mother's care – combine the ordinary with the exceptional. To revive *Redbook*'s declining readership, they must appeal to the ideal self-images of actual and potential readers of *Redbook*. As the text of the cover is expanded in the "People on the Cover" feature inside, details of everyday life combine with tales of the extraordinary. We become momentary voyeurs into the lives of these new "cover girls," comforted that they are like us, yet in awe of the exceptional in them. Although only one part of *Redbook*'s campaign to make itself more attractive to advertisers, this experiment with the cover is an important cultural symbol of the magazine's drive to compete with other women's service magazines in a period of declining ad sales, a soft economy, and changes in women's roles in society.

Redbook returned to the use of professional cover models in January 1982. In a matter of months the Charter Company, its parent, decided to divest its print media and in May 1982 sold *Redbook* and Charter Data Service to the Hearst Corporation for $23 million and a contingent sum based on *Redbook*'s future performance. *Redbook*'s advertising volume continued to decline in 1982, this time by 105 pages and its ad revenues fell 9 per cent that year.[6] In late 1982 glamorous, professional-looking women such as Isabel Rosselini in a business suit and tie appeared on *Redbook*'s covers. Hearst told advertisers that it was "making *Redbook* red hot," changing the magazine to keep up with the New American woman.[7] On Valentine's Day 1983 it began a $1 million advertising campaign to promote its new image with the theme line "At the Red Hot Heart of the Market." The campaign portrayed *Redbook*'s new audience as jugglers – women aged 25 to 44 who balanced their lives as wives, mothers and workers. Hearst hired Richard Sarno from *Harper's Bazaar* as

Advertising Director and Annette Capone from *Mademoiselle* to be the new Editor-in-Chief.[8] These replacements suggest that *Redbook* hoped to incorporate more elements of the beauty-fashion genre of women's magazines into its new image. With a declining market for women's service magazines, *Redbook*'s new publishers worked to update the magazine's image, beginning with the cover. By mid-1983 its covers began to resemble *Mademoiselle*'s in style with a close-up of a model's face and emphasis on beauty and self-improvement in the cover titles.

Another reflection of commercial and market factors is women's magazines' regular use of celebrities on their covers. Paul Rosenfield has pointed out that today the majority of these "cover girls" are TV stars. The most sought after audience is women aged 18–34, a group that watches a good deal of television. Consequently, magazines willingly participate in tie-in pieces and cover photos that connect to a TV movie or series because the star's current visibility will help their magazine sales: "A magazine will gladly time a cover to the airing of a TV movie, for example. Editors don't like to discuss such deals, however. Only [Martha] Schulman [Fashion Editor] of *McCall's* would acknowledge that her magazine makes such agreements," writes Rosenfield. The star with "pull" who will increase news-stand sales of a magazine is permitted certain privileges that appear to compromise editorial integrity, such as requesting the right to approve the photo and text that will appear on the cover. Sometimes the star may insist on a favorite writer for the piece, and even approval of the article.[9] Thus, in the drive to produce a cover that will promote impulse buys at the news-stand, magazines sometimes compromise their editorial independence.

Whether the "cover girl" is a TV star, a young model, or a "real person" whose name readers have submitted depends on the current market conditions of the magazine industry. More is at stake with the front cover "ad" than with any other advertisement in the magazine. If the cover image and text do not succeed in enticing large groups of readers, the reach of the other ads inside will be diminished. The commercial women's magazines will have failed in their principal goal – to deliver quality audiences to the advertisers who sustain the publications.

THE COVER AND GENRE IDENTITY

The front cover, in addition to being the magazine's most important advertisement, is the vehicle by which we distinguish one magazine from another. Genre is an important initial element of the positionality a magazine offers readers and helps to shape the reading process. Just as we bring different expectations to the reading of detective novels and poems, so, too, do we respond to the generic differences the covers signal as we are about to begin reading. Angela McRobbie's research, for example, shows that young girls in Britain perceive that magazines address different age groups; one 15-year-old in her study noted: "Well I buy *Jackie* and *Fab* now, but my sister, she's 17, buys *Honey* and *19* so I usually read them too. Once you go to work you start getting magazines with more on fashion than love stories."[10] Such preconceptions about genre, which the magazines themselves foster as part of the encoding process, help to position readers as they buy and consume the publications. Genre does not predetermine who the readers will be; crossover readership occurs as McRobbie's interviewee indicates. However, the code of genre affects one's self-perception during the experience with a magazine; when one's use of the magazine enters the public sphere, the cover serves to label not only the magazine but the consumer who possesses it.

The structured system of verbal and non-verbal signs on US magazine covers offers readers both a code of differentiation and one of similarity. The first enables prospective readers to distinguish various genres and the intended addressees: (1) preteen and adolescent girls: *'Teen*, *Young Miss*, *Seventeen*; (2) fashion and beauty for women 18–34: *Self*, *Mademoiselle*, *Glamour*, *Bazaar*, *Vogue*, *Cosmopolitan*; (3) service and home for women 25–49: *Family Circle*, *Woman's Day*, *Good Housekeeping*, *Ladies' Home Journal*, *McCall's*, *Redbook*, *Better Homes and Gardens*, *House & Garden*, *House Beautiful*; (4) salaried and career women: *Working Woman*, *Working Mother*, *New Woman*, *Savvy*, *Newsweek Woman*; (5) ethnic and minority audiences: *Essence*, *Latina*, *Buenhogar*, *Cosmopolitan en español*, *Vanidades Continental*, *Claudia*, *Tu*,; (6) women interested in health, fitness and sports: *Spring*, *Shape*, *Slimmer*, *Fit*, *Women's Sports*; (7) other special-interest groups: *Ms.*, *BBW*, *It's Me*, *Weight Watchers*, *Playgirl*, *Parents*, *Bride's*, *Modern Bride*, *Town & Country*, *Cuisine*, *Gourmet*, *Bon Appetit*. At the same time a code of commonality is at work which helps to generate expectations in readers about standard characteristics of the women's magazine genre.

Most covers try to create an idealized reader-image of the group advertisers seek to reach, by using the photo of a woman – usually a close-up of her smiling face. There is often an implied male presence, communicated through the woman's facial expression, make-up, body pose and clothing, as well as through the camera angle, lighting and color. Sometimes a man is explicitly present or the woman is pictured with a child. Often, an iconic sign, rich in secondary connotations accompanies the woman, or symbolically represents her by itself. Invariably, the verbal text of the cover consists of the magazine's title in large type and a series of headlines designed to attract the reader to certain features inside.

Specific genres of magazines present variational encodings to attract the readers they seek. A special-interest magazine such as *BBW* (*Big Beautiful Woman*) follows the main traditions of the fashion and beauty genre, featuring a close-up shot of the model's face as the main pictorial message. *BBW*'s eyecatching transgression is to substitute a "large-size" model for the traditional slender one. The *BBW* reader is to feel part of the discourse of the beauty-fashion magazine, yet recognize a message designed personally for her. Except for this departure from the normal generic rules, the *BBW* cover retains most of the previously established code for the beauty-fashion magazine.

The covers of *Woman's Day* and *Family Circle* reflect their special distribution requirements and define them as a subcategory of the women's service genre. Their extremely high circulations (approximately seven and eight million per issue respectively) are achieved primarily through supermarket and news-stand sales, allowing them to charge some of the highest advertising rates among women's magazines; large single-copy sales are especially desirable because they demonstrate the consumer's active decision to buy the magazine, instead of passively receiving it in the mail and perhaps not reading it.[11] The generic encodings of the covers of these two magazines promote continued high sales of single issues.

Often shelved near the checkout stand in supermarkets with other "impulse buys," both have covers that resemble a cluttered supermarket ad. In contrast to other women's service magazines whose covers usually picture celebrities, these often signify successful womanhood through the secondary significations of a semiotic icon – a cake or a quilt, for example. Smaller photos advertising various features surround the primary icon, and words such as "Bonus," "Exclusive," "Contest," "Rebate Offers," "Save," and "Free Sample Inside" add to the sense of supermarket clutter. The main photo usually communicates a project to do at home: a cake to prepare, a quilt to sew, tote bags to make, flower arrangements and Christmas decorations to construct. When the main photo pictures women directly, they are often demonstrating another such project: a blouse or vest to make, or ways to make one's hair look fuller. In 1981 the covers of *Woman's Day* portrayed beauty and fashion projects more than did *Family Circle*'s front photos. Because of the slumping market for women's service magazines, the publishers of *Woman's Day* worked to promote it as a beauty and fashion publication as well as a supermarket service magazine.[12] Its covers continue to reflect the distribution requirements of a primarily non-subscription publication of the home-service genre while increasingly utilizing cultural motifs from the beauty-fashion genre.

Sometimes a cover will more openly merge the characteristics of two genres. While *New Woman* is one of the new publications for women working outside the home, its cover format is similar to *Cosmopolitan*'s. Like *Cosmopolitan*, it uses a three-quarter or upper-body shot of the model instead of the usual close-up of the face common to beauty and fashion magazines. Headlines follow the *Cosmo* style in tone, the question-and-answer format, and the overuse of underlining and exclamation points. They are thematically similar to *Cosmopolitan*'s headlines, emphasizing relationships with men, marital life, and self-improvement. Overall, however, both in the photo and headlines, there is less of *Cosmo*'s emphasis on sex; a more subtle sex-symbol than the *Cosmo* model, the *New Woman* model wears less revealing clothes and more often has a closed-mouth smile and a less provocative head and body tilt. The *New Woman* cover model is a more businesslike "Cosmo girl," and there is a material explanation for this.

New Woman wants to attract monied women working outside the home and claims to have "the highest percentage of working women of any ABC [Audit Bureau of Circulation] magazine with over one million circulation – 89%."[13] Each month its cover prominently boasts "Over Four Million Readers" to encourage potential readers as well as advertisers. In effect, *New Woman* is aiming for both a "class" and a "mass" audience. By following the *Cosmopolitan* example, its cover will attract a large news-stand clientele, four times greater than its subscription numbers. Yet its cover also emphasizes the new woman worker, a "quality" reader, whose spending power is especially attractive to advertisers. By mixing the cultural images of two genres, the *New Woman* cover aims to attract both quality readers and large numbers.

Genre identity is crucial to a magazine's sales and readership, and plays a role in the reader's sense of self as she consumes it. The cover's generic encodings often operate in the public sphere, so that when making a news-stand purchase, reading in a public place, or displaying the magazine on a coffee table, one identifies oneself to others as a Cosmo girl or a *Family Circle* reader. While the cover's encodings of genre are primarily designed to sell magazines, they offer readers ideological positionalities as well, helping to shape both the reading process that follows and readers' self-presentation to others.

THE COVER AS SEMIOTIC SYSTEM

The Photographic Text

The principal image on every cover is a non-verbal one, a photograph that we see before or while reading the verbal messages. Erving Goffman has delineated several categories of "gender display" or "ritualized behavioral practices" which ads use to convey meaning at a glance. Cover photos often communicate through these 'hyperitualizations" as well, reinforcing cultural stereotypes and leading us to similar displays inside the magazine. Often the models exhibit "head and body tilting," or other "canting postures" that, in Goffman's view, communicate an acceptance of subordination through a lowering of the head with respect to the viewer of the picture. Several visual motifs attribute to women a lack of seriousness: the costume-like character of female clothing, "body clowning" and other childish or playful poses, and "ritualistic mollifiers" such as the broad expansive smiles which women display more often than men.

Some cover models, especially those pictured in three-quarter or full-length shots, exhibit the "bashful knee bend," a casual and trusting posture that presupposes the goodwill of others in the surroundings. Displays of what Goffman terms "licensed withdrawal" appear in cover photos: hands covering the face or mouth in moments of shyness, fear, or laughter, or a finger brought to the mouth which communicate that one desires to be psychologically cut off from the situation at hand; aversion of the eyes or "anchored drifts" which show women to be mentally drifting from the situation, a meaning also conveyed through the absent, unfocused gaze of many cover models; exaggerated expressions of delight, laughter and glee which imply a kind of "flooding out" on the emotional level – another sign of psychological withdrawal from the situation at hand into an enraptured emotional state.[14] Goffman's formulations offer one important method for decoding the photographic images of magazine covers, addressing the communication at the level of the initial visual perception of the photographic sign.

From the perspective of semiology, the gender-related poses that Goffman delineates are understood as connotational codes. In his study of news photographs,[15] Roland Barthes noted that often a photograph appears to be a "message without a code," that is, a perfect analogue of reality which faithfully reproduces the world without transformation or distortion. The news photo, for example, seems so analogous to reality that viewers often interpret it as purely denotative – a mechanical reproduction of reality with no added connotations. Other visual representations such as drawings, paintings, cinema or the theatre overtly add a connotated message (the style or artistic characteristics) to the denotated message (the image's analogous relation to the real). In mass culture, according to Barthes, the denotative, analogic message is conflated with the symbolic cultural message, so that it appears to be a reliable portrayal of reality. We often fail to notice the connotational procedures at work: trick effects, such as composite photography, the use of artificially arranged objects, the photogenia of the subject, the aestheticism of the photo, or the syntax of object-signs within a photo or in a series of photos. Barthes posits a "photographic paradox" in which the ideological, coded portrayal of reality that uses these connotational procedures coexists with an uncoded, denotative representation of reality. A photograph thus appears to represent reality objectively, yet at the same time it necessarily interprets reality. It is what Berger later terms a "way of seeing."

The poses Goffman discusses take on a great significance when we understand them as connotational procedures that are often naturalized by the analogous quality of the cover photograph. While it is true that the cover photographs of women's magazines are often more obviously stylized and appear less purely analogous than the news photo, the referent of most cover photos is real – someone we recognize either by name or at least as a real person. Often we see the model's poses, facial expressions, photogenia and accompanying semiotic objects as natural, non-coded aspects of this real person; we are misled by the apparent accuracy of the photo, its ability to naturalize and disguise its "ways of seeing." When a woman pictured on the cover of *Savvy*, for example, exhibits an exuberant smile and head tilting, as in the February 1980 issue (see Figure 1.1), we are encouraged to view the pose as natural and expected for women. That the woman is a public figure – Leslie Stahl, CBS White House correspondent – disguises and validates the connotational procedures further. Even when the cover photo does not depict a celebrity, it is precisely the real analogue that makes the symbolic messages more effective: "These are real women who are so glamorous," we are encouraged to think. The cover image is thus more credible, hiding the connotational code more effectively than would a painting or a cartoon.

The Photograph and Verbal Text in Interaction

The verbal and photographic texts of covers function together as a semiotic system through visual montage. In Eisenstein's theory of cinematic montage, the succession of two opposing images or "cells" (A and B) forms a third cell in the film viewer's consciousness, labelled "C," which constitutes a higher dimension of understanding.[16] In the case of the magazine cover, the eyes of the potential reader create a type of montage effect. The viewer produces the "C" cell of the montage, a level no longer limited to the mere sum of separate images.

The primary montage on these covers is that which the viewer forms from the two largest images – the "brand name" or title of the magazine and the photo. By virtue of their size, both enter the line of vision either simultaneously or in close succession and

Figure 1.1 Front cover of *Savvy*, courtesy of Family Media Inc.

are usually what lead the potential buyer to single out a magazine on the news-stand. The linguistic image modifies and is modified by the photographic image. The title *Working Woman*, for example, must be decoded differently from the usual meanings of the term when it is juxtaposed to the photo of a managerial woman on the magazine's cover. The publication is not, in fact, addressed to most working-class women, whose lower spending power makes them less attractive to advertisers than are executive and managerial women. In the new system of meaning, "working woman" comes to signify a female in a high-salaried professional position. Through montage, the title in turn modifies the meaning of the photo. We are to interpret, for example, the photo of a woman standing behind a desk in a

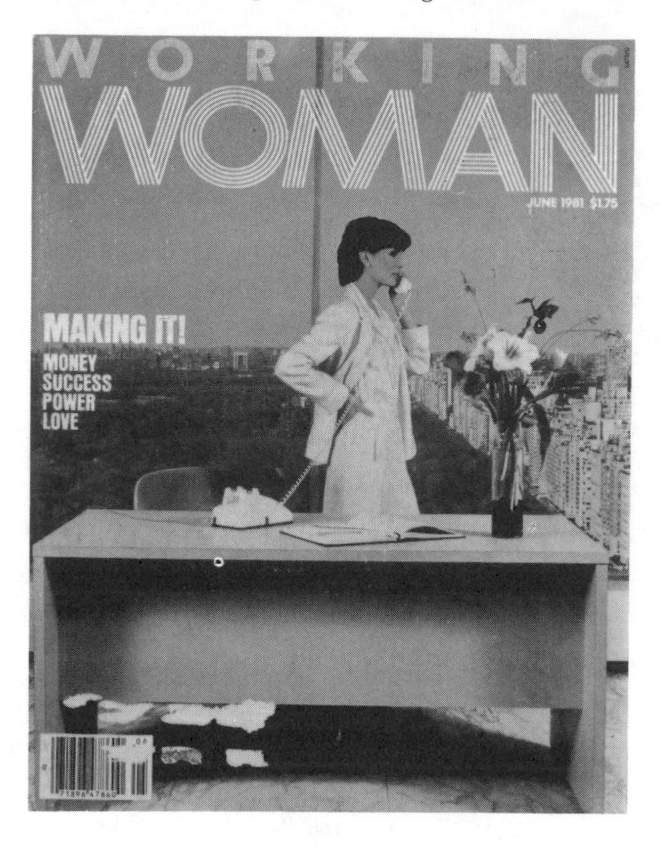

Figure 1.2 Front cover of *Working Woman*, reprinted with permission from *Working Woman* magazine. Copyright © 1981 by Hal Publications.

casual yet stylized pose on the June 1981 cover of *Working Woman* as indeed that of a working woman (see Figure 1.2). Sensing the disparity between the photo and the magazine logo, the Editor felt it necessary in her monthly column to remind readers of the desired decoding of the cover photo: "Playing the role of the symbol on our cover is a real working woman. Her name is Kathleen Buse and what she's doing standing there is hard work" (p. 4).

Semiology explains the interaction between verbal and photographic texts in terms that complement Eisenstein's formulations. In a 1964 study of the photographic and linguistic messages of advertising,[17] Barthes analyzed two operations that the linguistic text performs on the photograph: anchorage and relay. All images are polysemous, that is, they present a number of meanings from among which the viewer can choose; as a result, the originators of mass cultural messages often add a linguistic message to encourage viewers to select the desired meanings on the levels of both denotation and connotation. Sometimes, the linguistic message is part of another story or anecdote and, in effect, relays the viewer to that other text. In the comic strip, for example, the text in an individual bubble is part of a larger story. Here, the linguistic message and the image stand in a complementary relationship; the text presents messages that are not found in the image itself and are, in effect, part of the larger anecdote. In the case of magazine covers, the titles of articles can be understood as "relay texts" which send the viewer to other texts inside.

Thus, while Eisenstein's theory of montage shows how the viewer joins the verbal and photographic messages of the cover to create a higher dimension of meaning, Barthes' analysis of anchorage and relay addresses more specifically the levels of signification that the two texts create by working together. One effect of the montage of the magazine cover's title and photo, then, is the attempted anchorage of a specific meaning from among the many that the photograph offers. The title *Glamour*, for example, delineates the photo of a face on the cover as glamorous; when, as in the October 1981 issue, the model is pictured with a young child, the anchored meaning is that motherhood can be glamorous as well. The viewer, of course, brings her own interpretive lens to the text and may or may not accept the meaning that the verbal text attempts to anchor. Titles such as *Vogue*, *Mademoiselle*, and *Cosmopolitan* try to impart a sense of sophistication to the woman portrayed on the cover. Some viewers might ordinarily interpret as unsophisticated the sexually overdetermined poses of the *Cosmo* cover girls, but the title urges them to understand these visual signs as stylish, sophisticated and desirable. Viewers may resist or accept the attempted anchorage.

The headlines on the cover work in secondary systems of montage not only with the photo and the magazine's name but with one another as well. Ostensibly designed to lead readers to the articles inside, the headlines are relay texts, fragments of the lengthier texts inside. But they are also significant elements of the text of the cover itself; they serve to anchor the polysemous photo as well as the magazine's "brand name" or title which itself offers several significations to be delimited.

On the January 1981 cover of *Self* (permission to reprint denied), for example, the linguistic message of the title, repeated in the letters SELF on the chain around the model's neck, communicates a glamorized and openly narcissistic concern with the self, a sense of pride and self-confidence. At this point in the viewer's interpretive work on the cover, the title logo most likely refers to the model, shorthand for the third person "herself." However, the headlines framing the photo on the cover delimit the polysemous title in another way. The word "Yourself" appears in large type in the first title and is reinforced by second-person reader address in the other titles: "your looks," "your private life," "how to make yourself . . .," "your job," "your hair." "You" is also the implicit referent of titles such as "successful women's sexual needs and how to fill them" and "6-second fix for stress"; the potential reader is the "successful woman" here as well as the victim of the stress that the cover promises to remedy. Thus, the reader is to personalize both the title and the photo, anchoring the concept "yourself" as the desired interpretation.

Finally, montage functions among the headlines themselves. In examining the cover before reading the magazine, the viewer forms C cells from the titles as she perceives them in close succession. Often the titles develop a single theme, but they sometimes offer contradictory cells of meaning. The January 1981 cover of *Mademoiselle* illustrates the single-theme technique, developing the ideas of playfulness and women's lack of seriousness through the montage of succeeding titles that are childish in subject matter and rhythm: "How to get your way in bed," "The state of the date," "Vibrators: Today's love toy," and "Play the game – and win." Headlines on the cover of the December 1981 *Cosmopolitan en español* sold in the United States present contradictions when read together in montage. One title warns readers not to become the playgirl of the office party and risk "destroying in two hours what you've attained in two years!" Yet, an adjoining announcement tells readers to focus on their sex lives: "Prejudices, complexes and *stupidities* that ruin your sex life." A similar cell of contradiction is created between one headline, arguing that unrequited love can be cured with medicine ("Hopeless love is a *sickness*, and medicine can cure it!") and its companion which argues against drug taking ("Where the rainbow ends. A victim of those pills we all take tells her fatal experience").

The text of the headlines taken together can also stand in contradiction to the photographic image. The January 1981 *Self* cover portrays a carefree, natural-looking blonde woman gazing confidently into the eyes of the viewer. This image contradicts the inferiority implicit in the headlines – our bodies need to be stronger and sexier; we need "a diet that melts winter fat" and a "six-second fix for stress." Ostensibly the headlines refer to success, strength, talent, health and professionalism but their subtext is the reader's inferiority which can be remedied by purchasing the magazine and the products it advertises. It is precisely the contradiction between the inferiority implicit in the titles and the ideal self-confidence conveyed by the photo that creates desire and sells the magazine. This montage, although not always perceived consciously, establishes a cultural dialectic that will be at work throughout the magazine.

The Chromatic Text

Both the verbal and photographic texts are modified by an additional communicator – color. Uniting certain of the verbal and non-verbal elements, color imparts a structure of its own to the cover. The viewer's eyes are drawn to various images and words via coordinated tones or color underlining. Themes are established through color either by relying on stereotypical associations or by creating new color significations. Sometimes color also functions as a covert advertisement by reproducing a shade of lipstick or clothing advertised inside the magazine.

In her study of print advertisements Judith Williamson notes that color creates connections that the verbal text of an advertisement may not explicitly establish. Sometimes color develops a narrative on its own that can change or even reverse the meaning of the verbal text. Ads can use color to link an object to another project, to a person, or to a "world." Often, however, the predominant color is not the principal signifier; rather, a secondary color establishes connections, creating the primary chromatic meaning.[18]

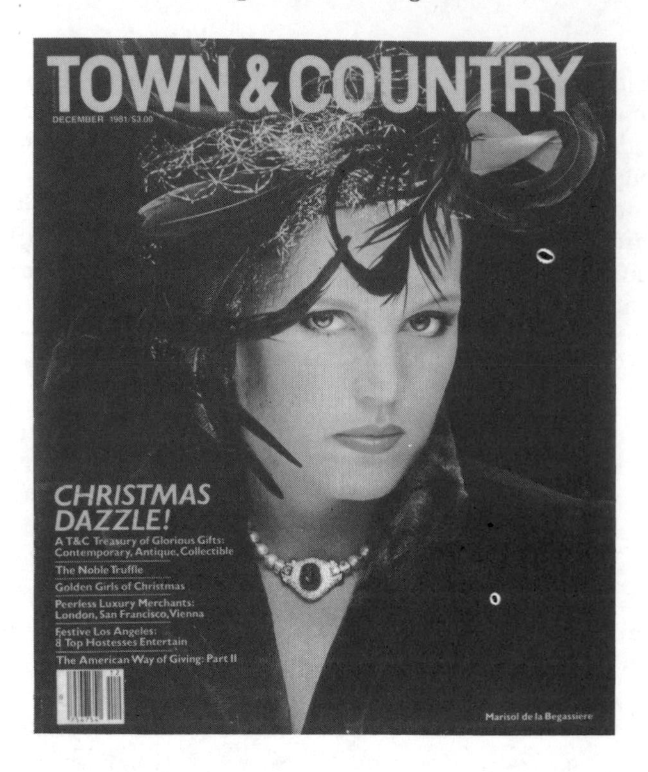

Figure 1.3 *Town & Country* Magazine, December 1981, Joel Baldwin, photographer, © The Hearst Corporation.

Although black is the predominant color, for example, on the December 1981 cover of *Town & Country*, it is not the primary communicator (Figure 1.3); rather than calling attention to themselves, the black background, hat and coat serve to set off the expensive jeweled necklace. The principal color communicator is the white–silver combination which links the title "Town & Country" to the netting on the model's hat, the whites of her eyes, several of the headlines, and, most importantly, to the necklace. A secondary chromatic text connects the blue ribbon and feather on her hat, her blue eyes, the alternating blue headlines, and the universal price code. By coordinating precisely with the color scheme of the model's clothing and accessories, the overall cover design becomes an extension of the significations of her picture.

The June 1981 cover of *Working Woman* (Figure 1.2) shows the use of color to alter the usual meaning of the verbal text. The predominant color white is used in all of the printed text, the model's clothing, desk, phone, appointment book, flowers, the office floor, and even the buildings we see through her window. Because white soils easily, its extensive use contradicts the normal connotations of the term "working woman." The message communicated through color here is an additional reason why, as we have seen, the Editor needed to assure readers that the woman pictured on the cover was indeed "doing . . . hard work." Here, the chromatic text has retinted the real world according to the mythical qualities of the product: the magazine offers women an idealized image of the working woman who is "Making it!" according to the principal headline on the cover.

Often, the January issues of fashion and beauty magazines use bright colors signifying newness and the coming of spring to encourage purchases that will assuage one in the dead of winter. The January 1981 *Harper's Bazaar* cover uses bright pinks, yellow, whites, and blues to support the verbal messages that emphasize newness (Figure 1.4). As in the *Town & Country* cover, the color of the verbal text extends the color scheme of the model's clothing, make-up, and accessories, establishing what might be termed a chromatic rhyme. The pink, blue, and white of the model's face (her lipstick, eyes, teeth, and earrings) coordinate with the pink, blue, and white of her sweater. The "look" that these colors combine to create is extended to the colors of the lines of verbal text. It is as if the text itself were dressed in the manner the model demonstrates. Two yellow lines of text stand out, one "the new YOU" in horizontal montage with the model's face and the other in the position of a caption beneath the model, "EXTRA! 88 HOT LOOKS/Spring preview from Milan, Paris, New York." These lines communicate not only through their verbal significations but through their shared color: the "new you" that will make us look like the model can be purchased through the 88 "hot looks" in the fashion preview inside. Color helps to create a system of montage between the two lines of text, and they, in turn, form a secondary montage with the model's face.

Figure 1.4 Front cover of *Harper's Bazaar*, January 1981, © Hearst Corporation, Courtesy *Harper's Bazaar*.

THE COVER AS FRAME

Individually and collectively, the verbal and non-verbal signifiers on the cover extend meaning to the material inside. After seeing them, even in a brief glance, readers carry a set of cultural prejudgments to their perceptions of the magazine's contents. As one French critic has pointed out about the covers of mass market novels, covers "delimit the arena of signification in which [the book] should be read."[19] The cover offers readers a strong, though not compulsory, interpretive frame for what is to follow.

The true beginning of the magazine is the cover, not the first ad page, the table of contents, or the first numbered page. Edward Said's observations on the beginnings of literary texts help to explain the framing function of the magazine's beginning. Said emphasizes an active, directional meaning of the term, in the sense that "The beginning A *leads* to B." By defining the beginning as "the first step in the intentional production of meaning," Said draws attention to its position in a sequence, that it signals "consequent intention": "a 'beginning' is designated in order to indicate, clarify, or define a *later* time, place, or action."[20] Thus, we focus on the beginning's power to define what follows; the cover continuously points ahead, and in so doing, shapes the reader's understanding of the subsequent material in the text.

Just as the magazine title delimits a certain interpretation of the polysemous cover photo, so, too, the title extends meaning to the words and photos inside. A given reader, for example, might interpret the photo of an unusually bizarre dress as "fashionable" because it appears on the pages of *Vogue*, yet judge the same dress to be in "poor taste" were it to appear in *Cosmopolitan*, despite the latter title's attempt to imply sophistication. In a more general sense, the titles of women's magazines have come to delimit the contents one is about to see as women's domain. Whether a magazine title specifically mentions women (e.g. *Woman's Day* or *Ms.*) or has acquired the signification of "belonging to women" (e.g. *McCall's* or *Essence*), it communicates that what follows is the concern of women. The title of the magazine presents an encoding frame within which the reader is to catalogue her perceptions of the material inside. As the product's brand name, it not only urges us to recognize, differentiate, and select the magazine, but it delimits in advance certain significations of the articles, features, and ads inside.

The headlines on the cover that advertise editorial content also extend structures of meaning to what follows. First, they suggest that the magazine is essentially reading material, even though most of the pages contain photographic and other non-verbal representations. The magazine can claim success when consumers merely flip through the pages, glancing at the ads, yet the cover suggests that what follows will be read, not merely seen. While ostensibly announcing only what one can read in the magazine, the headlines attempt to position us positively toward all of the magazine's contents. A second general code functions as well, the surge of excitement created through theme, tone, punctuation, and graphic design, intended to arouse the potential consumer's curiosity. However, as is the case with newspaper headlines, graphic and spatial considerations restrict content; the need for compression and the desire to attract readers often result in distorting or misleading phrases, so that headlines are frequently false leads or partial truths about what is to follow. For example, a reader who is attracted by the headline on the February 1982 cover of *Mademoiselle*, "Do Men Love the Women They Sleep With? By Shere Hite," will find inside that the real title of the article is "What men say about women (when women aren't around)." While the actual title of the article plays on women's generalized feelings of insecurity with respect to men, the cover headline specifies a sexual interpretation – men's judgment of the women they sleep with – and links it to love. The reader is likely to bring the sex/love interpretation to her reading of the article, searching the men's remarks in the article for the answer to the question posed on the cover. Similarly, the next cover headline, "Sex & Salary: Dirty tricks in the pay zone" adds sexual innuendoes to what is in fact an article on inequities in men's and women's pay.

To extend a concept that Stuart Hall has advanced with respect to news broadcasting, headlines or magazine covers present "pre-embedded definitions" of what is to follow; by connecting various events and themes with one another, they "'map' events into larger, wider frameworks of meaning." Hall notes that when viewers comprehend and decode the messages, they do so "on terrain which the broadcasters first define and delimit. In so far as audiences do not question the framework of assumptions within which these primary significations are made, they 'interpret' within the hegemonic 'definitions of the situation' which the broadcasters provide."[21]

Although there are always what Hall terms "negotiated" and "oppositional" interpretations of these definitions, it is important to study how these frameworks build upon one another and offer the consumer specific structures of interpretation. In one instance, as a means of attracting advertisers, *Better Homes and Gardens* promoted the concept of reader "action" as the structuring theme of its editorial matter: "*BH&G* editors demand action from readers through editorial material that cannot be accepted passively. . . . Each article says Do Something! . . . and here's how. . . . Advertising that performs best appears in active editorial atmosphere that preconditions readers to action."[22] "Action" and "doing" are euphemisms in the advertising world for buying; the magazine argues here that its editorial material conditions readers to buy goods and services. This ideology of "action" and "doing" is established as a structuring element as early as the cover.

Of the eight headlines on the January 1982 *Better Homes and Gardens* cover (permission to reprint denied), seven suggest activities that readers should engage in: food preparation, home decorating, adult education, houseplant arrangement, quiltmaking, craft projects, and home improvement. Because many of the readers of the service magazines today also work outside the home, in order to make ends meet, the language of the headlines sets up a structure in which the recommended activities can be done quickly and inexpensively but without loss of quality: "Timesaving recipes with great old-fashioned flavor," "Quick and easy decorating ideas," "Affordable open-plan house," "Create a classy home office," "Amish-style Quilt, Stitch it up in 5 hours for under $50," "Super-simple craft projects you can make in a jiffy." The ideology of action is established through the structural linking of time and money efficiency to high-quality projects:

Efficiency		*Quality*
Time	*Money*	
"Timesaving" "Quick & easy" "Stitch it up" "in 5 hours" "in a jiffy"	"Affordable" "for under $50"	"great old-fashioned flavor" "classy" "Amish-style"

The structure of action here offers what Hall terms a "pre-embedded definition" of what is to follow in the magazine; the articles and ads inside build upon this structure of interpretation (the majority show women performing one task or another), suggesting to readers a conventional definition of women's role. Disguising the fact that in each case to act means to buy in some form or another, the structure relies on the positive euphemisms of time and money efficiency with the retention of quality.

The photographic text of a magazine cover also extends meaning to the material inside. Usually a concrete representation of an idealized model of physical beauty, the cover photo whets the consumer's appetite for what is to follow. As a pleasurable visual representation, it invites us to enjoy further pleasure by consuming the magazine's contents visually, flipping through the pictures page by page. At the same time, it leads us necessarily to the verbal texts in the magazine, through which we will be given specific instructions for attaining the model of ideal beauty.

The covers that use the photo of a glamorous woman to represent physical perfection rely on readers' personal sense of inferiority, especially about their physical appearance. As Berger has noted, the consumer envies not only the glamorous model in an advertisement but herself as she will be in the future after having purchased the product advertised. According to Berger this relationship of envy "explains the absent, unfocused look of so many glamour images. They look out *over* the looks of envy which sustain them."[23] Sometimes the cover model appears to be looking directly at us, but a sense of superiority is still at work. Whether looking over us or directly at us, the model sustains our envy and feelings of insecurity, predisposing us to be receptive to the products advertised both overtly and covertly inside, as well as to the instructions for attaining beauty in the articles.

When covers represent women through the secondary significations of an iconic sign, feelings of insecurity and envy are also at work and carry through to the magazine's content. To achieve ideal womanhood, we must learn to prepare the ornately decorated food or make the crafts pictured on the covers of some magazines. In addition to framing our perception of the corresponding article and photo inside, these cover photos affect the meaning of apparently unrelated articles and photos in the magazine. Implicit is the notion that women's work in the home must always strive for the ornamental perfection of the cover photo. Many tasks are portrayed as unalienated labor in the ideal verbal and non-verbal representations which branch out from the cover photo to the magazine's contents. Just as we are to feel insecure about our failure to embody the image of physical beauty of the model on many fashion magazine covers, so, too, are we to idealize and envy the multitude of symbols of womanhood in the service magazines for which the cover signs set the stage.

The cover functions as an interpretive lens for what follows by offering us pre-embedded definitions through the magazine's title, the headlines, and the photo. Syntax, tone, color, visual images of ideal beauty and success, and covert images of consumption work to position us favorably to the magazine's content. Readers are not deterministically required to view the inside according to the cover frame, but a given model of interpretation is part of the cover's code and exerts strong influence.

The cover is the most important advertisement in the magazine, then, precisely through its roles as genre identifier, semiotic system, and frame. The interplay of the photographic, verbal, and chromatic texts on each cover creates a series of value-laden cultural significations but is primarily intended to attract revenues from advertisers and increase circulation. The cover's roles as a genre identifier, sign system, and frame are its means of achieving this revenue. Each role is closely connected to the commercial structure of the magazine industry and would be significantly different were the commercial goals of magazines to change.

Most of the "ways of seeing" or windows to the future self that the covers of magazines create are also linked to these commercial goals. The ideal images on magazine covers that women see on news-stands, in waiting rooms, or concealing the faces of others who are reading them, attempt to integrate women further into the consumer economy. Hidden beneath the glamorous ideals are subtexts that play on anxieties and encourage feelings of inadequacy, while promising pleasure and the acceptance and love of others if we purchase. If the cover photo is, in Berger's words, "a record of how *x* has seen *y*," it is an image of how the contemporary consumer society [has] chosen to see women in order to sell more goods and services.

2 Covert Advertisements

In his classic study of television,[1] the late British theorist Raymond Williams argues that ads only apparently interrupt television programs; in fact, commercials are crucial elements of televisual "flow" in which program segments, ads, and previews of programs to follow constitute a single continuum. While many of us perceive commercials as interruptions (including Williams himself both here and in earlier studies[2]), the important structuring device of televisual flow functions at the same time; it encourages us, as do the pleasures of both programs and ads, to continue watching an entire evening's sequence, although we may have initially intended to watch only a single program. Williams analyzes formal and thematic similarities between programs and ads as well as montage effects created by given juxtapositions between the two. This "organic relationship" between TV ads and programs marks, in William's view, a qualitative difference with previous systems of advertising, with the notable exception of glossy women's magazines.[3]

I would argue, however, that the flow or continuum between ads and editorial material in women's magazines is more profound than that of television. While TV commercials often frustrate us at their onset as interruptions and some viewers use them as breaks to do other things, many of us allow the pleasures of commercials to overcome our initial annoyance at the interruption. In contrast, ads in women's magazines are rarely seen as interruptions – only when one is intensely involved in what I have termed the reading II mode. While television commercials offer some structural support to the programs, a much more pervasive homologous structuration links ads and editorial material in women's magazines, so that ads seem a natural and logical extension of the editorial content.

A crucial element of this homologous structuration is covert advertising – the promotions disguised as editorial material or hidden in some other form so that they appear to be non-advertising. Covert advertising extends structural links to the purchased advertising, creating a harmonious, integrated whole. It can take specific forms such as the recommendation of brand-name products in an editorial feature or be more generalized as in the broad, thematic correlation of editorial content to advertising. Appearing in both verbal and non-verbal forms and often claiming only to present advice or information, covert advertising helps to position readers favorably toward the overt advertisements; the purchased ads appear to be natural extensions of the editorial material.

In fact, however, the editorial matter is often an extension of the overt advertisements, another crucial element of the reciprocal structural support that the two give each other. In one of the rare published interviews in which editors openly discuss how advertising affects editorial content, Máximo Simpson, Editorial Director of the Mexican magazine *Claudia* from 1974 to 1975, noted:

> The Advertising Director has veto power over the articles; if the material has some effect on or isn't agreeable to the advertiser, [the Advertising Director] can prevent its publication. On occasion, [the Advertising Director] himself has brought in articles that the advertisers are interested in seeing published.
>
> For example, he prevented publication of an article on the carcinogenic effect of products wrapped in plastic, and brought in one to be published on cemeteries and mausoleums sold in perpetuity.[4]

Consequently, while covert advertising and the entire editorial content extend structural links to the paid advertising, the latter contributes to the cultural formation of the editorial material as well. If many readers see advertising as the natural extension of a magazine's editorial content, it is because of the reciprocal structural links that the content and ads extend to one another.

Covert advertisements are crucial to this reciprocal structuration, occurring primarily in the editorial material but present at times within purchased advertisements as well. Most covert ads inaccurately label or disguise one thing as another: a make-up and clothing promotion is called a "cover credit," particular investments are recommended under the label of "financial advice," and an ad for one product conceals a promotion for another. When covert advertising is taken into account, the numerical proportion of ads to features is even greater than the standard ratios that only include figures on purchased advertising. Indeed, very little remains in most women's magazines that is not advertising, either covert or overt. In January 1981, for example, *Bazaar* had a total of 146 pages: only 59 had purchased ads but 96 others had covert ads; *Mademoiselle* that month had 180 pages, 88 of which contained purchased ads and 62 covert ads; and *Savvy* had 83 pages, 41 with purchased ads and 26 with covert ads.

It is important to both publishers and advertisers, however, that part of this large quantity of advertising be disguised, that magazines appear to have a balance between advertising and editorial matter. Although many readers may enjoy the ads, publishers want people to feel they are getting a good amount of editorial matter for their money. And, as one publication argued to potential advertisers: "For your ad to be read, the magazine must be read. When people skim through a magazine, chances are they skim through the ads."[5] Usually, purchased advertising makes up between 50 and 60 per cent of most women's magazines and editorial matter between 40 and 50 per cent. *Vogue*, with an especially small amount of editorial matter, 39 to 61 per cent ads, argues that most of its readers buy the magazine in order to read the ads.[6] Most publishers, however, aim for a balance between the two and in official statistics on advertising volume, do not include data on covert advertising.

A balanced amount of editorial material is important for other reasons. Advertisers realize that direct, overt advertisement is not always the most effective way to sell a product. The recommendation of a beauty advice columnist that readers try a specific brand of cosmetics is sometimes a more successful sales technique, or at least promotes a positive attitude toward cosmetics. As one newspaper Editor argued in comments that hold for magazines as well: "The biggest sales pitch a newspaper has going for it is that people believe what they read in a good newspaper. If they ever got suspicious about the integrity of the editorial product, then the next step is to be suspicious about the integrity of the advertising content."[7] Both publishers and advertisers believe that editorial material develops a confidence that readers carry over to the ads. Publishers also argue with somewhat strained logic that editorial matter is important because "a good editorial mix" stimulates diverse interests in readers and "readers with diverse interests [have] many consumer needs."[8] Finally, editorial material is important in a physical sense because it draws readers to see the ads. Research is conducted on the mean reading time that women spend on each issue, and magazines contend that if editorial material is read, ads are more effective. One promotion for *Seventeen*, for example, argues: "She spends about four days with every issue of *Seventeen*. Reads it word for word. That means she's more likely to read your entire ad down to and including the small print."[9]

For a number of reasons, then, both publishers and advertisers desire that strong editorial sections coexist with the ads. In practice, however, much of the editorial material in women's magazines contains one or another forms of covert advertising. Because these hidden ads are based on the mislabeling or disguising of one thing as another, it is important to unmask the varieties of disguise, cataloguing their forms and themes. By developing names for the techniques of covert advertising we attain a language in which to speak about these concrete practices, an important first step in an articulate criticism of women's magazines.

In learning to recognize hidden advertising, theories of ideology and infrastructural analysis are especially useful. Studies of ideology have taught us to look for, among other things, structures of meaning that disguise one level of content with another.[10] Covert advertising is best understood not as a series of separate instances of disguise in a magazine but as a system of mutually sustaining techniques and themes. Analysis of ideology in this sense directs us to look beyond the surface appearance of an article, photo, or credit for a subtext that connects to other parts of the commercial structure of the magazine. Further, we must study how the methods of disguise become naturalized through the traditions of genre that have come to be accepted in women's magazines. Complementing the study of ideology, analysis of the infrastructure of covert advertising directs our attention to factors such as a company's ownership of various products, some of which receive covert promotions while others are advertised directly; agreements between advertisers and editors such as that described by Simpson above; and a magazine's current advertising "health," including factors such as ad volume and revenue per issue, an important element in publishers' decisions to use certain forms of covert advertising. Together, analysis of the ideology and infrastructure of covert advertising can reveal it as an economically motivated system of mutually sustaining techniques and themes.

TECHNIQUES OF DISGUISE: THE SYMPATHETIC EDITORIAL STRUCTURE

The most important form of covert advertising is the editorial structure: magazines gear editorial content to complement the concerns of advertisers and predispose readers to the advertising messages. Accordingly, a general consumptionist ideology pervades the editorial content. Often the articles promote feelings of inadequacy in the reader and advise explicitly or implicitly that certain products will remedy the inadequacies. In most magazines, the editorial subject matter corresponds closely to the principal categories of advertising. This sympathetic structure helps to sell products. The fashion designer Bill Blass credits *Town & Country*, *Vogue*, and *Bazaar* with helping to create recognition for his fashions. Praising *Town & Country*, he notes, "We've had a terrific response from their editorials."[11] As we will see, editorial material gives general support to consumption through its format, subject matter, product recommendations, and promotions of feelings of inadequacy in the reader. Whether the editorial specifically publicizes Bill Blass designs or simply instills in readers a generalized need to beautify themselves through the advertised commodities, it helps to prejudice readers favorably toward the ads. By sharing the same goals and interests as the advertisements, the overarching sympathetic editorial structure works continuously to support purchased advertising in magazines.

The Magazine's Unique Image

"Mademoiselle. This Miss is a Hit." "I believe in my *Self*." "House Beautiful. Prosperity begins at home." "Think rich. Think *Cuisine*." "'*Teen* A true friend." "*Modern Bride*. She's determined to *spend* the rest of her life."[12] The special image that each magazine strives to project is an important element of the sympathetic editorial structure. Through editorial content and style, the magazine hopes to develop an image that will attract readers each month to see the advertisements inside. Subscription promotions mailed to current and prospective subscribers also play on the special image. The most extensive development of the magazine's image, however, occurs in the numerous slogans addressed to prospective advertisers. *Modern Bride* tells marketers: "Now that she's accepted his proposal, she's open to yours." The *Seventeen* reader is, according to the slogans, "Born to shop" and "Major[ing] in merchandise." Potential advertisers in *Bride's* are asked: "Do you still think they only buy for weddings?"[13] Publishers use the magazine's image as a ploy to attract advertisers, arguing that readers who identify with the image will spend money on related products.

The polymorphous "*Cosmopolitan* Girl," for example, whose characteristics change every month in the Hearst Corporation's promotions to advertisers, is said to "care about clothes, looking smashing, her apartment, travel, and entertainment," concerns that *Cosmopolitan*'s editorial material addresses. *House & Garden*'s changed, upscale image claims that its readers "serve everything from corn flakes to caviar . . . drive sports cars and station wagons, drink cognac and cola." One ad for *Woman's Day* pictures a model in a lace slip with the headline, "How's this for glamour?," arguing that the magazine not only offers service editorial but beauty and fashion features as well. *Vogue* projects an image of affluent, upscale readers: "The *Vogue* millions have the millions to buy what they want, when they want it. . . . She writes a check out for that Picasso jewelry, charges that new designer fragrance, puts those Ricci platinum pumps on her credit card."[14] Each magazine's unique image is designed to attract both readers and advertisers; not only will the image entice readers to see the ads but it assures marketers that readers have specialized buying habits that correlate closely to the editorial content.

The common denominator of these images is their link to consumption. As ideological projections, they present as natural and expected the magazine's promotion of consumption. The infrastructural foundation of a magazine's special image is also linked to consumer purchasing. To promote growth in advertising revenue the image must continue to attract readers who have spending power and convince them to consume certain commodities. If advertising pages and circulation are down, it is a sign that the special image is no longer working optimally. A magazine such as *Woman's Day* has modified its image slightly, to attract advertisers of beauty products, while others such as *House & Garden* and *Redbook* have begun major changes in their special images.

Placement

Besides giving general support to the ads, the editorial structure connects with the advertising both formally and thematically. Adjacency and placement are regularly used to enhance advertising messages, thus functioning as forms of covert advertising. Ads for food appear with food-related editorial, or even near articles on diet or exercise. An ad for a make-up product is placed next to a beauty article. In the April 1982 *Working Mother*, for example, an ad for Stresstabs vitamins appears on the page facing an article on fatigue and overwork (pp. 30–1), an article entitled "The healthy child" is enveloped by two ads picturing healthy-looking children – one for Carter's sleepwear and the other for Gerber's baby food (pp. 44–7), and an article on permanent waving hair is directly preceded by an ad for Gillette's Toni Silkwave home permanents (pp. 55–6).

Advertising Age Yearbook notes that requests for special placement increased in the early 1980s:

> Advertisers, who had always regarded with great concern the positioning of their ads in magazines, became even more so under the pressure of rough economic times. Agency and magazine people found that requests for specific ad positions were becoming more vocal and more sophisticated. Front-of-the-book treatment was being superseded, for some advertisers, by *insistence that their copy be placed opposite editorial matter (sometimes explicitly chosen)* and that separation from the advertising of competitors be maintained. One effect of this pressure was to force magazine people to *redesign their publications in order to offer more separation of units in the forward sections of their pages.*[15]

Especially in times of recession, then, when consumers spend less money, advertisers give greater emphasis to a covert technique such as placement. Sometimes the advertiser will even choose the editorial matter that will appear next to its ad. As a result, magazines are less able to preserve editorial autonomy and sometimes redesign their publications to please advertisers.

Even when related ads and features are not adjacent, placement can enhance advertising messages. Readers create links through recent and long-term memory. Many are likely to connect, for example, an ad for tourism in Trinidad and Tobago in the January 1981 *Bazaar* (p. 51) to a travel article on vacationing there (pp. 8–16) and a series of fashion features photographed in Tobago (pp. 116–31). Just as the cover is an interpretive frame for what follows, so, too, an ad early on extends links to the subsequent ads and features. The glamorous model in a make-up ad on one of the beginning pages of a magazine, for example, forms part of the system of mutually sustaining themes that structure the magazine. Her image affects the reader's perception of material not only in the beauty and fashion category but also in other diverse categories that use the concept of glamour to sell commodities. Whether an ad and feature obviously interrelate or whether the connection is more subtle, placement contributes to the connection and thus functions as a covert advertiser in its own right.

The Editorial "Tie-in"

Another technique whereby the editorial structure supports the purchased advertising is the "tie-in" feature. On the surface, an article entitled "Sexy muscles: 14 exercises to a seductive body" in the May 1982 *Self* (pp. 88ff) does not appear to be advertising a product. Because it directly follows a feature promoting swimwear, however, it presents an immediate thematic tie-in that supports the swimsuit promotion: readers who "shape-up," as the article advises, will be more likely to buy the swimwear presented in the feature and in other purchased advertising in the issue.

More obvious tie-ins occur when magazines publish articles on celebrities who also appear in the ads in the issue. In July 1981, for example, *Ladies' Home Journal* featured Brooke Shields on the cover, the table of contents page, and in the first feature article in the issue. And even in the middle of the article on herself, Shields appears in a full-page ad for Wella Balsam conditioner (p. 15)! In a sense, readers are drawn from the cover to the table of contents and then to the article that envelops the ad featuring Shields; one is relayed through a series of photographs of the famous model directly to the advertisement in which she appears.

The tie-in need not always be immediately obvious. In its first three issues, *Spring* published a series on buying small cars which, by promoting merchandise, was "designed to appeal to more cautious advertisers."[16] While on the surface the series appeared merely to offer readers information on compact cars, it was intended as well to "tie-in" with potential advertisers' messages: automobile manufacturers might purchase space in the new magazine once shown that *Spring*'s editorial material would give support to such ads. Tie-ins can even appear on the surface to be thematically unconnected to the primary advertising. The Editor of *Vogue* has argued, for example, that there must be articles on beauty and good health to make the fashion of interest.[17] Such articles function as subtle tie-ins to features and ads on fashion; their work of "making the fashion of interest" is really that of selling fashion through covert advertising.

Relay Texts

Another technique functions both on a formal level and thematically to support ads. Relay devices such as the front cover, the table of contents, and the Editor's introductory column openly send the reader to specific features and indirectly to ads. Adopting the techniques of advertising, these relay devices urge us to turn to an article or feature as overtly as many advertisements urge us to buy products. Relay texts are important parts of the planned integration of the editorial and advertising material first in a physical sense because they require us to look through several pages of advertising to find the indicated article. If requiring readers to see ads while turning to articles and features were not one important function of these relay texts, magazines could be edited in a less fragmented fashion, with ads placed after all of the editorial matter, for example.

As part of the integrated communicative chain at work in the magazine, relay texts often connect to the ads through theme as well. The links between an article on food and the ads for food, for example, usually have begun in the verbal and photographic signs about food on the cover and in the table of contents. Although the title of an article, "How to car-shop like a pro" on the table of contents of the March 1982 *Self*, for example, suggests through its language that the article will merely provide advice on buying a car, the title ultimately relays readers as well to the three purchased ads for cars in the issue. It functions as the beginning of a thematic chain of communication that urges readers to consume. The language of the title promotes consumption by its implied presupposition that the reader is car-shopping, needs a new car, and will, in fact, buy one. The tone of the article then builds on these presuppositions while the content supports them with other covert ads: the brand Ford is mentioned five times, a Ford Capri is shown in the photo, and the "pros" whose advice the article presents are two employees of Ford Motor Company. These specific covert ads for Ford are linked to a full-page color ad for the Ford Capri later in the magazine (p. 124). The relay text and article lead as well to other car ads in the magazine (Datsun, p. 64, and Chrysler, pp. 26–7).

The technique of relay prepares readers to be positively disposed to other ads and features through broader themes as well. Sometimes these themes surface unexpectedly in ostensibly unrelated features. Even the monthly horoscope, for example, can relay readers to other features and ads by both strong and subtle thematic underscoring. The January 1981 *Bazaar* horoscope (p. 146) relays readers to several articles and advertisements that promote Caribbean travel in the issue through such phrases as: "Early in January, good news breaks about travel. You will have more opportunities to see the world in 1981"; "You need to have a period of rest and relaxation . . ."; "Mars is your *Sun* sign" (my emphasis); "End of month will bring good news about travel . . ."; "a chance to plan glamorous travel in the next few months"; " . . . feel free to plan interesting travel in the next two months"; "arrange visits to new places."

The horoscope buttresses an article on investment advice (pp. 108ff) with such phrases as "You will see then how you can be secure in the years ahead"; "This is an extremely 'lucky' month for your money: You will earn more and you can expect a windfall near the 20th"; and "Soon money worries will be ended. . . ." Certain phrases support an article on remarriage: "This month you will be concerned about . . . a possible remarriage"; "marriage difficulties"; and "A romantic friendship that has already brought happiness could be threatened this month. Keep in touch by letter or telephone." Readers are relayed to articles and ads on health and beauty products by the horoscope's suggestion that "The days from the 6th to the 20th will be good for health treatment and for a new keep-fit routine"; and "Think of new health and beauty treatments in the last 10 days." Support of consumption surfaces in the horoscope in phrases such as: "Go bargain hunting"; "indulge yourself with a few luxuries"; "Spend on personal luxuries: good clothes and perfumes"; "If in a spending mood, you will find excellent bargains on the 29th and 30th"; "wait till the 20th to spend money on entertaining. Then spend as much as you find you must"; and "In bargain hunting make utility purchases early in the month but spoil yourself with personal luxuries in the last few days." Throughout the horoscope the phrase "Good News" recurs, reinforcing not only the main cover headline, "Good news issue," but several of the features whose titles and texts repeat the "good news" theme. Thus, while appearing not to be an advertisement, a feature such as the horoscope can function as a relay text to lead readers covertly to the ads and features, or to support the promotions readers have already seen in the issue.

Color functions as a relay device as well. In June 1982 the publisher of *New Woman* announced an editorial policy of "subliminal synergism."[18] Through this practice, the dominant colors of an advertisement are deliberately repeated in the tint block behind the editorial headline on the facing page. Color works here as a communicative sign to relay readers to the adjacent advertising and to promote the impression that the article and facing advertisement constitute an integrated, harmonious whole. Readers are to see the ad as a natural extension of the feature and vice versa. The publisher claims that the coordinated colors cause the reader's eyes to move automatically from the feature to the ad, creating an effect similar to that of a two-page ad spread while advertisers pay only for one page.

Indeed, most of *New Woman*'s editorial pages coordinate with the dominant colors of the ad on the facing page. Sometimes the magazine also combines subliminal synergism with other covert techniques. In February 1983, for example, the colors red, blue, white, and black in the ad for Chesebrough-Pond's Vaseline Intensive Care all appear in the article on the facing page. In addition, the article recommends the product by name. Thus, brand reciprocity works with a four-way color coordination to enhance the advertiser's message. Later in the issue, subliminal synergism is extended beyond color to coordination of graphics and layout. Not only do the Oil of Olay advertorial on page 29 and the article on the facing page share the same arrangement and typeface, but part of the headline in both is printed in blue. Thus, subliminal synergism through color works together with shared graphics and layout to suggest subtly to readers that the ad is a continuation of the editorial material.

Brand Reciprocity

Publishers often convince advertisers to buy space in their magazines on the basis of "editorial suitability," promising that products will be showcased in an appropriate editorial background. But it is not simply that manufacturers of cosmetics, for example, wish to advertise in publications with general articles on make-up application; the "appropriate editorial background" has come to mean much more than this. Not only are specific brands of cosmetics recommended in articles on make-up but they are mentioned by name throughout the magazine in the cover credit, fashion features, advice columns, and within advertisements for other products.

Thus, the editorial structure offers not only a complementary sympathetic backdrop for advertising but what has euphemistically been termed a "brand reciprocity" as well. Bona Campillo, Fashion Director of *Claudia*, described the process as follows:

> The [editorial] sections aren't sold to advertisers, all the material is produced by the magazine and obtained where the magazine wants, except that there exists a system of reciprocity for the brand names that are advertised throughout the year; the magazine gives them a feature in an issue without charging them. So, of every three articles in each issue of *Claudia*, one is a support for the advertisers; if there are six articles, two are for the advertisers.[19]

The brand reciprocity that Campillo describes takes both obvious and subtle forms. In *Claudia*, for example, Salomon sportswear, a division of Fuqua Industries, purchased a well-placed color ad for jogging outfits on the page opposite the table of contents in all of the twelve issues published in 1982. In the March issue the ad was visually "quoted" in the fashion feature (p. 88): an exact reproduction of the ad photo without the slogan and logo was reprinted as a photo in the feature. The traditions of the fashion feature format allow the sportswear to be promoted further in the accompanying verbal texts: "The Hit Line:

Salomon designs cheery and comfortable outfits for your favorite sport. . . . The outfits exhibited here are from the prestigious Salomon brand" (my translation). In "Spring 1982 makeup . . . eyeliner returns!" (*Cosmopolitan en español*, April 1982) the visual "quotations" are less obvious, but several are recognizable photos from cosmetics ads in other magazines. Although many of the cosmetics corporations named in the piece have not yet purchased advertising in the US Spanish-language *Cosmopolitan*, the publisher most likely hopes to attract such advertising in the future by initiating the process of brand reciprocity here.[20]

Brand reciprocity also includes the numerous promotions of products by name under the guise of editorial advice or information. The most obvious form is the recommendation of a product advertised elsewhere in the magazine. One feature in the June 1982 *Spring*, for example, "Water-works Wonders," promotes three Lever Brothers' soaps – Pears, Dove, and Caress – complementing Lever Brothers' purchased ad for Caress on page 21 of the issue. Similarly, the feature recommends Evian mineral water mist, reinforcing an ad for the product on page 9. A second, more subtle form of brand reciprocity occurs when there is a correlation between the editorial mention of a product and advertising in the same issue for other of the manufacturer's products. The June 1982 issue of *'Teen*, for example, recommends two Schering-Plough products in its "Dear Beauty Editor" column: Dr Scholl's Athlete's Foot Gel and Coppertone's For Faces Only. These recommendations are subtly connected to nine purchased ads and three other covert ads for Schering-Plough products in the issue.[21]

THE SHARED FORM OF ADVERTISING AND EDITORIAL MATERIAL: ADVERTORIALS, SPECIAL SECTIONS AND CONTESTS

The editorial structure supports the purchased advertising through such techniques as placement, tie-ins, relay texts, and brand reciprocity. In addition, ads and features sometimes share one another's form, offering each other covert structural support. Articles sometimes use the language of advertising. A feature may appear in ad-like form or an ad in the form of a feature. Finally, special hybrid forms such as "advertorials," contests, and other special sections unite the characteristics of ads and editorial material to produce new intermediary forms. This merging of the generic characteristics of advertisements and features blurs the traditional distinctions of the two principal categories of magazine content and is an important additional means of covert support for the purchased advertising.

Besides sharing themes with the advertising, features sometimes share language as well. The January 1981 issue of *Mademoiselle* contains an excerpt from a forthcoming book by Louis Gignac in a feature entitled "Turn on the lights in your hair" (pp. 110–13).[22] Besides mentioning eleven products and services by name, the feature uses the language we commonly associate with advertising in order to promote hair coloring and related products: "Women no longer want to radically change their natural hair color, they just want to improve on what nature gave them," Gignac notes. This generalization plays on readers' desire to be accepted, normal members of society, at the same time that it helps to shape popular opinion about what is normal. The contradiction between the first and second clauses, that women do not want to change nature yet want to "improve" it artificially, is glossed over by the appeal to feelings of inadequacy invoked through the word "improve." As Stuart Ewen has pointed out, advertising often promotes a sense of inadequacy in potential consumers precisely in order to recommend a product or service to remedy the supposed shortcomings.[23] After announcing the newly available remedies for the alleged problem, such as "sunbursting, tortoiseshelling," Gignac then employs the traditional imperative of advertising language: "So if you're *bored* with your natural color and would like to make it *livelier*, *brighter*, *be* adventurous and *try* a special effect" (my emphasis). The comparative adjectives "livelier" and "brighter" establish a thematic and syntactical opposition to the first adjective "bored." The opposition between the two states, the negative "before" and the positive "after," lends support to the imperative verbs "be" and "try," two traditional euphemisms in advertising language for "buy."

Later in the piece, Gignac promotes his profession, using the concessive mode common in advertising: "You can achieve simple sunlit effects with easy at-home treatments (see recipes, next page) but perfect highlighting requires the practiced technique of a professional colorist." Gignac's concession allows the magazine Editor to relay readers to haircoloring "recipes" on the following page containing ads for home haircolor products from Revlon, L'Oréal, and Clairol. Playing on stereotypical images associated with women, the magazine calls the mixtures "recipes" and gives them such food-related titles as "Color whip," "Lemon-lime swizzle," "Blackberry cocktail," and "Henna espresso." By using metaphors to which they suppose women will easily relate, the Editors imply that tinting one's hair is an extension of women's everyday task of preparing food; a woman must cosmetically prepare herself as she would an ornate meal. A more expensive, professional tint, however, is always better.

Besides buttressing the covert ads for products and services in the article, such language serves to naturalize and extend further the language patterns common to advertising. Although the shared language may make it appear that the ads are natural extensions of the features, the reverse is in fact true: the features are by-products of the advertising and of secondary importance in most commercial magazines.

Sometimes a feature appears in ad-like form, a phenomenon that also helps to naturalize advertising as a cultural model in women's magazines. The 27 April 1982 issue of *Woman's Day*, for example, lists on its table of contents a feature entitled "Special quilt kit: Applique-look country quilt" (p. 70). In appearance, however, the feature is much like an advertisement, with a large photo, headlines, an order blank, and the traditional command of advertising, "Capture the beauty of an appliqued quilt with less than half the work." But, like a feature, it relays readers to other covert advertising in the magazine with the phrase, "Information on furnishings, page 138."

Given that magazines usually strive for the appearance of a quantitative balance between advertising and editorial material, why would a feature (usually non-revenue producing) appear in ad-like form? Might it not add further to the advertising clutter of the magazine? On the contrary, as we have seen, many readers buy magazines precisely to look at the ads rather than perceiving them as clutter. Here, it is likely that *Woman's Day* is building upon its image as a service-to-readers magazine, one that will offer them something to do. No doubt editors hope that both the ad-like form of this feature and its recommendation that readers act through buying are carried over to the purchased ads in the rest of the magazine. Like the features that imitate the language of purchased ads, this feature gives covert support to the other ads by making the traditions of advertising more pervasive and apparently more natural.

Ads frequently appear in feature-like form as well. One classic example is the widely-run series for Richardson Merrill's Oil of Olay. So close is the ad's appearance to that of a normal editorial page that editors place the word "Advertisement" in parentheses at the top of the page. The ad, as it appears in *Family Circle*, 16 March 1982 (p. 56), uses type similar to the other editorial material in the issue and closely follows the editorial format of those features in *Family Circle* that are predominantly verbal: it has an enticing headline ("Remember how you looked on your wedding day?"), a lead-in paragraph in italics before the text begins, three columns of printed text per page, section headings in boldface type, the page number and issue beneath the text in the lower left corner, and two black-and-white photos of the model in a home-like environment. The ad appears on the left-hand page, the usual location of editorial material since advertisers prefer the more visible right-hand location. Richardson Merrill has had great success as a result of these ads disguised as features termed "editorial advertisements." Oil of Olay's sales of $10 million in 1960 reached $100 million in the early 1980s, and it achieved a 40 per cent share of the women's skin care market.[24]

From time to time Schering-Plough's Maybelline publishes an advertising booklet in *Cosmopolitan* in the form of a mini-magazine (April 1981, pp. 33–40). The cover of this magazine-within-a-magazine imitates the graphic design and layout of the *Cosmopolitan* cover with the word "Maybelline" replacing the title "Cosmopolitan." Following the mini-magazine's cover are four photographic features that also use the *Cosmopolitan* editorial style. By imitating these verbal and photographic editorial characteristics, Schering-Plough hopes that readers will give the ad the same credence they give to editorial material. Perhaps, in quickly flipping through the issue of *Cosmopolitan*, readers might not see the small-print label "Advertisement" on the first page, and mistake the section for an editorial feature in the magazine. At the very least, though, readers might sense an affinity between the magazine they enjoy reading and Maybelline products when looking at this feature, a connection designed to increase Schering-Plough's sales.

Ads in the form of features, or "advertorials," are "those advertiser-paid blocks of pages that combine clearly identifiable advertising with simulated editorial text"; editors prefer to call them "special advertising supplements."[25] According to this definition, the *Cosmopolitan* section discussed above is an "advertorial" while the Oil of Olay ad, a single page, is an "editorial advertisement." *Advertising Age* cites one Editor's admission of the deceptive nature of advertorials: "Fundamentally, advertorials were designed to deceive. They were designed to look like editorial."[26] Sometimes the deception is so effective that even a reader who is deliberately looking for covert advertising can be fooled; one university student, giving a report on hidden ads in the April 1983 *Seventeen*, mistakenly referred to one page of verbal text in an advertorial for Clairol's Sea Breeze as "the article on the page facing the ad" (pp. 60–1).

Although subtle, the deception is evident in the contrary ways in which editors present the section to readers and advertisers. *Woman's Day* tells readers at the beginning of its "Consumer Ad-Visor Section," that the magazine has invited advertisers "to supply you with more information than you normally receive from advertisers," (27 April 1982, p. 115). The magazine argues to advertisers, however, that the section is "a unique way to showcase a product by combining advertising, product information and promotion . . . your product gets exposed three times, three different ways . . . all for the cost of one four-color page."[27]

The advertisers in the "Consumer Ad-Visor Section" of 27 April 1982 are frequent purchasers of ads in the magazine throughout the year.[28] In addition, the spurious editorial texts employ several rhetorical devices to advertise products covertly. Coca-Cola has chosen a question-and-answer format to promote Minute Maid Frozen Apple Juice, using such pseudo questions as: "Are more people drinking apple juice these days?," and "Is Minute Maid Apple Juice 100 per cent pure?" Other advertisers in the supplement use the "how-to" format common to editorial material in women's magazines and standard advertising slogans that help to promote brand recall. Because some of these same rhetorical forms also appear in the accompanying advertisements, the techniques help to relay readers to other ads through both form and content.

Both publishers and advertisers recognize the advantages of the advertorial yet are concerned that it may eventually cause skepticism among readers, which could decrease consumer buying. Advertisers think that the editorial format gives greater credibility to the claims they make about their products. Publishers fear, however, that readers may perceive that the magazine is editorially endorsing an advertiser's product, especially if the magazine's editorial staff has helped to prepare the advertorial. By labelling these sections "Advertisement," editors hope to retain readers' trust in the publication's editorial integrity.[29] What editors are, in fact, concerned with is the degree of covertness that disguises these ads. Their fears of losing the readers' confidence in editorial objectivity surface only when a hidden advertisement is in danger of being readily perceived as such. Because it is standard editorial practice to promote advertisers' products covertly, editors and advertisers are understandably worried that obvious violations of the appearance of editorial objectivity might call into question other less obvious covert advertising as well. The concerns about advertorials have less to do with the preservation of editorial objectivity than with the preservation of the advertising dollars that sustain each magazine.

Contests, sweepstakes, and promotions are another group of special hybrid forms that mix the characteristics of advertising and editorial material and are ultimately covert ads. Although advertisers often sponsor their own contests and sweepstakes on purchased pages, these are not covert ads unless the reader mistakes them for non-advertising material. Contests promoted on the editorial pages of the magazine such as *McCall's* "Reader of the Year" (see Chapter 6), however, usually are covert advertisements for one or more of the magazine's regular advertisers. Here, the contest is a form of disguise for the promotion of products, often also functioning as a demographic survey for the magazine.

In August 1981, for example, *'Teen* sponsored a sweepstakes, "Win a Holiday in Hawaii" featuring United Airlines and Bolt Corporation clothing. Two models who are often pictured on the editorial pages of *'Teen* appear here wearing Bolt fashions and holding United tickets. The United logo and name appear six times and Bolt is named and pictured twelve times. On the four pages following this sweepstakes announcement, Bolt fashions are advertised in feature-like form, extending the covert ad begun in the sweepstakes. *'Teen* benefits from the contest by gaining data on its readership that will be useful in persuading other advertisers to buy space in the magazine – entrants must submit information on their clothing and shoe size and their age. Simultaneously, the contest enhances the image of one of *'Teen*'s principal advertisers, the Bolt Corporation.

Since 1976, *Seventeen* has conducted an annual special promotion, the "Tennis Tournament of Champions" in Mission Viejo, California. The magazine encourages prospective advertisers noting that "There's no better time to reach . . . fans – the thousands of young women who will follow every stroke. . . . With our special tournament issue and exciting promotions at over 500 department stores, your products could move as fast off the counter as our girls move on the court."[30] Three editorial features appear in each April issue to promote the products of the sponsoring companies beneath the guise of informing readers about the tournament. The 17-page special section on the tournament in the April 1982 issue (pp. 132–48) promotes through pictures and verbal recommendations the products of ten sponsors.

THEMES OF DISGUISE: EDITORIAL ADVICE AND INFORMATION

Two frequent ideological code words that women's magazines use to promote consumption are "advice" and "information." Through language and visual representations, these editorial codes subtly promote new needs for products and services or magnify already existing needs. Because the new codes through which these needs are presented correlate closely with the products appearing in purchased advertisements, the formats of advice and information function as covert advertisements.

The Ideology of Advice

The assumed objectivity with which editors present advice or information is an additional means of disguise of the system of covert advertising. In the case of advice, the presumed impartiality of the editor's recommendations is more serious: readers are in a more vulnerable state since often the magazine has urged them to feel inadequate so that a product may be recommended as a remedy. The advice appears to be offered in the spirit of friendship as a means of remedying real problems when, in fact, the problems are often artificially stimulated or magnified.

The most pervasive advice is on the subject of beauty. An obvious area of counsel in fashion and beauty magazines, beauty advice appears in other genres of women's magazines as well. Often the focus is on achieving an external beauty which is defined by market forces. Whether a beauty editorial recommends a particular shade of eyeshadow or a special hair-coloring agent depends on market factors such as a manufacturer's need to introduce a new product, the company's ability to make a profit selling it, and the publicity that the product is receiving and has received through standard purchased advertising. In addition to the general market factors affecting the definition of beauty that a given magazine promotes, each publication operates under a particular set of infrastructural factors that shape its beauty advice. The effects of purchased advertising on the advice given in the editorial sections are visible to anyone who studies the magazine closely, but only rarely do the magazines themselves publicly admit to the practice. As we have seen, Bona Campillo, Fashion Director of *Claudia*, described the system of brand reciprocity that exists at her magazine. In another example, an ad for *Woman's Day* argued that the editorial structure of *Woman's Day* increases the sales of beauty and fashion products:

> So we devote more editorial pages to beauty and fashion combined than to any other category.
>
> The results? Beautiful! For readers, advertisers, and people like Seligman & Latz (whose beauty salons did $750,000 in additional business from 25,000 new customers who responded to one *Woman's Day* beauty editorial).[31]

Even without such specific public acknowledgements of brand reciprocity or other editorial promotions, the effects of purchased advertising on editorial beauty advice are often evident. Beauty features often use photographs and language designed to promote consumption of cosmetics. In the April 1982 issue of *Elan*, a short-lived magazine for Black women, attractive photos of make-up artists applying the recommended cosmetics to models are set in the text of a beauty feature, with the results shown on the opposite pages. These photos sell the recommended cosmetics visually, while the text sometimes resorts to more direct advertising language: "From Gillette, the people who developed a self-adjusting shampoo, comes a self-adjusting moisturizer, *Silkience*. Developed for combination skin, it moisturizes dry areas without using oil" (p. 57) or "conditioned with *Ultra Sheen Conditioner and Hairdress*, because you don't need a heavy hairdress to achieve shine and body" (p. 59). It is hard to imagine the public accepting advertising slogans such as these in the non-advertising sections of a television or radio program but such language has come to be accepted as part of the beauty advice features of women's magazines.

Covert advertising for beauty products often takes the form of the monthly beauty advice column. An especially common format in magazines for younger women, the advice column plays upon adolescent readers' often exaggerated self-consciousness and their trust in the Beauty Editor's expertise. Under the pretext of answering letters from readers, the columnist recommends brand-name products as solutions to problems. In *'Teen* magazine the responses are so predictable that the observant reader can often guess in advance which product will be recommended for each problem, based on previous advertising in the magazine. The "Dear Beauty Editor" column in the August 1981 issue (pp. 116ff) notes that Super Strength Clearasil in the vanishing formula will allow readers to wear acne cream under bright classroom lighting without its being noticed. Cover Girl's Oil Control Translucent Blotting Powder will remedy an oily face. Cutex Creme Enamel will add "a professional touch to the home manicure" (p. 120). Maybelline's Dial-A-Lash mascara will remedy "gooky lashes," and Gillette's Aapri Apricot Facial Scrub is the solution for a reader who is "looking for a cleanser that will help my skin look healthy and feel soft and smooth." The Clairol Kindness Quartz Dryer for Curly Hair is recommended to the writer who asks, "What can I do to keep that just-permed look every day?"

Several purchased ads complement these recommendations: Clearasil (pp. 102–3), Noxell's Cover Girl (p. 11), three other full-page color ads for Noxell products (pp. 14, 17, and 134), Gillette's Silkience and Adorn (pp. 37 and 40), and Clairol's Sea

Breeze (p. 37). The advice column recommends Stri-Dex Medicated Pads for weekend trips and presents the details for obtaining a free case to carry them in from the company. Sterling Drug Inc., the parent corporation of Stri-Dex, purchased ads in this issue for two of its other products: Midol (p. 4) and PhisoDerm (p. 52). The recommendation for Clearasil not only coordinates with the ad for the product on pages 102–3 but with another Richardson Merrill product, Topex, advertised on page 122, one of the ad pages that interrupts the advice column. Of the seventeen responses to questions in this *'Teen* column, twelve recommend products by brand name and three generically advise the use of products. Illustrations of six of the products are set into the text as additional visual promotions of products.

The common "makeover" feature also uses the ideology of advice to promote products as well as the broad concept of glamor. Encouraging reader identification by using "ordinary" women from across the country as subjects, the makeover feature attempts to make women more self-conscious about their appearance through its conflation of glamor with the ordinary. Where the professional model presents a contrast to the way most women look, the subjects of the makeover appear to be transformed from ordinary to glamorous before the reader's eyes on the pages of the magazine. Thus, they give more credibility to the covertly advertised products that have purportedly enabled the transformation. In addition, the use of "ordinary women" as subjects encourages the "ordinary" reader to find fault with her own appearance.

The ideology of advice-giving permeates many other features. It promotes generic rather than brand-name product acquisition, for example, in a feature such as the August–September 1981 *Bride's* "Gift Registry Checklist" (p. 59), which tells the reader to be sure to list all her "needs" at the Wedding Gift Registry at a local department store. The list that the magazine publishes ostensibly in order to guide and advise readers, helps to instill pseudo needs, encouraging readers to be acquisitive as if it were natural and expected. Commodities such as parfait glasses and cocktail forks are listed with the implication that they are essential for a proper marriage.

Advice on food preparation and menu-planning appears in many women's magazines, especially those of the service genre. A monthly calendar of menu suggestions is offered in the *Woman's*

Day feature, "Twenty-minute money-saving menus" (27 April 1982, p. 134), which subtly suggests that readers buy specific food products, although brands are not mentioned. This and other advice features about food correlate closely with the surrounding food ads. In one unsubtle example, an ad for olives appears across from the menu recommendation for an antipasto salad. The suggested recipes and meals promote consumption of certain kinds of food-products that coincide with those promoted in paid advertisements. Thus, advice on meal preparation is an ideological disguise for a method of organizing patterns and habits of food consumption that places emphasis on some products to the exclusion of others.

Financial advice is a broad ideological code through which editors recommend certain investments – from upscale elite ventures to those more accessible to the general population, depending on the demographics of the magazine. *Elan*, for example, urges investment, names an investment company, and lists specific kinds of accounts, under the guise of presenting "Consumer Savvy" to assure "economic survival."[32] *Savvy*, another upscale publication, advises readers to avoid investing through discount brokers while purportedly presenting an objective report on two kinds of brokers (January 1981, p. 14). Magazines with broader audiences emphasize thrift and economy in their financial counsel. *Family Circle* advises women on methods of saving money in its "Cashing In" column. In the 16 September 1982 issue, readers are told: "You can cash in with *Family Circle* cents-off coupons – worth $2.05 in this issue; rebates total $3.00" (p. 12). Financial advice is used as an ideological code for covert advertising in "What every wife should know about money" (*Woman's Day*, 17 April 1982, pp. 64ff) – a promotion for insurance. Throughout the text runs the presupposition that a woman needs her husband's life insurance benefits to survive if he should die. It offers readers no suggestions on obtaining the training and education now that would enable them to support themselves should their husbands die. To promote the product, the article plays on women's fear of being alone and without support.

The Ideology of Information

As corporations introduce new products and services in accordance with market exigencies, the advertising industry promotes the concepts of the "new" and the "up-to-date" as ideological supports for these goods and services. The editorial material of many women's magazines follows suit, using these same concepts ostensibly only to provide information on products. Thus, one important use of the ideological code "information" is to promote in readers a sense of the new and up-to-date. Closely linked to its opposite, the old-fashioned and obsolete, the ideology of the new often helps to create feelings of inadequacy in readers which the new products are promised to remedy.

The information on new and up-to-date commodities can be traced ultimately to market factors. A corporation's decision to launch a new or modified product depends on national and international economic conditions, the performance of its other products and those of its competitors, and the advertising organs and retail outlets that are available to promote and sell the product. Manufacturers of cosmetics, for example, had to exercise caution in introducing new lines and colors in the hard economic times of the early 1980s because high interest rates made it difficult for retailers to obtain the financing to stock large quantities and varieties of cosmetics.[33] Although editorial promotions may appear to readers to be objective information on new products and services, market factors underlie the editorial statements.

Complementing the automobile industry's annual fall launch of new cars, for example, *Town & Country*'s October 1981 issue published an ostensibly informational piece, "The Best of the '82 cars" (pp. 185–8). Through photos, text, and price quotations, the article urges the reader to buy almost every one of the cars on which it reports. Four of the six domestic cars are made by corporations that have purchased advertising in the issue and the same Lincoln Continental that the Automotive Editor evaluates is advertised on pages 20 and 21.

Claudia disguised a "brand reciprocity" feature for one of its principal advertisers as an informational piece on a new line of furniture. The Dixy Furniture Corporation, which purchased the expensive back cover advertisement on every issue in 1982, received a special feature in the May issue, "The Freshness of

Rattan" (pp. 118–20). Claiming simply to present information about the "spectacular line of rattan" that Dixy Furniture is launching, the feature mentions Dixy by name eight times, recommending the furniture through positive language and attractive photos. The March, July, and October 1982 issues also contained "informational" features on Dixy Furniture (pp. 80–2, 94–6, and 116–18, respectively). Publicly, *Claudia* denies that it uses editorial material to advertise products: "Claudia does not accept editorial advertising. The mention of prices, products, brands, or well-known firms is a service for readers and implies no responsibility."[34] But in light of Campillo's statements to the contrary and the evidence in the monthly issues of the magazine, this disclaimer on the masthead lacks credibility.

Covert advertising also presents itself as factual information. "Vacations you can afford" (*Woman's Day*, 27 April 1982, pp. 52ff) overtly only offers information on money-saving vacations. Here the ideology is similar to that of most coupon promotions: one is urged to save money by spending it. The article promotes resorts and hotels by name yet claims to offer only facts and information. In October 1981, *Ladies' Home Journal* presented the "October recipe index," ostensibly to provide readers with information: "Here is a listing of recipes appearing in this issue including those from the *Journal* kitchen and *advertisements. All have been tested by our home economists*" (p. 122, my emphasis). Of the forty-three recipes in the index, ten are from ads. Through such an "index," *Ladies' Home Journal* encourages readers to conceive of advertising and editorial material as a single continuum. Readers are relayed to the purchased ads, under the guise of looking for recipes.

Certain standard editorial traditions are also part of the code of information. A relay text such as the "Report from the Editor," ostensibly only provides information on one or more of the magazine's features but in reality serves as a covert advertisement for these features and the products they in turn covertly advertise. The cover credit offers information about the cover but usually promotes several products as well. Book, movie, and record reviews often promote the cultural commodities that they claim to be reviewing. Book excerpts are subtle advertisements for the larger works. "Merchandise Information" (*Woman's Day*), "Where to Buy" (*Seventeen*), "Editorial Buying Directory" (*Modern Bride*), "High Point Shopping Information" (*Town &*

Country), and "Savvy Information Center" (*Savvy*) are some of the standard editorial features that tell readers where to buy the products advertised in the issue. Some magazines even include card inserts through which readers can send for further promotions from advertisers, under the guise of requesting more information.

Covert advertising, then, is a system of mutually sustaining techniques and themes that links the editorial material to purchased advertising. While varying in degree of concealment, covert advertisements always attempt in some way to mislabel or disguise themselves as non-advertising material. Because of their quantity and the variety of forms in which they appear, they interact almost continuously with the purchased advertising in the magazine. The examples discussed here should not be seen as individual instances of disguise but as elements of an integrated system. Since this system relies on concealment to one degree or another, it is important to develop terms that will aid in the recognition and analysis of covert persuasion. Decoding the numerous varieties of covert ads – adjacency, tie-ins, relay texts, and others – reveals the appropriateness of the term "women's advertising magazines" to describe these publications; when covert advertising is taken into account, very little remains in women's magazines that is not advertising. Besides increasing the quantity of advertising in a magazine, covert ads enhance the effect of the purchased ads in numerous subtle ways. As we move on to an analysis of purchased advertising in magazines – the lifeblood, in a manner of speaking, of these publications – we must keep in mind the strong editorial support that purchased advertising receives from these covert techniques of persuasion.

3 Critical Approaches to Purchased Advertising

ADVERTISING DISPLACES READING MATTER

The continuum of advertising that now underlies nearly 90 per cent of the pages of most women's magazines has not always been a structural constant. Like radio broadcasting in the early twentieth century, as Erik Barnouw shows, magazines began with very little advertising. During what Frank Luther Mott has termed the Golden Age of American magazines (1825–50) when several thousand new magazines were started, advertising made only a preliminary appearance and was confined chiefly to the covers of expensive magazines or to four- or eight-page inserts.[1]

After the Civil War, a new upsurge of magazines accompanied the growth of business and industry. Early forms of covert advertising appeared in this period such as "reading notices" – ads presented as if they were articles. Mott notes that one publisher tried to use his editorial columns to sell railroad bonds, for which he was to receive a percentage of sales. In the late nineteenth century magazines gradually became profitable businesses, selling more and more pages to advertisers. The Harper Brothers, for example, started *Harper's Monthly* (originally *Harper's New Monthly Magazine*) as a marketing aid for their book publishing house, using several pages of the magazine to advertise forthcoming books. In the 1880s *Harper's* began to include ads for other companies' products, sometimes as many as forty pages a month. In December 1891, the popular Christmas issue had 177 pages of ads. By 1892 the annual advertising revenue of another important magazine, *Ladies' Home Journal*, was about a quarter of a million dollars, and six years later that figure had doubled.

Before the 1880s most advertising in the United States occurred at the retailer's level in local newspapers. With the great industrial development of the 1880s more manufacturers began to advertise, and they were attracted to the wide readership of nationally circulating magazines. The 1890s saw a tremendous upsurge in national magazine advertising, although full-page ads were uncommon until the final year of the century. The average size of ads throughout most of the 1880s and 1890s was smaller than one-quarter page. *Ladies' Home Journal*, for example, ran 243 ads on eight pages in its September 1891 issue.[2]

Already in the 1890s advertising began to have a profound effect on editorial content. The practice of "tailing" fiction into the advertising pages, so that readers would be sure to see the ads, became common. Many magazines placed special editorial departments within their advertising sections which, it must be remembered, normally appeared at the end, after all of the editorial material. The home service departments of the magazines presented advice on purchasing consumer goods and correlated articles with the advertising columns. John Tebbel notes that the upsurge of advertising in magazines virtually ended the editorial independence of most publications. Because advertising revenues gradually replaced circulation monies as the primary source of income, magazines might risk their survival by offending advertisers even slightly: "When public relations dictated a particular working arrangement between advertising and editorial matter, no one was likely to question it."[3]

Indeed, as we have seen, one study has aptly termed contemporary women's magazines, "women's advertising magazines."[4] *McCall's*, an early example of this phenomenon, was founded in 1873 to promote the dressmaking pattern business of James McCall. *The Queen*, as it was originally titled, published a few notes about fashion on the first page while the remaining pages contained pictures of the clothes one could make with McCall's patterns. After the magazine's sale in 1893, the editorial content was broadened to include a children's section, literary notes, jokes and needlework – but fashion remained the principal editorial offering. By 1900, content had increased dramatically to 72 pages from the original eight because more advertising was sold. Not only did ad volume determine the size of the magazine but advertising soon assumed more prominent positions in each issue. In 1932 *McCall's* introduced "three-way make-up," an editorial layout that Mott claims "made a minor revolution in magazine journalism in the women's field." By dividing the magazine into three sections, each with its own cover page and special content, *McCall's* made it possible for advertisements to appear throughout the magazine instead of only in the back.

Other magazines followed suit and even when the special three-part format was dropped in 1950, advertising in the front remained a standard practice.[5]

Once linked inextricably to advertisers, magazines played an important role in the development of the consumer society. By the early twentieth century a number of specialized magazines had emerged, reflecting specific audiences with particular buying patterns. Advertising for household cleaning items, for example, was likely to work more efficiently in a magazine aimed at women than in a general-interest publication. Today, the advertising and editorial categories correlate closely. The editorial focus of a magazine about to be launched is often partially formulated according to which advertisers the publishers hope to sell space to. Advertising categories shape the cultural attributes of a magazine. While *Cosmopolitan*, for example, published 888 ad pages for toiletries and cosmetics in 1981, *Family Circle* only published 160 in this category. In contrast, *Cosmopolitan* ran only 34 ad pages for food and food products while *Family Circle* ran 479.[6] Magazines consciously develop their editorial material to offer an appropriate showcase for their advertisers' products. As occurred in *McCall's* early development, editorial pages increase as advertising grows.

WOMEN AND THE NEEDS OF INDUSTRY: INDUCED INSECURITIES AND THE MAGIC OF ADVERTISING

The "advertising magazine" continued to grow, in large part, because of industry's growth. In his historical study of the origins of modern advertising in the United States, Stuart Ewen has shown that with the advances in assembly-line mass production in the early twentieth century, the captains of industry increasingly needed outlets for mass distribution of the larger quantity of goods available. Modern advertising developed as a means of influencing human behavior in accordance with the needs of industry by instilling desires for new commodities.[7]

Crucial to the increased distribution of goods was the creation of "fancied needs"; businesses wanted people to buy not simply to meet basic human needs, but to satisfy those of industry. Ewen notes: "A given ad asked not only that an individual buy its product, but that [one] experience a self-conscious perspective [implying] that [one] had previously been socially and psychically denied."[8] Advertising then promised that consumer goods would alleviate these newly emphasized frustrations. Ads played on normal human anxieties, exaggerating them in order to promote consumption. Ewen cites an ad for Cutex Hand Preparations in the April 1920 *Ladies' Home Journal* which told women: "You will be amazed to find how many times in one day people glance at your nails. At each glance a judgment is made. . . . Indeed some people make a practice of basing their estimate of a new acquaintance largely on this one detail."[9] And because women were the major purchasers of consumer goods, making 80 per cent of family purchases, much advertising addressed women. Ads in the 1920s attempted to reverse the still predominant value of thrift which was now antithetical to increased consumer spending; soon, Ewen argues, "excessiveness replaced thrift as a social value."[10]

Several characteristics of early twentieth century advertising continue to underlie advertising in women's magazines today. Because women are still the principal purchasers of consumer goods, women's magazines constitute the largest group in the industry and contain immense numbers of ad pages. The quantity and kinds of ads in these magazines fluctuate according to the needs of industry to distribute various goods and services. Both covert and overt advertising attempt to create fancied needs and exaggerated self-consciousness in the primarily female audience of these publications.

Ewen's discussion of fancied needs parallels Raymond William's concept of the magic of advertising. In his study of the historical origins of advertising in England, Williams has analyzed the paradox that advertising in our materialist society is in fact not materialist enough. The material object that advertising tries to sell is never sufficient in itself: it must be validated, often only in fantasy, by additional meanings which Williams terms "magic." Added to material commodities in order to sell them is "a highly organized and professional system of magical inducements and satisfactions"[11] that have little if any material link to the products themselves. In fact, it is precisely because consumer goods often fail to satisfy many human needs and desires that advertising uses magic to associate consumption with human desires: women's magazines for example, promise that a shampoo will bring women male attention or that a dress will assure success on the job, although neither product will satisfy these needs in practice.

Ultimately, however, advertising does more than sell products, according to Williams. Not surprisingly, the cultural patterns of the system of magic begin to take root in a society, becoming a system of communication in their own right. Williams notes that once the magical pattern has been established, people respond to each other's "displayed signals" which symbolize one's having made the correct purchases. Consumers use commodities as a means of expression, a kind of language, and eventually come to depend upon the system of fantasy.[12]

Williams helps us to understand that the induced insecurities and fancied needs that Ewen describes can only be alleviated through the system of magic that advertising attaches to products. Ideas, not products, are the ultimate assuagers of fancied needs and induced anxieties. Nonetheless, we must purchase the advertised product or a similar one in order to gain communicative use of the idea. The magic associated with the possessed commodity then substitutes for some of our language faculties as we communicate information about ourselves through the products we own.

THE IDEOLOGY OF ADVERTISING AND THE FEMINIST CRITIQUE

These formulations of Ewen and Williams delineate only a few of the numerous ideological messages of advertising. Concepts such as fancied needs and magical inducements can be understood in the broad sense of the term ideology as an illusory, distorted picture of the world. Magical inducements, for example, disguise the actual inability of commodities to satisfy many human needs, as Williams shows. Jameson has suggested that we might term such illusions an inadequate "cognitive mapping" of social experience,[13] paralleling Althusser's formulation that ideology offers people an imaginary distortion of their relations to real historical conditions.[14] This view of ideology would argue, for example, that a magazine ad's depiction of a woman euphorically smelling the laundry she has just washed for her family, in fact disguises this often unpaid, repetitive household task as an instrument of happiness and fulfillment.

Ideology, of course, does not deterministically affect all who see an ad. Even when defining ideology in the somewhat reductionist sense of false consciousness, we must note that advertising and other ideological formations present certain distortions to people who, in turn, may or may not interiorize the misrepresentations. The point of analyzing ideology is to demarcate the various illusory strategies at work in an ad.

Several of the criticisms that cultural theorists have levelled against the Althusserian notion of ideology are useful in decoding magazine texts. Stuart Hall argues that Althusser presents the process of ideology as too "uni-accentual," that is, that the model is too functionally adapted to the reproduction of the dominant ideology. To explain how discourse reproduces other elements besides the dominant, distorted view of reality, Hall utilizes the theories of Voloshinov and Gramsci to redefine ideology as a "site of struggle." Meanings are constantly contested; what the dominant forces in society may "articulate" in a certain way is often "disarticulated" in what Hall terms "negotiated" or "oppositional" readings of texts.[15] What happens, for example, when a woman who has worked all day outside the home glances at an ad depicting the ideal homemaker ecstatically smelling clean laundry as she herself attempts to wash several loads of her family's clothes before going to bed? Can the utopian elements of this ad function at such a moment for her? Might not the ideological pleasure that the ad attempts to establish be strongly contested as the woman produces an oppositional reading of the text because of her present material conditions? De Certeau has argued that there exists a large field of resisting "practices" or "tactics" which apparatuses such as the media cannot fully repress. Although he is perhaps too optimistic in viewing such practices as "a mobile infinity of tactics,"[16] his work reminds us that social reality threatens constantly to disrupt what media strategies attempt to anchor.

For Hall, ideology is a site of struggle for competing definitions of reality, and ideological power is the power to signify events in a certain way. Viewed from this perspective magazines are part of a field of discourses, each of which is struggling to become the obvious or common-sense way of viewing reality; and within individual magazines and their constituent parts, competing discourses struggle as well. At both ends of the communicative process, a struggle for discursive power is waged, although we must remember that encoders and decoders do not hold power equally. Nonetheless, just as an ideological struggle takes place at the moment of decoding, so, too, are the encoders engaged in a semiotic offensive as they attempt to accent certain meanings over others. Chapter 7 will show, for example, that the first Editor of *New Woman* attempted to secure discursive control over feminist ideas by reappropriating certain elements of the women's movement and disparaging others. When the Editor of *Working Woman*, as we saw in Chapter 1, openly told readers how to interpret a cover photo, she desired to anchor a single, preferred meaning of the polysemous photo.

When the producers of magazines try to control signification in such ways, they exert cultural leadership – what Gramsci termed hegemony – rather than compelling individuals into adherence to dominant ideological views. Such elements as the pleasure magazines evoke and the implicit logic of verbal and photographic statements serve to attract readers into agreeing with the significatory presuppositions advanced, wining, as Gramsci theorized, the reader's active consent to ideological formations. Hall and others have argued, however, that although many cultural texts aim for such ideological closure, they can only attain it relatively; most texts are "leaky systems" which, although frequently attempting to suppress contradictions and obtain closure, often fail to do so.[17]

Fredric Jameson offers a model to explain how texts struggle to attain this discursive dominance. Arguing that ideology in one important sense is the structural limitation or closure of a text, he develops the concept of the "political unconscious" of the text – what a given cultural artifact represses, what it refuses to think or allow itself to say. By analyzing a text's "strategies of containment," we help to shatter its ostensible formal unity, its "ideological mirage," and discover, for example, how various levels in the text subvert one another. A structuralist model such as the Greimasian semiotic rectangle can be reappropriated, Jameson argues, to delineate "the limits of a specific ideological consciousness, the conceptual points beyond which that consciousness cannot go and between which it is condemned to oscillate."[18]

Even this understanding of ideology is incomplete, Jameson argues, when it only examines the negative work of the text, what the object of study represses and tries to prevent us from seeing. Simultaneously, we must analyze the positive, utopian elements through which these ideological texts attract us. Jameson suggests that mass culture, for example, offers audiences specific gratifications in return for remaining passive. While sometimes these gratifications allow us temporary participation in the forbidden or transgressive, it is precisely by awakening certain dangerous and protopolitical impulses that mass culture controls these impulses. Mass cultural texts engage in "a complex strategy of rhetorical persuasion in which substantial incentives are offered for ideological adherence."[19] The incentives and the impulses that mass culture both utilizes and strives to manage are utopian in character. While given levels of fantasy and pleasure are at work in the text, these utopian elements must ultimately serve certain ideological functions and be "reinvested by . . . the political unconscious."[20]

Jameson's formulations highlight the attractiveness of ideological representations, their internal structure, and their positions within other structures. The utopian element in ideology helps to assuage discontent with the inequalities of contemporary social organization and facilitates acceptance of the ideological representations as real or natural. In an ad that uses stereotypic gender distinctions to sell a product, for example, elements such as glamor, a sense of sexual transgression, the implicit promise of love and feelings of self-worth, and the aesthetic composition of the ad itself are some of the abstract incentives offered readers to make the stereotypical portrayal palatable and even desirable. Jameson shows that one can reappropriate certain literary theories to analyze both the internal structure of the ideological text and its larger function within other structures. What elements in an advertisement, for example, function as "strategies of containment" that both invoke and control oppositional impulses? In spite of the apparent formal unity of an ad, do its various levels in fact subvert one another? What are the broader structures that ads form with the other material in the magazine, other media, and other real-world phenomena?

Feminist theorists have expanded upon these rearticulations of the problem of ideology. Christine Gledhill argues, following Hall, that the process of meaning production must be understood as one of negotiation. Feminist criticism must perform two functions: first, "[use] textual and contextual analysis to determine the conditions and possibilities of gendered readings" but at the same time, "[exploit] textual contradiction to put into circulation readings that draw the text into a female and/or feminist orbit."[21] While respecting the text's capacity to negotiate in conjunction with the reader a number of ideological meanings, Gledhill argues that feminist criticism necessarily foregrounds certain of the text's semiotic possibilities over others.

Angela McRobbie, in a study of the British magazine for teenage girls *Jackie*, argues that such publications do not merely "[give] the girls what they want" but rather "try to win and shape the consent of readers to a set of particular values." Utilizing a concept of ideology as the site of struggle, McRobbie analyzes the magazine's work of "'framing' the world for its readers" by endowing importance to certain topics and not others.[22] Magazines work to set the agenda for cultural expression, engaging in a leadership role that guides readers' concerns to certain areas. Hegemony is achieved uncoercively in a cultural form such as women's magazines, a sphere of activity that readers view as an arena of freedom, free choice, and free time.

Theorists such as Tony Bennett have taken issue with the notion that the media function as definers of social reality by recurrently signifying events in certain ways; Hall, of course, posits that the preferred definitions of reality that the media attempt to maintain can never completely anchor the desired signification, but Bennett questions the implicit premise of a "duality between the plane of signification and that of 'reality'."[23] Rather than see the problem of ideology as one of the truth or falsity of images, one should focus on the relation between signs; "reality" is always already signified, that is, it is always mediated through codes.

Similarly, Valerie Walkerdine has argued that we cannot understand ideology as simply a distortion of an external reality which can be remedied by presenting people instead with correct images of the real world. Rather, she urges us to focus on the struggle for discursive meaning that takes place between text and reader and the role of desire and fantasy in establishing various "regimes of meaning." In fact, she argues, the very "unreality" of certain cultural texts is an important basis of their strength.[24] We will see in Chapter 4, for example, that ads that link cruelty (death, rape, and torture) to sexual excitement do not merely distort reality; rather, they reconfigure signifiers to displace the real experience of pain to levels of fantasy, allowing readers to conflate desire, abstract, "pleasurable" pain, and the product.

Herbert Schiller offers an important corrective to these and other views that audiences are not strongly affected by the ideological views that the media proffer. He suggests that media theorists who argue that audiences are active in producing their own meaning and resisting the dominant discourse are in fact reproducing a version of the "limited-effects" paradigm advanced by Lazarsfeld and others from the 1940s to the 1960s. Like its predecessor, the new, active-audience view, however, mistakenly assumes that the producers and receivers of messages have equal power. Arguments about the resistance and empowerment of the viewer fail to show that these activities have any effect on the real structures of power in society. They frequently focus on the production of meaning as an individual act and fail to take into account that "human beings are not equipped to deal with a pervasive disinformation system . . . that assaults the senses through all cultural forms and channels."[25]

I would argue that cultural criticism should combine Schiller's important emphasis on media power with some of the concepts about the audience's activity and pleasure. Theorists such as Hall and Morley[26] retain a concern with the power relations produced by class, race, and gender differences in their formulations about what audiences bring to the process of meaning formation. Lovell and Frith have noted that "the structures of power in the relationships into which individuals are inserted puts limits on the range of positions which a text can achieve"; one's reading of a text is shaped by one's material conditions.[27] As we move beyond the view of ideology as simply false consciousness, we move toward important hypotheses (and sometimes case studies) about how ideology in actuality functions. Cultural critics must continue the work of decoding dominant media strategies and recurrent structural systems that operate, while at the same time taking into account various modes in which audiences might read these messages.

For example, Schiller's argument that the media have convinced most Americans to believe in the Cold War and such concomitant enemies as Qaddafi, Arafat, the Sandinistas, and Castro is not incompatible with Hall's view that most of us perform negotiated readings of media texts in which our situational reference contradicts the hegemonic message. But, Hall argues, hegemonic definitions of reality often nonetheless prevail, "containing within them a great deal of negotiated exceptions." Historical evidence shows that people do not necessarily go on to construct counterhegemonic visions from their negotiated readings of texts.[28] Hall's contention that communicative systems are "leaky," that negotiated readings frequently exist, helps to explain the need for the constant repetition of ideological truisms, stereotypes and the other recurrent structures with which the media address us. The hegemonic vision is not secured easily because social reality often looms as a corrective. Women's magazines in the early 1980s, for example, were forced to contest such social pressures as feminism, the increasingly large number of employed women, and the movements of minorities for greater recognition and equality. In addition to such strategies as presenting depoliticized versions of feminism and exoticizing minority women, these magazines developed hundreds of thousands of repetitive, stereotypical images of women in an attempt to secure preferred meanings through easily understood semiotic systems that would work to sell consumer goods. It is precisely because a tired woman worker might read oppositionally a text such as the ad for laundry detergent discussed above that such stereotypes must so frequently be repeated.

Feminist criticism of mass culture has analyzed both the negative ideology in media images and the role of the active audience in the construction of meaning. Early studies offered quantitative findings about negative images of women, often without considering such factors as race and ethnicity.[29] Gaye Tuchman has argued that rather than cataloguing images, critics should use concepts such as Goffman's notion of frames or Geertz's theory of "ensembles of texts."[30] Following her suggestion, an analysis of the ideological myths that the media generate would analyze ensembles that exist between images, various media, and events in the real world. Goffman's concept of frames focuses attention on the media's attempt to predispose people to certain worldviews. It is not enough, for example, to say that a given advertisement in a magazine presents stereotypical images of women. How does an ad that shows women in a purely decorative role, for example, form an ensemble with similar and dissimilar images in the same mass cultural text, in other media, and in the world at large? Through what subtle and obvious frames does it attempt to anchor a given way of seeing the world?

Janice Winship also criticizes the standard content analysis of sex roles, noting that researchers who focus on images of women usually emphasize "*what* is represented at the expense of *how* it is represented."[31] Analysis of images implicitly assumes that certain images exist independently in ads and present transparent meanings to viewers. Instead, Winship argues, readers help to produce the meanings of ads. The "you" to whom ads speak usually has a gender and class; viewers' interpretations depend on whether they're women or men, working class or middle class, black or white. Winship suggests that we use the technique of reversal when analyzing the intended addressee of an ad. What words and images would the ad use were it addressing men instead of women, women of color instead of the usual white women, or women of a different socio-economic class?

Earlier Noreene Janus also argued against the liberal feminist bias common in most studies of women's portrayal in the media.[32] Janus insists that a fully critical approach to sexist portrayals must study the relationship between sexist images and social structures. The liberal approach confuses the mechanisms by which social relations are maintained with the underlying forces that promote the social relations and implies, for example, that the media would be less sexist if women advertised the same types of products as men, were shown in more types of occupations, or were used in the voiceovers of commercials as often as men are. Much content analysis studies all the male portrayals in a given medium in contrast to all the female depictions, thus failing to account for divisions such as class, race, or culture within the two groups.

One important debate among feminist researchers compares the usefulness of qualitative and quantitative approaches to the study of sex roles. Danish researcher Preben Sepstrup, for example, conducted an empirical study of advertisements in all Danish newspapers and magazines over a one-year period (February 1977 to February 1978) in an attempt to combine both the theoretical and empiricist approaches.[33] Five hundred and eight questions were formulated for coders to answer with respect to each ad, based on hypotheses that previous critical theoretical studies had presented. Highly significantly, the findings upheld most of the results of previous smaller-scale quantitative studies and those of qualitative studies that only examined a few ads. Sepstrup argues that qualitative analysis will always be necessary to understand in detail the content of advertising. Perhaps the concern that qualitative research is not representative should be laid aside in light of Sepstrup's findings. Critics should proceed with in-depth textual analysis of individual ads and small groups of ads, confident that the findings are quite likely to be representative. Periodically, researchers might join quantitative and qualitative techniques as Sepstrup has done to monitor the reliability of qualitative findings. Qualitative, critical study of small numbers of ads helps to reveal the subtleties of offensive portrayals in the media, the necessary first stage of articulate protest.

Other feminist criticism of mass culture focuses on the role of the audience in producing meaning. Dorothy Hobson, for example, has analyzed women's reappropriation of radio and television programs in the home as structural elements of daytime and evening domestic labor. Her respondents illustrate how "the ideology of femininity and feminine values over-determines the structures of what interests women."[34] The women in her study perceive news and current events programming to be of little interest and geared toward men yet view these programs as important. We must remember, however, that such perceived oppositions are learned as are one's interests. How might a companion medium such as women's magazines which rarely discuss news and politics help to shape women's interests away from current political events and toward a view that this is a masculine, albeit important, area of concern?

SEMIOTIC ANALYSIS OF ADVERTISING

One important method of qualitative analysis is the semiotic decoding of ads. A theoretical system with its basis in linguistics, semiology, or the "science of signs," extends linguistic analysis to other forms of communication. Roland Barthes built upon the Swiss linguist Ferdinand de Saussure's formulations that language is composed of signifiers and signifieds. In 1964 Barthes reversed Saussure's formulation that linguistics was only one part of the science of signs. Rather, Barthes claimed, semiology is a part of linguistics because signifieds cannot exist apart from language. Even non-verbal signs such as pictures "pass through the relay of language."[35] With linguistics thus established as its parent discipline, semiology was soon utilized and amplified by theorists in other fields such as anthropology, psychology, sociology, literature, and communications.

Several of Barthes' early semiotic studies – short essays written between 1952 and 1956 – appear, together with a longer theoretical piece, in the 1957 volume *Mythologies*. Predating by a few years Raymond Williams' study of the magic of advertising, they present a concept of myth in advertising and other forms of mass culture that complements Williams' notion of magic. Barthes' intent in *Mythologies* was to use semiology to demythologize and thereby repoliticize the mythic language of everyday mass culture. He expanded Saussure's semiotic chain to account for the mythic sign. In ordinary language, Saussure had noted, the sign is composed of the signifier (the acoustic image or its written form) and its signified (the corresponding mental concept). The sign "gold," for example, is composed of a signifier, "g-o-l-d" and a signified, the mental concept this signifier produces. In mythic language (which includes advertising and other mass cultural representations) the entire sign of ordinary language becomes merely the signifier in what Barthes termed a second-order sign system. The ordinary sign g-o-l-d/concept of gold, for example, has come to be a signifier in other semiotic chains, producing new signifieds such as wealth and success – what Williams would term "magic." Barthes' semiotic method in *Mythologies* was an attempt to demythologize the apparent naturalness and timelessness of these second-order sign systems by showing them to be "a type of speech chosen by history."[36] He claimed that semiotic analysis offered a metalanguage to unmask the mythic language of mass culture, showing it to be time-bound and historically specific, produced by second-order sign systems.

Barthes' concept of the second-order sign system places Williams' notion of the magic of advertising in the context of historically determined language. As part of a system of communication, the magical inducements of advertising are second-order meanings that the signs of advertising add to products. Although the second-order meanings may appear to be natural and eternal properties of the products, they are linked to a particular historical time. A bright shade of nail enamel, for example, may signify beauty, social acceptance, and a means of attaining love to a woman at one time period, while at another it may mean poor taste, the old-fashioned, and the possibility of rejection by others. To the consumer who has learned these meanings through advertising, they may appear to be natural, inherent qualities of the products. Semiotic analysis shows that, in fact, these myths and magical inducements are part of the secondary sign systems that advertising creates and are intentionally changed or retained in accordance with economic and market forces.

In her interdisciplinary study of contemporary advertisements, Judith Williamson builds upon Barthes' semiotic formulations, linking semiology to Freudian and Lacanian psychoanalytic theory, the structural anthropology of Levi-Strauss, several of Marx's works of the 1840s and 1850s, and the theories of his twentieth century successors, Gramsci, Brecht, Benjamin, and Althusser. According to Williamson, advertisements not only sell products but create structures of meaning; the messages of ads try to make the properties of commodities mean something to us. Ads provide a structure that can transform the language of objects into that of people and vice versa: "Thus a diamond comes to 'mean' love and endurance for us. Once the connection has been made, we begin to translate the other way and in fact to skip translating altogether: taking the sign for what it signifies, the thing for the feeling."[37]

Extending Freud's concept of "dream-work," Williamson emphasizes the important role that the audience plays in the creation of meaning in advertising. Secondary sign systems with less obvious meanings require the viewer to correlate additional signifiers and signifieds. We perform the work of transferring meaning from one signifier to another. I will argue in Chapter 4, for example, that although the preferred encoding of the ad series for Hanes hosiery may appear to rest upon the central motif of a woman made glamorous by wearing this product, in fact the ads urge us to activate a secondary system of signification. Within this secondary discursive structure, the apparently central model only exists in relation to her opposite – the negative pole established by another model in the ad who does not wear the product. The oppositional structure that the advertisers have preferred here depends on viewers to activate its semiosis whether consciously or unconsciously. Instead of presenting a completed meaning, the ad invites us to make a given transaction, to perform "advertising work," and participate in the system of creating meaning.

Williamson argues that the first task of advertising is that of differentiation. Because there is so little real difference among most products within their respective categories (shampoos or toothpastes, for example), ads attempt to create apparent differences; each pseudo-difference is defined explicitly or implicitly by its opposite. Williamson cites the example of an ad for Chanel perfume that juxtaposes two signs: a picture of the product with a picture of Catherine Deneuve. The ad is part of a communicative system in which its opposite is implied – the ads for the less expensive Babe cologne that picture Margaux Hemingway. Ads appropriate and use the distinctions of current social mythologies to differentiate similar products. In a type of reverse totemism, people are used to differentiate objects in ads such as these. (Subsequently, however, as Raymond Williams noted, things are used to differentiate people, as we communicate to one another through the products we have purchased.)

Williamson links this process of pseudo-differentiation to the formation of ideology in advertising. When ads juxtapose two signs such as Catherine Deneuve and Chanel perfume, we often assume the connection to be natural. Similarly, advertising falsely links people's internal feelings to an external object through what comes to be seen as a logical connection; the unattainable is associated with what can be attained – the purchased product. Instead of seeing that this connection is ideological, based on an artificial system of pseudo-differentiation of similar products, we come to view the abstract quality as an inherent, natural attribute of the product.

One of the principal techniques of advertising's system of communication is interpellation. Ads often address us through the implied phrase, "Hey, you!" Expanding Althusser's discussion of the technique, Williamson notes that just as we learn to associate a product with an emotion, so do we associate ourselves with the way we are addressed in ads.[38] This learning process helps to explain the concern of many women about sexist stereotyping in the interpellations of ads. The "Hey, you" address is a cornerstone of the ideological system of communication in advertisements; historically rooted patterns of language and thought appear to be natural and eternal. In his 1975 study of advertisements, Lawrence Bardin delineated three common forms that the "Hey, you" interpellation in ads can take: (1) the vocative case which marks the one addressed (direct address); (2) the imperative case which urges the addressee to become what she is addressed as; and (3) more subtle mechanisms such as characters in ads who face readers, speaking to them, or psychological devices that permit the reader to identify with the hero or heroine.[39] In Chapter 4 we will see, for example, that interpellation in ads often establishes structures of opposing elements that mark the limits of a given way of thinking about reality. When we learn to conceive of ourselves according to the way we are addressed in ads, we frequently learn as well to situate ourselves between the poles of an arbitrary structure of opposition.

Theorists such as Williamson have expanded Barthes' early semiotic analysis and have begun to demonstrate in specific terms how the mythic language of mass culture is historically specific and time-bound. One can critique Williamson's interdisciplinary model for conflating the critic's interpretation of certain advertising texts with the work that the audience performs when viewing ads, that is, of seeing the audience's work somewhat unidimensionally. More recently, cultural theorists have amplified such critical models to hypothesize about how different audiences perform semiotic work when viewing mass culture. Focusing on the polysemous nature of such texts, critics analyze a number of sometimes contradictory semiotic strategies at work in a text which offer various meanings for readers to appropriate according to their own circumstances and preferences. But theorists must be careful, as Williamson has been, to ground the critical semiotic optic in historical specificity. And as we delineate some of the discursive positions that readers may activate in a given text we must remember, as Hall and Schiller point out, that certain linkages have been reinforced more than others throughout history. The repeated couplings of select signifiers and signifieds help to secure certain articulations over others.[40] The text is not a completely open field in which discursive power awaits anyone who will anchor it in whatever way she or he chooses. While one cannot presume that the critic's readings of a text is coextensive with those of the text's everyday audience, the critic sometimes succeeds in decoding certain of the important historical couplings that a given ad or magazine feature attempts to naturalize.[41] Although some semioticians allude to the historical nature of the verbal and photographic signs of advertising, they often place more emphasis on delineating the signifiers and signifieds of second-order sign systems than on precisely demarcating the historical specificities of these signs. For semiotics to succeed in its goal of repoliticizing the mythic language of mass culture it must link its observations to other theoretical models and techniques of analysis. Indispensable is the study of the infrastructure of the advertising industry.

INFRASTRUCTURAL ANALYSIS OF ADVERTISING

Many view advertising in women's magazines simply as a series of pleasurable images, even though conscious to some degree that its purpose is to sell products and services. Semiotics decodes these pleasurable images as elements of secondary sign systems. But the images are rooted as well in the economic system of consumer goods distribution. The information, for example, that a magazine charges over $100,000 for an ad on its back cover, a cost that is often passed on in some form to consumers who buy advertised products, materially reconfigures the pleasurable signs of the ad.

Analysis of the infrastructure of advertising in women's magazines focuses primarily on the economic underpinnings of the magazine industry and the advertisements it publishes. Proceeding from the general to the specific, the analysis begins with economic information about the women's magazine industry as a whole and the fiscal health of individual magazines in this group. Second, one examines the material underpinnings of individual purchased ads, analyzing such factors as the price of the advertising space, the ad's location in the issue, and its structural relation to other ads and features in the magazine. Finally, the infrastructure of the particular advertised product is analyzed – its price, parent corporation, assumed potential consumers, and the current market conditions affecting its sales. Study of the infrastructure of advertising reveals the women's magazine to be an integrated cultural whole in which covert and overt ads interact continuously with one another and with the minimal non-advertising material in each issue.

The Infrastructure of the Magazine

The Women's Magazine Category and Group Ownership

As advertising vehicles, women's magazines are among the most desirable of publications. They are aimed at the sector of the population traditionally most responsible for purchases. Today, despite some changes in the division of labor in households, many women continue to carry the primary responsibility for buying. The publishing industry has made changes that are, for the most part, minor. Traditional women's magazines have updated their methods of urging women to buy and some claim to attract male readers as well. Several new publications address more specialized sectors of women with high purchasing power. The strength of the women's magazine category rests principally on the crucial role of women in the consumption process and on the ability of this magazine group to adapt, albeit superficially, to social change.

The business of directing advertising messages to women is so profitable that some corporations own several women's magazines. Data on group ownership facilitate the infrastructural decoding of both overt and covert ads. Often an advertiser has obtained special rates for buying space in two or more of the publisher's magazines. Until the end of 1982, for example, the "Conde Nast Package" offered discounts for combined advertising in at least four of its six women's magazines.[42] In the case of covert ads, when an editorial promotion for a product or service occurs in two or more publications owned by the same parent corporation, each with its separate editorial staff, it is likely that the editorial mention has been suggested by the publishing staff rather than coincidentally by the separate groups of editorial workers.

Many women's magazines are also part of larger media conglomerates. The Conde Nast Group is a subsidiary of S. I. Newhouse and Sons, the country's seventh largest media company, whose media revenue during 1982 *Advertising Age* estimates to be $1.35 billion. Also owner of Random House books, numerous newspapers, cable-video interests, and *Parade* Sunday supplement, Newhouse is the largest privately owned media company in the country.[43]

Hearst Corporation, the country's ninth largest media company, made an estimated $1.3 billion in media revenues in

1982. It publishes six women's magazines: *Cosmopolitan, Good Housekeeping, Harper's Bazaar, House Beautiful, Redbook,* and *Town & Country*, and owns five television stations, seven radio stations, cable-video interests, numerous other magazines, newspapers, book publishers and comic strip syndicates. The company has established a "Gold Power Package" to compete with the "Conde Nast Ltd" special advertising discount. For advertisers primarily wishing to reach women, Hearst offers the "Power Package" which includes *Cosmopolitan, Redbook*, and *Good Housekeeping*. With twelve pages in each of these magazines, the publisher claims, advertisers will not only earn discounts but will reach 70 per cent of all women between the ages of 18 and 49. In 1982 Hearst made $595 million in revenues from its fourteen magazines and six of its top seven moneymaking magazines are women's publications.[44]

The Magazine's Fiscal Health

The financial viability of a publication is a primary determinant of the kinds and quantity of ads published in it. Here, annual profit figures do not reveal as much as do specific data on advertising, circulation, and growth. The number of advertising pages sold per issue is one of the most important signs of a magazine's fiscal health and advertisers' confidence in the publication's ability to promote products. *Vogue* and *Cosmopolitan* have the highest number of ad pages of the women's magazines and were ranked tenth and seventeenth respectively of all US consumer magazines by ad pages for 1982.[45] When ad volume is down, as was the case with the home service magazines in the early 1980s, there are more instances of special advertising sections, stabilization of ad rates, and editorial innovation – concerted attempts to increase ad volume.

Figures on annual and per-issue advertising revenue also reveal a magazine's fiscal health. Statistics for 1982 ad revenue place ten women's magazines among the top twenty-five of all consumer magazines in the country: No. 8 *Good Housekeeping* ($110,465,000), No. 9 *Family Circle* ($106,197,000), No. 12 *Better Homes and Gardens* ($100,289,000), No. 13 *Woman's Day* ($88,909,000), No. 18 *Cosmopolitan* ($67,615,000), No. 20 *McCall's* ($62,001,000), No. 22 *Glamour* ($46,917,000), No. 23 *Vogue* ($45,154,000), No. 24 *Redbook* ($45,095,000) and No. 25 *Ladies' Home Journal* ($43,385,000). Even though *Better Homes and*

Gardens, *McCall's*, *Redbook*, and *Ladies' Home Journal* suffered declines in ad revenue that year, their multi-million dollar ad revenues enabled them to remain among the top twenty-five consumer magazines. In an outstanding example, the November 1981 *Better Homes and Gardens* earned the highest advertising revenue of any magazine issue in the medium's history, $12,315,582.[46] These women's magazines have successfully combined high advertising rates with a proportionately large number of ads sold. Thus, the number of ad pages factors with the rates that a magazine is able to charge to determine ad revenue rankings.

Ad rates, the amounts that magazines charge for advertising space, also indicate financial viability (see Appendix, Table A2). In general, magazines with larger circulations can charge advertisers more than lower circulating publications. Newer titles such as *Self* and *Working Woman* gradually increase their ad rates as their circulations grow. Advertisers are concerned with CPM figures, that is, the dollar cost for reaching 1000 consumers, and large circulation magazines usually have the lowest CPMs. The four-color CPMs of *Family Circle* and *Woman's Day*, for example, are very low – approximately $8–$9 – while those of *Savvy* and *Working Woman* are high – $29.51 and $23.91 respectively.[47]

As a number of advertisers became more concerned with reaching a "class" rather than a "mass" audience, however, some magazines deliberately lowered their circulations in order to offer advertisers a more select readership as well as to economize on production and distribution costs.[48] In 1982 *House & Garden* underwent a radical upgrading, raising its cover price to $4 and cutting its circulation rate base of one million to almost half. A magazine such as *Vogue* with a moderate circulation of approximately one million per issue charges only $20,000 for a four-color ad. However, it sold more ad pages in 1983 than any other women's magazine (3104), partly because advertisers were interested in reaching its upscale readers – women with high spending power. In contrast, a magazine such as *Better Homes and Gardens* had fewer ad pages in 1983 (1353), yet its immense circulation of approximately eight million per issue allowed it to charge the highest ad rates of any women's magazine – $78,985 for a four-color page and $110,715 for the back cover.[49] In general, ad rates rise in proportion to the number of women whom the magazine reaches, although sometimes magazines that reach "class" women with high spending power earn higher rates and sell more advertising space.

Circulation figures on subscription and news-stand sales are another important factor in the fiscal health of a magazine and of great concern to advertisers and publishers. Some place more value on news-stand purchasers, arguing, as we have seen, that such readers have made a conscious decision to buy an issue rather than receiving it automatically in the mail and perhaps not looking at the ads inside. *Family Circle* and *Woman's Day*, the first and fourth respectively among women's magazines in the 1983 *Folio* 400 overall ranking, can boast of almost complete news-stand circulation. *Good Housekeeping* and *Better Homes and Gardens*, the second and third overall of women's magazines in the *Folio* ranking, rely more heavily on subscription circulation, although *Good Housekeeping*'s distribution is divided more closely between the two kinds.[50] Advertisers are also concerned about factors such as discounted subscriptions and the news-stand cover price. Strong use of discounted offers to attract subscribers not only means that readers assume less of the production expense of the magazine but often signifies as well the declining popularity of the publication. Conversely, some magazines experiment with higher news-stand cover prices not only to help defray production costs but to suggest to advertisers that women who purchase the higher-priced issues are more motivated to look at the ads inside and likely to have more money to spend on products.

Besides circulation figures, publishers utilize even more detailed information about readers to draw advertisers. Data on the number of readers per copy, the time the average reader spends with each issue and the other magazines read each month are made available to encourage advertisers that readers in fact see the ads and constitute an audience that is not duplicated by other magazines. Sometimes surveys of readers' attitudes toward current social issues are presented; *Cosmopolitan*, for example, offers advertisers figures on the number of its readers who are "active *involved* citizens," those who have written to elected officials, magazines, newspapers, radio or TV stations, addressed a public meeting, or worked for a political party. Here, the implication is that active, involved women will purchase more advertised products.[51]

Perhaps the most comprehensive studies are those of the

readers' buying patterns. Figures abound on those who purchase consumer goods such as televisions, appliances, sports equipment, clothing, automobiles, cosmetics, liquor, cigarettes, men's products, household cleaning products, food items, insurance, and jewelry. *Mademoiselle*, for example, offers advertisers an in-depth beauty and health survey with documentation, on its readers' purchase of cosmetics, fragrances, and products for the hair, complexion, hands, nails, and bath. The booklet gives data on the frequency of use of various products, the average prices paid, and the places of purchase; it breaks down a category such as "fragrance," for example, into such detailed subcategories as: "types of fragrance used," "when worn," "number of bottles on hand," "received as gifts," "layering fragrance," "keeping fragrance at work," "carrying fragrance when they travel," and "use of men's cologne."[52] It is not coincidental that these subcategories correspond thematically to the editorial features *Mademoiselle* publishes about fragrance. Not only does covert advertising in editorial sections directly recommend brand-name fragrances for gifts, travel, and work, but it gives structural support to advertisers' promotion of fancied needs in consumers through thematic parallels to the above survey subcategories.

The infrastructural data on readers are important in decoding advertising because they provide information about the audiences that advertisers think they are addressing through ads. These surveys do not inform one accurately about the magazines' real readers – the thinking, feeling human beings who are far more than a function of the amount they paid for their last bottle of shampoo. But in analyzing the advertising text, these surveys are invaluable because they catalogue and delineate the intended addressee of the communicative process. At the same time, they contribute to the development of stereotypical conceptions of women, abstractions that continue to permeate contemporary consciousness, in part, because of their frequent use in marketing and selling products.

Potential advertisers are also interested in a magazine's growth. Factors such as advertising volume, revenue, rates, circulation and the demographics of the readership continue to improve or decline according to current economic and social factors. *Folio* ranks magazines in a number of growth categories both overall and in comparison to other similarly sized publications. In 1982, for example, *New Woman* and *Working Mother* were the two fastest growing women's magazines by total revenue, having increased overall 76 per cent and 74 per cent respectively from 1981. In total revenue they were the fifth and sixth fastest growing consumer magazines in the country. Nonetheless, their 1982 revenues of $29.5 and $26.2 million respectively were less than *Parents*' $38.2 million in the same period. *Working Woman*, which had been the fastest growing women's magazine in 1979 with 61 per cent total revenue gain, by 1982 had slowed to 48 per cent with only $16.4 million in total revenue. When growth in advertising revenue alone is considered, *New Woman, Working Woman*, and *Working Mother* were among the top ten in the country in 1982 with increases of 77 per cent, 72 per cent, and 69 per cent respectively.[53]

In contrast, most of the women's service magazines showed either minimal growth or substantial declines that year. *Family Circle* and *Good Housekeeping* had 12 per cent and 7 per cent ad revenue growth respectively and the former grew only 1.5 per cent in ad volume in 1982. In total revenue *Good Housekeeping* grew only 11 per cent, *Family Circle* 9 per cent, and *Woman's Day* 2 per cent, while *McCall's, Better Homes and Gardens, Ladies' Home Journal* and *Redbook* each declined between 2 per cent and 8 per cent. Even these slight increases in total revenue and ad earnings are not accurate representations of growth, however, since inflation accounts for much of the ostensible increase in these categories. *Family Circle* and *Ladies' Home Journal* declined 4 per cent in news-stand sales per issue, as did *Better Homes and Gardens* (7 per cent), *McCall's* (−8 per cent), and *Redbook* (−15 per cent), while *Good Housekeeping* increased only 4 per cent in this category and *Woman's Day* only 0.2 per cent. *Good Housekeeping, Woman's Day, Redbook*, and *Ladies' Home Journal* were also down in subscription growth that year.[54]

While newer magazines such as *Working Mother* and *New Woman* can be expected to experience growth in more categories than do the well-established magazines, lack of growth concerns both publishers and advertisers. Declines or only minimal growth suggest that certain magazines fail to reach new consumers, especially the highly sought women who have recently entered the paid workforce. Lack of growth also suggests that commitments from other advertisers are not increasing; this undermines the general climate of confidence in a magazine's effectiveness as an advertising medium.

A publication's growth or lack of it produces cultural effects on the advertisements inside. The successful magazines continue to expand, often increasing their ad volume and rates, and adding new product categories. In early 1982, *Self*, for example, in order to increase further its growing advertising volume, began to solicit ads for cigarettes and liquor – categories it had previously excluded because of its health orientation. Magazines that are experiencing a decline or standstill in advertising often promote new special advertising sections such as *Redbook*'s "Gifts for the Man." In January 1982 *Redbook* promised that there would be no ad rate increase through the first half of 1982, an additional sign of its advertising declines.[55]

Another practice helps to associate current advertising sales with further increases in ad volume: often a magazine's publicity to potential advertisers names other companies that have purchased space in the publication. To encourage new advertisers, for example, *Cosmopolitan* lists forty of the top fifty advertisers in the country that buy space in the magazine. In its publicity, *Newsweek Woman* names fifty-five companies that use its special demographic edition for women.[56] Declines in advertising promote the opposite psychological effect – the sense that advertisers have found better ad vehicles elsewhere. In short, growth or lack of it affects the kinds and quantity of advertisements in a magazine.

The Infrastructure of the Purchased Advertisement

To decode properly the purchased ad as text one must also examine the material underpinnings of individual ads: the price of the advertising space, the regions of the country in which the ad appears, the agency in charge of the ad campaign and the overall ad budget, the production costs of the ad, the other magazines and media in which the ad or a related one appears, the ad's location in the issue, and its structural relation to the rest of the magazine.

Information on the price of advertising space is available on the rate cards that publishers issue and in Standard Rate and Data Service (SRDS). Prices for the prime back cover ad range from the most expensive *Better Homes and Gardens* ($110,715), *Woman's Day* ($105,210), and *Family Circle* ($103,500), to the least costly, newer and lower circulating magazines such as *Women's Sports* ($3620), *Fit* ($2875), and *Buenhogar* ($1135).[57] The rate card lists the prices for black and white ad pages, two- and four-color ad pages, and fractions thereof.

Most publishers offer a number of discounts on the full fees. Ad agencies receive a 15 per cent discount and a 2 per cent reduction reward for timely payment. Frequency discounts exist for advertisers who purchase space more than once during a twelve-month period. A one-page, four-color ad in *Ms.* in 1983, for example, cost $9880 if run once but dropped to $8920 if run six times. Another special ad price available from large publishers who own several women's magazines is the "combination rate." Charter Publishing Company offered a *Ladies' Home Journal* and *Redbook* combination discount in 1981 in addition to the "Loyalty Discount" and the "Multiple Impression Discount" in both its standard national editions and its upscale advertising editions, *Redbook Gold* and *Ladies' Home Journal Prime Showcase.* The Conde Nast "Package of Women" offers six combination packages for advertisers who buy space in four of its women's magazines.[58]

Another option, "split-run" advertising, allows advertisers to experiment with ad texts and layouts. A coupon, for example, can be inserted on the ad page in editions of the magazine reaching certain sections of the country and the response measured. *Family Circle* charges advertisers between $250 and $2100 extra for each copy change involved in split-run advertising. *McCall's* offers a number of split-run options for extra fees between $1500 and $2000: (1) the Two-Way Random Split, (2) Geographic Copy Splits, (3) News-stand/Subscription Splits, (4) Subscription Circulation Only, (5) News-stand Circulation Only, and (6) the VIP ZIP Split.[59]

"Test-run" advertising is available in the larger magazines for companies that wish to test a product or an ad in various areas of the country. *Good Housekeeping*, for example, offers 152 standard test markets and has set-up charges for each market ranging from $100 to $1000. Its rate card lists the estimated subscription circulation in each test-market area.

Approximately twenty women's magazines offer geographic and demographic editions through which advertisers can reach the regions and income-level areas appropriate to their product. Safeway Stores Inc., for example, buys ads in regional editions in the areas where its supermarkets are located. Similarly, an advertiser may wish to reach only women in a certain income level. Using zip-code demographic figures, the magazine will run the ad only in the copies sent to women living in the most affluent areas, for example. *Family Circle* offers twenty-six regional editions with sixty sub-regions. *Ladies' Home Journal* has eleven regions. In both magazines, space is sold to advertisers according to CPM figures corresponding to the circulation in the region(s) that the advertiser wishes to reach.[60]

After ascertaining the approximate price of an ad – for this study, the standard price the space costs before the various discounts are applied – it is helpful to determine which advertising agency handled the account. Agencies, more often than corporate clients, are responsible for creating the cultural images in magazine advertisements; agency personnel are usually held accountable for campaigns that succeed or fail in selling a product. This information helps to particularize one's understanding of the initial stages of the communicative process of advertising, showing that a specific group of workers, rather than an anonymous sender, produced the message. Sometimes this information is also useful in relating the ad under study to other campaigns the agency has developed. When available, data on the budget figures for the campaigns of the most widely advertised products can also help to make the advertising message less of an abstraction.[61]

Seldom does an ad appear in a single publication or medium. Most ads are part of an inter-media structure of communication in which an ad relays us to its companion ads through a system of intertextuality. Sometimes a special series of ads develops a unified theme. In a $10 million ad campaign for Mrs Paul's Kitchens, for example, the slogan, "It doesn't leave my kitchen unless it's delicious" was developed to add the impression of a personal touch to the image of mass-produced frozen foods. The campaign created three ads for television, five radio spots, newspaper ads with coupons, and a casserole ad in women's magazines.[62]

Thus, women who saw the ad in a magazine were likely to have heard or seen the slogan in at least one other media source. Similarly, an individual ad in a print series does not communicate to women entirely on its own, but rather in conjunction with its companion ads. Series such as the long-running Maidenform campaign ("You never know where she'll turn up") or the Virginia Slims ads ("You've come a long way, baby") modify the visual image in succeeding months while retaining the slogan. These ads function as serial narratives, attracting the consumer with a new episode each month. Each ad relays the reader from those that have preceded it in the series to those that are to come. Rarely does a consumer see only one ad in the series and interpret it apart from these cultural frames that come before and after it.

A similar process occurs in spin-off ads developed for Latina and Black readers for women's magazines. One well-known campaign for Kent cigarettes uses visual substitution to liken the taste of cigarettes to such foods as the olive in a martini, butter on a stack of pancakes, or chocolates in a gift box. In the Spanish-language variation of the ad series in such magazines as *Buenhogar* and *Vanidades*, Latin American symbols of pleasant taste are substituted: a bowl of tropical fruit or coffee in a manual grinder. Latina women in the United States who see these ads in the Spanish-language magazines sold here are likely to understand these symbols in the context of the English-language series, perhaps interpreting the change from United States to Latin American symbols as the advertisers' special effort to personalize the communication for Latinas here. Black readers are likely to interpret similarly ads that use Black models.

An ad's position in a magazine in an important infrastructural factor. Often advertisers request the right-hand pages, the side of the magazine most often seen. Fees are charged for certain special positions such as the covers, the centerspread, or the page adjacent to the table of contents. *Ms.* charges $22,500 for a four-color centerspread, *Parents* $66,530, and *Young Miss* $23,240. Magazines such as *Modern Bride* and *Buenhogar* charge 10 per cent and 20 per cent extra respectively for all special positions.[63] A number of magazines try to accommodate advertisers' placement preferences but do not guarantee them. Usually ads are placed near appropriate editorial content – food ads in the food section and cosmetics ads near articles on make-up, for example.

Position is a significant factor in advertising communication not only because of the degree of visibility it gives an ad but because it is a crucial material aspect of the interaction between ads and features. Because of position, relations of montage often exist between ads, producing new cultural semes. The sexual innuendoes of one ad, for example, can be concretized and expanded by those in an adjacent one. The May 1981 issue of *Mademoiselle* ran an ad for Givenchy underwear opposite a beauty editorial entitled "Your looks" and a smaller ad for Princess Gardner leather goods with the slogan, "Princess Gardner does it 3 ways" (pp. 36–7). Readers may consciously or unconsciously establish a montage between the title "Your looks" and the visual image of the model in the underwear ad; similarly, the sexual innuendo of the Princess Gardner slogan works in montage with the sexual hints presented in the Givenchy photo and text. In addition, we have seen, position is especially important in the cases of covert advertising in which editorial recommendations support nearby purchased ads for the same or related products.

The Infrastructure of the Product

The product's price and the assumed potential consumers are two important infrastructural factors that affect the communication of the ad. Lower-priced cosmetics, for example, are usually advertised in magazines that reach women with moderate spending power, such as *'Teen*, *Seventeen*, and the "seven sisters," while ads for more expensive make-up lines appear on the pages of *Vogue* or *Town & Country* – magazines with upscale readers. Conde Nast's research shows that the average reader of *Mademoiselle* spends $3.49 for mascara, while the average *Vogue* reader spends $5.09. Identifying the product's price allows one to relate the ad's communicative process to the economic stratification of US society. Certain sectors are addressed with relatively expensive magazine advertising for more costly products. For example, advertisers pay a four-color CPM of $29.51 to reach 1000 *Savvy* readers and $21.42 to reach the same number of *Bazaar* readers. In contrast, the average four-color CPM for *Seventeen* readers is $13.00.[64] Whether or not a woman will be addressed by an ad and which advertising vehicles will be used to speak to her depends on her specific position within a stratified social organization.

Advertisers are also concerned with the percentage of a given magazine's readership that uses their products. Simmons Market Research Bureau (SMRB) provides detailed information on product users and the magazines they read. Publications such as

Better Homes and Gardens, *Family Circle*, and *Woman's Day*, for example, reach large percentages of the US female population who use eye shadow. In contrast, magazines such as *House Beautiful*, *Bazaar*, *Mademoiselle*, *Parents*, *Vogue*, *Town & Country*, and *Working Mother*, although reaching small percentages of the US users of eyeshadow, have high percentages of their readers who use this product. While the first set of publications can offer marketers of eyeshadow large numbers of women who buy the product, the latter group offers an efficiency in reaching a concentrated group of readers who wear eyeshadow:

	Total US female readers	*Used eyeshadow in last seven days*	*% of US users*	*% of readers of this magazine*
Better Homes and Gardens	16,226,000	9,534,000	20.4	58.9
Family Circle	15,673,000	9,152,000	19.5	58.4
Woman's Day	14,827,000	8,548,000	19.1	60.3
House Beautiful	3,526,000	2,243,000	4.8	63.6
Bazaar	2,869,000	2,133,000	4.8	74.3
Mademoiselle	3,407,000	2,710,000	5.8	79.5
Parents	3,117,000	2,410,000	5.1	77.3
Vogue	4,262,000	3,086,000	6.6	72.4
Town & Country	894,000	689,000	1.5	77.1
Working Mother	806,000	652,000	1.4	80.9

Source: SMRB *1982 Study of Media and Markets*, Vol. P-28, "Women's Beauty Aids, Cosmetics, and Personal Products," pp. 0096–0097

SMRB gives even more detailed data such as figures on readers who are heavy, medium, or light users of eyeshadow and which brands they use. Of *Vogue*'s three million readers who use eyeshadow, for example, 387,000 use Avon, 363,000 Cover Girl, 285,000 Max Factor, 785,000 Maybelline, 759,000 Revlon, 454,000 Aziza, 538,000 Estée Lauder, and 286,000 Mary Kay.[65]

Ascertaining the parent corporation of the product is another crucial task of infrastructural analysis. Often, one discovers that the same corporation owns competing products and that a sole advertiser accounts for dozens of advertising pages in an issue of a magazine. Procter & Gamble, the largest advertiser in the country, for example, successfully "competes" with itself in product categories such as toothpastes, deodorants, shampoos, soaps and detergents. Maker of Crest and Gleem toothpastes, Sure and Secret deodorants, Prell and Head and Shoulders shampoos, Procter & Gamble also markets numerous laundry detergents such as Dash, Salvo, Oxydol, Cheer, Era, Duz, Ivory Flakes, Ivory Snow, Tide, Bold, Bonus, Dreft, and Gain; four dishwashing liquids, seven hand soaps, and several food and paper products. Sometimes a product that is covertly advertised in an editorial section of the magazine is owned by the parent corporation of a seemingly unrelated product advertised elsewhere in the magazine. Similarly, information on a product's parent corporation allows us to connect various purchased ads for apparently unconnected products. Figures on the parent corporation's annual earnings, those of its individual products, and its advertising and promotion budgets are helpful to give us a material understanding of the role of the ad and its success or failure in selling merchandise.

One final infrastructural aspect of the product is the material interdependence of various products. To wear a new shade of nail polish correctly, for example, magazines advise that one wear clothing in coordinating colors and vice versa. Thus, the purchase of one new product often leads to other purchases. Similarly, the recipes that most women's service magazines suggest in their editorial sections direct women to buy certain kinds of coordinated foods. It is unlikely, for example, that one would serve Jell-O for dessert after a gourmet meal, yet this General Foods product seems to be the natural accompaniment of a meal of hot dogs or General Foods canned spaghetti. In effect, an advertisement for one product, whether covert or overt, can help to instill the perceived need for another. This material interdependence of products contributes to the structural homogeneity of the magazine; one's conception of a magazine as structurally cohesive is often due in large part to the material support its ads give one another.

This detailed infrastructural analysis of the magazine, the advertisement, and the product works together with the companion critical approaches discussed here to aid the decoding of the attractive advertising messages that magazines present. While each critical method reveals important parts of an advertisement's subtext, used together the methods allow one to transcend surface appearances and first impressions, linking the material to the ideological and decoding these through semiotic and feminist optics. These critical approaches enable one as well to understand the editorial material in women's magazines as part of the same cultural continuum as the advertising texts, a continuum based first and foremost on the financial exigencies of magazine enterprises.

4 The Codes of Overt Advertisements

Turning back the cover of the October 1982 *Redbook*, we are drawn into an enticing sight of luxurious well-being (Figure 4.1). The camera lens positions our vision before two carved wooden doors opening to a spacious room. We might be looking at a movie screen in a darkened theatre, so real is this large two-page image that seems to place us at the room's entrance as we hold the magazine at reading distance. Whites and golden browns predominate, while green indoor plants extend the room beyond its boundaries by directing our vision to the trees outside in the background. At middle distance the woman of the house appears enraptured in a daydream. Bathed in sunlight and dressed in white as are her furniture and walls, she presents a model of affluent leisure – the woman who need not work. Stretching between us and this fantasy of ourselves is the predominant image in the photograph, the expansive Armstrong floor "Solarian Supreme." By purchasing it, the ad suggests, we will attain both the affluent appearance of this room and the life of leisure that the woman signifies.

Each day millions of women engage pleasurably with ads such as this. Like any language, the systems of meaning configured in advertisements are value-laden; beneath the pleasurable and ostensibly innocent appearance of purchased ads are subtexts and codes that articulate ideology. Beyond their overt role of selling products, ads present selected value systems as merely "common sense." Position is one of the first modes of configuring such systems of value.

THE ADVERTISING FRAME: COVER POSITIONS

After the magazine's most important self advertisement, its cover, the purchased ads on the opening and closing covers are key. The outside back cover (cover four) is the most expensive advertising space since many see it even without buying or opening the magazine. Next in importance and cost is the inside

Figure 4.1 Ad for Solarian Supreme flooring, courtesy of Armstrong World Industries Inc.

Figure 4.2 Ad for Tiffany flooring, courtesy of Armstrong World Industries Inc.

front cover (cover two), followed by the inside back cover (cover three). Together with the front cover, the ads on all three of these prime spaces frame the reading of the magazine; they are the advertising images with which one usually begins and ends. The heavier paper of the covers imparts a special aura to these ads. Often, large cosmetics companies, cigarette and liquor concerns, and home furnishing corporations purchase both cover two and the first page so that the initial paid ad functions as an expansive gateway to the rest of the magazine.[1]

Armstrong Floors often buys the opening space in women's service magazines, presenting large, double-page images that make abundant use of signs that stand for women. The perfectly arranged family room, kitchen, or playroom with numerous symbols of material success serves as a showcase for the floor and together these signs are a material representation of the ideal homemaker and mother. Images of a privileged class and race overlay the gender stereotypes. One Armstrong ad opens several women's service magazines (for example, *Ladies' Home Journal*, October 1981, Figure 4.2), highlighting the elegant playroom of a blonde child serving tea to her blonde doll and white teddy bear. Whites and other light shades predominate in the room's decor – even the leaves of the plants are retinted white and together with the other fuzzy and misty images contribute to the aura of magic and childhood fantasy that appears innocently to entice viewers.

While it encodes itself as childhood fantasy, the ad turns pivotally on an adult fantasy – a pleasing sign of ideal motherhood. Readers of *Ladies' Home Journal* from different economic classes and ethnic backgrounds are all to idealize themselves through this single class- and race-based gender stereotype. And this commercially constituted ideal motherhood must be witnessed, the ad's discourse of sight implies. We, the readers, form one such observer group and the position of the camera conflates the perspectives of several other potential admirers: the self-satisfied ideal mother and homemaker (ourselves in the future) who gazed admiringly at her daughter and well-appointed playroom; a visitor to the home who looks approvingly at these signs of material success; and the loving glance of a husband, appreciative of his wife's childcare and home management.

Like the front cover, opening advertisements serve as a lens through which we view and interpret what is to follow. Figuratively – and because of the photograph's immediacy, almost literally – we are entering an ideal home, like the one that the magazine and its opening advertisement will help us to create for ourselves. Most of the ads and features that follow will seem to be parts of this already concretized ideal. Whether the initial ad spread symbolizes successful womanhood through well-appointed homes, women's caregiving function (*Redbook*, January 1981), or ideals of youth and beauty (*McCall's*, May 1983), readers carry elements of the corresponding stereotype to their interpretations of the rest of the magazine. Other editorial and advertising messages are enhanced by these important "gateway" ads. Eventually, these initial images work with the ads on covers three and four to form a signifying bracket around the magazine's contents.

The front cover of *Good Housekeeping* in November 1981, for example, which offers Debby Boone and her young son as an image of ideal womanhood, is followed by the Armstrong ad depicting the young girl's tea party and additional pages of ads for Armstrong floors. This first advertising lens through which we see the magazine, then, is reinforced and developed for several pages before we reach the editorial contents of the issue. The remainder of the advertising bracket around this issue consists of an ad for Purina Cat Chow with a smiling housewife on cover three and an ad for Pine Sol on cover four, again with a smiling woman cleaning grease (symbolized childishly with the block letters GREASE on the oven door). All four covers, and the pages that extend them, connect the successful, happy woman to apt management of household and family. Whether the magazine lies on a table with its front cover up or its back cover showing, it communicates a similar message. In both opening and closing the issue, the reader sees an ideal image of herself linked to the proper care of household and family.

Another of *Good Housekeeping*'s primary advertising frames links personal beauty to home and family maintenance. The April 1981 front cover pictures an attractive model who "Shows you the new pastel makeups" and cover two along with page one extends the theme of beauty with an ad for Clairol Loving Care. Cover three advertises Dow Bathroom Cleaner and cover four, Procter & Gamble's Lilt Soft Perm, picturing an attractive woman three times in close-up, middle-, and long-distance shots. The three purchased ads in this frame suggest that successful womanhood can be achieved by outwitting the passage of time. Signs of aging can be eliminated by coloring grey hair with Loving Care. The ad for Dow Bathroom Cleaner tells readers, "Let us do your dirty work . . . make short work of your toughest job. . . . And you can take it easy" and the Lilt ad begins, "Introducing soft, full body that stands up to time." The model, pictured in shots of varying distances, stands on progressively later dates on a calendar to symbolize the passage of time, while her permanent lasts indefinitely. The ads in this frame also tell readers that these domestic and cosmetic ideals are logically contiguous. Cleaning the bathroom with Dow is, in this utopian scenario, letting someone else do one's unpleasant work, freeing time for self beautification.

INTERNAL AND EXTERNAL MONTAGE

Most purchased advertisements communicate through the interaction of verbal and photographic texts. As occurs on the magazine cover, the slogans and copy in the advertisement form a montage with the photograph. The reader creates a third, new meaning or "C" cell by mentally joining the verbal and visual messages. Montage can also occur between two or more visual images in an ad and between entire ads and their surroundings in the magazine.

An ad for Chesebrough-Pond's Chimere perfume (*Mademoiselle*, February 1981, p. 27), juxtaposes two large visual "cells." The upper photo shows a businesswoman dining with several male associates. Their glances, her own blank stare, low neckline, and body position with hand on hip, leaning slightly forward, combine to sexualize her; but the caption to the right asks us to decode this image as signifying discretion and elegance. The lower photo depicts a private (although here made public) moment of sexual intimacy in the woman's life to contrast her public "discreet" image. The perfume mediates these two personas, allegedly permitting the women to be both discreetly and openly sexual at different moments. The lower photo carries the image in the upper photo forward in time and imagination. In effect, the second cell actualizes the subtle sexual implications of the first. The reader mentally constructs a new cell of signification: Chimere will keep you sexually enticing in a socially acceptable way in the business world and help you attain love, male acceptance, and sexual intimacy later.

Some ads use pictorial montage to heighten women's insecurities and thereby encourage purchases. Johnson & Johnson's Sundown sunscreen breaks the usual advertising conventions of emphasizing glamorous images and playing only subtly on the fears and insecurities of potential consumers. Instead, the Sundown ad (*Ms.*, August 1982, p. 12), divides a woman's face into two halves: one, normal and attractive, and the other, badly scarred, wrinkled, and burned. Captions beneath the halves anchor the meaning we are intended to draw from the counterposition of the two images: "Sundown" below the attractive normal-looking side and "Sundamage" under the badly burned side. The damaged half is so badly disfigured that the woman appears to have been injured in a fire or explosion. Viewing this antithesis of the usual glamorous image of make-up advertisements here, we are to fear not merely the failure to be beautiful but that we might be deformed. A subtle, underscoring image heightens the contrast between the two cells of the montage: a man plays with a child in the background behind the half of the "Sundown" face, while there is no one behind the damaged face. Besides disfigurement, we are to fear the lack of human contact and male attention as well.

Sometimes montage in an ad links more than two images and imitates the motion of film. Revlon's ad for European Collagen Complex beauty cream (*McCall's*, October 1981, cover 2 and p. 1; Figure 4.3) promises silkier skin in ten days. Ten progressively larger slices of the model's face fan out across the page, culminating in the beautiful whole. Several kinds of motion underlie this montage series: (1) a temporal progression from day one to day ten; (2) a representational progression from black-and-white images to a full-color photo; (3) a physical progression from fragments of the face to a close-up of the full face; (4) an implied progression from the present (soon-to-be-past) you with inadequate skin to the future (soon-to-be-present) you with silkier, more youthful-looking skin. All of the motion, change, and progression from the negative "before" to the positive "after" are predicated on purchase of the product.

The verbal and photographic texts of adjacent ads sometimes

function in montage. Two ads for Schering-Plough's Maybelline appear on facing pages in the May 1981 issue of *Ms.* (pp. 10–11), subtly undermining the feminist ideals of the magazine. *Ms.* has argued on its editorial pages against the veil as a symbol of women's oppression, yet in this ad encourages women to view literal and figurative veils as glamorous (Figure 4.4). On one level, the veil across the model's face in the right-hand ad might be decoded as innocuous fashion. In montage with the facing ad which urges readers to "Run for cover" by purchasing a product to camouflage circles beneath the eyes, the veiled face enters into a new semiotic system. The "C cell" suggests metaphorically that cosmetics are a kind of glamorous veil behind which women are to hide. Where the veil on the right covers the model's face up to the level of her eyes, the cover stick on the left will hide the area that the other veil has left uncovered.

Sometimes an ad's own verbal text and photograph create a contradictory montage. Often, in ads for Seagram's whiskey, large-size drinks appear in the photograph while the last line of the verbal text cautions readers to drink in moderation. One ad promoting Seven Crown pictures a drink as tall as the 12-ounce Seven-Up can on the right (*Glamour*, June 1981, cover 4). Another shows two large drinks in the foreground while a man holds an even taller drink in the background (*Cosmopolitan*, April 1983, p. 185). The verbal text of the first ad cautions, "Enjoy our quality in moderation," and the second claims, "It's one combination, in moderation, that . . . you'll never forget." The larger and more striking visual images in these ads eclipse the ostensible disclaimers – Seagram's unconvincing effort to insist that its ads do not encourage excessive drinking. Like the Surgeon General's warning that must appear in cigarette ads, the messages promoting moderation here are hardly noticed. To focus on the contradictory montage between the verbal and photographic texts helps us to understand that Seagram's goal is precisely the opposite of the verbal encouragement of moderation; the company aims to persuade us to consume more, not less.

FORMS OF ADDRESS

All advertisements address us with one or more signifiers. As we have seen in Chapter 3, Althusser and Williamson argue that we

Figure 4.3 European Collagen complex advertisement courtesy of Revlon, Inc.

[illegible]

Figure 4.4 Ad for Maybelline cosmetics courtesy of Maybelline Inc.

learn to identify ourselves according to the way we are addressed. If we respond when someone calls to us, "Hey, cutie," for example, we are admitting the possibility that this signifier may refer to us. When we respond to a given form of address, be it a proper name, a title, a diminutive, or an advertising image, we are tacitly agreeing that this is a conceivable and even appropriate means of addressing us; whatever we allow ourselves to be called, we must, in a sense, already be.[2]

In the case of advertisements, if our self-concept does not already correspond to the form in which we are addressed, the ad encourages us to learn to see ourselves in this way. Some women who see the Maybelline "Run for cover" ad discussed above, for example, may never before have worried about circles under their eyes. The ad's task, as it works in montage with the glamorous, veiled woman on the facing page, is to convince women to see this alleged problem in themselves and to feel the need to purchase the cover stick. The interpellation's potential to refer to us is to be actualized.

Ads utilize a variety of modes of address. Frequently, the slogan or headline speaks to us declaratively in direct address, for example, "It's more you" (More cigarette ad, *Self*, June 1983, pp. 156–7) or with an imperative, "Find the perm that's right for you!" (ad for Gillette's Toni Silkwave permanent, *Good Housekeeping*, July 1981, p. 47). Ads address us through their visual images as well and often the visual and verbal elements work together to interpellate.

One famous ad series for Chesebrough-Pond's Bass shoes uses the single verbal imperative "Go Bass or go barefoot." Usually several women are shown barefoot in the background of the ad, having left their Bass shoes displayed for us in the foreground (see *Mademoiselle*, January 1981, pp. 20–1). In each ad, however, there is at least one more pair of shoes than the number of women in the picture. The extra pair of shoes is a subtle means of calling out to us. It addresses us visually with the message that this pair is for us. In one Bass ad we see several women trying on clothes in a store's dressing rooms. One woman has removed her shoes but two pairs rather than one are beside her feet (*Bazaar*, August 1982, p. 66). Another variation reverses the interpellation using the same signifiers; here we see the feet of eleven women; ten are wearing Bass shoes while one is barefoot (*Mademoiselle*, February 1982, p. 103). Now the visual image of bare feet, rather than the extra shoes, addresses us, suggesting that we are inadequate like the woman without shoes in the photo who, in addition, does not have painted toenails as do the other models. Without Bass shoes, these ads imply, we might as well be barefoot. This either–or dichotomy intends to arouse feelings of inadequacy in the potential consumer while at the same time offering a concrete alternative that calls out to us directly. The extra pair of shoes or the single pair of bare feet invite the reader to become part of the group of attractive women in these ads who wear Bass shoes.

Sometimes the direct address misleadingly appears to constitute the principal interpellation of the ad. The headline of one ad for Quaker Oats' Aunt Jemima Pancake Mix (*Ladies' Home Journal*, October 1981, p. 112; Figure 4.5) asks: "Do you remember your first bite of an Aunt Jemima Pancake?" But this nostalgic evocation of the audience's own childhood is of secondary importance to the primary interpellative icon of the ad – the photo of the blond child; here, the smiling face and the forkful of pancakes address us as arbitrary signs of ideal motherhood. The evocation of past time in the headline is, in fact, a means of speaking about the future time represented in the primary interpellation in the photo – the moment when the ideal white reader will gaze at her happy blond child about to eat the product she has purchased. The accompanying slogan "Some things never change" reinforces this merging of past and future.

Ads often address us through signifiers of male approval. The promotion for Gillette's Adorn Hair Spray (*Mademoiselle*, May 1981, p. 115; permission to reprint denied) pictures this approval through metonymic signs of men. Three smiling women gaze at us, each with a man's hand reaching into the picture to touch her hair. The intrusive yet naturalized hands momentarily become ours as we survey the models; in effect, we assume the position and vision of the approving male. We are to judge ourselves – these three future images of ourselves from the perspective of the men whose hands we see. While gazing at the ad, as Berger has pointed out, we are both the surveyor and the surveyed.

Besides addressing us through an approving male vision conflated with our own, the ad interpellates with a verbal text, "Come on, touch it." On one level, the models are inviting the men whose hands we see to survey and judge them. On another level, however, the headline teaches us language. The phrase

Figure 4.5 Ad for Aunt Jemima pancake mix, courtesy of The Quaker Oats Company.

appears in quotation marks, indicating not only that the models are saying it but that we can speak this way to men as well once we purchase the product.

In some ads, interpellation urges us to learn a language in which products speak for us. Consolidated Foods Corporation's promotions of its L'Erin cosmetics tell us to "Say it with the 'Sentiments Collection,'" (*Cosmopolitan*, April 1983, p. 321) and "Say it without saying a word. Let L'Erin Color Glaze do the talking" (*Ms.*, August 1982, p. 216). Both ads picture a man directly whom we are to understand as the intended addressee of the new language we are to learn.[3]

An ad for Playtex Body Language underwear implies that the

product will substitute for one's deteriorated communicational skills (*Mademoiselle*, October 1981, p. 93;). The headlines bracketing the top and bottom of the ad – "Now Playtex speaks Body Language. Because your body has a language all its own" – use interpellation to encourage us to let our bodies, once dressed in the product, communicate for us. The photographic message shows a woman wearing only the Playtex underwear, sitting in an awkward position so that she can display the product for the camera. Trying unsuccessfully to compose a letter to "Mark" while in this awkward, tilted position, she has strewn the evidence of her inability to communicate through words in crumpled pieces of paper on the floor. No matter that she lacks the skills of verbal communication, the ad implies; the Playtex underwear will speak to Mark for her. Additional interpellation in the verbal text of the ad reinforces the photographic message: "Speak softly. But speak out. In Body Language . . . from Playtex. . . ."

A three-page ad for Phillip Morris' Benson & Hedges cigarettes (*Working Mother*, July 1982, pp. 107–9) uses physical layout as a means of interpellation. Page one pictures a wrapped gift box with the imperative headline, "Open a box of deluxe." By turning the page, one, in effect, opens the box as the headline has commanded and is face-to-face with a close-up shot of the interior of the gift box which displays still another unopened box, the Benson & Hedges. The text of the ad closes with another command: "Open a box today." This time it is the cigarette package that we are to open, that is, buy. Thus, the ad sets up a chain of commands and follow-up actions that lead us to consume the product. The ad teaches us to "open" the product by first having us do so symbolically as we turn the page.

Some perfume ads use "scentstrips" to address us through smell. A sample of the fragrance is enclosed in an insert to allow readers who so desire to try the perfume. In fact, however, the strong fragrance pervades the entire magazine and affects how one reads the other articles and ads. An insert scented with Giorgio perfume in *Ms.* (November 1983), for example, addresses us both visually and through smell. The pervasive odor functions as a signifier, communicating to us continuously as we read the articles and ads. To those who find it unpleasant, the strong smell is an annoying distraction from the serious feminist themes discussed in several of the articles. The culturally weighted significations of ideal femininity attached to this olfactory form of address might appeal to other readers of *Ms*. For these readers, the smell of the perfume might enhance and uphold several other messages of ideal femininity that appear in the ads in this issue of *Ms*. The issue displays long polished fingernails (cover 2, pp. 3 and 11), several make-up and cosmetic ads (pp. 8, 9, 13 and 55), an ad for another fragrance that promises to be "the essence of romance" (p. 4), and an ad for Slenderalls control top underwear that pictures a fragment of a woman's body to illustrate how the product will rid one of "bumps and bulges" (p. 77). In either case, one cannot escape from this pervasive olfactory signifier by turning the page.

Jameson, as we have seen, argues that cultural texts often establish structures of opposing elements that mark the limits of a given way of thinking about reality. In this structural view of ideology, sets of oppositions in a text demarcate the limits beyond which a given consciousness cannot go. Often, ads in women's magazines create such structural oppositions as they address the reader, asking that one first vacillate between the opposing motifs, and ultimately distance oneself from the negative pole by purchasing a product or service.

The photographic images in an ad for Procter & Gamble's Duncan Hines Cookie Mix (*Family Circle*, 3 February 1981, p. 3; permission to reprint denied), begin to establish such an opposition with motivated and metonymical signs. The most prominent image is an enormous cookie that is offered to us out of the picture, almost three-dimensionally. Holding the spatula on which the cookie rests is a woman's hand signified by a painted thumbnail; in the visual metonomy here, the decorated nail communicates not only the idea of a woman but her place in the kitchen as producer of this spurious homemade cookery. Disproportionately small in the upper left-hand corner, a package of store-bought cookies comes to signify negative womanhood in the ad's system of structural opposition.

These visual forms of address are buttressed by two verbal imperatives in headlines that unequivocally demarcate the poles of the opposition: "Don't take cookies out of a bag," near the tiny image of the bag, and above the giant home-baked cookie, "Take Duncan Hines out of the oven." Together the oversize, three-dimensional cookie and another line of text beneath it, "Tastes so mmm-much better," appeal to the reader's senses of sight and taste and give greater emphasis to the second pole of the oppositional structure:

bag → packaged cookies → store-bought taste → guilt
↕ ↕
OVEN → DUNCAN HINES COOKIE MIX → FRESH, BETTER-TASTING → PRAISE

Symbolically, this system of verbal and visual oppositions interpellates the reader as either a good or bad person based on the kind of cookies she offers to her family. By addressing her through images of guilt and praise, the ad asks her to oscillate between arbitrary oppositions that through visual and verbal representations are more heavily weighted toward the declared positive pole. Ultimately, she is to distance herself from the negative images by purchasing the Duncan Hines Cookie Mix. The ad has already begun the process symbolically by picturing the cookie bag as distant and far-off while the giant home-baked cookie is within immediate reach.

In the next issue of *Family Circle* (24 February 1981, p. 8), an ad again addresses readers by linking food to guilt (Figure 4.6). Promoting H. J. Heinz's Weight Watchers' pizza, the ad plays precisely upon guilt to sell the product, contradicting the headline "Pizza without guilt." The main photo communicates the negative oppositional pole visually by showing a woman punished and forcibly restrained to prevent her from eating pizza. The cloth and rope that gag and bind her coordinate visually with the tape measure tied around the package of Weight Watchers that we are urged to buy. By encircling the "waist" of the package, the tape forms a verbal–visual pun with the word "weight" in the brand name. The heavy ropes binding the overweight woman who is about to consume pizza and feel guilty will be transformed, after the reader purchases the product, into the opposing signifier of the slender measuring tape around the "waist" of the product that will allegedly produce a slim waist and attain praise for the potential consumer. Again, the ad establishes poles of opposition between which we are at first to vacillate:

PIZZA
WITHOUT GUILT
NOW YOU DON'T HAVE TO RESTRAIN YOURSELF FROM EATING THE FOOD YOU LOVE WHEN YOU'RE ON A DIET.
It's here. The last thing you ever thought you could eat on a diet. The food people call "junk." The one they hate to love. It's pizza. The hot bubbly kind you have to tilt your head back to eat. The kind worth burning your mouth for. And since it's made by Weight Watchers, you can eat a whole one without feeling guilty.
You see, Weight Watchers Frozen Meals believes if we bring you the foods you used to go off your diet for, you'll have no reason to go off your diet. So we make all 28 of our meals the kind that tempt you.
We give you rich brown gravy with our beef. We give you Lasagna. Baked Ziti. We give you fragrant herb-scented stuffing with our turkey. And satiny sauces with our fish. Essentially, you're eating the foods you once considered no-no's. Only we make them so they'll fit into any sensible weight loss program.
To wit, our pizza.
We twirl our dough thin and crispy instead of thick and soggy.
We give you herbs and spices that taste delicious. Instead of empty calories that don't do a thing for the flavor.
Or the figure.
And, surprise of surprises, our frozen pizza is actually good for you. Fresh mozzarella is a natural source of calcium and protein. Our tomato sauce is ripe with Vitamin A.
Now,
Next mealtime when you're walking down the street and you happen to get a warm whiff of hot cheesy pizza and your tastebuds start to tingle, what do you do? Do you give in? Do you buy a slice? Do you suffer that bizarre paradox of remorse and enjoyment as you eat it?
No.
You keep walking.
And you don't stop till you get to your freezer.
WEIGHT WATCHERS® FROZEN MEALS.
THE TEMPTATION YOU DON'T HAVE TO RESIST.

Figure 4.6 Ad for Weight Watchers frozen pizza, courtesy of Weight Watchers International Inc.

pizza → guilt → restraint → thick ropes, gag → overweight condition

↕ ↕

Weight Watchers → praise → freedom → slim tape measure → slim waist

Just as the misleading title "Pizza without guilt" in fact encourages guilt in the reader, so, too, the apparent freedom that the ad attributes to Weight Watchers' products uses another image of restraint, the tape measure, to misleadingly imply freedom. In effect, the forms of address in this ad urge women to escape one image of restraint only to acquire another.

Fascinación, a De Armas magazine that Spanish-speaking women in the US read, ran an ad for its sister publication *Cosmopolitan en Español* that also addresses readers through structural oppositions (February 1983, p. 3.) Here, visual and verbal messages of fear are counterposed to the stereotypical image of the liberated "Cosmo girl." Promoting a self-defense manual to appear in the April *Cosmopolitan*, the ad's main visual image imitates a magazine cover but adds violence to the usual image of glamor: a male attacker's hand grabs the blonde model's face. Verbal appellation on the mock cover commands, "Read this guide and survive unharmed!", establishing parallel oppositions between buying *Cosmopolitan* or not buying it, and being harmed by an attacker or escaping unharmed. Other block-lettered headlines reinforce the negative pole by reminding us to fear rape and attacks in our home or car. Ultimately, however, the ad enlarges the system of oppositions it has initially established, counterposing our fear of attack to the ostensibly liberated "Cosmo girl": "Read *Cosmopolitan* and liberate that Cosmo girl inside you!" With this interpellation, the poles of the opposition become violent.

Whether ads address us through an extra pair of shoes, the smiling face of a child, a language that we are to learn, a fragrance, or an arbitrary set of oppositions, it is important to remember that these forms of address are race-, class- and gender-based. The implicit or expressed "you" in ads represents an ideal "you" for readers to strive to be. If we do not already see ourselves in terms of the smiling blond child or the dichotomy between home-baked vs. packaged cookies, ads encourage us to learn to see ourselves in these ways. All the readers of a given women's magazine are to view themselves according to the class and race the ad uses in its system of address; rarely do the ads in the mainstream women's magazines picture Black, Latina, or non-middle-class women. Janice Winship suggests that we employ the technique of reversal in order to become conscious of the gender, race, and class stereotypes that a given ad uses to address us. What images might an ad use were it trying to address other audiences?[4] Does the image of a blonde, smiling child sell pancake mix to Black, Latina, and Asian women? How do working-class readers respond to images of opulence that address them in the ads for Armstrong flooring or Playtex Body Language underwear? Do women from all classes and backgrounds learn to conceive of themselves in terms of the images that ads use for interpellation?

THE MALE PRESENCE AND THE POWER TO SEE

Men's visual reification of women permeates many levels of contemporary society. Although staring is generally considered discourteous in our culture, men's staring at women is usually exempt from this proscription. In the mass media, the position of the camera often coincides with a male perspective of the women portrayed. Because of the frequent conflation in mass culture of the denotative, analogic message with the symbolic, cultural code, we usually fail to notice connotational procedures such as the implicit male vision. These media images then help to naturalize further the male stare in real life. As Berger has noted, women frequently internalize the male surveyor's view of their appearance so that this cultural construct becomes their own view of themselves. In women's magazines there are numerous varieties of the implicit male vision which, although part of the symbolic code, are often presented as natural, objective pictures of women.

Explicit signifiers of the male vision in women's magazines include pictures of men openly gazing at the women in the ads or back at us, the readers, and parts of men's bodies which metonymically represent the male surveyor's view. Among the common implicit signifiers are the camera's angle of vision, an object such as the crab in the ad in *Good Housekeeping* for Round-the-Clock hosiery discussed below, whose secondary signification is the male surveyor, and arbitrary signs such as the headline "The most beautiful thing next to nothing" which accompanies the photo of a woman in a nightgown lying across a bed in an ad for lingerie (*Modern Bride*, June/July 1981, p. 75). Whether explicit or implicit, the male vision in ads comes to signify acceptance and love or the fear of losing these. The male line of vision reifies women and sometimes moves from reification to the hint of imminent violence.

Examples abound of explicit images of men in the act of visually consuming women. The long-running ad series for Procter & Gamble's Secret deodorant depicts a man staring with an approving smile at a woman standing in a sexualized, off-balance pose, holding the product (see, for example, *Ms.*, August 1982, p. 36, or *Seventeen*, April 1983, p. 109). Ads for Schering-Plough's Coppertone suntan lotion show a group of eight men who grin with approval as they stare at a woman in a bikini who opens her towel to exhibit her suntan for them and us (permission to reprint denied). The headline, "Flash 'em a Coppertone Tan," urges women to play at the male-flasher role, thereby trivializing themselves as well as the sexual aggressions of male flashers. But the model's reified state extends to the eight male surveyors who themselves function as totems; in effect, the model invites us with her direct glance to be part of the group of sexually desirable women who have in their possession both a Coppertone tan and a large number of approving male surveyors. Both the product, pictured in multiple images to convey a spurious choice, and the reified men function as totemic symbols of membership in the group of desirable, approved women. The reifying stare of the male surveyor has returned to objectify him as well.

Some ads use the surveying glance of an explicit male to encourage competition between women. The long-running campaign for Consolidated Foods Corporation's Hanes hosiery promotes competition with photographic signs and the judgmental verbal slogan, "Gentlemen prefer Hanes" (see, for example, *Working Mother*, April 1982, p. 15, and *Essence*, May 1981, p. 38; Figures 4.7 and 4.8). In each ad, we see two couples at a public event; one woman's legs in Hanes stockings are highly visible at the center of the ad while the other woman's are covered. According to the logic of the ad, then, it is only natural that the latter's partner be staring at the other woman's legs, made desirable by the product; Hanes will assure one woman of being preferred over another. The ad invents its own system of positive and negative role models for the reader, predicated on the approbatory power of the male surveyor. The ideology of the ad is to urge readers first to oscillate between these two opposing poles, to use Jameson's formulation, and then to reject the negative pole. We are either the visually consumed or the visually non-consumed, the desirable or the non-desirable one, depending on whether or not we use Hanes stockings.

Ads for frilly, lacy underwear often explicitly depict the approving male, since the product is primarily designed not to be

Hanes
Gentlemen Prefer Hanes.
Sensuously smooth, luxuriously
sheer, undeniably silky,
unmistakably Hanes.

Figure 4.7 Ad for Hanes hosiery, courtesy of Sara Lee Hosiery

functional but to please a male surveyor; indeed, some ads contend, women are always to be ready for an unexpected situation in which the surveyor will scrutinize their underwear. In the words of the notorious Maidenform ad series, "The Maidenform woman. You never know where she'll turn up."[5] The campaign pictures models engaged in various public activities such as descending a staircase at the opera or theater (*Cosmopolitan*, February 1983, p. 71), walking a dog (*Vogue*, May 1983, p. 108), on a sailboat (*Essence*, May 1981, p. 24), or at the racetrack (*Vogue*, June 1983, p. 54). In each scene, the women are inappropriately dressed, either wearing only Maidenform underwear or opening clothing to expose it. Whatever the situa-

Hanes
Gentlemen prefer Hanes
Sensuously smooth. Luxuriously sheer. Unmistakably Hanes.

Figure 4.8 Ad for Hanes hosiery, courtesy of Sara Lee Hosiery

tion, at least one man is present to remind readers for whom they are to wear the product. In contrast to the overpowering image of incongruity that the women provide in each public situation, the men are only subtle symbols of male voyeurism; in most cases they seem hardly to notice the exposed women and continue with their activity as if the exposure were natural. Nonetheless, by depicting as ordinary an incongruous situation in which the underwear has "turned up," i.e. become an object for men to see, the ad urges women always to be on their guard, femininely dressed even under their clothes, continually prepared for the male surveyor.

An ad for the VF Corporation's Vanity Fair underwear explicitly portrays not only a man in the act of staring at a woman who does not look back at him, but the image he would see were the woman undressed. (*Self*, June 1983, p. 45; permission to reprint denied). Tinted only in black and white, except for the inset of the woman wearing the product, the ad contrasts the negative past, when the underwear is not visible, to a bright, desirable future. One of the available meanings of these polysemous photos – before we allow the verbal text to anchor the signification the advertisers prefer – is a visual narrative in which a male-voyeur figure stares at a woman, mentally undressing her; what he sees is revealed in the color inset. The verbal text of the ad modifies this initial visual narrative, however. Above the inset, forming a montage with it, are the words: "Life isn't always fair. There are times when confrontation seems to be the only way to clear the air. At times like that, how you feel about yourself can make all the difference in the world." Using "fair" to play on and underscore the brand name of the product, the ad text implies that wearing the pictured undergarment will give women confidence when confronting or arguing with a man. In fact, however, the ad as a whole works to decrease women's self-confidence, urging the internalizing of the scrutinizing view of the male surveyor and implying that the product will give an advantage. One is assured of winning an argument when properly sexualized in the Vanity Fair underwear. The photographic text of the ad teaches us to assume this male vision, measuring ourselves against what the man sees beneath the clothes of the woman in this ad.

The power to look at and visually consume a woman who does not look back as an equal becomes associated in a number of ads with the hint of imminent violence about to befall her. We are to displace the suggestion of danger onto feelings of excitement, fear, elegance, or male approval. The ad series for El Greco Leather Product's Candie's shoes offers several examples of the ominous, explicit male. In Figure 4.9 (*Mademoiselle*, February 1981, cover 3), two women appear in awkward, sexualized poses, one on the floor talking on the phone and the other leaning over a bed with a blank stare. As Goffman has noted, ads depict children and women lying on floors and beds more frequently than men and often show women talking on the phone, exhibiting "licensed withdrawal," and psychologically away from the situation at hand.[6] Here, the situation decodes as an imminent danger – the mirror reflects a man lurking in the background, apparently unobserved. He gazes, while the women are in sexual poses with their attention distracted. In the lower corner of the mirror, sharing the same visual frame, is the reflection of a piece of one woman's leg – a segment of her sexualized pose on the floor. Shadows across the entire ad increase the sense of danger surrounding the dark image of the male voyeur. The ad subtly suggests as well that if we, the audience, can see the man's reflection in the mirror, he, too, can see ours; although only fictionally part of his vision, we are linked to the women in the ad. The same male attention, which the ad delimits as both desirable and pleasantly dangerous, will be ours if we buy Candie's shoes.

The potential for violence becomes much more explicit in an ad for Candie's in *Mademoiselle*, September 1982, p. 81 (Figure 4.10). In the left-hand frame, the model applies make-up while standing in an awkward position to display her boot for us. In the background, a man's hand presses ominously against the outside of her window. The right-hand frame moves us ahead in time and gives us a closer, larger view of the room and window. Here, the woman's legs are lifted on the window sill while the shadowy figure outside the window appears to stare up her dress as he tries to open the window. Not only does the male voyeur threaten violence explicitly here, but the woman is depicted as freely participating in what is portrayed in an almost game-like manner. She is the temptress who teases the intruder with her make-up, boots, and open legs.

The male voyeur blocks the doorway in another ad which hints at imminent danger – Chesebrough-Ponds' Aviance Night Musk (*Cosmopolitan*, June 1983, p. 49). Again we see part of a woman's body – her legs, which form a triangular frame around the man standing in the doorway. His upright position suggests strength in contrast to the reclining woman, whose crossed, bare legs and red stiletto heels signify sexual availability. The ad overtly suggests that the fragrance will entrap the man just as the woman's legs have done visually for us in this photo. But in reality it is the man who entraps in this picture, as he blocks the doorway and gazes ominously at the partially clothed woman.

The male gaze can structure an ad even when it is represented only metonymically. A black and white ad for shoes sold at Nordstrom department store in *Vogue* (August 1981, p. 53; permission to reprint denied) shows a pair of trousered legs lurking behind the clothes in a woman's closet. This fragment of

Figure 4.9 Ad for Candie's footwear, courtesy of New Retail Concepts

the male surveyor signifies not only the complete man but, secondarily, his strength, power, and the potential of imminent violence. Admittedly the ad reduces both the woman and the man to their lower legs, but these metonyms are socially over-coded with semes of strength and weakness; the man is in a position of potential aggression and the woman apparently ignorant of the impending danger. The ad trivializes women's well-grounded fears of violent attack by anchoring the picture with the caption "Surprise!" Together with the non-photographic quality of the drawing, this caption urges women to displace the suggestion of danger and their normal fears of impending violence onto feelings of fun and game-playing.

Figure 4.10 Ad for Candie's footwear, courtesy of New Retail Concepts

An ad for Mombasa mosquito netting in *Cosmopolitan* (June 1983, p. 62) also uses a sign of a man to suggest voyeurism and imminent violence (Figure 4.11). Here, instead of legs in a closet, we see if we look closely a man's hand in the foreground among the jungle plants. This metonymic icon suggests that a man is gazing at and approaching the semi-naked woman who lies beneath the netting in a sexual pose in this nearly deserted jungle. The ad asks us to imagine ourselves not only beneath the mosquito netting but as the object of the gaze of the man and his imminent approach. In effect, we are to envision this dangerous situation as romantic and sexually enticing and to look at our future selves through the vision of this potentially aggressive male.

Figure 4.11 Ad for Mombasa mosquito netting, courtesy of Yungjohann Hillman Inc.

Sometimes an ad signifies imminent violence and the male vision using neither a man nor an explicit sign of him. We see a partial view of an undressed woman standing before an uncovered window in an ad for Zip Wax depilatory (*Self*, June 1983, p. 22; Figure 4.12). Drawings of other fragments of a female body appear on two boxes of the product on the window sill. Also draped on the sill is the bikini the woman has just removed, captioned with the headline "Bare Essentials." Together, these icons suggest a vulnerability and the possibility of imminent violence as she undresses before the uncovered

zip
zip
Wax Hair Remover
Bare Essentials
Don't bare it 'til you ZIP* it!
Because ZIP wax depilatory is
a year-round bare essential
for that sleek and sexy look.
Removes unwanted hair from legs,
face, underarms, bikini line
Safely. Smoothly. Lasts longer, too.
Up to sixty days or more.
You owe it to yourself to discover
the luxury salon method used by
sophisticated women the world over.
And try ZIP Creme Bleach,
to lighten face and body hair.
It's easy to mix, gentle to use.
For smooth, sexy silky skin,
nothing bares up better than ZIP

Figure 4.12 Ad for Zip Wax depilatory, courtesy of Lee Pharmaceuticals

window. As in the Mombasa ad we see outside the window large plants that might conceal a voyeur or intruder. The sexualized signification of these individual motifs of fragmentation and imminent danger enter into an oppositional structure of presence and absence. The white tan line across the fragment of the model's hip in the photo, signifying both the absence of the sun and the presence of the bikini, is both the inverse and the mark of the bikini, itself present on the sill; the bikini appears to be tossed aside casually but in fact is arranged perfectly to allow us imaginarily to reconstruct the absent torso of a reclining woman framed by the two parts of this minimalist garment. Similarly, the "marked" fragment of the model's hip and leg joins with the other bodily fragment depicted on the picture of the product here. The oppositional structure carries through to the absent yet somehow ominously present figure of the voyeur who might lurk outside the window.

FRAGMENTED BODIES

Fragmented versions of the self are not always linked to overt violence. Numerous ads utilize an ostensibly innocent fragmentation that appears only to relate to companies' needs to market products for certain parts of the body. The almost magical fetishization of eyes or lips in cosmetics ads may appear necessary for the visual semiotics of marketing products for these body parts but, as Williamson has argued, such ads in fact separate and appropriate parts of us and then invite us to buy them back in a transformed state.[7]

In an $8 million ad campaign for Nestlé Corporation's L'Oréal Crème Riche lipstick launched in spring 1983, McCann Erickson Agency pictures a woman's hand (communicated through her painted nails) holding a mirror that reflects her lips (Figure 4.13; *Vogue*, May 1983, pp. 22–3). Although this is a version of an everyday ritual of many women who wear lipstick, the idealized photographic rendering of the hand, lips and lipstick taken apart from the other accoutrements of everyday reality, adds a phantasmagoric level to the images. Like the lipstick tubes that appear to float autonomously to the right, the large lips seem to exist in suspension, apart from the face. The double frame of the mirror, itself framed by the model's hand, in one sense has captured the previously free-floating lips. But one can only repossess this fragment of the face through the mediation of the product. Readers are invited to buy back this part of themselves which the ad has separated and appropriated ostensibly only because the fragment corresponds to the product being marketed. The angle of the model's hand and its position on the page suggest that these larger-than-life lips and hand are our own; we are almost literally cradling this separate piece of ourself in our hand as we gaze at the image. Through this visual semiosis, the ad urges us to develop a narcissism centered on a

Figure 4.13 Ad for L'Oréal Crème Riche lipstick, courtesy of Cosmair Inc.

fragment of ourself. By purchasing the product we, too, can hold an image of these beautiful lips in our hand and admire ourselves through them.

While ads for cosmetics notoriously fragment women into faces and parts thereof, underwear and hosiery ads commonly depict women as torsos or legs. An ad for Givenchy underwear, made by Esmark's Playtex International, shows a model from her shoulders to her thighs (*Mademoiselle*, May 1981, p. 37). Because her head is excluded, we see her without the fictional possibility of her seeing us, and our viewpoint coincides with the perspective of an implied male surveyor. By omitting the head, the fragmentary image denies reciprocal vision and establishes a relation of power between the viewer and the viewed. This body without a face is an especially useful fragment for advertisers because each reader can more easily imagine it as her own without its face.

The raspberry-colored bra and panties form symbolic brackets around the body fragment and connect by color to another set of symbolic brackets at the ends of the model's arms – fingernails painted in the identical shade. Color connects two other objects – the body fragment bracketed in a shade called raspberry and the raspberries themselves that she holds. Through this color connection the ad invites us to consume the model visually as if we were being offered a raspberry from her fingers. Verbally the ad upholds this connection through the imperative interpellation, "Indulge in a rare delicacy. French raspberry." By commanding us to buy using the euphemism "indulge," the ad encourages us to think of ourselves as this headless torso, a fragment that will be desirable to the male voyeur who shares our position as addressee and is invited to consume both the raspberry and the fragment bracketed in the raspberry-colored underwear and nail polish. The sexual significations of the fragment wearing Givenchy underwear are heightened by the innuendos of the headline of an adjacent ad, "Princess Gardner does it three ways." Underscoring the invitation to consume the raspberry and the underwear is the title of the article "Your looks" on the facing page. In montage the messages on the two pages suggest that this fragmentary image can become "our looks" and enable us to "do it" with style.

Although a woman's entire body appears in an ad for Round-the-Clock's Givenchy panty hose, much of the body is difficult to see, shrouded in black, while the legs stand out in stark contrast (*Mademoiselle*, March 1981, p. 99). The model's large black hat prevents us from seeing her face and her from seeing either us or the implicit male for whom her legs are displayed in this awkward position. She simulates the act of consumption, playing at the appearance of drinking the contents of the cup, while the real purpose of her awkward position in this chair is to exhibit her legs, to offer this fragment of herself to us in magically fetishized form. Other body fragments in pictures lie on the floor. Just as her hand is reflected on the table, so are her legs reflected and multiplied in these images on the floor. They keywords in the text, "collectible" and "collect them all," where collect means buy, also encourage us to see ourselves in pieces that we need to gather together or collect.

One of the most violent of the ads that fragment women's bodies is another in the Round-the-Clock series that pictures a woman's legs from the waist down, the upper body buried in the sand (*Good Housekeeping*, March 1981, p. 93). Her legs are crossed in a sexual pose not normally assumed when one is alone, and the camera position again suggests the line of vision of a male viewer who stands above her. In addition to the Round-the-

Clock hose, which, the ad tells us, were "Too elegant to take off," she wears high stiletto-heeled shoes that would have been extremely difficult to walk on the sand in. A crab crawls ominously toward this fragment of her. We are asked to decode as "Sheer radiance" an image of death or near death as she lies buried in the sand from the waist up. "There are 17 spring shades, so you can bury yourself in color," the ad tells us, implying that the woman has done this violence to herself. While the word "bury" is used here in a figurative sense, the photographic image depicts the concept literally. Together these significations urge us to conceive of ourselves as a fragment and link the image to physical harm or death.

All of these images of fragmentation substitute a part of a woman's body for the whole and often the reader's vision of that part coincides with the perspective of the implied male surveyor. By encouraging women to think of themselves in fragments, advertisers only hope to sell products but such repeated images do more than this. The constant reinforcement of fragmented ways of seeing the self teaches a reified consciousness in which lips, eyes, legs, and other body parts fetishistically stand in for the whole.

FROM PLAYFULNESS TO VIOLENCE

As we have seen, the theme of women's playful nature often begins on a magazine's cover and continues in the ads and features inside. When editorial features develop a theme such as playfulness, they give further covert support to ads that emphasize this view of women. The fashion feature "Briefer encounters" in the March 1981 *Mademoiselle* (pp. 174–81), for example, supports purchased advertising not only by presenting pictures of underwear, verbal descriptions, manufacturers' names and list prices, but by developing a theme often used in purchased advertising: playfulness that hints at violence. This covert ad for underwear is part of a larger series of features in the issue titled "A walk on the wild side" which urges women to play at being "wild" and at having "brief encounters of the sexual kind" but ultimately cautions them to stay within the accepted moral standards. Here, as in much of the editorial material and advertisements in women's magazines, we see at work what

Jameson has termed the ideological double standard.[8] Articles and features allow readers a brief taste of eroticism and transgression, only to uphold the dominant moral order in the end.

Playfulness rapidly turns to violence in the covert ad "Briefer encounters." The first photograph shows four women either reclining, sitting in an off-balance pose, exhibiting what Goffman terms a coy knee bend, or fondling their hair. The men pictured, in contrast, are dressed, ready for activity, staring at the exposed women who pose in underwear and wait to be visually consumed. On the subsequent pages the women assume gestures and poses that Goffman analyzed such as wide beaming smiles, bashful knee bends, canting heads, hands placed over the mouth in licensed withdrawal, and puckish, clowning body positions. Two of the photos (pp. 178 and 181) link violence to this playfulness. The men assume positions of attack while the women smile coyly. Goffman suggests that this mock assault usually hints at what men could do if they got serious about it.[9] Thus, covert ads such as these contain a veiled threat toward women and add an implicit violence to what at first appears to be harmless fun.

Playful poses in ads are numerous and sometimes hint at the seductive little girl. An ad for Bonne Bell's Lip-Smackers lip gloss shows a childish-looking girl with her hair braided and tied in bows, winking at us and saying, "I'm crackers over Lip-Smackers!" (*Young Miss*, July 1982, p. 33). Contradictory iconic signs here encourage the young readers to retain childish, playful gestures and behavior yet decorate themselves with cosmetics for the implied male. Revlon's two-page ad spread on cover two and page one of *Mademoiselle*, April 1981, shows an adult woman dressed as a little girl in a ruffled party dress holding a balloon. Promoting Rouge lipstick and nail polish, the ad's headline reads, "Little girls wear pink until they're ready for Rouge." The theme of the sexually enticing little girl here is heightened by a picture inset on the left-hand page showing a woman's pink lips with one fingernail, painted in the matching shade, in her mouth. This childish yet seductive gesture works in conjunction with the image of the adult little girl on the facing page who, with her ruffled dress and balloon, might be on her way to a birthday party.

The models in an ad for You Formfit underwear stand in childish playful poses and appear to be either trying to hold down their dresses which have blown up, revealing their underwear, or coyly lifting them up to show us the product (*Good Housekeeping*, April 1981, pp. 68–9). They exhibit ritualized behavioral practices that Goffman found were frequently used to depict women in advertising such as coy knee bends, body clowning, and covering their faces in embarrassment or shyness. Further, the interpellative "You" in the headline, the product's name, and the shape of the package in the letter "u" constitute a series of playful homonyms, underscoring the models' childish poses. The stiletto heels and lacy underwear suggest the presence of an implied male so that the image of the playful little girl is linked to that of the seductress.

Signs of playfulness merge with those of violence in ads for Interco's Esprit clothing. An ad in the August 1981 *Vogue* (p. 228) depicts a model with her mouth opened in surprise, shyness, or fear, trying to pull her skirt down as the two men beside her pull it up. Similar to the sexualized little girls in the Formfit ad, the woman here pushes her skirt down defensively while the men appear strong, calm, and on the offensive. The playful theme of many Esprit ads crosses the boundary to violence in a two-page ad spread in *Mademoiselle*, November 1981 (pp. 140–1). A woman lies supine across an ironing board and a man presses an iron to her pelvic area while kissing her. The man, completely in white, contrasts the woman who wears a multicolored dress. The Esprit logo across his shirt leads us to several innocent, "playful" interpretations of this ad that has no ad slogan to anchor the photographic images. We might interpret the photo to mean "Esprit loves you," "Esprit kisses you," or "Esprit wants you to look perfect as you're ready to leave, purse in hand." Where, normally, words anchor selected meanings of photographs and drawings, here, the photographic image of the man anchors the logo "Esprit," conflating the signification of the linguistic sign with that of the affection of a desiring man. But the signs in this photograph personify the product as both a male lover and torturer. We must interpret the iron in a symbolic, non-real sense if we are to avoid cringing in pain at the sight of this image. The ad has reconfigured signifiers to displace the real sensation of pain to levels of fantasy, thus enabling readers to conflate desire, abstract, "pleasurable" pain, and Esprit clothing. In effect, the ad transforms playfulness into violence while attempting to obviate the violence by showing the woman smiling

Figure 4.14 Ad for Jovan lipstick and nail polish, courtesy of Quintessence Inc.

during her torture. Merging eroticism and violence, it conflates the childish and the seductive. An ad for Jovan lipstick and nail polish shows six pictures of a woman with ostensibly playful objects in her mouth, (*Vogue*, June 1981, p. 38; Figure 4.14). The last image shows her with a firecracker between her teeth as she lights the fuse with a match. The photos have progressed from a popsicle and party favor in the model's mouth to this final image of violence. The text of the ad reinforces a violent decoding of the photo by using the rhetoric of war: "Six whole new rounds of ammunition added to Jovan's potent arsenal of 24 luminous colors. Match your lips and nails today. And you're armed for any match." While Jovan hopes that this violent image will excite us, the company does not wish us to interpret the final image in a literal sense. As in the Esprit ad in which the man irons the woman, a literal interpretation would likely promote feelings of physical pain that might not increase sales of the product.

Images of cute, childish women in playful poses appear frequently in women's magazines. The impending violence in some of these images is cause for concern because the surrounding context of playfulness and the attractiveness of the images cast an aura of innocence and harmlessness on what we see. As we learn to view ourselves as childish and playful, we are at the same time learning to naturalize violence toward women. Further, whether ads use male voyeurism, female fragmentation, or ostensibly innocuous playfulness to overcode the seme of violence, they present what Walkerdine, following Coward, has termed "regimes of meaning" that link cruelty to sexual excitement, and encourage a passive heterosexuality.[10]

IDEAL AND DISTORTED MIRRORS

We have seen that advertisements, whether they be the front cover, a covert ad disguised as a feature, or a purchased ad, usually present the reader with a symbolic mirror image of herself, an ideal supposedly attainable for the price of the product. As Williamson has pointed out, the eyes of many models in ads are level with our own and stare back at us as if they were our reflection in a mirror.[11] Often the image is ostensibly positive – a desirable, glamorous, and often unattainable version of the real women who read magazines. But some ads, such as those for Sundown sunscreen and Weight Watchers pizza discussed above (see Figure 4.6), utilize a negative mirror image to deter readers from not using the product.

A number of ads go beyond this implicit suggestion that the photograph is our future mirror image by directly portraying a mirror. We have seen that cosmetics ads often fragment a woman's face and use a mirror image to draw attention to one part of it. The woman in the ad for L'Oréal lipstick discussed above holds in her hand a mirror that contains her lips, asking us to develop a narcissism based on a fragment of ourselves. An ad for Christian Dior make-up carries these images one step further by showing a woman embracing her mirror image (*Vogue*, August 1981, p. 77; Figure 4.15). The model appears to be wearing no clothing, exuberantly embracing her ideal self in the mirror in an exaggerated narcissism. She loves this image of herself so because it has been glamorized by the product. We, too, will love ourselves this ecstatically, the ad implies, if we purchase the make-up.

Essence advertises TCB hairdressing products (May 1981,

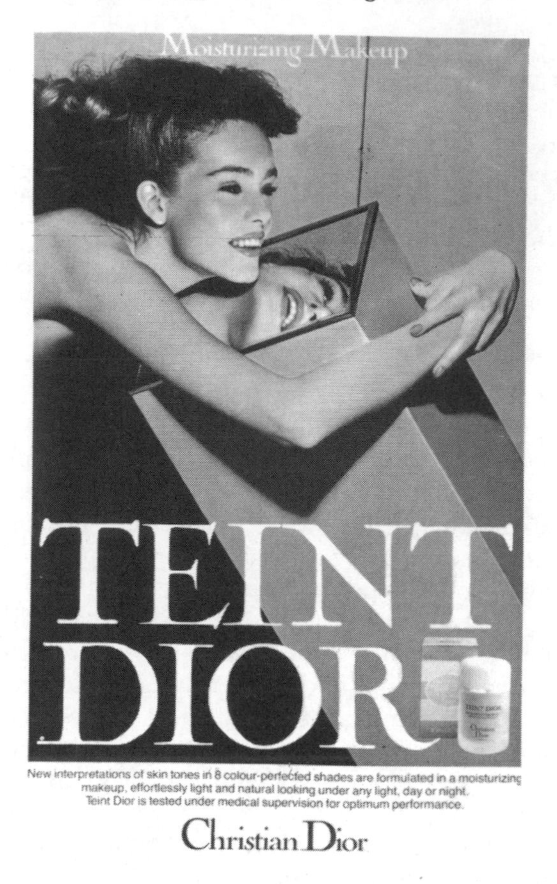

Figure 4.15 Ad for Teint Dior make-up, courtesy of Christian Dior Perfumes, Inc.

p. 79) with the image of a magical mirror that remakes reality before our eyes (Figure 4.16). Here, as the model's male hairdresser combs her hair, she gazes at her future self in the mirror before her. There, she has been transformed by different clothes and placed in a jungle setting with another admiring male gazing at her. The ad headlines direct the viewer, along with her, to "See all you can be" in the ideal, changed reality reflected in the magical mirror. It is a politically charged ideal, however, in which the image of the Black as jungle savage is exoticized. Afro-American readers of *Essence* are encouraged to go back instead of forward historically into an in fact non-existent,

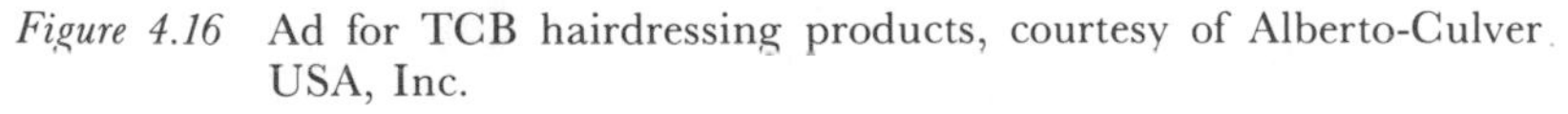

Figure 4.16 Ad for TCB hairdressing products, courtesy of Alberto-Culver USA, Inc.

exoticized past. Her fantasies are to become the viewer's, to be magically attained through purchase of the product.

As we study the creation of meaning in ads, focusing on the value-laden systems that structure the pleasurable images, we begin the work of becoming critical, articulate receivers of mass culture. Advertising texts may still attract us, but when we are aware of their value systems and subtexts we will read them differently. Images that suggest imminent or actual violence toward women such as the Candie's shoes ad with the man ominously lurking outside the window or the Esprit ad in which the man irons the woman use pleasurable images to encourage us to view ourselves as victims. These ads would fit well in the "No Comment" column in *Ms.* to which readers submit blatant examples of media sexism. But, while publishing negative visual representations of women in such a column is an important first step in actively protesting these media portrayals, this column, in one sense, renders women inarticulate in the face of sexism: "No comment" is all one can say. Instead, we must work to develop articulate critiques of these negative images and learn to communicate the objections to those responsible.

In critically analyzing ads we must remain aware, as well, of the utopian elements at work in many advertising texts. How does an ad present us with attractive fantasies and scopophilic and other pleasures as inducements to buy a product? While often these levels of pleasure remain intact even after critical analysis of an ad, it is helpful to understand this utopian pleasure and fantasy, as Jameson has theorized, as the rewards that mass culture offers for our consenting to remain passive.[12] Utopian fantasies in ads can tyrannize us at the same time that they give us pleasure. Our often unconscious consent to remain passive in fact contributes to the status quo of women's portrayal in advertising. We can struggle against this link between pleasure and passivity by also examining what attracts us to a given ad as we analyze the structures of meaning the ad uses to communicate to us.

Part Two: Editorial Texts: The Continuum of Commodity-Based Culture

5 Fashion and Beauty: Transgression, Utopia, and Containment

We have come to think of advertising pages and editorial material as distinct entities. With the increasing commercialization of magazines, however, these divisions have become blurred. Today in most women's magazines, advertising and editorial content form a continuum; many of the patterns at work in advertising appear as well in the editorial pages.

This cultural continuum is especially well developed in one of the strongest categories of women's publications, the fashion and beauty magazines. It is a unique category because it spans several age groups of readers. Young girls learn patterns of consumption early on with *Young Miss*, *'Teen*, and *Seventeen*. (Since December 1983, the category reaches even younger girls – 4 to 11-year-olds – with the appearance of *Barbie*, a magazine copyrighted by Mattel Inc., that promotes the company's dolls and accessories along with sex roles and ideals of fashion and beauty.) *Mademoiselle*, *Glamour*, *Self*, and *Cosmopolitan* address the important group of prime spenders aged 18–34. Competing for the somewhat older, affluent audience are *Bazaar* and *Vogue*. Because the magazines in this genre are usually the first that a young girl seriously reads, the cultural continuum between advertising and editorial material here plays an especially important role in teaching women lifelong habits of consumption. When, in rare instances, the advertising conflicts with the editorial material, as occurs in *'Teen* and *Seventeen*, the overriding message of consumerism remains nonetheless unendangered.

One of the key inducements to consumption in the fashion and beauty magazines is the pleasure they offer readers. Bright colors, exciting headlines and layouts, elegant fashions and flawless faces draw the reader in as she turns the pages of a *Mademoiselle* or *Vogue*. Ideal images of the future self encountered on the front cover are multiplied and reinforced in feature after feature. Free to indulge in a narcissism based on fantasy, one can, for a moment, forget one's actual appearance in the mirror, replacing that memory with the magazine's concrete examples of ideal beauty. Ostensibly, these images are positive projections of the future self, for few would buy these publications were they overtly to present negative images.

Structuralism has taught us, however, that systems of opposition are frequently at work in even the most simple of cultural forms. The apparently straightforward and positive ideals of fashion and beauty here are often subtly intertwined with their opposites – the non-fashionable and the non-beautiful. The attractive presentation frequently disguises the negativity close at hand: within this discursive structure, to be beautiful, one must fear being non-beautiful; to be in fashion, one must fear being out of fashion; to be self-confident, one must first feel insecure. This oppositional strategy helps to assure the continued purchase of commodities; one product or even several will never completely alleviate insecurities and the fear of being non-beautiful. One must always return for more goods and services.

The economic root of this cultural configuration is industry's continued need to sell products. Because of that need, the pleasure of magazines must only be transitory. Both the magazine as a cultural commodity and the goods it advertises must never give complete satisfaction or one would not need to buy further magazines or products. Magazine editors do not consciously link beauty and glamor to their structural opposites in order to heighten fears in readers deliberately. Rather, the logic of the magazine industry leads them in an ostensibly natural mode to this path.

From *Young Miss* to *Vogue*, the beauty and fashion publications encourage one to enjoy certain transgressive and utopian pleasures, each magazine developing its own specific configuration of both forbidden and acceptable arenas of enjoyment. Simultaneously, however, each publication finds a means of containing these pleasures, harnessing them to consumerism. After releasing both subtle and overt subversive elements for readers to enjoy, the magazines attempt to secure ideological closure to accompany their consumerist containment of the transgressive.

A few large companies dominate this lucrative magazine category, which earns millions in revenue each year from this oppositional structure. Triangle Publications, Petersen Publishing Company, and Gruner & Jahr compete for the young female audience with *Seventeen*, *'Teen*, and *Young Miss*, preparing young girls to purchase consumer goods now and in the future. Conde Nast (*Mademoiselle*, *Glamour*, *Self*, and *Vogue*) and Hearst (*Cosmopolitan* and *Bazaar*) compete with one another for the post-teenage market. The most lucrative magazines in the category, *Cosmopolitan* and *Vogue*, have immense ad volumes. As we will see, both offer readers unique escapes from everyday life, fantasies that ultimately reaffirm dominant moral values and women's role in consumerism. Together, the nine publications in the fashion and beauty genre constitute a wide-reaching cultural force that helps to socialize women during several decades of their lives; through an oppositional structure that links positive beauty ideals to images of female inadequacy, women learn both their expected social role and their duties as consumers.

CHILDREN AND YOUNG ADOLESCENTS AS FUTURE CONSUMERS

Young Miss and *'Teen*: Consumerist and Ideological Closure in the Privatized Space of Subculture

In 1981 Gruner & Jahr, USA, publisher of *Parents*, began a magazine aimed at older children. Petersen Publishing Company markets a competing monthly, *'Teen*, whose readership overlaps with that of *Young Miss* and extends to girls a few years older.[1] The two magazines employ childish advertising and features to initiate readers into the world of female consumption. Cosmetics, fashion, food preparation, and romance are the predominant themes that prepare girls for their future roles as wives and mothers, when they will be responsible not only for their family's consumption but for decorating themselves with cosmetics and fashion to secure a man's love. The underlying theme that sustains this consumption is female inadequacy.

A male Editor of a prominent women's magazine has argued that magazines do not create insecurity in women: "If women's anxieties are there, shouldn't their magazines try to help? We're not creating anxieties. We're reacting to them."[2] In fact, however, beginning with *Young Miss* and *'Teen*, most women's magazines help to develop insecurities and anxieties in women by constantly repeated themes in features and advertising. While magazines are not always the initial cause of anxiety, they often encourage and exacerbate these feelings, and suggest that increased consumption is the remedy. As we have seen, the logic of the magazine industry as it is currently organized leads Editors to this path.

The keynote of beauty and fashion magazines is an exaggerated concern with physical appearance so that other aspects of the complete human being are undervalued. In order to stimulate sales of cosmetics and apparel whose advertisers sustain these magazines, editorial features encourage readers to dissect themselves conceptually into fragments that various products are promised to improve.

A case in point is the monthly "Dear Beauty Editor" column in *Young Miss* which offers advice on a plethora of pseudo-problems: fading eyeshadow, pale eyebrows, full lips, smudged polish on toe nails, bitten fingernails (May 1983, p. 66); droopy hair, white bumps on the face, dry hair and skin (April 1983, p. 74); red splotches on the face, powder blush that wears off before noon, eyes that seem to disappear behind glasses, a long narrow face and pointed chin (February 1982, p. 80); dark hair on legs, thin eyelashes, bushy eyebrows, "goopy," uneven make-up, and fat stomach, thighs and hips (September 1982, p. 74). The columnist often recommends brand-name products to alleviate the problems, frequently the same brands that appear in the purchased advertising. The technique of question and answer encourages readers to think that their peers have written to the magazine with such problems. If a reader hasn't yet thought about herself in these fragmented terms, she should begin to do so if she wishes to be beautiful and share the concerns of her peers.

Even the fiction in *Young Miss* reinforces the concern with visual appearance. The protagonist in an April 1983 story notes:

> I changed my image quickly, too. I got a short, sleek haircut and lots of sundresses. Steph, with her eye for color and style, helped me shop and sew. I felt like a new person.
>
> One day even my yellow sundress stood out brightly against the tan I had slaved over since moving to Florida. Eat your heart out, Hal Matson, I thought, as I slid gracefully into my seat in Latin class. Smart does *not* equal ugly (p. 4).

The primary lesson here is that external changes make one a "new person." The girl's friend, like a magazine advice columnist, teaches her to remedy alleged inadequacies by shopping. The "slaved over" tan, together with the bright sundress and her gracefully sliding into her seat, will draw male notice, that is, visual consumption of her physical appearance. The message is that girls who are intelligent must decorate themselves to win male approval, for one's intelligence is not enough to secure love.

In *'Teen*, the commodity-based beauty advice constitutes an especially pervasive form of covert advertising and appears even in the horoscopes. Readers born under each month's astrological sign are to identify with a "best feature" such as "shapely shoulders" or a "trim body." The June 1983 horoscope notes that Gemini is "flighty in the make-up and fashion departments . . . seldom wears clothes in the same way more than once [and] figure[s] out six or seven ways to wear her newest scarf" (p. 15). An April 1983 article offering advice on preparing for one's prom urges readers to be preoccupied with physical appearance and self-criticism several weeks before the prom. Besides watching one's weight so that "extra pounds don't creep up on you . . . once you've invested in a dress," one is to carry an "emergency kit" containing a blemish cover, cosmetics, safety pins, and a breath freshener, and not wait until the last moment "to defuzz unwanted hair" (pp. 64–5). The commodity base of the insecurities that *'Teen* introduces each month becomes evident at the end of the numerous advice columns. Whether "Dear Jill," "Dear Jack," "Dear Beauty Editor" or "Dear Doctor," each column ends by inviting readers to join *'Teen*'s Research Gang. Along with a membership card, readers will receive a questionnaire about beauty, fashion, and entertainment products and, perhaps unknowingly, provide market information that the magazine can use to attract advertisers.

Young Miss teaches readers at an early age to look critically at their bodies and be ashamed of parts that do not fit the established model. Questions and answers in advice columns often assume the presence of a surveyor who continually judges. Readers are advised to use clothing and accessories to draw attention (i.e. visual consumption) to certain parts of their bodies and away from others. In May 1983, for example, the monthly clothes-advice column negatively entitled "Hiding your figure problems" begins with the question: "I have heavy hips and thighs so I prefer not to wear pants or mini-skirts – or any clothes that *emphasize* my *figure problem*. What's *new* and interesting this spring that will *conceal* my hips and thighs?" (my emphasis, p. 18).

Each month questions and answers in the clothes column also emphasize the ideology of the new and its companion the obsolete to draw attention to physical appearance: "Q. I have several old skirts . . . but I'm tired of the style. A. Be sure to wear it with the new low-heeled or flat shoes" (March 1982, p. 68). "Q. . . . I never know what styles are the most popular. Do you have any hints? A. This spring, legs are the center of attention" (April 1983, p. 9). Induced insecurities about the shape of one's body and the obsolescence of clothing already owned encourages further purchases. Pre-teens who read the magazine learn to look self-consciously at their bodies even before they enter adolescence. Early adolescent readers, more than likely already self-conscious about their changing bodies, learn to be even more self-critical through the magazine's emphasis on visual appearance.

Besides selling commodities both *Young Miss* and *'Teen* engage in especially transparent attempts at ideological closure. The advice columns in *Young Miss* emphasize self-criticism as they work toward ideological socialization. The monthly "What's the Problem" column invokes an authoritarian tone, placing blame and guilt on readers. In September 1982, the columnist asks one advice-seeker: "Are you doing anything that he could interpret as flirting?" (p. 12). Other warnings such as "Don't jeopardize the trust your parents have in you by dating behind their backs" (April 1983, p. 81) attempt to regain social control over some of the transgressive elements that readers have been allowed to enjoy on other pages in the magazine. *'Teen* promotes properly socialized behavior with such articles as "Drinking and driving: A ticket to disaster" (May 1982), "Shoplifting: Taking a losing chance" (August 1982), "The truth about cults" (April 1983) and "Teens and sex: Too much, too soon?" (May 1983). In March 1983, the "Dear Jack" column warns against sexual activity by stating authoritatively: "Your friends have the mistaken belief that engaging in sexual behavior is a sign of growing up" (p. 48).

These pieces stand in contradiction to other ads and features in the magazines that encourage girls to become sex objects. Like the Seagram's ad that advises readers to drink in moderation yet pictures an extra-large glass of liquor, *Young Miss* and *'Teen* encourage girls to consume goods and services that will make them sexually attractive, yet in certain editorial features caution them to avoid sex. These socializing articles that advise readers against drinking, smoking, cults, sex, and shoplifting give the magazines a wholesome image that is likely to please the readers' parents. Together with the family, schools, and churches, these publications teach girls to engage in moral and socially acceptable behavior but unlike these other institutions, engage openly in an ideological double standard. In addition, however, and perhaps more important to the economy, they teach girls to be good consumers.

The monthly advice column of Eric Carlson in *Young Miss* attempts to socialize readers in a less contradictory mode because it parallels so closely the induced insecurities that sustain the magazine's other glamorous images. "Just what makes a guy look twice?" (February 1982), for example, advises readers to imagine themselves through the eyes of a male surveyor: "Take a look at yourself. Does your appearance say, 'I'm interesting and interested'?" (p. 22). The September 1982 column "Coping with a busy boyfriend" advises readers to refrain from pressuring their boyfriends and to be patient, learn to compromise, and not be "unreasonable." Setting up a power hierarchy in which the boy's priorities predominate over the girl's, Carlson underscores the power with a veiled threat: "if you continue to nag him you may find he doesn't need you either" (p. 26). Sometimes, however, Carlson's advice contradicts ads and features that encourage sexual reification. "What guys think about flirts" warns that "once you're labelled *a flirt*, it's pretty hard to be known as anything else" and "most guys don't take [them] seriously." In order to market commodities, *Young Miss* and *'Teen* release on some of their editorial and ad pages elements of transgressive sexuality that the dominant moral order tries to forbid young girls. The magazines attempt to regain ideological closure over these elements in columns such as Carlson's.

This releasing of transgressive elements only to harness them more securely to dominant ideological constraints works more effectively as a socializing tool because it occurs within the privatized subcultural space allowed teenage girls. As McRobbie and Garber have shown,[3] the secretive space within the home –

one's own bedroom or a friend's – is an important site of girls' subcultural expression. But it is also here that the transgressive is harnessed to consumerism and ideological socialization. Girls experiment elaborately with make-up, clothes, hair products and accessories and enjoy recorded music, posters, videos, and magazines. Experienced as constituent of one's subculture and often enjoyed in one's own privatized space, magazines such as *Young Miss* and *'Teen* are especially effective agents of socialization and consumer culture.

Although *Young Miss* tells advertisers that "its editorial aim is to help the individual realize her own potential . . . to open up her mind to the variety of options she has, to help her achieve a sense of self-confidence and self-achievement . . .,"[4] the magazine in fact uses numerous techniques to make girls feel insecure about themselves so that they will buy products to remedy the alleged shortcomings. Rather than offering readers a variety of options for realizing their potential, it emphasizes fashion, beauty, food preparation, romance, pets, and entertainment stars; concern with physical appearance predominates to the exclusion of articles that would develop broader interests such as national and world politics, literature, the arts, science, and the life of young people in other countries. In *'Teen* as well, this emphasis on commodity-based glamor and the underlying induced insecurities offer girls limited rather than diverse options for development.

The parallel strategy of employing transgressive elements to sell products while attempting ideological closure to contain these elements in other sections of the magazines has proven a lucrative technique for both publications. Gruner & Jahr increased *Young Miss*' circulation 50 per cent in one year. In March 1983 it announced a 7 per cent rise in its rate base to 750,000. That year *'Teen* charged $16,625 for a back-cover ad and its low CPM of $2.26 was only two cents higher than 1982.[5] The glossy, glamorous images in both publications serve as a pleasant sugar coating on the pill of insecurity that young girls are asked to take each month as part of their induction into their important role as primary purchasers in the consumer society. Ordinary adolescent insecurities become magnified, entering a new discursive system of "figure flaws," "droopy hair," and "red splotches" for which purchases are the only remedy. If, as *'Teen* argues to advertisers, readers "hang on our every word,"[6] the ideological and consumerist training of young girls will be successful; in a few years readers will be ripe for other beauty and fashion magazines that will continue this formation.

Seventeen: Wholesomeness and Consumerism in Contradiction

Begun in 1944, *Seventeen* has a long tradition of correctly socializing young women. It is edited for 16- to 17-year-olds and, according to SMRB, reaches 5.13 million girls aged 12–17 and another 2.3 million women between 18 and 24. In recent years with its teenage audience declining, the magazine has worked to update its editorial sections, adding features on health, fitness, nutrition, and sex to its usual fashion and beauty features. In keeping with the wholesome image it strives for, *Seventeen* declines over 100 ad pages a year for products such as liquor, cigarettes, birth control, bust developers or ads with an overt sexual pitch. Its principal advertised products are cosmetics, toiletries, and fashion – also the primary subjects of its editorial material.[7]

Even while turning away advertisers deemed inconsistent with its editorial image, *Seventeen* produced $25.8 million in ad revenue in 1982 for its parent corporation, Triangle Publications, owned by the Annenberg family. Triangle, whose main publication is *TV Guide*, earned over $549 million in revenues that year. *Seventeen* attracts advertisers by emphasizing how much its readers consume. Besides reducing its readers to slogans such as "Calculating consumer," "Purchasing agent," "Born to shop," "In a class by herself,"and "Speaker of the house," the magazine tells advertisers that *Seventeen*'s readers are "branded for life" because 33 per cent use the same brand of nail polish that they first bought as teenagers, 29 per cent drink the same brand of coffee, and 34 per cent use the same mouthwash. Because 66 per cent of its readers have mothers who work outside the home, the magazine argues, these readers are responsible for some of the family shopping. Most important, however, is what *Seventeen* calls "the Scholar Dollar": in 1982, the magazine claims, teenage girls spent $7.9 billion on their way back to high school or college. Apparel marketers who advertise in the August back-to-school issue, *Seventeen* promises, reach one out of every two teenage girls in the country and receive extra support for their products from the over 600 retail stores that participate in related promotions for *Seventeen*'s back-to-school merchandise.[8]

Seventeen's promises to advertisers correlate with the consumerist ideology that structures the magazine's editorial material. Indeed, the magazine addresses its readers as young purchasers, giving them a "seminar on spending" while also teaching accepted social values. Thus, the monthly "Now You're Cooking" food section and annual contest, for example, not only attracts food advertisers to this fashion and beauty publication but helps to integrate young women into their expected role in the kitchen. Meal preparation is as important as beauty and fashion concerns, the magazine implies. Correctly done, it will also attract "boys" and allow teenage readers to integrate themselves into the residual unpaid household labor that much of contemporary society still expects women to perform.

Although *Seventeen* is edited for an audience somewhat older than that of *Young Miss* or *'Teen*, an aura of childishness pervades the magazine. A column on food in the December 1982 issue instructs readers how to make "Teddy bear bread" (p. 8); the decorating-crafts feature in the issue uses a *double-entendre* with sexual implications in its title "Bear-ing it!" and gives instructions for making clothes for teddy bears along with teddy bear address books, diaries, wallets, and chocolate (p. 130). The models in fashion features often appear in childish poses; "In the pink" (December 1982, pp. 92–105), shows girls in awkward positions of exaggerated playfulness, on the floor with their legs up, holding balloons, and emerging from a gift box wide-eyed and open-mouthed, childishly covering their mouths. An ad for Bass shoes shows a group of women playing "ring-around-the-rosy" (January 1981, pp. 10–11), and a number of the other childish ads discussed in Chapter 4 often appear in *Seventeen*.

As in *'Teen*, these images of childishness coexist with messages that encourage a sexual self-positioning. An ad for Candie's shoes, for example, pictures a woman lying across a rumpled bed with her legs crossed and skirt up, in a sexualized pose that suggests the presence of a male observer (March 1982, p. 99). Fashion and beauty features in *Seventeen* often refer directly or indirectly to the critically observing male surveyor, urging readers to be sexually alluring by first scrutinizing themselves. In May 1983 one feature shows swimsuits that will correct "figure problems" (p. 32) and articles such as "Back talk" (p. 78) and

"Flirty back views" (p. 174) not only remind readers that their backs will be seen in summer clothing, encouraging more self-consciousness but conflate discursive and visual reification as a metonymic substitution of verbal speech.

In further contradiction to these messages that girls should be both childish and sexually alluring is *Seventeen*'s sex advice. "An open letter to *Seventeen*'s readers and their parents," (July 1982) announces a new monthly column about the "sexual concerns and problems of young people." The purpose of the column, "Sex and Your Body," the announcement notes, is "to inform and enlighten . . . in a prudent, discreet manner . . . so that you can deal responsibly, as teens and adults, with your sexuality" (p. 16). In contrast to both the childish and sexualized images in much of the magazine, then, these columns claim to advise readers to be responsible and adult about their sexuality. However, a number of the columns subtly and sometimes openly discourage girls from having sex. In May 1983, for example, the column's headline reads: "What happens to you physically – and emotionally – when you lose your virginity." In addition to using a value-laden term such as "lose," the column employs a stereotypical dichotomy to describe the effects of sex: "Physically it means . . . that if you are male you now have put a female at risk of pregnancy; that if you are female you now may have begun the creation of a new life in your womb" (p. 58). The column does not mention birth control, even though later in the issue, a report of the results of a previous survey of *Seventeen*'s readers shows that 63 per cent approve of sex before marriage (p. 92).

Two years earlier the magazine had published a column about birth control (October 1981, pp. 142–3 ff), also using the piece to subtly discourage sex. One answer advises: "[a girl] should think long and carefully about becoming sexually involved. . . . The resulting guilt and other worries that she may have, along with her fears of pregnancy, can turn out to be a very heavy burden" (p. 175). Another answer notes that "78 per cent of the top high school achievers, academically and socially, [have] chosen not to have sexual relationships during high school." Even though *Seventeen*'s own poll shows that the majority of its readers approve of premarital sex, this column, ostensibly intended to inform readers about birth control, implies that one won't succeed as well in school and will feel guilty if one engages in sex.

Ostensibly oblivious to its own "mixed messages," the magazine entitles its December 1982 sex column "How to sort through those mixed messages you're getting about sex – and decide what's right for *you*"; it cautions: "Too many . . . young women . . . in the heat of sexual excitement, have given up standards that they had meant to uphold – and thereafter have had to carry a burden of guilt and disappointment." Telling readers that contraception often fails for teens, the column ends, as do the majority of *Seventeen*'s sex advice columns, with the reminder that the decision to have sex is a very complicated problem related to individual development and maturity. By emphasizing repeatedly the theme that teenagers are not emotionally ready to engage in sex, *Seventeen* helps to socialize its readers according to the predominantly accepted values.[9] Nonetheless, the magazine continues to contradict this message by publishing ads and features that encourage girls to be both childish and sexually alluring.

As does *'Teen*, *Seventeen* trains young girls to engage in other socially and morally acceptable behavior at the same time it teaches them to function as consumers. Columns such as "Volunteer work does pay off" (March 1982, p. 52), "Do nice girls swear?" (January 1981, p. 96), "Am I eating with the right fork, Mabel?" (October 1981, p. 146), "Are you ready for marriage?" (February 1982, p. 150), "Don't lower the drinking age for teens!" (August 1981, p. 90), "How to handle anger" (June 1982, p. 128), and "Driving is a privilege not a right" (February 1983, p. 83) complement the advice on social problems that appears each month in the column "Relating" by Abigail Wood. Wood's column often tries to build up readers' sense of self while giving advice on socially correct behavior.

As have a number of women's magazines, *Seventeen* has begun to include pieces that touch on feminism. In the February 1982 issue a column by a 15-year-old reader urges readers to work for the passage of the Equal Rights Amendment (ERA) (p. 112). The December 1982 article "Do teachers treat boys differently from girls?" (pp. 106ff) cautions readers that teachers often praise boys for academic accomplishments while complimenting girls on good penmanship, neat desks, and tasteful wardrobes. Later in this issue, however, the short story "Christmas Eve" undermines this feminism. When the protagonist cannot think of ideas for a paper she must write on *Julius Caesar*, her date gives her his analysis of the play. She replies, "'I wish I could help you with your math.' I felt very stupid" (p. 144). So, while *Seventeen* publishes occasional articles and letters with a feminist orientation, it undercuts them with much of its editorial content and advertising.

One key to the magazine's real preoccupations is the title on the binding of each issue. Frequently these titles remind young girls that they are being scrutinized: "Party-perfect looks" (November 1982); "Camouflage is in" (January 1981); "Fun looks for summer" (May 1982); "Terrific looks for '82" (January 1982); "Good looks all year long" (January 1983); and "Look great this winter" (November 1981). This preoccupation with physical appearance pervades many of the editorial pages – not only the beauty and fashion features, but fiction, articles, features, and even the food section. Here *Seventeen* shows girls how to prepare attractive-looking meals, a visible symbol of their worth as women, and to dress up to serve the meal to their date (February 1983, pp. 45–8). Another food feature advises: "How to make your picnic extra-pretty" (June 1982, p. 147), a reminder that the food we prepare, like our clothing and make-up, reflects on the self. This emphasis on physical appearance upholds the interests of the magazine's primary advertisers – cosmetics and apparel companies.

Seventeen continues the predominant themes of *Young Miss* and *'Teen* – exaggerated emphasis on physical appearance and feelings of insecurity – as a means of integrating young girls into the consumer society. Because its audience is young (*Seventeen* notes that some of its readers are below ten[10]), the magazine tries to project an image of wholesomeness to reassure parents. At the same time, the magazine's primary concern is to secure advertising revenue and, consequently, a number of contradictory images appear. While officially it accepts no ads for liquor, cigarettes, or other products that it considers inappropriate, many of its ads urge readers to become sexually enticing for men. Although the beauty and fashion features also encourage this and promote childish images, other editorial features caution readers to behave maturely and avoid sex until they are married. If such editorial features help to socialize young girls correctly, it is only of secondary concern to the publisher. First and foremost is the securing of advertising and circulation revenue; messages of socialization are useful only if they advance these goals.

BEAUTY, HEALTH, AND PSEUDO-LIBERATION FOR WOMEN 18 TO 34

Mademoiselle: Beauty in the Service of Consumerism

Addressed to readers who are no longer children and young adolescents, the other fashion and beauty magazines need not appear concerned with the moralistic socialization of readers. Instead, a magazine such as *Mademoiselle* can emphasize beauty in editorial material and avoid the frequent contradictions of *Seventeen* between editorial content and advertising messages. Boasting that it publishes more features about beauty than any other magazine, *Mademoiselle* consciously attempts to attract advertisers of beauty products. It argues to advertisers that its readers "admire so many beautiful things. And acquire them."[11] More accurately, then, *Mademoiselle*'s editorial concern is with beauty in the service of consumerism.

Adapting itself to the current popularity of health and fitness, the magazine has renamed its beauty section "Good Looks and Health" and tells advertisers that *Mademoiselle* will give them a "healthy climate" in which to promote their products.[12] Articles in the updated beauty section include advice on hair and skin care, makeovers, cosmetics, fragrances, exercise, weight-reduction, and some medical problems. These features commonly have an ostensibly positive tone but at the same time subtly undermine readers in order to promote goods and services. In the November 1982 section, for example, articles such as "Tips on coping with perspiration," "How to sleep with a man," "A new body for the New Year – Remake your shape in only 10 weeks," and "The fat trap – How to escape" presuppose the reader's inadequacy or lack of knowledge and offer to remedy these. The negativity remains subtle, however, beneath the display of bright colors, glamorous images, and exciting phraseology on the cover and throughout the magazine. Learning about beauty in the service of consumerism on the pages of a glossy women's magazine is a pleasurable and attractive experience that often distracts one from the feelings of inferiority evoked beneath the attractive surface.

One monthly feature, "What went wrong here? How to make it right" pictures several improperly dressed women and explains how they could have dressed correctly. After we identify with these "ordinary" women who, in spite of trying, fail to achieve the correct fashion "look," the magazine guides and advises us, to prevent our repeating these mistakes. To the right of each "wrong" photo is a picture of the correct look, a concrete image that we are to strive to attain. Here again, proper consumerism allows us to valorize ourselves – but only after we have been made to feel inadequate and self-critical.

Not obliged to project the image of wholesomeness of magazines for younger women, many of *Mademoiselle*'s editorial features underscore rather than contradict the sexual implications of the ads. Fashion features show no reticence in overtly linking childishness to sexuality; where *Seventeen* urges young readers to be both childish and sexually alluring, *Mademoiselle* encourages older readers to regress to childish behavior as a means of becoming sexually attractive. The April 1982 feature "Pretty baby" plays on the theme of childhood prostitution from the movie with the same title. The models wear white, with their hair arranged in childish styles. One lifts her skirt in a coy, seductive gesture and a young boy accompanies each. "Dressed to thrill" (March 1982, pp. 128–85), plays on the title of its intertext – the violent movie "Dressed to Kill" – and links childhood to sexuality in a more aggressive mode. A covert ad for lingerie, this feature pictures models dressed to represent various roles with their underwear showing, some holding children's toys. While overtly coded as adult/children figures playing the game "dress-up," these women at the same time hint at prostitution and imminent violence evoking the cinematic intertext "Dressed to Kill."

Just as the magazines aimed at homemakers also have several articles on beauty and fashion to attract these advertisers, so do the fashion and beauty magazines publish features on food. Sometimes recipes for fattening foods directly follow articles on diets and exercise in *Mademoiselle*'s "Home and Food" section. In June 1982, for example, "The last-chance diet" and "Last-chance exercises," are followed by "The scoop on ice cream" (with one subheading entitled "New ways to sin") and "The icing on the cake." Then appears "Diet News" and an ad for Tab with a slender model and the slogan "Body by Tab." Not only are there internal contradictions among the articles in the food section but some of these articles contradict the pressures to be slim that structures other features. Readers are to vacillate between eating and dieting. Regardless of these contradictions, the main purpose of the "Home and Food" section is fulfilled – to secure advertising revenue from the makers of food and home products for a magazine whose editorial material relates principally to beauty and fashion.

Mademoiselle publishes some articles on current social issues such as nuclear war, the right-to-life movement, and feminism. In May 1982, for example, an article by Louise Bernikov, "Fearless and female," discusses the courage of some prominent figures in women's history. In the same issue, however, "The fine art of flirting" makes anti-feminist statements such as "I continued flirting when my feminist sisters were wearing hobnails and a scowl," and "I am refreshed by this world . . . where . . . a man and a woman know the parts they are expected to play and each plays the part with a special relish" (pp. 118–19). In extremely poor taste, *Mademoiselle* placed a September 1982 column "Are women writers worth more dead than alive?" (p. 80) across from the ad for Candie's shoes discussed in chapter 4 that pictures a man ostensibly trying to break down the window of a woman's room while she is preoccupied with applying make-up. Not only is the column critical of feminism which, the writer claims, identifies "so avidly with victims and sufferers," but the ad on the facing page tries to sell shoes by showing a woman as a potential victim, and suggesting that imminent danger is glamorous.

For a women's advertising magazine such as *Mademoiselle*, then, editorial features that provide a "healthy climate" for advertisers are the primary concern. Thus, beauty and fashion features predominate while other articles that do not undermine the advertising are published to try to increase circulation. Be their subject feminism, nuclear arms, movies and records, or health and exercise, the new features are an attempt to update the magazine as contemporary women's lives change. The new interests of college-educated, working women between 18 and 34 – the prime spenders that *Mademoiselle* seeks for its advertisers – must be taken into account. At the same time this audience must not be allowed to forget its crucial role in the consumption of beauty and fashion products or *Mademoiselle*'s advertising might decline.

Glamour: Fashion and Beauty Linked to Social Issues

In mid-1983 *Glamour*, another Conde Nast publication aimed at working women 18–34, announced a more serious image. It promised advertisers "relevant" surroundings for their promotions and labelled itself "the fashion and beauty magazine that takes on issues." Noting that news agencies reprinted a number of articles from its pages, *Glamour* claimed that "more and more involved women are turning away from fluff and looking to *Glamour*." With an average of 38 per cent of its editorial dedicated to fashion and beauty, the magazine began the campaign about its "serious"editorial as a means of attracting more car, cigarette, food, and alcohol advertisers.[13]

While it is true that *Glamour* has a varied editorial content,[14] the magazine also presents much "fluff." The November 1982 cover, for example, lures readers with such editorial hooks as "How to stay thin forever," "The most exciting evening looks in years," and "19 Beauty habits that zap your good looks." Often *Glamour*'s covers attempt to attract readers with references to the magazine's beauty and fashion editorials, not the socially relevant pieces. Bright, diagonal banners across the covers promise "Thin thighs in 30 days" (July 1982) or "Legs, eyes, breasts, smiles: 100 Men tell what they love about women" (April 1983). While only about one-third of *Glamour*'s editorial content relates to fashion and beauty, the covers give disproportionate emphasis to these themes, establishing an interpretive frame through which to view what follows inside.

Like other magazines in this genre, *Glamour* helps to exaggerate feelings of inadequacy in readers through its beauty and fashion features. The regular column "Please Make Me Over," with titles such as "Help! I hate my glasses" (February 1981, p. 22), "Help! I'm tired of the 'Schoolmarm' Look" (June 1982, p. 34), or "Help! Can you change my hair texture?" (June 1981, p. 20), links negative self images to commodity remedies. Value-laden words in a title such as "Do your feet stand up to sandal scrutiny?" (April 1982, p. 30) urge readers to remain self-critical and concerned with external appearance. Like the *Mademoiselle* column "What Went Wrong Here?," *Glamour*'s "Do's and Don'ts" presents negative role models for us first to identify with in shame and then to reject through new purchases;

ultimately, we are to identify with images that *Glamour* deems the correct ones.

Glamour tries to keep its editorial content up-to-date with articles on current social and political issues. The "Washington Report" column provides information on current events in the capital and encourages readers to become aware of and involved in political issues. In May 1983, *Glamour* published two articles on unemployment and recession. The magazine conducts monthly reader-opinion surveys on such topics as the social security crisis, student aid cutbacks, violence on TV, surrogate mothers, nuclear arms, as well as more usual *Glamour* topics such as the impact of beauty, men's sexual needs, and "what turns you on when you meet a man." The results of the issue-oriented surveys provide information about the political views of some *Glamour* readers. In October 1982, *Glamour* reports that 85 per cent of those who completed the survey think that the military or foreign aid budgets should be reduced to fund student loans (p. 49) and the November 1982 issue shows that 70 per cent favor a nuclear freeze.

Glamour often includes feminist articles, although sometimes the attempt results in pseudo-feminism. The "Education" column in April 1982 (pp. 303–4) reports on the growth of Women's Studies Programs on college campuses and urges women who do not live near colleges to form their own study groups on women's issues. In a small block of unfilled advertising space on the facing page, boldface print asks readers: "The ERA was introduced in Congress in 1923, three years after women were granted the right to vote. Isn't it about time it got passed?" These feminist messages are undercut, however, by adjacent pictures of women in sexual poses modelling underwear in an ad for Frederick's of Hollywood with the headline "Be outrageously sexy!"

Glamour's inclusion of feminism and other socially relevant themes stems from the magazine's desire to keep up with the interests of the large number of women now working outside the home. Like *New Woman*, which, as we will see, uses a few feminist ideas enveloped in many parafeminist ones, *Glamour* wants to attract employed women who have discretionary spending power. *Glamour* assures advertisers that the 80 per cent of its readers employed constitute "the largest working audience among all women's magazines."[15] Beauty and fashion editorial is no longer sufficient to attract women workers; one *Glamour* survey found that only 55 per cent of the respondents had grown more concerned with personal appearance over the past year, while 82 per cent were more concerned with the economy, 69 per cent with personal finance, 62 per cent with personal health, and 57 per cent with energy and conservation.[16]

Adding socially relevant articles to the magazine creates contradictory constellations. One of *Glamour*'s ads to advertisers joins two starkly opposing photos, both with the caption "That's *Glamour*." The first shows a woman washing her face and the other a police chalk outline of a woman's body on the pavement. The ad copy tells advertisers that *Glamour*'s readers are concerned with beauty but also with "the not-so-pretty" side of life: "The article on rape, robbery, and murder that accompanied this picture was the highest read *Glamour* article in five years. To have your message read seriously, put it in an environment eight million readers respect – That's *Glamour*."[17] In effect, *Glamour* sees its articles on social problems as a way to attract advertisers; even rape and murder help to sell commodities. The juxtaposition of these two contrasting images of women in this ad parallels the themes and images joined in the monthly issues of *Glamour*. In effect, skin care, beauty and violent crimes against women are equally important editorial subjects.

Self: Beauty and Health for Young Workers

Although it has some characteristics of a new magazine for working women, Conde Nast's *Self* launched in 1979 is much closer in editorial content to magazines in the beauty and fashion genre.[18] *Self*'s innovation is to link so extensively traditional beauty and fashion themes to the current interest in health. In the difficult economic climate of the early 1980s when many new magazine ventures failed, Conde Nast read the times well. The publisher believed that young employed women, a primary target for advertisers of beauty and food products, could be drawn to such advertisements more successfully through editorial that integrated health and fitness to traditional beauty concerns. However, the usual preoccupation with beauty of most magazines in this genre has merely been updated and partially disguised beneath the ostensible emphasis on health and fitness.[19]

Self modifies other conventions of the beauty and fashion genre as well. Where the covers of these magazines usually picture a close-up shot of a model's face to draw attention to cosmetics, *Self* in 1981 and 1982 often used a middle-distance shot, usually of a model posing at exercise, play, or work. *Self*'s cover headlines employ a youthful, contemporary tone, emphasizing up-to-date concerns that are broader than *Mademoiselle*'s or *Glamour*'s traditional topics of beauty and fashion. The largest headlines project in capsule version *Self*'s new lifestyle image: "Intimacy," "Self-power," "Personal style," "Pleasure," "Persuasion," "Self-change," "How to attract," "Your body appeal," and "Confidence" aim to promote positive feelings and excitement among potential readers who glance at the cover.

Inside, the traditional fashion features and advertising of *Vogue*, *Glamour*, and *Mademoiselle* are replaced by occasional promotions of exercise attire, sportswear, or a "dress-for-success" wardrobe for work. Sometimes letters to the editor praise *Self* for expanding the focus of fashion magazines: "It's about time women's magazines shifted the emphasis from thin to health – both emotionally *and* physically . . . your magazine is setting an example for the industry by giving us . . . informative articles that help us realize our potential" (September 1982, p. 12). But the writer is praising a June 1982 article entitled "A woman's body character: How to develop physical charisma" which, although arguing against the usual ideals of thinness, still encourages self-consciousness in readers about their physical appearance.

One ad for *Self* in a trade journal exemplifies this contradiction by picturing a woman hastily applying make-up and styling her hair as she is about to leave for work (Figure 5.1). In stark contrast to this image of insecurity and preoccupation with physical appearance, the magazine's slogan printed above says "I believe in my *Self*."[20] In effect, the self-confidence that the magazine claims to promote is one based on the correct use of cosmetics, self-criticism, and excessive concern with physical appearance.

In December 1982, a special section entitled "Confidence" included such articles as "Sleek muscles, sensual movement for only 6 exercises," "Your people sense: How to make confident moves others miss," and "The body's five stations to success: Your senses." Readers are told that confident, successful people – "the happily coupled, the people lovers, the movers and doers, the enthusiasts of life" – are more intensely aware of their

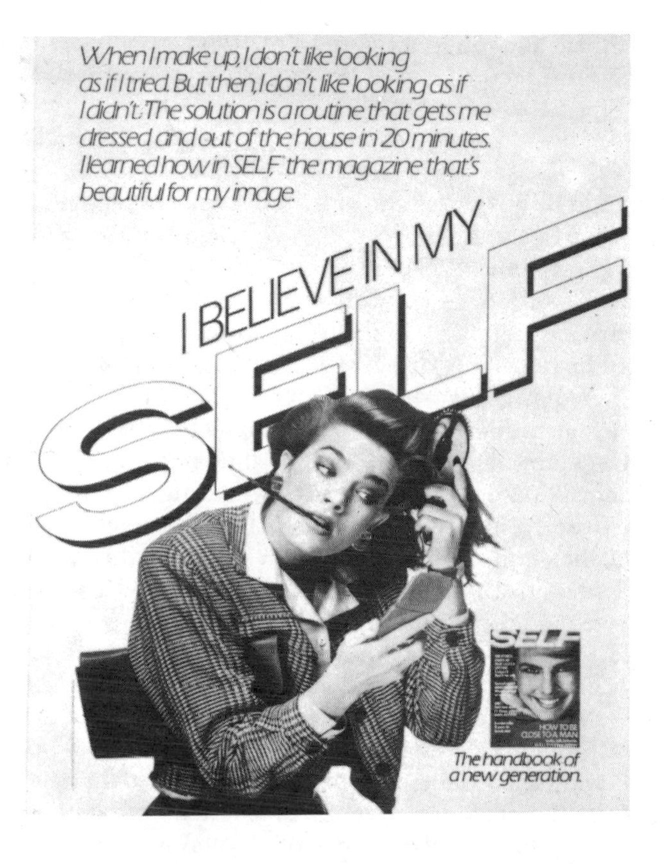

When I make up, I don't like looking as if I tried. But then, I don't like looking as if I didn't. The solution is a routine that gets me dressed and out of the house in 20 minutes. I learned how in SELF, the magazine that's beautiful for my image.
I BELIEVE IN MY
SELF
The handbook of a new generation.

Figure 5.1 Ad for *Self* magazine, courtesy of Conde Nast Publications, Inc.

senses. The exercise article promises to give readers confidence through such movements as the "Pelvic rock for sexier walking and dancing," and "Neck and spine awareness for sinuous movement." Like many articles in *Self*, these features ostensibly claim to encourage self-confidence, but only do so after undermining it. Continuously, readers are directed to look critically at their bodies under the guise of healthful exercises, dieting, or beauty. One May 1981 article in the "Health Watch" section, "How to take it all off," advises women on methods of removing hair from eyebrows, nipples, upper lip, chin, underarms, stomach and legs (pp. 38–42). Self-criticism serves as the basis of the beauty advice given in this article ostensibly about health. Although *Self* uses abundant bright, cheery colors, attractive photos, upbeat language and an overtly positive tone, much of its message indirectly teaches women to view themselves negatively.

Like *Mademoiselle* and *Glamour*, *Self* occasionally includes elements of feminism and other political issues. Usually these subjects indirectly help to augment the magazine's advertising revenue. A May 1981 article, "Who plays politics with your private life – How to keep your right to choose career or motherhood or both," encourages women's economic independence – advice that will make them more desirable to advertisers. Similarly, a September 1982 article, "New price tags on success," encourages working women by arguing that successful women are healthier and live longer. The "Money Watch" column that month presents a table showing how few jobs are created per billion dollars of military spending and urges readers to support the Kennedy–Hatfield nuclear freeze resolution.

We see the limits of *Self*'s concern with feminism and other political issues in an ad for Tab (September 1981, p. 107) that pictures a female construction supervisor wearing a hard hat and drinking Tab with her fellow male workers. But beneath her image appears a glass of Tab that has been narrowed in the middle to symbolize the desirable woman's waist. As often occurs in *Self*, the Tab ad is in the middle of the monthly exercise article. Just as the magazine wants its readers to be employed so that they will be attractive consumers for its advertisers to reach, so are its interest in health and the few positive images of women in its ads ultimately linked to its desire to increase advertising volume. The contradictions within the Tab ad and its relation to the exercise feature help us to understand that feminism is only of concern to *Self* when it leads women to purchase more products.

Self's upbeat emphasis on lifestyle, health, exercise, beauty, and contemporary issues nonetheless offers attractive messages to readers and has contributed to the magazine's rapid growth. It is unlikely that the 3.5 million readers that *Self* claims to have would be attracted to a publication that emphasized self-criticism and negative feelings without disguise. Instead, the magazine offers women a sense of reading about contemporary subjects, expanding their personal potential, and attaining physical beauty, health, happy relationships with men, and success on the job.

Readers' letters reveal how the magazine appeals to different groups. "It's wonderful to find a magazine that also speaks to adult women who are not mothers" (September 1981, p. 12). "I look forward to more articles on infants and toddlers in *Self*; they are great for working mothers like me" (September 1982, p. 12). "Just seeing how other women are thinking, coping and living was a real eye-opener. And the advice from the experts has helped me set new goals and get to work on them" (September 1981, p. 12). "I have to confess: I recognized myself as a number five, the nonstop questioner . . . I plan to tone down my excesses!" (February 1981, p. 10). "After ten years of marriage to a beautiful man, I found myself alone. . . . Much of my strength comes from years of subscriptions to *Self*. Keep up the good work." "Please continue your type of medical coverage; it's a big help for people like me with no medical background" (January 1983, p. 15). "Thanks for attempting to set straight those who think being single is one big party" (May 1982, p. 10). "My husband and I both felt better after reading your article in the December issue 'How to Shake Money Stress.' We may not be able to control inflation but thanks to your advice we've spent less time worrying and fighting about it and more time thinking up strategies to help us cope" (February 1981, p. 12).

Although correspondence published in the Letters to the Editor column is not an accurate survey of readers' opinions, and negative letters appear only infrequently, we can use the column as an initial gauge of why the magazine attracts some women. The first two examples suggest that by publishing occasional articles on pregnancy and motherhood, *Self* appeals to mothers without overwhelming non-mothers. Reading about others who share one's problems seems to encourage readers, as does advice that promises to eliminate the problems. Some readers see the magazine as a source of strength in the face of problems such as divorce and inflation. Articles often contain a germ of truth that the reader identifies with – for example, the piece on singles praised in May 1982. Some readers feel that the magazine provides information about inaccessible subjects such as medicine. Sometimes the information is incomplete and misleading, or, as in the case of the article on inflation, deals with the surface of the problem rather than its roots, but the readers' perceptions of the articles help us to understand the magazine's appeal.

Self's success results from its visual attractiveness and its ability to focus on the contemporary lifestyle issues in which many young working women are interested. The concern with beauty that many women have learned from an early age is expanded here to include health, physical fitness, sex, food, and decorating. With this experiment Conde Nast was able to gauge successfully the interests of a significant group of young women workers in the 1980s so that *Self* has become one of the few new magazine ventures in the 1980s to survive.

Cosmopolitan: Pseudo-liberation, Vicarious Eroticism, and Traditional Moral Values

In 1965 Helen Gurley Brown, the recently successful author of *Sex and the Single Girl*, convinced the Hearst Corporation that she could remake *Cosmopolitan* into a best-seller like her book. Her innovations worked so well that the magazine's monthly circulation rose from 775,782 in 1964 to 2,848,339 in 1981. In 1982 *Cosmopolitan* had 2273 ad pages, the highest volume of all women's magazines, with nearly $68 million in ad revenues. In addition, 92 per cent of the issues are purchased at news-stands, allowing Hearst to earn more circulation revenue than it would through discount mail subscriptions.[21] What accounts for the enormous success of the new *Cosmopolitan* in attracting readers and advertisers?

At first glance, *Cosmopolitan* seems to contradict the traditionally accepted ideals of female beauty and fashion. The cover model often resembles a garishly dressed, inelegant woman with long bouffant hair, heavy make-up, gaudy jewelry, and a plunging neckline. Her clothes are usually styles with low social acceptance – a gold lamé tunic and shorts, a black leather halter top, or a purple feather jacket; rarely worn by most women, the clothing lacks the elegance and sophistication of the apparel in other fashion and beauty magazines. If the *Cosmopolitan* cover photo presents women with an ideal image of their future selves, it is an image at the other end of the social spectrum from that of the affluent *Vogue* or *Bazaar* cover.

Nonetheless, the chameleon "Cosmopolitan girl," the image that the magazine has developed both to attract advertisers and for readers to identify with, projects a spurious elite culture with overt links to consumerism:

How do you rationalize loving Judith Leiber hand bags and Ralph Lauren hacking jackets with also loving humanity? Well, eschewing beautiful possessions doesn't make you a Certified Superior Person and *liking* them doesn't make you shallow or selfish. My favorite magazine says care . . . be generous . . . write checks for people who need you to but don't get the guilts about the checks you write for *you*. You earned the *money*! I love that magazine. I guess you could say I'm That COSMOPOLITAN girl.[22]

In practice, the connotations of cultural sophistication of the magazine's title are only superficially fulfilled inside by occasional pieces such as the June 1982 quiz, "How much do you know about music?" (p. 304).

In fact, it is precisely *Cosmopolitan*'s lack of both sophistication and traditionally accepted fashion and beauty images that helps to account for its immense success. The magazine allows women the impression of a pseudo-sexual liberation and a vicarious participation in the life of an imaginary "swinging single" woman; however, this idealized image is more a male stereotype of the desirable woman that it is a female construct. The "Cosmopolitan girl" on the cover and inside each issue embodies an implied male's vision of female sexual desirability more overtly than do most other women's magazines. In the words of one subscription promotion, "*Cosmopolitan* shows you the way to bring out the ravishing you . . . the real and lovable sexy you . . . to help you find and keep love in your life . . . to be a better and more radiant person, and, win the man of your dreams."[23] Helen Gurley Brown was able to harness the sexual upheaval of the 1960s and 1970s to commercial ends and sell this modified version of sexual liberation to several million women each month. Although most readers will never dress or behave as the magazine urges, *Cosmopolitan* offers them momentary opportunities to transgress the predominant sexual mores in the privacy of their homes. A woman can dream of an adulterous affair or a *ménage-à-trois* with no threat of social stigma.

Unlike its competitors, *Cosmopolitan* publishes few fashion features. In 1981, almost half of *Cosmopolitan*'s advertising pages were for toiletries, cosmetics, apparel, footwear and accessories, but it does not need to publish a large number of fashion and beauty features to attract such advertisers. In effect, the latent implications of the fashion and beauty features in other magazines are fully unleashed here in a variety of editorial features. Where other magazines imply that one will attract male sexual desire by wearing a certain fashion or make-up look, *Cosmopolitan* expands these sexual implications to features as diverse as "What girls want most in a lover" and "Instant pasta magic: He'll swoon as he savors your fun feast" (March 1981).

"Sexual signals at work" (December 1981), for example, presents a series of male fantasies about women workers beneath the guise of a factual report about the workplace. Describing the body language of the secretary who has been called into her boss's office, the author's male vision recounts:

> To clarify a point she begins moving around the desk toward him . . . leaning forward over his desk, reviewing the report. Her hips are about eye level, mere sensual inches from his face. The sleeve of her blouse whispers in his ear. He can view her breasts from an angle usually not available to him. . . .
>
> The fondling of jewelry or clothing are important signals. A long necklace is an extension of the breasts. . . . Adjusting the collar of a blouse and toying with the top button whispers a fantasy that the blouse may be removed (p. 88).

Where other beauty and fashion magazines merely advise women to "dress for success" at work, only subtly implying that the correct clothes and cosmetics will please one's male supervisors, this article openly develops these themes. In contrast to standard fashion and beauty features which encourage a degree of self-consciousness in women, this article carries the concern with the self to an extreme, suggesting that accessories, gestures, and body positions will send messages of sexual availability to one's supervisors. It is not surprising then, that *Cosmopolitan* attracts a large number of apparel and cosmetics advertisers even though it publishes only three beauty and fashion features each month.

Besides the sense of pseudo-sexual liberation, *Cosmopolitan* provides numerous voyeuristic glimpses into the more exciting or successful lives of others. Frequently, these articles emphasize the exotic or unusual: "My life with a playboy" (May 1981), "I was a Lolita" (March 1983), "My lover was an Italian smuggler" (April 1983), "My lover was crazy for swinging" (March

1981), and "My love affair with a best-selling author" (December 1982). Others in this genre present personal testimony about methods of making oneself more desirable to men: "I had a nose job" (May 1981), "How I erased deep laugh lines (and got my Madonna smile)" (November 1982), "I joined Overeaters Anonymous" (February 1983), and "I had breast reduction surgery" (July 1982). We enjoy voyeuristic looks into the lives of women with more exciting careers than ours in articles such as "The prostitute is a cop" (May 1982), features on stars and celebrities, and the monthly "Cosmo Cover Girl" columns which present a few details about the private life of each cover model.

The opportunity for voyeurism extends to pieces on scandal such as "The Yale Murder" (June 1982) and "When romance turns to terror" (August 1982) as well as to intimate glimpses into the lives of our peers: "Irma Kurtz's Agony Column" and "Analyst's Couch" answer letters from people with psychological problems that either resemble our own or allow us to participate vicariously in the unusual, exotic ones of others. All of the numerous voyeuristic pieces in *Cosmopolitan* offer readers occasions for fantasy that contrast their everyday lives. Whether pseudo-sexual liberation, exotic love affairs, drastic modifications in one's physical appearance, scandals, the lives of stars and celebrities, or the emotional problems of people like ourselves, the subjects of these voyeuristic pieces are far-fetched yet conceivable fantasies that few of us will ever experience. The narrator of "My love affair with a best-selling author," for example, is a TV talk show host – the profession of only a small number of women in the country – who almost magically begins an affair with her favorite author after interviewing him. Similarly, in "My lover was an Italian smuggler" a glamorous man approaches the narrator as she vacations in Italy and the two begin a whirlwind affair, travelling to exotic places. The improbability that most readers will attain such fantasies is less important than the special opportunity for vicarious pleasure that each piece presents – a chance for readers to escape for a moment from their everyday lives as workers in ordinary, unglamorous jobs.

Although *Cosmopolitan* makes much use of pseudo-sexual liberation, eroticism, and voyeuristic fantasies, the magazine ultimately offers women conservative messages. Readers are allowed temporarily to experience social transgressions and the exotic, to derive pleasure from reading about such themes, but by the end of these pieces are reminded of the correct behavior pattern. The Italian smuggler is finally arrested, admits bigamy, and the narrator realizes that her affair with him will not last. In a piece of fiction, "One step forward, two steps back" (June 1983), the protagonist experiences problems with the man with whom she lives and decides to move out. By the end of the story, however, the two decide to marry, their problems magically solved and the dominant social order upheld. Many of *Cosmopolitan*'s sexually daring pieces are based on male fantasies about women that have habitually structured women's view of their own sexuality. Thus, although much of *Cosmopolitan*'s editorial material appears on the surface to counter traditionally accepted social values, it ultimately upholds many of them.

Cosmopolitan describes its average readers to advertisers as "young women, single or married, interested in self-improvement, careers, clothes, beauty, travel, entertainment and the arts – with special emphasis on the world outside the home. [*Cosmopolitan* is] edited to help young women realize the very most of themselves."[24] The magazine's range of editorial content and the upbeat tone it boasts about here that will allegedly help women achieve their potential combine with other factors to account for *Cosmopolitan*'s enormous success under Helen Gurley Brown: pseudo-sexual liberation, opportunities for exotic voyeurism, the appearance of culture and sophistication, and the promise of love and winning the man of one's dreams. Like other fashion and beauty publications, *Cosmopolitan* often induces insecurities and self-dissatisfaction but the glamorous, sexually daring appearance of the magazine helps to disguise these negative emotions. Again, *Cosmopolitan*'s success with readers and advertisers is the result of its ability to link its attractive elements to the consumption of goods and services. As one writer has noted, "Sex for the Cosmo Girl is attainment of desirability, not through the quality of her existence as a woman, but through collecting the symbols of sex: perfumes, clothes, figure, atmosphere."[25] Ultimately, *Cosmopolitan*'s messages of sexual power and liberation serve to disguise women's lack of real power in contemporary society.

HEARST AND CONDE NAST COMPETE FOR THE AFFLUENT MARKET

Bazaar: The Utopian and the Real

In contrast to *Cosmopolitan* with its immense circulation, Hearst's *Bazaar* sells only 684,000 copies each month. *Bazaar*, however, is aimed at a select, upscale group of women, a "class" rather than a mass audience. It is part of Hearst's "Cadillac" division, which includes the upscale *Connoisseur*, *Town & Country*, and *Motor Boat and Sailing*. Hearst offers a "Gold Power Package" to advertisers, allowing special discounts for groups of ads in these publications. In comparison to other women's magazines, *Bazaar*'s four-color cost-per-thousand (CPM) of $21.42 is especially high[26] but nevertheless, its ad volume has continued to rise. In the first quarter of 1981, when many women's magazines were suffering advertising declines because of the sluggish economy, *Bazaar* had a 23 per cent increase in ad volume. In ten years the magazine nearly tripled its ad pages, which rose from 520 in 1972 to 1382 in 1982.[27]

Advertisers' growing confidence in *Bazaar* reflects an important trend in the 1980s: more and more companies prefer to spend greater sums to reach a quality audience with high spending power than to pay a lower CPM to reach a large mass audience with mixed spending abilities. *Bazaar* claims that the household income of its average reader is $47,739, that 61 per cent of its readers have household incomes of $25,000 and over and 49 per cent, $35,000 and over.[28] The Editor-in-Chief describes the intended audience as "women of sophistication and awareness who have at least two years of college, combine family, profession and travel; often maintain more than one home; and are active and concerned about what's happening in [the] arts, their communities and the world."[29] *Bazaar* addresses this ideal upscale reader each month with images of opulence and elegance.

The magazine's primary editorial focus is fashion and its publishers boast to advertisers: "*Bazaar* concentrates on style. Not lifestyle." Accusing its competitors of diluting their editorial content with articles on "cooking, coping, and copulating," *Bazaar* claims that 73 per cent of its editorial material is about fashion while its closest competitor, *Vogue*, has only 54 per cent, *Mademoiselle*, 47 per cent, and *Glamour*, 40 per cent. *Bazaar*'s emphasis on fashion begins on the cover and like *Vogue*, it extends the standard cover credit to a lengthier column, "Our Cover Fashion," that promotes designer clothing such as a Bill Blass evening outfit costing $1830 (February 1981). *Bazaar*'s lengthier fashion features often promote famous designers' fashion that is sometimes as expensive as $5500 (October 1982, p. 141) and pictures the designer posing with the model. Oscar de la Renta, for example, holds a model wearing his dress ($2850) as if she were a small child in an October 1982 fashion feature (p. 140). In its publicity to potential advertisers, *Bazaar* quotes designers such as Geoffrey Beene, Halston, and Albert and Pearl Nipon who testify that the magazine is a useful place for them to advertise.[30]

Even if *Bazaar*'s average readers have a household income of $47,739, it is unlikely that they can afford such expensive clothing. The 61 per cent of its readers who, according to *Bazaar*, have total household incomes of $25,000 or over are not likely to spend nearly one-fifth of it on a $5400 evening dress, or even buy the $2000–$3000 dresses often pictured in the features. Utopian elements are at work in many of *Bazaar*'s fashion features. Readers can momentarily enjoy the opulent garment, its prestigious name and price, and the glamorous model who wears it, even while they know it is out of reach.

The magazine describes one dress, for example, as follows: "*The body never got more attention*. . . . With all-over, silver, fringed beading on a body-hugging slip of a dress, Anita's in perfect form for a dazzling performance. From Fabrice with beads on crepe de chine, about $3470. To order at Saks Fifth Avenue NYC . . ." (May 1983, pp. 148–9). Dreams of exclusivity and unlimited spending power are the signifieds of the high price of this dress, its fabric, and its availability only by special order at an expensive New York City store. These signs are conflated with the promise of approving attention on the reader's body, as she imagines herself wearing the dress, in "perfect form." The garment is "body-hugging," further suggesting that it will bring her the feeling of physical affection. Much of the pleasure involved in reading fashion features such as these stems from such momentary utopian visions of the self. One knows that they are unattainable but the dream is nonetheless compelling. Roland Barthes has argued that when the garment is expensive and readers cannot easily obtain it, the language used to describe it is strong in connotations, like the phrases in the above descriptions. This system of connotations facilitates utopian investment in the image. However, cultural investment is only possible, Barthes argues, when the image is also somehow within the means of the audience. In the best connotative systems there is a tension between the real and the dreamed. "Though utopian," Barthes notes, "the dream must be near at hand."[31]

How does a magazine such as *Bazaar* make the dream near at hand at the same time that the fantasy is alluringly beyond one's reach? The names of the designers promoted on many of *Bazaar*'s fashion pages also appear on less expensive items shown in the magazine such as blouses, shoes, fragrances, and accessories. For a much smaller investment, the reader can participate in part of the utopian vision, projecting some of the connotations attributed to the $3000 dress onto herself as she carries a purse or wears a less-expensive blouse with a designer's name. Even if she never buys a less-costly designer item, at least she is aware that the possibility to do so exists.

Bazaar also makes the fantasy of its fashion pages more accessible to readers with features on bargain or lower-priced items. In November 1982, for example, a feature entitled "Looking rich when you're not" (pp. 228–31) displays clothes that range in price from $50 to $340, hardly low-cost items, but nonetheless accessible to a number of *Bazaar* readers. Another example, "Cooling trends from $16 up" (April 1982, pp. 226–7), begins: "The best part of summer is that big fashion looks can be had for a small investment." The text refers to the $16 item as "a slip of a dress," the precise phrase used to describe the $3470 dress discussed above. This feature is photographed in black and white so that the reader must mentally link the previous images of full-color opulence to this partial fashion vision in order to complete the fantasy. The clothes do not need to be depicted in color because there are so many other fantasy visions in the magazine. In these ways, then, *Bazaar* establishes a tension or equilibrium, to use Barthes' terms, between the real and the dreamed.

In a similar vein, *Bazaar* publishes a number of pieces on accessories. In April 1983, for example, "75 Money-saving summer finds rev up your wardrobe" (pp. 240–7) promises that we can participate in the magazine's fashion ideal for the price of a few accessories. Barthes has pointed out that French women's magazines often portray the accessory as "a little nothing that changes everything." By calling the accessory "a find," Barthes notes, the magazine enables the low-priced item to share in the dignity of fashion. Portrayed in fashion magazines, accessories fit "a democracy of budgets while respecting an aristocracy of tastes."[32] Again, *Bazaar* presents a concept of fashion that is both utopian and near at hand by linking features on accessories to the idea of high fashion.

The fashion features are utopian on temporal and geographic planes as well. Barthes has noted that fashion articles often evoke festive times – spring, vacation, or the weekend – along with two geographical sites: a "utopian elsewhere" that consists of exotic though not necessarily distant places and a "real elsewhere" that is more accessible, usually inside the country.[33] Utilizing *Bazaar*'s temporal utopia, spring clothing promotions begin in January each year and the magazine often recommends apparel for vacations and weekend trips. To establish further the prestigious, upscale image of its covertly advertised fashion, *Bazaar* often sets its fashion pieces in a major world capital: "Cutting loose in Milan! The best of Italian design for spring" (January 1983), "Paris power: Black plus color" and "New York: news for fall," (July 1981). The European locations correspond to Barthes' exotic "elsewheres," while New York is a more utopianly real site for US readers.

Especially significant is that these temporal and geographic elements of utopia in *Bazaar*'s fashion features position readers favorably to *Bazaar*'s travel advertisers and the covert ads disguised as travel features every month. An interest in fashion thus appears to lead naturally to an interest in travel and vice versa. Like the opulent fashion features, travel articles sometimes recommend things that are inaccessible to most of *Bazaar*'s readers such as the $400-a-night hotel in Paris suggested in "First-class passport" (April 1983). At the end of each travel feature is a coupon that readers can send to *Bazaar* in order to receive promotional brochures about the resorts. These articles and coupons make both exotic and familiar vacation spots seem accessible, even though many are too expensive for most readers.

Articles on beauty in *Bazaar* follow a similar pattern. "Beauty report" (February 1981) advises readers where to go for "beauty fitness" in New York, noting which stars and celebrities frequent each salon. If one cannot afford professional skin care at Make-

Up Center Ltd., which serves celebrities such as Catherine Deneuve and Liza Minelli, one can at least nurture fantasies about doing so. The opposing pole of accessibility to which Barthes refers is formed by other beauty features which recommend brand-name cosmetics such as Estée Lauder, Lancôme, and Germaine Monteil (March 1981, pp. 100ff). Although these brands are also expensive, individual make-up items are likely to be within the range of readers.

Certain features in *Bazaar* use the bi-polar utopian structure to induce insecurities and sell products. "Nobody's perfect" (January 1982) reminds readers that "even the most glamorous cover girls" have beauty flaws. Each model confesses to a serious "problem" such as "my weight" or "my hair," and tells how she remedies it. The celebrity remains a superior being to imitate, at the same time humanized to facilitate identification with her. She gives testimony about beauty products and techniques, a covert promotion for *Bazaar*'s beauty product advertisers. Later in the issue "How to love the way you look" (pp. 103ff) presents Meryl Streep as a role model: "By her own admission she is not beautiful in the classical sense and has said repeatedly that she didn't feel beautiful enough to play Sarah in *The French Lieutenant's Woman*." Again we are to identify with a celebrity who is flawed like us, at the same time that we learn about beauty ideals and techniques that will make us good consumers. Like the fashion features, these pieces allow utopian identification with what is impossible to purchase (the beauty of celebrities) while establishing a pole of the real through a few accessible items. Here, the stars are temporarily brought down to our level, though they remain above to insure utopian desire.

Besides fashion, beauty, and travel advertisers, *Bazaar* also seeks liquor marketers. Promotional editorial features include "Enjoying the gin game" (April 1983), "Aperitifs for openers" (September 1982), "A single woman's wine guide" (June 1982), and "Drink wine and live longer" (March 1981). Each September, however, *Bazaar* publishes a special issue on women over 40 that includes an article about alcoholism. Pieces such as "Closet alcoholics" (September 1981), "Could you be an alcoholic?" (September 1982), and "How I freed myself from alcohol" (September 1983), contradict the numerous articles in *Bazaar* that promote liquor consumption. *Bazaar* presents liquor in the opulent sophisticated light in which it presents fashion, beauty, and travel. Its occasional pieces on alcoholism probably do little to deter liquor consumption among readers who encounter so many other attractive messages about drinking in the magazine.

While it is true that some of *Bazaar*'s readers are "upscale" in marketing terms, the magazine offers certain images that are out of the reach of even this audience. By linking utopian dreams to real ones, however, the magazine facilitates other kinds of consumption and attracts a growing number of advertising pages. Although it has not achieved the large advertising volume of its closest competitor *Vogue*, it works together with the upscale *Town & Country* to help Hearst reach the desirable, "class" audience of female consumers. Since Hearst's purchase of *Redbook* in 1982, the company promises advertisers that its seven women's magazines reach an unduplicated audience of over one-third of all women between the ages of 18 and 49 in the United States.[34] *Bazaar*'s small, select circulation of nearly 700,000 plays an important role in Hearst's overall circulation claims.

Vogue: Affluent Fantasy, Intelligence, and Consumerism

> I'll bet that I'm a "country bumpkin" by your standards, but when I have your magazine in my hands I am transformed – I am chic, sensual, rich and racy. (In reality I'm a married mother-of-two real estate agent from rural Pennsylvania.)
>
> *Vogue* is my escape. Even when I'm pinching pennies in groceries, I splurge on *Vogue* – to me it's worth it! . . . I may not be model perfect, or a fast-paced executive doing terribly important things, but as I said, when I read *Vogue*, I'm *very* exciting and *very* beautiful and *very* rich, rich!!![35]

> Every time I read *Vogue*, I want to go shopping. It never fails. The other day I read *Vogue* at work and sure enough, as soon as I got off, I went to the department store to look for clothes.[36]

The comments of these two readers crystalize the key reasons for *Vogue*'s success. The images of affluence, sophistication, beauty, and success offer women a utopian vision of themselves that ultimately leads to the marketplace. Although conscious of the disparity between her real, everyday self and the chic, imaginary self that she envisions while reading *Vogue*, the first reader revels in the pleasure of these images all the same. Though she must "pinch pennies" to buy groceries, for a mere $2.00 – the 1981 news-stand price of *Vogue* – she can feel "sensual, rich, and racy." The second reader is conscious that the magazine's beautiful images lead her directly to purchase clothing and accessories. For *Vogue*'s publishers, her remarks constitute the epitome of the magazine's success, assuring advertisers that pages purchased in *Vogue* lead directly to sales of products. As *Vogue* boasted to advertisers: "When she meets you in her book, her interest is up. Her resistance is down. She wants to know you better. Wants to know how you can make her life better."[37]

Vogue outpaces its closest competitor, *Bazaar*, in a number of areas. Its monthly circulation of 1,217,453 surpasses *Bazaar*'s by 78 per cent. Where *Bazaar* sells only 37 per cent of its subscriptions at full price, *Vogue* earns full revenue from 79 per cent. *Vogue*'s 1981 ad volume was 104 per cent higher than *Bazaar*'s and that year *Vogue* published 880 four-color editorial pages while *Bazaar* published only 461.[38]

SMRB figures show that despite the upscale image of their readers that both *Vogue* and *Bazaar* project to advertisers, the majority have household incomes of only $20,000–$25,000.[39] Like *Bazaar*, then, *Vogue*'s numerous images of affluence are beyond the reach of many of its readers. The "Fitness now" article in January 1983, for example, advises the use of private exercise instructors, personalized exercise videotapes and large projection-screen televisions which most *Vogue* readers cannot afford. Like those in *Bazaar*, the opulent images in *Vogue*'s ads and features are savored and imitated by many readers who can afford only lower-priced likenesses. The sense of participation in luxury and affluence continues to attract readers while they view the magazine, even though the prices prohibit them from acquiring much of what they see.

Vogue extends the image of affluence in its fashion, travel, and entertainment articles to a variety of other features. Barthes has noted that the rhetoric of fashion offers women an ideal identity by implying, "If you want to be this, you must dress like this."[40] In *Vogue* this ideology appears as well in features on culture, home furnishings, food, beauty, and health. One major division on its table of contents page, entitled "People are talking about," includes short pieces on culture which imply that if the reader wants to be like the ideal, affluent *Vogue* reader, she must be familiar with the recent cultural developments the magazine has chosen to highlight.

Significantly, these articles appear in the first editorial section of each issue, setting the tone for what is to follow. Beginning after an average of forty-four ad pages, they cast an aura of "culture" on the substantial body of fashion, cosmetics, and liquor advertising just seen. Thus, *Vogue* expands the cultural spectrum to include advertised fashion and beauty products besides the traditional movies, art exhibits, books, and records. Within the *Vogue* ideology all of these become equal: high culture and high fashion are logical extensions of one another. The intelligently written pieces on culture and the aura of sophistication and affluence of their subject matter extend the impression of high cultural achievement to *Vogue*'s other ads and features. We learn that to be like the *Vogue* ideal we must consume both culture and consumer goods.

The selection of letters to the editor printed in *Vogue* each month adds to this impression by reflecting the thoughtfulness and intelligence of readers. Nearly every month *Vogue* prints at least one letter strongly critical of the magazine's negative images of women, often demarcating *Vogue*'s internal contradictions. In November 1982 a reader complains that the magazine printed an impressive piece on the imbalance of power between men and women while simultaneously using "explicit scenes of violence to advertise the latest shoe fashions" (p. 141). In February 1982 a reader criticizes the now famous photograph of Natassia Kinski lying naked with a large snake running between her legs, its tongue licking her ear (see *Vogue*, October 1981, pp. 494–5). Terming the photo "repulsive and verging on the pornographic," the reader charges:

> All this degradation and explicit nudity has a primarily sensationalistic value, since the ostensible purpose of the photograph is to illustrate the rather large plastic bangle about her wrist. Surely the extravagance of the visual message is completely out of proportion to the commercial aim of selling the merchandise in question. The viewer might actually wonder what is the merchandise actually being offered in your photograph (pp. 20, 121).

Rejecting another series of images of violence toward women, a reader in the May 1983 issue protests about

> the unnecessarily sadistic and sensational photographs . . . of beautiful female models ostensibly allowing themselves to be

> abused (one photograph shows a tennis ball being smashed into the model's face). . . . The tragic results of anti-female attitudes can be seen in shelters for battered women throughout our country. I don't want to see fashion photographs which depict stylized violence, and perhaps help perpetuate the dangerous image of woman as victim (p. 46).

Vogue continues to publish negative images of women at the same time that it prints letters from readers criticizing these portrayals. Controversy helps to sell the magazine and might draw more readers to see the ads inside. Even negative responses show that various pieces draw the readers' attention. An editorial mix of intelligent, progressive articles with offensive photographic representations is likely to reach many more women than would either all positive or all negative views of women. In addition, printing one or two of the responses from feminists gives the magazine the image of a fair, evenhanded treatment of the issues, as well as the appearance of the incorporation of pro-feminism into its editorial pages. The publishers perhaps hope that both feminists and non-feminists will find something to their liking on the pages of *Vogue*.

Vogue's publication of these and other intelligently written letters is part of its overall attempt to attain an image of sophistication and cultural enlightenment; just as the ideal, imaginary *Vogue* reader wears the latest high fashion and cosmetics and consumes the correct movies, books, records and television programs, she reads *Vogue*'s articles with careful thought and concern; she writes articulate, analytical responses to what she sees in *Vogue* at the same time that she dreams about her ideal self dressed in *Vogue* fashions. The woman who wrote that reading *Vogue* transforms her from a "country bumpkin" to a "chic, sensual, rich and racy" person represents the ideal reader who not only fantasizes as she views *Vogue* but is intelligent enough to be conscious of that fantasy and verbalize this consciousness. As *Vogue*'s frequent slogans to advertisers exaggeratedly contend: "*Vogue*'s millions are the most educated, most affluent, most influential women in America. The women other women would like to be like." "*Vogue*'s 5.2 million have the millions to get what they want and go where they want." "She knows *Vogue* knows. Month after month, they introduce her to places she never dreamed of. People she always wanted to meet.

They help make her healthier, wealthier, prettier, wittier."[41] Whatever the dimensions of the fantasy projected about the ideal *Vogue* reader, it is ultimately rooted in consumption. Women's intelligence is tolerated and even encouraged as long as it leads to the purchase of goods and services.

Throughout several decades of their lives, then, women encounter attractive messages of the transgressive and utopian, harnessed to consumerism and socialization in the fashion and beauty magazines. From late childhood on, many female consumers spend a portion of their leisure time enjoying the elegant fashions and flawless faces in the advertisements and features of these publications. They learn to conceive of themselves as inherently in need of improvement and that the most direct path to pleasure and fulfillment is consumption. Even if their purchases are low-cost items, women can at least vicariously participate in more expensive consumption while turning the pages of these magazines. In addition, the pleasurable images, even the socially transgressive ones, often contribute to women's proper socialization. Whether offered as the appearance of sex education in a magazine such as *Seventeen* or spurious sexual liberation in *Cosmopolitan*, the messages contain socially accepted moral values beneath the surface. Together, the tropes of consumption and proper socialization prepare women for their expected dual roles as socializers of children and purchasers of goods and services. In the short run the important goal of selling advertisers' products is met as well, enabling these magazines to prosper as lucrative businesses.

6 Service and Home: The Seven Sisters Adapt to the 1980s

The economic recession of the late 1970s and early 1980s profoundly affected one of the strongest magazine categories – the "seven sisters." After years of leading the industry, it suffered significant declines in growth and profitability in 1979. By 1980 advertising volume was down for all but *Good Housekeeping* and *Woman's Day*, and only *Better Homes* and *Woman's Day* had not suffered drops in circulation.[1] The declines continued throughout the early 1980s while publishers and editors tried a number of new ploys to attract advertisers and readers.

Industry analysts offered several explanations for this sudden change of fortune. Some argued that grocery product marketers, the principal advertisers in the seven sisters, were now spending more of their advertising dollars on promotions in supermarkets. The executives of several women's service magazines blamed the economic recession, arguing that both consumer and advertiser spending was down. Competition from other media was another factor; some advertisers who had turned to magazines when television rates skyrocketed now bought more TV ads as rate increases for this medium slowed. In early 1981, the publisher of *Woman's Day* noted that the largest loss of advertising in his magazine was in the cigarette category. Affecting the other service magazines as well was the tobacco industry's decision to move many of its magazine ads into newspapers, billboards and regional publications. *Good Housekeeping*, which publishes no cigarette advertising, was the only women's service magazine to sell increased ad pages in early 1981; besides its lack of dependence on tobacco advertising, industry analysts speculated that the magazine was one of the first choices on many advertisers' schedules and therefore not likely to be cut.[2]

Besides contending with the effects of the economic downturn on advertisers and consumers, the executives of the seven sisters faced demographic and attitudinal changes in the female population. With over half of all US women in the paid workforce by

1980, time constraints and changing interests contributed to a drop in readership for the traditional home service magazines. The feminist movement's critique of traditional sex roles and women's exploitation under the free household labor system caused some women to look with disfavor on the standard messages presented in the seven sisters. While a group of readers continued to be attracted to the traditional magazines, others began to buy publications they perceived to be more up-to-date. A decade later in May 1990, *Woman's Day*, one of the group's leading publications was put up for sale, with speculation that its lack of viability might lead to a "fire sale" mentality among potential purchasers.[3]

In response to the drop in readership in the early 1980s, the publishers of the seven sisters took several steps. Most attempted to create a more modern image without alienating traditional readers. Peter Diamandis, then Publisher of *Woman's Day*, argued that a major repositioning of his magazine was unnecessary and attempted to change the magazine's image from, in his words, "old and dowdy" to "young and vital"; he would introduce only "nondisturbing" editorial innovations to preserve the large loyal audience yet attract new readers.[4] Most of the seven sisters added a few editorial features about jobs, financial management, and new lifestyles, and introduced minor changes in print and graphics.[5]

Economic measures were necessary as well. *McCall's*, *Redbook*, and even *Good Housekeeping* froze their ad rates, hoping to attract more advertisers. In December 1982 *Woman's Day* raised its cover price from 69 to 79 cents, and *Family Circle* soon followed; when asked why, *Family Circle*'s Publisher is said to have remarked: "Greed is always a factor."[6] This statement reminds us that although their ad volume and circulation dropped, the service magazines remained immensely profitable enterprises; the recession meant only that profits were slightly lower and rates of growth had slowed. Even during the recession Diamandis predicted that *Woman's Day* would make $10 million in pretax profits in 1982 on total revenues of $125 million. That year each of the seven sisters had a higher total revenue than most other women's magazines; figures ranged from *Family Circle*'s $190 million to *Redbook*'s $86 million. In 1983 the total revenues of all the seven sisters except *Redbook* rose substantially; *Family Circle* earned $209 million and *Good Housekeeping* $207 million; and the circulation of each, including *Redbook*, was far greater than all other women's magazines even during the slump.[7]

So, while the economic recession and other factors affected these traditional home service magazines more than other women's publications, the seven sisters remained highly profitable enterprises. The use of the term "greed" demonstrates the logic that underlies such multi-million dollar enterprises: economic growth and profitability must consistently be increased to insure an adequate return on investors' funds. To reach this goal, executives take gambles such as editorial innovation, reduced or frozen ad rates, or higher cover prices. While the seven sisters' decline in the early 1980s was real, the effects were relative because the home service category was the strongest group of women's magazines to begin with. Nevertheless, the group was forced to instigate a number of changes in order to adapt to the times.

FAMILY CIRCLE AND *WOMAN'S DAY*: SUSTAINING THE DUAL ECONOMIES OF THE SUPERMARKET AND THE FREE HOUSEHOLD LABOR SYSTEM

Although many magazines are sold in supermarkets, in a number of stores two women's titles tempt shoppers from special racks above the checkout stands. Indeed, *Family Circle* and *Woman's Day*, unlike other supermarket commodities that are on the shelves primarily for their own sale, perform the additional important function of encouraging the sale of other supermarket products. Fostering the paradoxical ideology that one can save money by spending it, these widely circulating, inexpensive magazines play crucial roles in the dual economies of the supermarket and the free household labor system.

Both publications began during the 1930s Depression as promotional devices to draw women shoppers away from corner stores into supermarkets. Sanitary Grocery Company (now Safeway) started *Family Circle* in 1932 as a free weekly, distributed in New York and Washington grocery chains to promote products. *Woman's Day* began as a menu leaflet published and distributed by the Great Atlantic and Pacific Tea Company grocery store chain.[8] Today, these giveaway publications from the Depression rank among the top moneymakers in the industry. Throughout most of the 1980s, large media conglomerates owned them: the New York Times Co. continues to publish *Family Circle* and until 1987 CBS owned *Woman's Day*.

The roots of these magazines in the Depression gave rise to a special ideological sales tool still at work in these publications. With millions of Americans in the 1930s hard-pressed for money to purchase even the barest essentials, the early *Woman's Day* argued that supermarket shopping would allow money to go further and that even minimal purchases would enable women to prepare appealing meals.[9] Today, these magazines continue to foster this paradoxical notion of spending in order to save, now to working- and middle-class audiences.

Unlike the new "class"-oriented magazines, *Woman's Day* and *Family Circle* promote low-cost, mass consumer goods rather than elite, high-priced items which would be beyond the low-to-average income levels of their readers. The notion of thriftiness joins the ideology of spending to save to encourage greater consumption of these mass goods. Fashion features such as "Looking great for less $$$" (*Woman's Day*, 7 June 1983) and "Repair and wear: How to make your old clothes new" (*Family Circle*, 19 April 1983), allow readers to practice thrift while simultaneously spending what the magazines code as small sums of money. In the same issue of *Family Circle*, "Priceless cook-booklets you can get for free" ostensibly encourages thrift while in fact promoting purchase of the brand-name products required for the recipes. These frequent articles function similarly to coupons; playing on consumers' real need and desire to save money, they in fact stimulate spending.

Within this ideological system, time replaces money. The full-time working- or middle-class homemaker is expected to contribute additional unpaid labor beyond her daily household duties in order to save her family money. She can obtain the "high fashion . . . at low prices" in the above feature by spending many hours sewing her clothing at home; her time must also be invested to make the repairs suggested in the above *Family Circle* feature. "How to be a successful shopper" tells readers, "You won't reap the benefits of competent shopping . . . until you make up your mind to invest the time and energy it requires" (*Woman's Day*, 11 August 1981, p. 12).

The numerous expository features on making crafts also rely on the notion that time replaces money, yet often disguise the labor required with concepts such as ease and the homemaker's supposed unlimited free time. "Lazy-day needlework" tells readers: "You can pick up your needlework whenever you're in the mood to make these rapturous things for house, baby, and you" (*Woman's Day*, 11 August 1981, p. 76). A piece in *Family Circle*, "The best new summer crafts" begins: "Whether you're home in your own backyard or sunning at the beach, we've got satisfying projects to do" (8 June 1982, p. 91). No doubt, crafts offer some readers a sense of personal creativity in a society based on mass production but features such as these presuppose that women who work in the home have "lazy days" during which to crochet whenever the mood strikes them and that they spend breezy summer days sunning themselves. While far from the reality of many women in low-to-average income families, these scenarios create an ideal pleasurable space in which the homemaker can fantasize while performing unpaid household labor and fulfilling her role in the consumer economy. One large-print feature extends craft instruction to children, inviting young readers to "Make your own water garden" (*Family Circle*, 27 April 1982). In one sense, many of the crafts articles here imply that women working at home are like children, needing projects to occupy their apparently ever-expandable free time.

Contradictions arise when the service magazines attempt to appeal both to those who work outside the home and those who do not. "Perfect makeup in just 10 minutes" (*Woman's Day*, 11 August 1981) and "Quick-to-fix meals from what's on hand" (*Family Circle*, 21 July 1981) contradict the "lazy days" presumed available in other features. While the cover of *Woman's Day*, 5 April 1983 pictures time-consuming activities such as baking and hat decorating, the Editor's column in the issue announces a new section titled with childish lettering and repetition, "QUICK! QUICK! QUICK!" Noting that readers have complained about "the time crunch," Editor Levine describes the new section: "Everything . . . will be streamlined for the time-tight woman. Meals that can be fixed in a flash. Fashion and crafts that take only a few hours to make. Even fiction that takes only minutes to read" (p. 15).

Thus, these traditional magazines walk a fine line as they attempt to modernize in response to women's new work patterns. While directing features to workers both in and outside the home, the magazines must entice one group without offending the other. In both cases, traditional values are upheld; employed women are to sew, make crafts, and read magazine fiction even though they now have less time to do so.

The ideological constructs of both magazines seek a delicate balance between the traditional and the modern.[10] In its 50th anniversary issue (1 September 1982), *Family Circle* recounts its own modernization decade by decade, also showing inadvertently how the magazine buttressed the dominant ideology in each period. In the 1940s, the magazine contends, the family pictured on its cover "symbolized what we were fighting for. . . . Domestic chores became acts of patriotism. . . . In industry: 'Women [were] proving themselves in dozens of callings heretofore closed to them'" (p. 84). In the 1950s, the magazine reminds us, it encouraged women to go "Back to the kitchen." During the 1960s "more women were finding an escape from that trapped housewife feeling in part-time jobs, but for many, a woman's place was still in the home." As *Family Circle* adapted itself for new ideological ends in each decade, this delicate balance between traditional and modern messages enabled it to reassure readers who felt threatened by social change, while simultaneously allowing them the sense of being up-to-date. And the modern facade made the orthodox ideological messages more palatable for less traditional women.

But the veneer of modernity in both *Family Circle* and *Woman's Day* is quite thin. Surprisingly, *Woman's Day* advertised the traditional article "Back from the brink of divorce" as part of its 1983 "new look." Ellen Levine, hired as Editor-in-Chief in mid-1982 to revitalize the magazine, planned "an evolution, not a revolution."[11] Backed by a $10 million promotional budget, the magazine would now emphasize emotional subjects and health and medical topics. The emotional topics were quite traditional, however, including stories about unfaithful husbands and "how to make them stay" and "ways to avoid divorce."[12] At the end of 1982 the magazine had announced an aggressive campaign to attract younger women. In ads in trade publications, a woman carries a baby in a halter on her back with a bag of groceries and a copy of *Woman's Day* in her arms. Although most of the food products advertised in *Woman's Day* are prepared foods, only fresh vegetables appear in this woman's bag. Here, the healthy, outdoors, active look is intended to connote modernity, while the underlying images of women remain traditional: grocery shopping, magazine reading, and childcare.[13]

Both *Woman's Day* and *Family Circle* sell about seven million copies per issue, the majority of which are highly desirable single-copy sales. What accounts for the continued appeal of these supermarket magazines for over fifty years? One important factor is their ability to channel women's desires to select symbols of the ideal self. As Berger has argued, when one looks at an ad one is envious not of the model herself but of a future version of oneself attainable after purchasing the product.[14] Similarly, *Woman's Day* and *Family Circle* create such a system of desire in which aesthetically pleasing food arrangement, home decoration, and self-adornment are the principal visual components. Thorstein Veblen's 1899 critique of women's aesthetic role in the leisure-class household continues to obtain: "woman's sphere . . . is within the household, which she should 'beautify,' and of which she should be the 'chief ornament.'"[15] Just as women are to create aesthetically pleasing meals and household decor so, too, are they to adorn themselves with the proper clothing, jewelry, hairstyles, cosmetics, and toiletries. An essential part of their value is ornamental, the magazines imply, like that of the food they prepare and the homes they maintain and decorate.

Family Circle's and *Woman's Day*'s emphasis on the physical appearance of food, the home, and the self leads to consumer purchases and to the reader's envy of a future version of herself demarcated by these limiting terms. The visual symbols that configure this system are extremely attractive, but by overemphasizing external appearances, they subtly equate readers with objects such as food and home decor. The images ostensibly represent non-alienated labor but occlude the difficult, repetitive work involved in preparing such food, maintaining such homes, and adorning the self in such ways.

In order for this created desire to convince one to buy, it must be rooted in the practical. These magazines meet several traditionally assigned needs of women who perform household labor, as the letters to the editor and the high circulations attest to. Hundreds of ideas for recipes, furnishings, gardens, sewing, self-adornment, and childcare appear, including features with readers' own practical advice to others. Sometimes recipe features even contain a "Market list" with products to buy and a "Work plan" with detailed instructions for meal preparation.

Both *Family Circle* and *Woman's Day* attract readers as well with frequent sensationalist pieces that allow a voyeuristic look into the lives of others. "I didn't know my son was deaf," "I lost 259 pounds and 85 inches," "I saved his life" (*Woman's Day*, 8 March 1983, 7 June 1983, and 5 April 1983) are similar to *Family Circle*'s "Against all odds" (1 September 1981), the story of a woman who was shot, knifed, and raped, and its regular feature "True-life Drama" which recounts, for example, the story of a couple who lost their four sons in a home fire (4 October 1983). These features take one step-by-step through people's suffering while teaching important ideological and consumerist messages. "I saved his life," for example, tells the story of a woman who administered CPR to her husband when he had a heart attack. The article defines woman's role as that of nurturer, caregiver, lifesaver, and, most of all, cook, for it begins and ends by recounting the preparation and consumption of the spaghetti her husband had asked her to make that day; in the face of this tragedy, as the paramedics worked on her husband, "she put the cheese torte in the oven" (p. 142). On the adjoining page appears a huge first-person view of a slice of Bisquick "Impossible Ham 'n Swiss Pie," as a fork breaks off a mouthful implicitly for the reader. Fittingly, the key structural motifs in this story correspond to food, the subject of many of the ads in this supermarket magazine. As one reads these spellbinding stories and vicariously participates in the tragedies of others, the pleasure experienced helps to shape one ideologically and encourage participation in consumerism.

For several decades, *Family Circle* and *Woman's Day* have been huge revenue producers for their parent corporations – seventh and ninth respectively of all consumer magazines in the country in total revenues for 1983.[16] The ability of the supermarket magazines to adapt to the times while remaining traditional and to meld idealist fantasies with the practical has been their key to success. Besides producing vast advertising and sales revenues for CBS and the New York Times Co., they play other crucial roles in the US economy. By giving numerous buying incentives, brand-name promotions, and recommendations of generic products in their editorial material, they benefit the supermarket industry and manufacturers.[17] Through ideological justification and support, they help to sustain the free household labor system, as unpaid homemakers continue to bolster the economy with their work. As women stood in supermarket lines in February 1981 and saw the headline across *Family Circle*'s cover "This magazine can save you $90 at the checkout," the 59-cent cover price seemed a small investment for a $90 return and several hours of pleasurable reading. While the slim magazine functioned that month as a kind of coupon for many of the women who purchased it, it played an immensely greater practical and ideological role in the overall US economy.

GOOD HOUSEKEEPING AND *MCCALL'S*: SAFE CONSUMERISM AND IDEOLOGICAL FORMATION

Two of the oldest women's magazines, *Good Housekeeping* and *McCall's* have survived since the 1880s. At their inception, both emphasized traditional roles for women: *Good Housekeeping* claimed to serve "the interests of higher life in the household,"[18] and *McCall's*, originally called *The Queen*, began as a promotion for the dress patterns of a Scottish immigrant to the US, James McCall. Hearst later purchased *Good Housekeeping* and Norton Simon bought *McCall's*,[19] but even adapted and updated, the two magazines continue to focus women's attention on traditional topics. Both present guidelines for proper consumerism and homemaking, all the more convincing because the advice appears to have been passed down from our foremothers.

Good Housekeeping's aura of wholesomeness has continued to attract readers. Unlike other women's magazines, it has foregone the lucrative revenues of cigarette advertising, yet maintained high ad volume. Thus, it was free to publish an informative article "Can your husband's cigarette give you cancer?" (May 1981) without pressure from advertisers. In a letter to the editor in the April 1983 issue a reader praises *Good Housekeeping* for its refusal of cigarette ads, noting that in a recent month the other seven sisters ran 8–12 per cent of their ad pages for cigarettes.[20]

Indirectly related to the absence of cigarette advertising, the famous *Good Housekeeping* Seal of Approval also contributes to the image of wholesomeness. A limited warranty covering most products advertised in the magazine, the Seal was devised in 1909 to bolster the consumer's declining confidence in the honesty of magazine advertising.[21] In the February 1983 issue, for example, an ad for six Lever Brothers products recently "awarded" the Seal appears across from the monthly explanation of the guarantee which overtly enhances the products' saleability. While *Good Housekeeping* presents the Seal to readers as the magazine's desire to protect them, the argument to advertisers is that the guarantee increases sales: "Periodic marketplace tests . . . conclusively prove that the Seal is a positive and powerful persuader that helps sell merchandise."[22]

Not only would cigarette advertising counter *Good Housekeeping*'s image of wholesomeness, it would clash with the Seal's guarantee policy for products. The credibility of the Seal would be undermined were the emblem to appear on cigarette packages. By foregoing one source of ad revenue from a product that cannot be guaranteed, the magazine increases advertising in other areas. This policy is so successful that *Good Housekeeping* was number one among the seven sisters in 1983 in both ad volume and revenue with 2097 ad pages and $127.2 million in ad sales.[23]

The frequent "*Good Housekeeping* Institute Reports" also foster an image of integrity in order to increase product sales. "GH rates those best-seller diets" (February 1982), for example, condemns every diet book and program it examines except Weight Watchers, while an ad for Weight Watchers' frozen meals precedes the article. Thus, a tautological continuum develops in which editorial features and ads uphold each other's wholesomeness: of all the diets, Weight Watchers is the best; because Weight Watchers is the best, it is advertised in the magazine and covered by the famous limited warranty.

While *McCall's* has no Seal of Approval program, it offers much advice on consumerism. Like *Good Housekeeping*, it presents tips on beauty, home-decorating, money management, and food preparation, including quick meals for working women. Somewhat more up-to-date than *Good Housekeeping*, *McCall's* also runs advice columns such as "You and the Law" and "*McCall's* Handywoman." The monthly "Movie Guide for Puzzled Parents" imparts to *McCall's* an aura of reliability and wholesomeness like *Good Housekeeping*'s. The practical advice about consumer and life problems in both magazines, together with their long history and implicit association with stable family life bolster confidence in their recommendations for consumption; along with devices such as the Seal of Approval, they assure us that we can participate in safe consumerism.

Both magazines attempt to secure women's ideological formation, engaging in a struggle for discursive power and presenting certain views as the obvious, common-sense way of understanding reality. The process involves a struggle because reality lurks constantly as a corrective to mass cultural images. Here, this discursive struggle is couched within an overarching code of pleasure. In the 1950s a *Good Housekeeping* study noted that women read service magazines not only for practical information but for the pleasures of daydreaming, self-identification, and escape from daily routine.[24] Numerous features in *McCall's* and *Good Housekeeping* give readers these pleasures, but meld them with morals and lessons to contain the dangerous elements that readers have temporarily been allowed to enjoy. In *Good Housekeeping* these features offer voyeuristic pleasure while establishing patterns of structural opposition between everyday protagonists and celebrities, fiction and non-fiction.

One popular feature, "My Problem and How I Solved It," uses personal testimony and a black-and-white photo that lend it an air of authenticity. Marital and family issues predominate, with the figure of the husband as the structural center: "My husband's secretary won't leave him alone" (February 1982), "My husband and I shared too much" (January 1982), and "Our marriage had gone stale" (May 1981). Suspense and the lure of a tale about a life either like one's own or potentially so draw readers into each story; the narrator teaches a lesson to apply to life, either a remedy or a preventative measure. One can combat the danger of the over-attentive secretary by nurturing one's marriage, the column counsels. Wives must make time alone for themselves if marriages are to survive, advises the January 1982 story, but if one's marriage has "gone stale" one must patiently wean her husband away from a distraction such as television into activities both spouses can do together (May 1981).

Closer inspection reveals that these are not true stories, however, despite their veridical trappings. No author's name claims responsibility either on the feature or in the table of contents. Fiction and real life are blended here, creating pleasure to accompany the ideological socialization. The episode is more credible and carries greater weight when one inadvertently assumes it to be a true story. To realize that it is fiction is to lose some of the voyeuristic pleasure. But the lesson remains effective either to guide readers out of a similar problem or to help them to modify behavior that might lead to such a situation.

Openly at the pole of non-fiction, in contrast, are *Good Housekeeping*'s other voyeuristic features that deal with both ordinary people and celebrities, and here strategies of containment are diligently at work. Stories abound about extraordinary events that happen to ordinary people. "Terror at noon" (February 1982), for example, ends with a moral: "My ordeal taught me that while the will to live is God given, the strength to survive is self given" (p. 104). "I froze to death – but lived" (January 1982), "The woman who trusted too much" (June 1983), and "Marjorie Graham's last-chance baby" (April 1983) allow readers to enjoy the apparently impossible – both good and bad events that happen to ordinary people, but ultimately employ strategies of containment to secure discursive power. The strength of the lessons in these stories lies in their non-fictional character – the confirmation that the impossible is indeed possible.

McCall's fairy-tale-like feature, "Reader of the Year" parallels these accounts of the exceptional in *Good Housekeeping*. After announcing in fall 1981 a search for readers who wanted their homes redecorated and new wardrobes furnished, *McCall's* received over 10,000 letters from readers with pictures of themselves and their houses – parallel entities that need renovating in the logic of consumerism.[25] A lengthy feature in the September 1982 issue shows "before and after" pictures of the winning reader who is ordinary as is her house; after transformation, the two become parallel signifiers on the continuum of self-perfection, ideals that other readers also can attain by purchasing the sponsors' products. The elegant formal dining room is available from Sears, the new clothes from J. C. Penney. The remodeling process extends even to new make-up, recipes, and exercises. Just as the ideological socialization in *Good Housekeeping*'s extraordinary stories about everyday people is more effective when one believes the protagonists to be real, so, too, does the ordinariness of *McCall's* Reader of the Year draw one more effectively into consumerism. The feature's advertising slogan, "Fairy tales do come true,"[26] applies not only to the contest winner but to the magic that proper consumerism promises to produce in all readers' everyday lives.

Features about celebrities and stars are structurally parallel to the tales of extraordinary events. Where *Family Circle* and *Woman's Day* often show inanimate signs of ideal womanhood on their covers, *McCall's* and *Good Housekeeping* consistently picture celebrities. The follow-up features offer voyeuristic pleasure as did the stories of extraordinary events, but here one's voyeurism is directed to traditional and stable aspects of the stars' lives. Goldie Hawn notes that "having children is the most important thing you can do in your life" (*McCall's*, October 1983, p. 178). "The real story of the playboy prince" (*McCall's*, February 1983) argues that Prince Andrew is an ordinary, friendly but lonely man who has simply made a few youthful mistakes.

Good Housekeeping presents lengthier and more numerous features about stars, often focusing on older figures such as Cary Grant, Bob Hope, and Lana Turner. Like their counterparts in *McCall's*, these features usually offer occasions for voyeurism that ultimately reinforce the predominant social order. In "Joan Kennedy: Life on my own" (April 1983), the voyeuristic details are encased within an overarching moral; here, one such strategy of containment functions when Kennedy stresses that her family and children come first in her life.

The fiction in both magazines is realistic, utilizing reader identification, emotion, and fantasy to create pleasure that draws one to the ideological messages. Relations between mothers and daughters, the importance of marriage and family, and standard romance themes surface continually. Frequently the central conflict is between two generations of women, recounted from the daughter's perspective. The birth of the daughter's own daughter exacerbates the conflict but ultimately the protagonist learns appropriate lessons from her mother and the conflict is resolved.[27] The stories thus address two sets of readers, both younger and older women, using the common cultural denominator of childcare and familial relations.

In one *McCall's* story, "Mother-in-law" (March 1981), the husband's mother performs the role of guiding the young wife back to traditionally accepted values. Here the poles of the traditional and modern are confused: although the young protagonist intelligently questions childbearing, the story portrays her as old-fashioned because she is a respected classics teacher with a severe hairdo and drab clothes. Modernity comes to equal having a child at age 42, a new hairdo, bright clothes, and replacing antique furniture with modern. The mother-in-law advises the protagonist to hide her professional achievements behind beauty so that her boss won't feel threatened. Surprisingly, the protagonist is immediately convinced by this argument even though she has been characterized heretofore as intelligent and sensible. By labelling the traditional "modern" and the modern "traditional," this story utilizes up-to-date thinking about childbearing and career issues to reinforce traditional roles for women.

Frequently stories in *McCall's* and *Good Housekeeping* encourage both transgressive and socially accepted romantic fantasies. "The man who got away" (*McCall's*, October 1983) provides details about a married woman's date with an old boyfriend. Like *Good Housekeeping*'s "Second chance" (April 1983), where a romantic setting helps to remind a wife that her current husband is better than her ex-spouse, "The man who got away" uses transgressive fantasy to uphold the traditions of marriage and family. "Where my tomorrow waits" (*Good Housekeeping*, May 1981) suggests that women should stand up for themselves against familial and social pressures but posits romantic love as the solution to class differences.

Despite these traditional messages, both *Good Housekeeping* and *McCall's* adapt to the times to remain profitable. Both strive for a balance that will attract new readers while retaining traditional audiences. *Good Housekeeping*'s "30-Minute Entree" and *McCall's* "No Time to Cook" offer monthly menus to prepare quickly with packaged foods. Although in tune with the time constraints of many contemporary working women, the presuppositions that these features try to anchor as "common sense" imply that women should be responsible for preparing meals, sometimes consisting of several courses and always decoratively arranged. Other features continue to present time-consuming foods to prepare, often with products advertised in the magazines. *McCall's* launched a special campaign in 1984 to reach baby boomers. Its ads to advertisers showed "typical mothers" such as Tina Turner, Cher, and Carly Simon to suggest that the magazine appeals to others besides traditional homemakers.[28]

Good Housekeeping included a feminist article about housework by Letty Cottin Pogrebin in October 1983 which argues that housework should be viewed as a valuable economic activity. Unlike many other features in the magazine which romanticize home labor, Pogrebin notes: "Those who reminisce sentimentally about old-fashioned Thanksgivings . . . are clearly not viewing the holiday through the eyes of the housewife" (p. 64). *McCall's*, in contrast, published anti-feminist articles such as William Novak's "What do women really want?" (February 1983) and Annie Gottlieb's "What men need that women can't give them" (October 1983). The first claims that women wish to have it both ways, wanting men to be driven yet gentle. The article denigrates feminism by denigrating women, focusing concern on men's emotional problems of adjustment. It fails to consider the power that men wield and women's systematic exclusion from that power. The second article argues that feminist gains have caused the loss of "a special vibrancy, vitality, gusto, pride that we once recognized as distinctly masculine" (p. 166). Gottlieb contends that men, more than women, need a clearly defined difference between the sexes and suggests methods by which women can help to affirm men's sense of power. Under the guise of being up-to-date, this piece undermines women's struggle for equality. It asks readers not only to accept men's power but to help secure it. Both *Good Housekeeping* and *McCall's* will have to do much more authentic, in-depth modernization if they expect to attract younger women.

LADIES' HOME JOURNAL AND *REDBOOK*: NEW OWNERS FOR THE LEAST POPULAR SERVICE MAGAZINES

In the early 1980s, Charter Company owned the two poorest performers of the seven sisters. From 1981 to 1982, *Redbook* lost $4.3 million in ad revenue and 248,000 readers, while *Ladies' Home Journal* dropped $6.1 million in ad revenue, and lost 352,000 readers. Charter, a billion-dollar conglomerate with oil, real estate and publishing subsidiaries, had purchased *Redbook* from Norton Simon in 1975, intending to become a major communications corporation. But by early 1982 there were rumors that both magazines were up for sale; in May the Hearst Corporation bought *Redbook*, and in July *Ladies' Home Journal* was sold to Family Media Inc., publisher of *Health* and *1001 Home Ideas*.[29]

Chapter 1 delineated some of the changes Hearst initiated in *Redbook*. Although continuing to emphasize motherhood, the new owner sought an updated target audience – mothers in the now-grown baby boom generation. Hearst termed its new ideal reader "the young dynamo who manages to juggle husband, child, and career,"[30] and recruited personnel from *Bazaar* and *Mademoiselle*. *Ladies' Home Journal* made fewer changes, eliminating a dozen staff positions and offering advertisers a special 20 per cent discount for combination ads. In December 1982, however, the magazine announced a 5 per cent increase in its ad rates with no additional guaranteed circulation and the following February tested a lower cover price in the midwest.[31]

Ladies' Home Journal's minor changes achieved greater economic success initially than did *Redbook*'s major ones. Although the *Journal* had trailed *Redbook* when both were owned by Charter, it showed a 27 per cent rise in ad pages in 1983 while *Redbook*'s rose only 4.7 per cent. *Redbook* lost $597,000 in ad revenue that year but the *Journal* earned $14 million more, a substantial 32 per cent increase. In total revenues *Redbook* was down 2.3 per cent in 1983 while *Ladies' Home Journal* was up 32.1 per cent.[32]

We have seen that *Redbook*'s attempt to modernize under Hearst was initially visible on the cover, where close-ups of young models' faces and a new typographical design hint that the magazine is similar to a fashion and beauty publication such as *Mademoiselle*. While *Ladies' Home Journal* introduced bright yellow tint blocks on its table-of-contents page, it made few changes in the style of its cover. *Redbook* initiated more substantive changes in its content, such as including articles on non-traditional mothers. In November 1983, "I was a better mother when I was a single mother" (pp. 90–1) points out the advantages of a one-to-one parent–child relationship. Another piece terms single mothers "The strongest women in America" (p. 87).

Occasionally the new *Redbook* publishes feminist articles such as "How would your life be different if you'd been born a boy?" (February 1983), which urges readers to experiment with sex-role reversal and offers other advice on how to remedy latent sexism in one's children. The new *Ladies' Home Journal*, in contrast, rarely publishes pieces with a clear feminist perspective.

Instead, an essay by Betty Friedan appears in July 1983, after the writer has revised some of her previous feminist stands. In the same issue, "Could a woman be President?" argues that only the vice-presidency is a possibility, encouraging women to be temporarily content with the second-best position.

Redbook cosmetically modernizes with such pieces as "The food of the future" (February 1983), and "How to break the salt habit" (June 1983). Sometimes these articles clash with the surrounding advertisements for prepared food products, traditionally the staple of the women's service magazines. The article advising against salt, for example, appears across from an ad for a salty packaged potato mix.

Neither magazine abandoned its popular monthly "triumph-over-trauma genre,"[33] which offers voyeuristic glimpses into people's problems along with the closure of a happy resolution. The *Journal*'s famous opening feature, "Can This Marriage Be Saved?" spuriously poses the question in its title each month, referring both to the real-life cases recounted in the article and to the readers' own marriages. The message with which it attempts ideological closure is that most marriages can be saved, no matter how troubled, if spouses will compromise and sacrifice. Like soap opera viewers, readers are caught up in the day-to-day details of other people's marriages. One quickly turns the voyeurism on oneself, having learned from the article that one's own marriage might be endangered. Unlike *Redbook* which now publishes a number of features on divorced and single women, *Ladies' Home Journal* has continued to valorize institutionalized marriage.

Redbook's monthly "A Young Mother's Story" entices readers with such titles as "I was a leaky-hose spender but now I have control of my cash" (February 1983), "We had everything we wanted and lost it all" (November 1983), and "I went back to work – and took my baby with me" (June 1981). Readers are invited to submit their own stories for the feature and promised $500 upon acceptance. This opportunity allows each story's ideological frame to function more effectively: readers examine their own lives through the optic of the narrator–protagonist to see if they might not have a similar episode to recount to earn $500. The story's ideological framework thus shapes readers' perceptions of their daily lives more strongly than do other "triumph-over-trauma" features that do not offer monetary remuneration for applying the frame to one's life.

The *Journal*'s regular "It's Not Easy to Be a Woman Today" parallels *Redbook*'s "A Young Mother's Story" by recounting extraordinary events in ordinary women's lives and inviting readers to submit their own stories. "What I have to be thankful for" (November 1981), for example, tells of a woman whose husband collapses with encephalitis the very day she discovers that she is pregnant. Although her mother-in-law suggests an abortion, the protagonist–narrator decides against it; eventually her husband recovers and the family lives happily ever after. Here, the attempt to secure the dominant ideological order harnesses accepted moral values to the narrative pleasure of reading about an extraordinary tragedy that someday might touch one's own life.

Related to the monthly "triumph-over-trauma" features are other articles in the *Journal* that present moral and ideological lessons in voyeuristic trappings. "Anatomy of a road accident" (November 1981) and "The $300,000 medical bill" draw readers in with tragic stories about one family's death in a car accident and a catastrophic illness that strikes another, encouraging campaigns against drunken drivers and augmenting one's medical insurance. "Unfaithful wives" (November 1981) claims to be a report on "Why more and more 'nice' women are having affairs" (p. 58) but labels adultery a "narcissistic pursuit" and strongly cautions readers to avoid being unfaithful or risk divorce.

The *Journal*'s conservative ideology sometimes extends from such traditional issues as faithfulness in marriage and strong family life to overt political indoctrination. Strong anti-Communist themes surface in "The long journey home" (February 1983) about the attempts of a couple to get their young daughter to the US from Viet Nam after the war. James Clavell's "The children's story," (November 1981) originally published in the *Journal* in 1963, is a dystopia in which the Soviets have taken over the US; they send an attractive teacher to indoctrinate the school children, who are easily persuaded because they haven't learned the meaning of the Pledge of Allegiance they recite before the flag. In these two cases, a "triumph-over-trauma" human-interest piece and the moral lesson of a short story are linked to the attempt to politically indoctrinate readers with anti-Communist attitudes.

In 1982 fiction was *Redbook*'s largest editorial category, comprising 30.1 per cent of its editorial material and centering on romance themes.[34] In describing the monthly novella, the Editor claimed contradictorily: "Since 1933 we have been the only women's magazine to publish regularly a full and complete novel 'condensation'" (September 1981, p. 16). The August 1982 issue reported that fiction is one of the main reasons many buy the magazine. Because it attracts readers and helps to sustain *Redbook*'s commercial goals, the fiction changed little under Hearst. The predominant themes of romance draw readers to ads for romance novels and to other features that use romance to promote products. For example, a series in June 1983 included a fashion feature "A touch of romance for you," a decorating feature, "A touch of romance for your home," two features on men – "Why can't men be more romantic?" and "Dream lover" – and an interview with a romance writer.

Both *Ladies' Home Journal* and *Redbook* have weathered the crisis that the seven sisters experienced in the early 1980s. While *Redbook* has undergone more changes under Hearst than has the *Journal* under Family Media, its economic recovery has been slower than the *Journal*'s. Perceptual stereotypes that have developed about a magazine over many years are difficult to change. Perhaps *Ladies' Home Journal*'s rapid increase in ad volume after its sale had more to do with the combination discounts the magazine began to offer with *Health* and *1001 Home Ideas*, than with the minor editorial changes it instigated. Regardless of which is ahead in the statistics, both magazines are exceedingly lucrative enterprises: in 1983 *Ladies' Home Journal*'s revenues totalled $128.1 million and *Redbook*'s were $84.1 million.[35]

BETTERING THE HOME TO ATTAIN PERFECTED WOMANHOOD

Classified as one of the seven sisters because of its service editorial and extremely high circulation, *Better Homes and Gardens* is also a shelter magazine similar in many ways to *House & Garden* and *House Beautiful*. Its emphasis on home improvement and the accompanying devalorization of readers' current homes creates a pattern similar to that of the fashion and beauty magazines. Where the latter emphasize improvement of the body, wardrobe and interpersonal relations, *Better Homes and Gardens*, as its title indicates, promotes the notion that one's home and yard are inadequate and can be bettered through increased consumerism. Like the other seven sisters, the shelter magazines, and the fashion and beauty publications, *Better Homes* presents a constellation of signs of ideal womanhood. Whether it be a perfectly prepared meal, a well-decorated and -landscaped home, up-to-date appliances, an ideal family and marriage, stylish clothing or correctly applied make-up, the images of perfected womanhood in these magazines constitute a single cultural continuum whose material base is consumerism.

Established as *Fruit, Garden and Home* in 1922 by E. T. Meredith, former Secretary of Agriculture under Woodrow Wilson, *Better Homes and Gardens* grew steadily and by 1928 had a circulation of one million. It became even more popular after World War II with the numerous suburban housing developments and increased home ownership, and today claims a circulation of eight million. It now competes with *Family Circle*, *Woman's Day* and *Good Housekeeping* for first place among the seven sisters in revenues, ad volume and circulation. SMRB calculates the total female readership of *Better Homes* at 16.2 million.[36]

Better Homes' huge advertising business[37] provides strong evidence of the consumerist roots of the cultural signs of ideal womanhood on the editorial pages. Although some features address men or husband and wife together, most readers are women and ads and features are directed primarily to them. The articles on home decoration, entertaining, food preparation, children and health present idealized images of women's labor. In spite of the high female readership and the women-oriented content of most of the magazine, each issue begins and ends with male-authored columns – "Editor at Large" and "The Man Next Door." This cultural frame encloses the numerous signs of ideal womanhood in each issue and imparts to them an aura of implicit male approbation.

The home, properly appointed with the latest consumer goods, is the principal icon of ideal femininity in *Better Homes and Gardens*. Each month features on decorating, furnishings, and remodeling urge readers to change what they currently have. Frequently, suggestions for remodeling focus on the primary female space in the home – the kitchen. The October 1981 issue published four articles on kitchen remodeling. Whether the focus is the kitchen, another room, or the entire house, the predominant theme is that of updating the implicitly old-fashioned and inferior. Obvious examples such as "Rehabbing an old brick bungalow," and "An updated family room," (May 1983) appear along with more subtle recommendations for up-to-date household products. "Space-saving spots for your microwave" (November 1983), while ostensibly about kitchen redecoration, presupposes that readers own microwave ovens or that they should purchase them in order to fit into the group of ideal women addressed directly in the title.

The idealized spaces of the home for which women are responsible extend beyond the kitchen in the *Better Homes*' cultural system. "Affordable elegance" (October 1981) urges room-by-room redecoration, knitting, arranging food properly for parties, and making everyday foods appear elegant. Time-consuming female labor is made invisible here beneath the catch words "affordable elegance" and the enticing pictures that predominate on these pages. The feature collapses together these four separate areas of women's work beneath the rubric of ideal femininity implicit in the trope "affordable elegance."

As in the other seven sisters magazines, enticing visual displays of prepared food encourage readers to purchase grocery products, the largest ad category in *Better Homes*.[38] "Apple buymanship" (October 1981), for example, correlates with a recipe feature, "Extra special apple salads." *Better Homes* shows food preparation to be primarily women's domain, although one small monthly feature, "My Turn to Cook" highlights recipes that men have submitted. This editorial proportion suggests that men may take an occasional turn at cooking but that it need never be their full responsibility. By implication, the numerous other food features constitute the norm – women's responsibility for cooking – to which this column is the exception. One can imagine the shock this feature would cause were it to focus on recipes submitted by women beneath the title "My Turn to Cook." Even a feature on remodeling a house, "Turning their dreams into reality" (July 1983), pictures food that the wife has prepared and her recipes, again emphasizing that food preparation is women's domain.

Better Homes and Gardens calls itself "The Do Something! Magazine" and argues to advertisers that its "active editorial atmosphere . . . preconditions readers to action" (i.e. buying products).[39] This emphasis on readers' action, a euphemism for buying, shows that *Better Homes*' primary concern is to assure its own profitability as it offers women ideological messages. In a few features, however, a strong conservative ideology is the predominant concern.

The July 1983 issue, titled "A Celebration of the American Spirit," begins with direct ideological messages in the "Editor at Large" column. With his words printed around a picture of the American flag, the Editor links today's American family to the founding fathers' dream of "Life, Liberty, and the pursuit of Happiness," and argues that Jefferson would be pleased with the families featured in this issue. The articles in the "American Spirit" series highlight individual families who embody traditional values. One retired couple remodels a country house in order to create an extended-family home for their children and grandchildren. Another family embodies the "American Spirit" by "Creating a colonial home on a limited budget" (p. 40); linking himself to history on a purely formal level, the husband argues: "We take the past and make it work for us today" (p. 44). Another feature, "Pride in the symbols of freedom," highlights a woman who makes calico American flags. Other features praise the work ethic, showing how enterprising families have started businesses, remodeled homes, and planted gardens.

On one ideological level, this exaltation of the traditional American family (no minority or single-parent families are shown) appears simply to be linked to the patriotism of the Fourth of July holiday; its placement following the report on *Better Homes and Gardens*' survey on the state of the American family, however, shows its deeper role in the struggle for discursive power. About 200,000 of *Better Homes*' eight million readers responded to this survey published the previous October, six times more women than men, and mostly middle-income homeowners. In contrast to *Better Homes*' celebration of the ideal American family, 80 per cent of respondents thought family life to be in trouble in the US, blaming the absence of religion and moral decay as the greatest threats; only 17 per cent of respondents (and few were poor, it will be remembered) cited economic hardship as a threat. In the context of this pessimism among readers about family life, the "American Spirit" features directly following in the magazine can be understood as an attempt to alleviate fears and secure discursive power. In fact, the very concerns the readers voice contribute to this editorial mission by helping to hegemonize precisely the values perceived to be in danger of disappearing. The strong ideological images of the ideal American family linked to Fourth of July and the founding fathers will also help to sell consumer goods and future issues of the magazine. Here, however, ideology is the first concern and product promotion is second – the reverse of the usual priorities of magazine publishers.

Besides these idealistic images, a good deal of useful information attracts readers each month. Instructions for installing plumbing for a washtub, information on energy-saving fireplace inserts, and tests for determining if furniture is well-made offer immediate applications to readers' lives. Like the numerous pieces that promote images of ideal womanhood and strong family life, these features lead readers to consume as well. The key theme – that readers need to improve their homes – which extends from the first word of the title to the end of each issue has enabled *Better Homes and Gardens* to become one of the top money-making enterprises in the publishing industry.

The response of the service magazines to the economic and demographic changes of the 1980s has been, in general, one of cautious change. Because many women remain responsible for consumer purchases for the home whether they hold an outside job or not, and large numbers of women read one or another of the home service magazines, many advertisers continue to purchase space in the seven sisters. Unlike the fashion and beauty publications which easily appear up-to-date because of the seasonal – although spurious – changes in fashion and cosmetics products, the home service category openly tries to appear traditional, employing only the requisite tinge of modernity. The category's failure to grow in the early 1980s meant that the magazines had to integrate more modernity, or at least the appearance of it, in order to attract readers. The resultant cultural constellation links together images of ideal womanhood as disparate as aesthetically pleasing meals, household decor and personal appearance, successful marriage and childraising. The configuration of such varied elements is made to appear natural, thereby not only selling consumer goods but upholding the free household labor system so vital to the present economy.

7 New Workers and Career Women: Tapping a New Generation of Spenders

In the 1950s and 1960s many magazines engaged in a protracted battle with television for advertising dollars. By increasing circulations and lowering CPMs (cost per thousand), publishers hoped to compete with the wide exposure television gave advertising messages. By the end of the 1960s, however, many magazines abandoned this drive for massive readership,[1] emphasizing instead their ability to reach special, affluent segments of the market; the new trend was to be a "class" rather than "mass" publication.

Advertising Age labelled the movement to special-interest publications "the biggest single change in magazine thinking today."[2] By cutting circulation, a magazine reduced production and distribution costs yet could raise advertising rates because it now targeted an affluent audience. Advertisers could avoid spending money to reach people unable to purchase their products, as frequently occurred when ads addressed mass segments of the population.

At the same time as this reverse trend from "mass" to "class" audiences occurred, large numbers of women were entering the workforce. By 1980, 44.7 million women were employed, over half the US female population, where in 1960, only one-third of the women in the country worked outside the home.[3] This material change in many women's lives along with the attitudinal changes evidenced in the women's liberation movement signalled the transformation of the traditional female consumer. Magazines that addressed women principally as homemakers receded in popularity. Many women no longer had time for or interest in the traditional seven sisters. In 1980 all of the seven sisters suffered declines in ad volume, except *Good Housekeeping* which only had a slight increase of 0.7 per cent, and all were down in circulation as well, except *Woman's Day* with a small increase of 1.7 per cent and *Better Homes and Gardens* whose circulation stayed the same.[4] It is true that magazines in general suffered in 1980 and 1981 because of the recession, but the seven sisters experienced some of the most serious erosions, partly attributable to the changing female population. The fashion and beauty magazines, in contrast, did well during this period.[5]

Realizing that massive circulations were not enough to attract advertisers away from television and that women's material conditions and attitudes had changed by the 1970s, publishers began to take new approaches to reaching female consumers. William J. Abbott, Marketing Director of *Self*, noted in 1979, "The women's market is now segmented. . . . You don't advertise to a stockbroker in the same way you do to a field worker."[6] This need for new ways to advertise to women led to the appearance throughout the 1970s of several new, specialized magazines. *Woman News*, intended as a twice-monthly national news magazine for working women, tried to find financial backing in the early 1970s. *Executive Female Digest*, previously the newsletter of the National Association of Female Executives, was converted in 1978 to a glossy, bimonthly business magazine. *Family Circle* experimented with an annual publication, *Women Who Work*. Even earlier, *Ms.*, launched in 1972, sought an educated, feminist audience. Billie Jean King began *Woman Sports* in 1974 for women interested in participatory and spectator sports, and she faced competition from another bimonthly, *The Sportswoman*.[7]

Besides these special-interest magazines which had varying degrees of success, a new genre of publications developed addressed specifically to the growing group of women who had entered the workforce. A new generation of spenders, these women were earning money that allowed them to buy more than the usual household and family products advertised in the home service magazines. They constituted a new market for what had traditionally been male-oriented purchases such as cars, liquor, insurance, travel, and financial services.[8] Five magazines directed themselves to specific sectors of this group of workers and thereby attracted substantial advertising revenue from marketers who wished to address these new consumers. Within this specialized audience, each magazine carved out an even more specific readership. *Newsweek Woman* and *Savvy* focused only on extremely upscale executive and professional women; *Working Woman* at first sought all women and then narrowed its focus to career women; *Working Mother* decided to address both working and career women but limited its audience to workers raising young children; *New Woman* sought the broadest audience of the group, and focused its editorial pages on the personal problems of these new women workers.

It is useful to study this group of successful magazines for working women beginning with the most elite and proceeding to the least, rather than following the chronological order of their publication. Although each has targeted a special group of consumers with different desires and more spending power than the audience of the traditional home service publications, some seek a more elite audience than others. *Savvy* and *Newsweek Woman* limit their circulations to 300,000 and 500,000 respectively; their readers are affluent and constitute a "class" audience in the strictest sense. At the other end of the group, *New Woman* aims for a larger "mass" readership within the group of new spenders; its official circulation in 1983 was about one million although it claims on its front cover to have six and sometimes even eight million readers. Both *Working Woman* and *Working Mother*, in different ways, also attempt to reach "mass" as well as "class" audiences while remaining special-interest publications.

As is the case for the majority of new magazines, survival was extremely difficult for most of these publications in their first years. That they have succeeded is testimony to the changing marketplace and women's continuing role as purchasers. One analyst noted in 1983, "Mass Marketing as we know it is over."[9] Although mass marketing to women for all but mass consumer goods may be obsolete, what has not changed is that women are still the primary consumers and continue to be addressed as such even in these new magazines for working women.

NEWSWEEK WOMAN: GENDER-SEGREGATED ADS AND THE CONSTRUCTION OF MEANING

If you are a woman who subscribes to *Newsweek* and happens to live in an affluent or "upscale zipcode" area, once a month your issue will be different from the editions others are reading. Because your high income makes you attractive to advertisers, you will see certain ads that men and non-affluent women will not see in their copies. Although you are probably unaware of it, you are a subscriber to *Newsweek Woman*.

Begun in February 1980, this special advertising edition of the news magazine was a response to the growing trend among advertisers to seek "class" rather than "mass" audiences. In its publicity for the edition, *Newsweek* promises to deliver to advertisers "the cream of the contemporary women's market . . . women of intellect, enterprise and means," 500,000 high-income readers, 80 per cent of whom are employed in professional and managerial positions.[10] In contrast to the mass audiences of the seven sisters and the fashion and beauty publications, *Newsweek Woman*'s controlled circulation allows advertisers to spend money efficiently by paying only to reach a select group of monied consumers. Where, for example, a one-page color ad in *Family Circle* costs $69,000, the same ad is only $12,980 in *Newsweek Woman*.[11] And while the *Family Circle* ad allows the advertiser to reach millions of women, some of those addressed may not be able to afford the product. For less money the advertiser can target the small group of *Newsweek Woman* readers, all of whom are affluent and who, *Newsweek Woman* claims, constitute an unduplicated audience.[12] An efficient medium for advertisers and an additional revenue producer for *Newsweek*, what does *Newsweek Woman* represent for the upscale women who unwittingly subscribe to it?

Newsweek's national and international news content, as one source of information about world politics, can help women to participate more knowledgeably in contemporary society. The time expended reading beauty magazines to learn about the latest make-up and fashion might more productively be utilized in reading a variety of news sources, among them weekly news magazines. But this special advertising edition of *Newsweek* does not in itself entice more women to read about international events; the women who read *Newsweek* do so whether or not the extra ads addressed to them appear. This special magazine exists not to inform women about world events but to sell commodities. In fact, because of the principle of montage at work between the editorial material and advertising in magazines, the current news in *Newsweek Woman* is mediated and somewhat altered by the special gender-oriented advertising.

A typical edition of *Newsweek Woman* contains one or more sections of ads interleafed between pages of the regular edition. The 17 May 1982 issue,[13] for example, included four extra ads between pages 10 and 11: Chanel Creme Extreme Protection,

Kelvinator Appliance Company, Adia Temporary Services, and Stouffer's frozen dinners (pp. 10a–10d). Later in the issue an ad for Gibson Appliances appeared (p. 104d). Often these new ads combine with the editorial text, creating secondary meaning systems not available to readers of the regular edition.

At the height of the 1982 Falklands/Malvinas crisis, for example, two pieces on the war that followed one another immediately in the regular edition (19 April 1982, pp. 40ff) were separated in *Newsweek Woman* by a four-page advertising section. An elegant ad for Chanel waterproof mascara starkly contrasts the details of the impending war described on the preceding pages and is followed by a two-page ad series from the American Dairy Association which patronizingly addresses the intelligent, upscale reader of *Newsweek Woman* with playful rhymes: "Fake on your bake? Phony on your macaroni? Imitation on your fine creation? Never!" (pp. 46b–46c). The final intervening advertisement promotes an Avon book, *The Kahn Report on Sexual Preferences*. By asking women to read about "the astonishing results of a two-year survey [about] what American men and women really want in bed," the ad reinforces both the language and concerns of traditional women's magazines and forms a contradictory montage with the title of the second article about the Falklands war on the facing page: "Of principle – and power." Readers of the regular editions of *Newsweek*, seeing this headline directly following the first piece on the Falklands, are likely to decode the word "power" here directly, as Britain's rightful response to the invasion, as the article's preferred encoding would have it. *Newsweek Woman* readers, however, experience the confusing mediation of the ad's emphasis on acquiring a type of sexual power. Their reading about the war is interrupted by a constellation of trivial messages about cosmetics, dairy products and books on sexual preferences. If the upscale reader of *Newsweek Woman* wishes to be well-informed about current international events, she must also not forget the traditional concerns assigned to her in the consumer society – beauty, meal preparation, and attending to another's sexual preferences.

A similar but even more jarring constellation occurs in the 4 October 1982 edition of *Newsweek Woman* in the middle of "The making of a massacre," an article about the Israeli role in the September 1982 massacre in West Beirut. Following the pictures of piles of dead bodies, *Newsweek*'s affluent female readers encounter the exposed "Maidenform woman" in a hospital scenario, "making the rounds in elegant delectables" (p. 26c). Pens by Cross are advertised on the next page with the slogan, "Elegance a woman can use everyday," along with a public service ad urging readers: "Do something selfish. Support the arts" (p. 26d). Across from these, another ad shows an elegantly attired model promoting a Pendleton suit. The last ad page in this series also plays on the notion of elegance by using a French word and arguing that purchasing Stouffer's frozen crepes is "Improving on the French" (p. 26f).

This ad series sharply contrasts with the continuation of the article about the massacre in Beirut on the next page, creating a jarring montage for *Newsweek Woman* readers. The sentence that the ad series insensitively interrupts illustrates this: "When Western journalists entered the camps two days later, they observed scores of Palestinians in" (p. 26) "grotesque attitudes of death" (p. 27). The passage continues, noting that the Christians "chained a group of men to the back of a pickup truck and dragged them into a garage. Inside the same garage they left a pile of corpses, one with its genitals ripped away" (p. 27). Fragmenting this sensitive passage are the glamorous images in the ad series urging women to be preoccupied with a pseudo-elegance. In addition, the headline of the Stouffer's ad "Improving on the French" works in montage with photos on the facing page of Ariel Sharon and General Eitan to offer an optional meaning system most likely unintended by the Editors of *Newsweek*. The notion that the Israeli presence "improved" on the former French presence in Lebanon is a subtle meaning available for some *Newsweek Woman* readers to choose.

Other ads in the affluent women's edition of *Newsweek* encourage competitive feelings between women. The classic "Gentlemen prefer Hanes" ad in the 27 December 1982 issue (p. 18a) depicts a woman wearing Hanes stockings attracting the desiring gaze of a man who ignores the woman he accompanies because she has failed to wear the product. In the 1 November 1982 issue, another Hanes ad depicts a woman's legs as its central motif but this time shows the competing woman without the stockings pouting off to the side, gazing at the Hanes woman with a look of pain (p. 88f). On the previous page another ad encourages a more subtle form of women's competitiveness. One professionally dressed woman says to another, "Hey, look – I just got my American Express Card." The other responds, "Great. Now all you need is a desk." On one level a friendly joke, this rejoinder also valorizes one woman's undercutting another, especially in the context of the strong allusion to women's competitiveness in the Hanes ad on the next page.

Further, the ad for American Express works together with another ad in this special section to suggest that success and freedom can be attained through consumer commodities. "Maybe you just got a new job. Or a promotion . . . But while you're getting established, you need the American Express Card. . . . Because it helps you handle all kinds of situations competently and gracefully" (p. 88e). Here, the green card, a sign of success like the suits the models are wearing in the ad, will allow upwardly mobile women to purchase goods and services that will assure success. Another ad in this series promotes Stouffer's food by using the persona of an implied working woman: "For me, freedom comes in a bright red package," the headline reads (p. 90). Next to the product is a set of car keys; within the rhetorical system of the ad, the two images are symbols of freedom for the successful working woman. The arbitrariness of connecting the idea of freedom to commodity consumption parallels the synasthetic image in the ad text's endline: "Freedom. It's delicious." Just as readers are asked to imagine that freedom has an identifiable taste, so too are they to believe that freedom can be obtained through purchase of a commodity.

The effects of montage between the ads and editorial pages in *Newsweek Woman*, the fragmenting of articles, and the messages of triviality, spurious, commodity-based success and freedom undercut the positive effects of the opportunity *Newsweek* offers for women to learn something about current world events. More serious, however, is the element of deception involved in this special advertising edition. Virginia M. Mueller, *Newsweek Woman* Sales Manager, noted: "We do not believe that the subscriber has any idea that she is receiving an extra-ordinary copy of *Newsweek*."[14] If the 500,000 "women of intellect, enterprise and means," as the publicity brochure calls them, are to be used in this fashion to sell more advertising space, they should at least be made aware that they are buying gender- and income-segregated issues of the magazine. Although Mueller contends that *Newsweek Woman* contains the same editorial copy as any other edition of *Newsweek*, in fact the editorial content is changed by the intervening ads and the montage effects they establish with the news articles. Readers should be notified that their copies of *Newsweek* are "extra-ordinary"; the ultimate message to women here is that they may inform themselves about world events so long as they continue to play their important role as consumers.

SAVVY: PALATABLE FEMINISM FOR UPSCALE PROFESSIONALS

With an average monthly circulation of only 300,000, the smallest readership of the new magazines for working women, *Savvy* fosters a strong sense of elitism. On the surface it is addressed to an extremely small, albeit growing, audience – executive women with top salaries – but lower-paid women who read it can vicariously participate in the privileged world it presents. Besides offering less-monied women imaginative pleasure, *Savvy*'s elitism also attracts advertisers. Willing to pay a very high CPM of $29.51 (the cost to reach 1000 women with a four-color ad), *Savvy*'s advertisers primarily seek the ideal woman the publisher promises; "the 34-year old, well-paid, urban dweller with a managerial job in a corporation or a bank."[15] Since its debut in November 1979, *Savvy*'s annual ad volume has continued to rise: from 181 pages in 1980 to 511 in 1982.[16]

The success the magazine would have in attracting readers and advertisers was not foreseen by financial backers when Judith Daniels conceived of the idea in 1975. While there were an increasing number of women in the mid-1970s who had entered the workforce at professional and managerial levels, Daniels had difficulty convincing potential backers that these women would respond to a magazine about work issues. In April 1977, she succeeded in publishing a 44-page preview issue of *Savvy* as an insert in *New York* and *New West* magazines. After an extraordinary response of 13,000 subscription orders, Daniels formed a partnership with Alan Bennett as Publisher and twenty-eight limited partners, securing the $2 million needed to launch the magazine in November 1979. In less than a year, and in spite of the bad economy, *Savvy* had doubled its monthly circulation from 125,000 to 250,000 and nearly tripled its ad volume to 426.5 by 1981. By 1983 its annual ad revenues were $3.7 million, up 50 per cent from 1982.[17]

Such a magazine venture could only have succeeded given the demographic and attitudinal changes caused by the women's movement of the 1970s and the simultaneous entrance of large numbers of women into the professional workforce. In response to these changes, *Savvy* incorporates certain elements of feminism in its editorial material but its principal concerns are money management, business trends, and career development. *Savvy* might be termed a gender-oriented trade magazine; its listing in Standard Rate and Data Service is in the "Business and Finance" category and many of its articles address an implicit executive reader who is already knowledgeable about the upper levels of the business and finance community. *Savvy*'s debt to the feminist movement is overshadowed by the magazine's principal concern of addressing executive women as members of the business sector.

As a result, an underlying political conservatism coexists with certain progressive feminist elements in the magazine. The readers' letters section in June 1982, for example, opens with three letters highly critical of an article about the progressive mayor of Santa Monica, Ruth Goldway. "It is ironic to find a paean to . . . Ruth Goldway, who says, 'private property has no rights,' in a women's business magazine," one letter notes (p. 6). On the same page, however, another reader criticizes *Savvy* from a progressive perspective for its stereotypical portrayal of Irish women: "In the future I trust you will leave the more trite and tasteless commentary to *Playboy* and other magazines devoted to such folderol." Because many of *Savvy*'s readers are conservative, only a modified, palatable feminism can be included in the magazine.

In most features, for example, "she" and "her" are used as generic terms to replace the traditional "he" and "his." There is also a feminist bent to the monthly column of short anecdotes from readers, "Facts of Life." Different from most of the other articles in the magazine, the short vignettes here are easy to read, humorous, and pleasurably anecdotal. Most make a point about gender inequities in society but fail to analyze this problem or suggest remedies. Like the "No Comment" section of *Ms.* magazine in which examples of sexist advertising are reproduced without critical comment and analysis, "Facts of Life" uses the device of the quick surprise effect to attract readers. In the March 1983 issue, one reader, Dorothy J. Mahon, relates an anecdote about her dissatisfaction with hotel service on a recent business trip. After filling out the standard complaint form at the hotel, she wrote a more extensive letter on the plane, signing her full name: "In the weeks that followed, Dorothy Mahon was refunded half of her room cost and D. J. Mahon was refunded (his) room cost in full" (p. 88). Readers must take the time to analyze this episode on their own, however, if they are to profit from it: even though a more extensive, thorough complaint letter was submitted by the woman, the party whom the hotel thought was a man received the larger refund by only filling out a complaint form. What action can women take against such an inequity? Might not *Savvy*'s readers be an ideal group to initiate a boycott against this hotel to protest its unequal treatment? Unfortunately, the structure of "Facts of Life" works against this sort of analysis; the column encourages one to read through the short episodes quickly and avoids thorough feminist analysis of the very problems that allow readers to laugh here.[18] Like the generic use of "she" and "her," the feminism in this column is presented as a surface-level philosophy, one compatible with the political conservatism of much of the rest of the magazine.

In keeping with its primary function as a women's advertising magazine and its narrow, elite audience, *Savvy* promotes an upscale consumerism that sometimes also conflicts with its limited feminism. Complaining about a fashion feature, "Suited for the fast track" (March 1983), a reader criticizes being asked to spend "a quick $2000 on clothes as though it were just a drop in the ocean. Maybe it is to the 'successful executive,' but to me that sum represents a year's taxes on my house plus one month's mortgage. For the average woman battling out there on her own, spending that kind of money is just not possible" (May 1983, p. 8). Here the reader focuses on the conflict between *Savvy*'s articles and the limited spending power of many women supporting themselves alone. It must be noted, however, that this reader's ability to pay a mortgage and property tax of $2000 already distinguishes her from many working women. She is privileged, but her spending power has limits. Nevertheless, she points out the contradiction between the upscale consumerism *Savvy* promotes and the reality of many women's lives.

In January 1983, the feminism in another reader's letter

conflicts with an ad for Ultra Sense pantihose a few pages later. *Savvy* had asked readers to complete a survey about executive dress. This reader was offended because the models wore high heels in the survey pictures: "Heels are worn for the purpose of making the calf and leg more attractive to men. . . . What wearing heels has to do with being a successful executive is beyond me" (p. 8). On page 19, however, the ad for pantihose pictures as its central motif a woman's legs in a seductive pose with high heels; she tugs at the hose and the slogan reads: "With new Ultra Sense you've got pull!" Contradicting much of *Savvy*'s editorial advice about succeeding professionally (including, for example, warnings against sexual liaisons at the office), this ad suggests that a product and the seductiveness it imparts will aid women in achieving success.

Complementing the paid ads for expensive liquors, cars, jewelry, office equipment and investment opportunities, are covert advertising features such as the attractive two-page spread "Consuming passions." Here, beautiful photography emphasizes the aesthetic qualities of consumption, as large pictures of harmoniously arranged products eclipse the high prices listed in small print. The aesthetic pleasure of this consumption is expensive: a $1550 suitcase (January 1981), a $250 silk scarf (March 1981), $225 gardening shears (May 1981), and a $98 key ring (April 1981). Upscale consumption is presented here as the natural outcome of professional success. Readers do not uncritically accept this equation, however, as one letter about the June 1982 feature reveals: "Are you seriously suggesting we spend between $130 and $298 on a single maternity outfit, a necessity for only three to four months? I make a very comfortable living but don't believe in spending for the sake of spending. Is this dressing for success?" (September 1982, p. 8).

Although *Savvy*'s readers may be monied, they are not always willing to spend exorbitant amounts on upscale products. Part of *Savvy*'s role in this stage of the consumer society, then, is to convince women with newly attained levels of spending power that they should indeed spend. Even after some women have achieved financial independence, magazines addressed to them still regard them first and foremost as consumers.

Interspersed between messages that urge consumption are editorial pieces that depart from the tradition of most women's magazines by addressing readers intelligently. The articles are often lengthy, encouraging a longer attention span than that needed for most articles in women's magazines. In October 1982 a long essay on peace activist and defense specialist Randall Forsberg educates women about the nuclear freeze issue and offers a role model for channeling one's professional talents into politically progressive businesses. A monthly advice column on executive problems replaces the beauty advice column of traditional women's magazines. Other articles address business and finance, work problems, lifestyle issues and current events.

Savvy attracts upscale, managerial women as well as those who desire such jobs. The magazine must continually walk a fine line, however, between incorporating some of the feminist changes of the 1970s and 1980s and alienating the conservative political views that many of its readers hold. That *Savvy* tries to have it both ways is evident in two opposing letters from readers in September 1982. One supports a previous *Savvy* editorial that lamented the defeat of the ERA and promises that women will continue to fight for it. Immediately following is an opposing letter that complains: "Having equality pushed down one's throat is extremely unpalatable. It is killing the free enterprise system that has made our country great (p. 8). Indeed, these two letters point to the central contradiction of a magazine such as *Savvy* which is indebted in part to the women's movement for the new monied audience it addresses yet is constrained by the loyalty of much of that audience to the current economic system. *Savvy* must try to balance these opposing concerns of its audience so that it can continue its primary work of promoting advertisers' products.

WORKING WOMAN: CONSUMER-BASED SUCCESS FOR "MASS" AND "CLASS" WOMEN

Beatrice Buckler was at the vanguard of her profession in 1973 when she conceived of the idea of a magazine addressed to working women. Executive Editor and Vice-President of *Family Circle*, Buckler saw that the traditionally widely read women's service magazines were no longer adequate to reach the large numbers of women entering the workforce in the 1970s. Advertisers now needed a vehicle to address the new "part-time housewives"[19] – women who held jobs outside the home, with increasingly less time for or interest in the traditional service magazines. Buckler argued: "37 million of us are working today. We haven't *left* our homes; we just want to be in both worlds . . . Sophia Loren, Elizabeth Taylor, Jackie Onassis and Princess Grace are no longer role models."[20]

When *Family Circle*'s owner, the New York Times Company, decided not to finance the new magazine Buckler proposed, she raised money privately. Along with Elizabeth Forsling (who had briefly been the Publisher of *Ms.* magazine) as President and Co-publisher, Buckler announced the November 1976 debut of *Working Woman.* By June 1976 the magazine had secured eight orders for ads and eleven verbal commitments from advertisers, many of whom were concerned about the rising cost of television ads and therefore willing to try the new magazine whose rates were only $1600 for a four-color page. To the advertisers, backers, and founders, the time seemed ideal for such a publishing venture. *Working Woman* got off to a rough start, however, before skyrocketing into success in the early 1980s.[21]

Less than a year after the November 1976 premiere issue, financial backer J. Jay Frankel forced founding Editor Buckler to resign and by December 1977 *Working Woman* was in bankruptcy court. Frankel and Buckler had taken each other to court over financial disputes several times during the magazine's first year. In June 1977 Frankel announced Buckler's resignation along with fifteen of the magazine's staff of seventeen. Kate Rand Lloyd was hired as Editor-in-Chief, having held top editorial posts at both *Vogue* and *Glamour.* Even with the new Editor, the magazine was forced to file under Chapter XI of the Federal Bankruptcy Law at the end of 1977. It was purchased by Dale W. Lang and his newly formed corporation Hal Publications on 30 January 1978 for a mere $100,000 cash and a $300,000 three-year promissory note. Lang, a Group Vice-President at 3M Company, had begun in the late 1960s Media Networks Inc., a magazine placement service for advertisers, which merged with 3M in April 1977 with Lang remaining its Chair. In the early 1980s a number of ads for 3M products appeared in *Working Woman.*[22]

During 1978 Lang invested $1.5 million to promote the magazine (by 1982 he had spent more than $5 million of his own money) and by November 1978 the circulation was up to 300,000. Carol Taber, who had been Sales Manager at Lang's Media

Networks from 1970 to 1975 and New York Advertising Sales Manager at *Ladies' Home Journal* since 1975, was hired for the crucial post of Advertising Director in July 1979. That year *Working Woman*'s ad volume increased 29.5 per cent followed by a huge 55 per cent in 1980, and another 37.6 per cent in 1981. *Working Woman* called itself "the fastest growing magazine."[23] Its 1983 ad volume was the highest in the "women-in-business" category – 1192 pages according to *Folio 400*; that year its total revenue was $22.3 million.[24] In November 1983 Taber was promoted to Publisher, one of the few women to hold the head business post in a magazine.

It was not only Lang's infusion of capital into the bankrupt magazine that accounted for its remarkable success but also the publication's decision to seek a smaller, elite audience. As James Horton, former Publisher and now President of *Working Woman* noted, the magazine succeeded because it decided not to address all working women as the founders had envisioned. Instead, it is principally geared to women who want to get ahead in business. Since 1978, under Kate Rand Lloyd, the magazine has tried to appeal to only 10 million of the 43 million American working women, those who are considered upwardly mobile and achievers.[25]

Working Woman's readership, however, is broader than the elite group its publishers overtly address. Simmons Market Research Bureau's figures indicate that 83 per cent of the magazine's readers are white and 36.7 per cent hold professional or managerial positions. However, 24.8 per cent are employed in clerical or sales positions, 17.3 per cent in other occupations, and 21.2 per cent are not employed. Only 24.9 per cent have household incomes of $40,000 or more.[26] While *Working Woman* has more high-income readers than many other women's magazines, a good number of its readers are not in professional or managerial positions and one-fifth are unemployed.

Consequently, *Working Woman* uses both "class" and "mass" appeal to reach this varied group. The magazine benefits from projecting to certain advertisers the image that it has a narrow, elite audience, yet appealing as well to many average- and low-paid working women to gain additional circulation revenue. It continues to employ its original broad title alluding to all working women, rather than a more specific, narrow name such as "Executive Woman" or "Professional Woman"; it also notes each month on its title page the current total number of women in the workforce in the US – not merely the number of professionally employed women. As we have seen in Chapter 1, by picturing professional, affluent women on its cover and throughout its pages, this magazine encourages a new, more narrow definition of the term "working woman"; this elite decoding appeals to advertisers, women in well-paying professions, and also less-affluent women who can imaginatively transform their circumstances while reading the magazine. As occurs in upscale fashion magazines such as *Vogue* and *Bazaar*, lower-income readers can purchase the less expensive products also advertised while retaining the sense of participation in affluent lifestyles. Corresponding to this dual audience, there appear in *Working Woman*, along with ads for expensive computers, investments, cars, and jewelry, ads for less costly items such as cosmetics, pantihose, and office supplies which both affluent and lower-income readers can purchase.

Working Woman is less elite than *Savvy* yet more "class"-oriented than *New Woman* or *Working Mother*. But as occurs in *Savvy*, the upscale consumerism that *Working Woman* advocates draws complaints from readers. One letter points out the contradictions between *Working Woman*'s own admission that few working women earn over $30,000 and the March 1983 fashion feature that promotes clothing ranging from $300 to $1000 (June 1983, p. 16). Another reader complains that *Working Woman* emphasizes the same stereotypes of ideal youth and beauty as other magazines. The reader proposes that the magazine validate role models such as the successful keynote speaker she saw at a recent seminar: "[The speaker] was overweight, not dressed in the professional woman's 'uniform' and did not color her hair. She was neat, clean, and obviously intelligent . . . at the top of her profession. . . . She has not let false expectations of her appearance stand in the way of her success. Perhaps she has concentrated on what was really important" (September 1983, p. 28). On the page facing this letter, however, *Working Woman* has placed an ad for Charles of the Ritz Age-Zone Controller, with the headline "It's never too soon to start."

At the center of the contradiction between this letter and the facing beauty ad is *Working Woman*'s financial dependence on encouraging women to consume. Although claiming to depart from other women's magazines, it promotes similar consumerist patterns. Along with ads for Maidenform underwear and Oil of Olay, a "Good Looks" column frequently appears in *Working Woman*, and another column "Health: Your Skin" (May 1982, pp. 56–8) appears between ads for Neutrogena soap and Oil of Olay.

Working Woman must update the consumerist model of traditional women's magazines, however. Employed women consume differently from unemployed women, using fewer bath additives, for example, since they are more likely because of time constraints to take showers; but they use more cosmetics, perfume and grooming aids than women who work at home. In addition, although career women have more money to spend, they often lack time to shop.[27] *Working Woman* capitalizes on these time constraints by serving as an intermediary marketing agent: a feature such as "Access: The working woman executive shopping service," for example, markets products with a toll-free number for orders.

The non-glamorous model of success that the reader saw in the keynote speaker described above is incompatible with the model that *Working Woman* promotes in order to earn advertising dollars. While the magazine gives readers practical advice about success on the job, consumerism is often the base of this success. And features such as "At Home" and "Working Woman's Kitchen" with ads for floors, towels, dishes and furniture, give *Working Woman* the appearance of an updated women's service magazine, reminding the working women of her double day and her double duty to consume.

Besides the attractive photos of consumer goods in ads and features, *Working Woman* offers useful editorial bait to entice prospective consumers. Columns such as "Can This Career Be Saved?" and "Can This Business Be Saved?" replace the famous "Can This Marriage Be Saved?" of *Ladies' Home Journal*. Articles on job interviews, networking, business travel, salary increases, current business trends, investments, and opening small business respond to certain real needs and interests of women. These articles entice both employed and unemployed women who buy the magazine in growing numbers each month and see the many ad pages as they read. Beatrice Buckler's concept of a new magazine addressed specifically to working women proved an extremely useful marketing tool. While the seven sisters found that articles on homemaking were not enough to attract women to consume in the 1970s and 1980s, *Working Woman* developed an up-to-date, narrowly focused editorial bait that drew large numbers of readers and advertisers.

WORKING MOTHER: THE DIALECTIC OF THE EVERYDAY AND THE GLAMOROUS

The photograph on the cover of *Working Mother* each month is much like *Working Woman*'s cover. An attractive, professionally dressed young woman appears, often with a briefcase or another symbol of white-collar work. A smiling child is usually present as well, but because of the naturalness with which many associate women with children, the impression of the woman as an upscale, professional worker is preserved. After the cover, however, the magazine's ostensible similarity to *Working Woman* disappears.

If *Working Woman* is primarily aimed at professional workers and secondarily has begun to include service themes each month, *Working Mother* attempts the reverse; it is, in essence, a service magazine which tries to capture upscale readers as well. Indeed, both the editorial material and advertisements in *Working Mother* have more in common with magazines like *McCall's* and *Parents* than they do with *Working Woman*, *Savvy*, or *Newsweek Woman*. What *Working Mother* shares with these new magazines for female workers, nonetheless, is the desire to tap into this new group's increased spending power.

Like *Working Woman*, *Working Mother* had its origins in the declining appeal of the seven sisters magazines. Where *Family Circle*'s parent corporation decided not to finance a new publication aimed at the part-time housewife, *McCall's*, in contrast, began to publish a monthly column for working mothers after a 1976–7 survey showed that many of the magazine's readers were both employed and raised children. In October 1978 McCall Publications began an offshoot of this column, the quarterly magazine *Working Mother* which was to grow steadily to a bimonthly, become a monthly publication in 1981, and finally make a profit for McCall in 1983. In late 1983 *Working Mother* spawned both a cable television series and a special edition of the magazine for day care centers. A month before *Working Mother*'s five-year anniversary (October 1983), the magazine officially increased its circulation rate base to 500,000.[28]

Working Mother does not yet earn as much money for its parent corporation as does *McCall's*, but its continued growth means extra profits and the opportunity for advertisers to reach employed homemakers no longer attracted to the century-old *McCall's*. Although the second-lowest of the seven sisters in ad volume in 1983, *McCall's* with 1107 ad pages does not seem so far ahead of the relatively young *Working Mother* which had 815 that year.[29] The launching of *Working Mother* was an opportunity for *McCall's* to redirect a specialized yet growing part of its audience which was in danger of falling off, while at the same time attracting new readers who were uninterested in buying *McCall's*.[30] The new magazine would allow McCall Publications to retain old readers in the corporate fold, gain half a million more, and keep the profits in-house. *McCall's* could sell its advertisers additional space in the new magazine, offering attractive discounts almost as if *Working Mother* were a new demographic edition of *McCall's*, but with modified editorial material. And by offering its advertisers an extra discount for buying matching ad pages in the two magazines, *McCall's* helped its sister publication to get off the ground.

It is not surprising, then, that the advertising in *Working Mother* is similar to that in *McCall's*. The largest category of ads is for food and household products, followed by childcare ads. Beauty products and toiletries are the next largest category, and there are a few ads each month for cigarettes, women's apparel and cars.[31] The buying habits of *Working Mother*'s readers are somewhat different from those of *McCall's* readers, but the two groups share certain consumer patterns. SMRB data show, for example, that 61.6 per cent of *McCall's* readers used eyeshadow seven days prior to the survey, while a larger 80.9 per cent of *Working Mother*'s readers did.[32] Although consumption of the product is higher for the group who reads *Working Mother*, both audiences show substantial use of eyeshadow. Similarly, because women's homemaking and childcare responsibilities do not disappear when they enter the paid workforce, the two groups of readers have similar patterns of consumption of household goods and childcare products.

The editorial material correlates closely with *Working Mother*'s advertising categories. Like the seven sisters, *Working Mother* publishes beauty and fashion features but more editorial pages are devoted to food and meal preparation, including columns on quick breakfasts and dinners, lunches for the office and school, as well as more elaborate recipe features. The monthly "Bulletin Board," which contains many promotions for advertisers' products, uses the ideology of the new and the up-to-date to encourage readers to consume.

Approximately 15 per cent of *Working Mother*'s readers are single mothers,[33] a group whose problems the editorial features frequently address. "When the father's gone before the baby comes" (June 1982), and "The nuts and bolts of home repair" (April 1982), along with the allusions and examples in other features do not presuppose that readers belong to a stereotypical nuclear family, as often occurs in *McCall's*. In "What's wrong with this picture?" (May 1983), for example, the writer rejects the nostalgia of those who argue for full-time motherhood and the traditional nuclear family. Instead, she notes, this image represents a "commercially generated sentimentality" (p. 80) that is financially attainable only by the well-heeled middle class.

Working Mother shows a magazine's willingness to adapt to the times because consumers have changed. Traditional ideologies are updated and sometimes even abandoned if the audience one's advertisers seek no longer subscribes to them. A magazine's concern for upholding the dominant ideology is less important than its desire to attain its commercial ends.

This is not to say that *Working Mother* is free of ideology. In fact, in abandoning one ideological system traditionally used to address women, *Working Mother* establishes another. The new ideological constellation is based on a dialectic between concrete everyday problems and a glamorized, commodity-based ideal of the working mother. This dialectic is at the heart of women's attraction to the magazine. Although the articles and columns reflect the real problems of the double day and parenting, they contain attractive images that feed one's fantasies as well.

The pole of the ideal is constituted by the majority of the visual images in *Working Mother*. Ads for the elegant Armstrong flooring discussed in Chapter 4 appear in *Working Mother* along with pictures of enticing foods and perfectly made-up faces. An ad for Eureka vacuum cleaners (January 1981) presents a sense of well-being through a picture of a similarly attired mother and daughter, each posing with a vacuum. While some readers might be offended at this image of the early inculcation of sex roles, others view the child with her miniature battery-powered vacuum as an ideal of a middle-class home. Indeed, little in the ad signifies work or dirt; both mother and daughter are dressed in non-work clothes and pose next to their vacuums rather than operating them. For a number of readers this image is attractive, representing an image of ideal femininity to be attained by purchasing commodities.

But such idealized images are not the sole reason women are attracted to *Working Mother*. Concrete, everyday problems form a thematic that continuously interacts with the glamorous ideals of motherhood and femininity. Readers may need and desire the releases fantasy provides, but they need as well a sense of self-recognition, practicality and usefulness. Since, for example, a number of working mothers are divorced, features often discuss the problems of disputes over visitation rights, late child-support payments, the children's special psychological needs, and relations with one's former husband. A monthly column "The Guilt Department," said to be the most popular feature,[34] offers arguments to assuage readers about the impact their job has on raising children. Often, features give advice on overcoming working mothers' stress. The fiction also provides answers to the readers' concrete problems. "A sense of loss" (June 1982), for example, advises directness as the best method for telling one's child that the father has left for good; "Welcome to paradise" (April 1982) describes a divorced mother's battle with loneliness, her decision to go to a singles' bar, and her preservation of her sense of self while there.

Working Mother is careful to envelop the discussion of these everyday life problems in an optimistic tone; if its discussion of these problems were too negative, its circulation might decline. Just as the insecurities fostered in fashion and beauty magazines to stimulate consumption are enveloped in bright colors and a sense of excitement, so, too, are the concrete problems *Working Mother* discusses often attenuated by an optimistic ending, a series of possible solutions, and the use of anecdotes about other women with similar problems. Thus, an internal dialectic between the real and the ideal functions in the features on everyday life problems, along with the external dialectic that exists between the problems recounted and the images of ideal motherhood presented in the ads and other features.

Similarly, the idealistic ads in *Working Mother* often contain a subtle internal dialectic that turns upon a practical element. While the image of the mother and daughter vacuuming in the ad discussed above is an idealized one, for women who fulfill the duties of the "double day," the image of the child with a toy vacuum might also signify a means of occupying one's small daughter while trying to complete household labor. And no doubt there are many negotiated readings of this ad in which overworked women substitute their young sons as the pretended laborer who vacuums here, transcending the sex-role closure the ad attempts. Couched within the many other idealistic and sexist signifieds of this ad, then, is a practical seme that interacts dialectically with the glamorous pole.

Working Mother's success stems not only from its focus on a specialized segment of the women's service market but from its ability to attract that audience by mixing the banal and the glamorous. McCall Publications saw an attitudinal and demographic change in women homemakers in the 1970s and developed a new magazine to attract that group. If the number of working mothers continues to rise as is expected,[35] *McCall's* might well find that its young sister publication has replaced it as one of the lucrative seven sisters magazines.

NEW WOMAN: A MODERN VENEER FOR THE TRADITIONAL

When the first issue of *New Woman* appeared in 1971 readers found pictures of a male nude inside. Now the "Pin-Up" feature contains only memorable quotations to post on a bulletin board, but *New Woman*'s spirit of modernity and daring remains. Encouraged by Helen Gurley Brown's successful revamp of *Cosmopolitan*, the changes in women's attitudes inspired by feminism and the sexual revolution, and the large numbers of women entering the paid workforce, *New Woman* attempted to provide an alternative to the traditional women's service magazines. By the early 1980s, it had achieved remarkable success, claiming on its front cover to have over six million readers.[36] By seeking a wider readership than the other magazines for working women, *New Woman* has made substantial inroads into the traditional readership of the beauty and fashion publications and the seven sisters. To do this, it has employed the ideology of modernity as exciting bait for its often traditional messages and developed editorial topics of interest to a wide range of income- and age-groups.

New Woman's path to success was difficult. When Margaret Harold announced the publication in November 1970, her intended audience was women aged 17–54 who were neither women's liberation enthusiasts nor contented housewives. These middle-of-the-road women, according to the publicity brochure, were to find in *New Woman* "a land inhabited exclusively by exciting females with brains and money."[37] Harold planned to distribute 100,000 free copies of the new magazine to beauty salons, department store buyers, and women's clubs.[38]

In June 1972, however, only a year after its first issue, *New Woman* suspended publication. Arguing that her idea for the magazine was "a great concept . . . but poorly executed," Harold wanted time to reevaluate and start over.[39] Along with Wendy Danforth as Associate Editor and Publisher, Harold began publishing *New Woman* again in October 1973, promising in an editorial column to "satisfy the deeper interests of the hard-working business and professional woman as well as to provide surprise, titillation, inspiration, entertainment" (September–October 1973, p. 4). Using this formula to create a business-like version of *Cosmopolitan* and proceeding cautiously, publishing only bimonthly for the next eight years, Harold and Danforth were able to build *New Woman* steadily so that it earned $25 million in total revenue in 1983. In May 1984 they sold the magazine to Rupert Murdoch's News Group Magazine for $22 million.[40]

New Woman's editorial categories parallel both those of *Cosmopolitan* and those of *Self* and *Working Woman*. Along with regular features on "Image-Building," and "*New Woman* Astrologer," are pieces about "Power Dressing," "Financial Advisor," and "Working Mother." *New Woman* also tries to attract readers in the home service category by emphasizing a dichotomy between the "old" woman and the "new" as a continuous editorial theme. In the "Publisher's Platform" in the first issue, Harold subtly disparaged the seven sisters by telling readers that other publications already exist for women who enjoy raising a family "as their sole or prime challenge"; *New Woman*'s readers, she noted, are "a select audience of thinking women who want to contribute more to an already overpopulated society than three or four well-bred or ill-bred youngsters" (June 1971, p. 3). When it claimed to have "over eight million readers" on its June and July 1982 covers, *New Woman* implicitly asserted itself as a strong competitor of the seven sisters, the only other women's magazines with such high circulations. How is it that *New Woman* has attracted readers from this wide variety of magazines from the health and beauty, seven sisters, and new working women categories?

New Woman's editorial material is aimed at a much broader age group than other magazines – women 17–54. To attract women with such different interests it includes features on a wide range of traditionally female topics and utilizes numerous elements of popular appeal to draw women in. Frequently, it assumes a middle-of-the-road position on controversial issues, in effect "playing it safe," while at the same time projecting an image of novelty and excitement. On closer inspection, the "new woman" is, in fact, quite traditional beneath her appearance of modernity.[41]

Rather than addressing only the upscale and the young, *New Woman* includes articles aimed at less monied women and older readers. A monthly column "The Right to Be Your Own Boss" urges readers to start their own businesses, giving examples in which little or no start-up capital is needed: a restaurant one woman began with only $1000, a cookie business run from one's home, and writing romance novels. A May 1982 piece, "I was 40 years old when we had our first baby," the October 1982 "Age cannot wither a new woman," and a photo of a grey-haired woman in a beauty feature (May 1983, p. 70) are among *New Woman*'s techniques for attracting older readers. While such features psychologically build up older women, they contradict the numerous idealized images of youth in other ads and features in the magazine each month.

Readers are attracted as well by numerous features on traditionally female topics. Month after month diet articles promote gimmicks and quack weight-reduction schemes. In "Three little (two-minute) tricks that will shrink your tummy," women are advised to rub their stomachs slowly in circles thus creating "electricity from your own hand," so that "the superfluous areas of your stomach and abdomen are literally rubbed away" (September 1982, p. 80). There are many articles on marriage, divorce, and love-affairs – most often the affair that the woman fears her husband is having. The April 1983 issue, for example, has four articles on "How to keep your man," three on "Breaking up," and one man's story of "The *language* that led to my divorce." In almost every issue there is a version of the February 1981 article "Is your marriage drifting into trouble? (5 early warning signs)." In *New Woman*, articles on love relations, marriage, affairs, and divorce are so numerous that they are comparable to the articles on children and homemaking in the seven sisters magazines. Most of these articles on relationships present a powerfully attractive opportunity for voyeurism; laden with enticing stories, they allow readers to participate vicariously in emotional events in the lives of others and to apply the correct lessons to their own lives.

Throughout *New Woman*, traditional messages predominate, although they are often disguised by a veneer of the modern and up-to-date. A May 1983 article "How (and why) 'Respectable' wives cheat on their husbands," for example, offers five pages of exciting narrative about extramarital affairs yet ultimately counsels against them. A feature in an ostensibly up-to-date editorial category, "Working Mother," in the July 1983 issue heightens readers' sense of guilt with its title "'Latchkey' children," and its subtitle invoking a frightened child's voice: "I'm scared in the house all by myself!" (p. 47).

This wavering between the modern and the traditional is partly rooted in *New Woman*'s desire to reach a wide range of readers who have varying viewpoints. By being both modern and traditional, *New Woman* aims for a safe, middle-of-the-road position that will not alienate readers, yet be exciting enough to entice them to the magazine. This course is not always successful. An article on lesbian relations drew critical letters from some traditional readers but there were then objections to these letters from some lesbian readers. In July 1983 several readers complained about a May 1983 piece "Why I am not willing to pursue a full-time career outside my home." One reader called the piece "deflating," arguing that it left her feeling like an unfit mother. While four letters that *New Woman* printed strongly opposed the article, one commended it for "pointing to God as the answer" (p. 8). It is difficult for a magazine that seeks a broad readership through an image of modernity to avoid offending some. Wavering between the traditional and the modern is not a workable solution.

New Woman's treatment of feminism is an especially notorious example of this vacillation. The magazine attempts to have it both ways, utilizing a spurious feminism to enhance its image of the "new woman," yet frequently undercutting women's liberation as well. In the first issue of the magazine Margaret Harold announced in her "Publisher's Platform": "we dedicate ourselves to the elevation of the status and image of women" (p. 3). She was quick to note, however, here and in several other early issues, "we do not intend to build up the image of women by putting down the image of men" (p. 3). *New Woman* was not beyond putting down the image of feminism, however, when, later in the issue, a guide to the women's movement asked readers: "Are you a secret sympathizer of the women's liberation movement but don't know which is witch [*sic*]?" (p. 82).

Already in the first issue, *New Woman*'s spurious feminism and vacillation between modern and traditional images of women were evident. Harold noted: "We sincerely believe that the day will come when gentlemen will prefer brains. And that the idea of women as sex objects will be mercifully laid to rest" (p. 3). But this statement appears across from a cigarette ad that gratuitously pictures a woman smoking in a bathtub, thus using a woman's bare body to sell a product unrelated even to bathing. Harold's version of feminism is limited by the commercial goals of her magazine enterprise. She notes that *New Woman* has turned down eleven ads because they were damaging to the image of women. Arguing that this is a costly policy, she then defends women's use of cosmetics, perfume and toiletries to enhance personal beauty. Because of the growing women's movement, Harold was forced to respond to widespread complaints about women's portrayal in advertising; but rather than publicly telling advertisers to change their images to suit readers' new concerns, Harold chose in this column to try to change readers' views to coincide with advertisers' needs to sell products.

Harold's spurious feminism comes full circle when, in her attempt to exonerate men, she blames women themselves for not having succeeded in business. Expressing concern that men are faulted for "the shallows that exist in some women's lives,"

Harold notes: "women themselves are largely to blame for much of their own limited opportunities in business . . . most women in the past really have followed like woolly little sheep, and worked only until they got married or had babies. . . . So the fault, dear Brutus, is not in our birth but in ourselves" (July 1972, p. 3). Appearing to be unaware of the social and economic forces that have pressured women to remain out of the paid workforce at various periods in US history, Harold urges women to blame themselves and even to see themselves as traitors.

In every issue, *New Woman* uses selected aspects of feminism to enhance its image as a magazine for "new women." Numerous cartoons appear, most of which play on concepts of women's liberation. In June 1982 a cartoon shows a woman in a bar telling a man, "Yes, I could use a little company. Did you have one for sale?" (p. 40). A monthly feature "Swap the Old Lady for a *New Woman*" counterposes several quotations that degrade women to more positive ones. In March 1983, for example, the negative side includes an instance of Norman Mailer's hatred of women: "[He] announced in a speech: 'A little bit of rape is good for a man's soul.' He then invited 'all the feminists in the audience to please hiss.' When a number had obliged, he commented: 'Obedient little bitches'" (p. 12). Like the "No Comment" section in *Ms.* and *Savvy*'s "Facts of Life," this feature, by merely juxtaposing quotations, remains at the surface of the problem. Even this incipient criticism of sexism, however, stands in sharp contrast to the magazine's other negative portrayals of women.

In its search for a large, yet specialized readership of working women with new attitudes, *New Woman* has arrived at a successful money-making formula. Under the appearance of novelty and excitement, the up-to-date and modern, the magazine in fact assumes a safe, middle position which allows it to attract more readers than it alienates. Its pseudo-feminism appeals to a number of women who wish to be considered modern, but stops short of offending them. Its articles on psychology, diets, love relations, and self-enhancement offer numerous opportunities for voyeurism and the compelling pleasure of reading stories about others. Features on finances, investments, small businesses, and the problems working women have at home and in the office appeal to the large number of women now in the paid workforce.

New Woman's vacillation between the modern and the traditional and between feminism and negative images of women has enabled the magazine to become both a "class" and a "mass" publication.

While not a homogeneous group, the magazines directed to the growing number of women working outside the home all aim to earn high advertising revenues by attracting "class" rather than "mass" audiences, or at least a combination of the two. Ostensibly more modern than the seven sisters, the new magazines for working women often present traditional messages beneath the veneer of modernity. The elite readers of *Newsweek Woman*, for example, are encouraged to learn about world news only if they simultaneously view gender-segregated advertising that emphasizes their traditional role as consumers. Although *Working Mother* makes significant ideological adaptations for the times, it nonetheless presents a glamorized, commodity-based ideal of the working mother which interacts dialectically with articles about readers' concrete, daily-life problems. Often, the traditional ideology disguised beneath the modern in these publications reaches women from different social classes; while the magazines in this group can guarantee advertisers a number of upscale consumers, less-monied women also read several of these publications, participating in the dreams of elite consumption that constitute each magazine's ideal image of the future self.

8 Reaching Minority Women: Language, Culture, and Politics in the Service of Consumerism

Glossy magazines for minority women are not available on all news-stands. With the exception of *Essence*, the successful magazine for Black women, most of these publications are difficult to find outside areas with large minority populations. These magazines are important, however, because they reach a substantial, growing sector with consumerist messages that are ostensibly personalized with the specific cultural heritage of minority groups. By harnessing selected elements of Black and Latino culture to a glamorized presentation of consumer goods, the magazines try to become lucrative enterprises through convincing readers to buy more. As a result, their commercial messages sometimes conflict with the positive elements of ethnic and racial pride they present.

The two principal English-language magazines for minority women, *Essence* and *Latina* (the latter founded in 1982 by Chicana women in Los Angeles), continue the heritage of the struggles of the Black and Chicano Movements of the 1960s and 1970s. To succeed financially, however, the publishers must sell advertising space, and both magazines include advertising messages that undercut the progressive ideas presented in the editorial material. In contrast, the major group of Spanish-language magazines read by Latina women in the US contain only superficial elements of Latin American nationalism and instead use transnational cultural models to sell products for advertisers. Owned by a Miami firm which publishes women's magazines throughout Latin America, the principal Spanish-language magazines sold in the US serve to remind recent immigrant women of the countries they have left, and Spanish-speaking women born in the US of the culture of their forbears. The transnational consumerist messages that lie beneath the superficial trappings of Latino culture also focus on the elite experiences of the upper classes in Latin America. When purchasing an inexpensive product advertised in the magazine, then, the Spanish-speaking reader in the US can simultaneously feel that she is participating in the upper-class lifestyles presented on the editorial pages and remaining loyal to her Latin American heritage. In spite of the low wages she may be receiving, she participates briefly in the American Dream of upward mobility, while apparently, at the same time, retaining her own national culture. The Miami-based transnational publishing group and the producers of the transnational commodities the magazines advertise are the real winners.

ESSENCE: THE CONTRADICTORY CONSTELLATION OF BLACK NATIONALISM AND CONSUMERISM

The Civil Rights and Black Power Movements of the 1960s raised the political consciousness of millions of Black men and women in the US and drew national attention to Black issues. Before long, business and investment sectors began to see this large minority group as potential consumers. These two forces – Blacks' heightened consciousness of themselves as a political group and their national visibility as a potentially lucrative consumer market – combined in 1970 to enable the successful launch of *Essence*, a new magazine for Black women.

Backed by more than a million dollars in capital from the brokerage firm Shearson, Hammill & Co., the Hollingsworth Group, made up of the four Black businessmen who held the executive positions at the new magazine, previewed *Essence* with a dummy issue in February 1970. Besides this strong financial backing, *Essence* had received support from other media corporations such as Time Inc. which loaned six full-time executives. Aiming for the 18- to 34-year-old women's service market, the magazine hoped to attract the substantial non-white readership of the seven sisters; at the time, *Good Housekeeping*, *Ladies' Home Journal* and *McCall's* each had over one million minority readers. *Essence* hoped to distinguish itself from the usual service magazines by including articles on Black heritage and folklore. Publisher Jonathan Blount promised advertisers that the new *Essence* reader would buy products; he described her as: "the young, inquisitive, *acquisitive* black woman" (my emphasis).[1] These dual concerns of Black nationalism and consumerism became the poles of a constellation of contradictions that *Essence* continues to offer readers each month.

As is usually the case, advertisers were slow to purchase space in an untried medium. The first issue ran fifteen ad pages, while the second and third had only five each. Circulation was good, however, and *Essence* increased its press run to 220,000 in August 1970. The magazine announced that its ad pages would be up 60 per cent in the first quarter of 1972, arguing that it had begun to attract airline, automobile, and tourist-board advertising.[2]

The successful start of this new Black media venture was marred shortly after its first year of publication, however, by a public protest over *Playboy*'s investment in the venture. In May 1971 Jonathan Blount, the founder of *Essence*, charged that he had been dismissed as President when he alleged that *Playboy* was attempting to take over the magazine. At a press conference he gave with several staff members who had resigned in sympathy, Blount circulated photocopies of a *Playboy* inter-office memorandum written by Bob Guttwillig, *Playboy*'s representative on the *Essence* board of directors:

> I [Mr Guttwillig] am, of course continuing to advise the *Essence* staff in the areas of my competence, and we continue effectively to dominate the board of directors with what now appears to be a solid coalition of five out of seven directors.
>
> In short, it looks as if we'll get a damn good run for our money.[3]

According to Clarence Smith, who replaced Blount as President of the board of directors, *Playboy* invested $250,000 in *Essence*, controlling 10.8 per cent of the total shares. A *Playboy* spokesman called Blount's charges "absurd." Playboy Enterprises continues to be listed as a stockholder in *Essence*.[4]

In spite of this early scandal, *Essence* today has become a leading women's magazine. Its average monthly circulation in 1983 was 700,237 and its total revenues that year were $20 million; $12.3 million of this was from advertising. That year, *Essence* surpassed both *Self* and *New Woman* in its monthly averages of ad pages and ad revenue.[5]

One key to the success of this minority magazine is its appeal to diverse concerns of Black women. The covers of *Essence* often illustrate concisely the different audiences the magazine wishes to attract. In June 1982, for example, four headlines are superimposed on a photograph of an ideal Black nuclear family – mother, father, and daughter. The largest line, over the mother's head, uses the words of a popular song to reinforce the primary meaning of the photograph: "We are family!" Directly beneath the woman's image, however, is a contradictory line which allows viewers to isolate the face of the attractive model, Iman, in a secondary meaning system: "Single and satisfied!" Readers choose individual decodings of Iman's photograph in accordance with their personal desires: part of an ideal nuclear family or "single and satisfied." Regardless of marital status, heterosexual female readers are likely to be attracted by the headline beneath the man's face, "true love: The myths, the reality." Finally, the upwardly mobile are addressed with overtones of black nationalism in the lower right corner with the line: "Big money: A black folks guide to making it." The different decodings available for readers here reveal the varied audiences *Essence* seeks.

Essence consistently breaks new ground for women's magazines each month with articles on key political issues affecting the black community. "Southern shame: Local 882 on the line" (March 1981) informs readers about a long, difficult strike of black women poultry workers in Mississippi for safe working conditions. In November 1981 an interview with black judge Bruce Wright provides an excellent analysis of the inequities of the criminal justice system for blacks and whites.

Essence also informs readers about international politics that affect Blacks here. Alexis De Veaux's excellent informational pieces on such subjects as Haitian refugees (January 1983), Zimbabwe (July 1981), and Namibia and SWAPO (March 1982) are evidence that *Essence* functions as an alternative mass medium to counteract the lack of information on these topics in the mainstream media. Pointing out, for example, Namibia's proximity to South Africa and the United Nations' recognition of SWAPO as the sole representative of the Namibian people, De Veaux asks why there is so little news of SWAPO in the daily press: "Does 'the Western press' ignore SWAPO because the West supports South Africa? I want the news. What happens in Africa happens in me" (p. 168). With respect to the plight of Haitian refugees in the US, De Veaux prods readers: "Is there a 'family gap' in our politics when it comes to the Caribbean? Are reggae and West Indian food, tropic beaches and dark rum all we identify with when it comes to 'the islands'?" (p. 64).

Readers of *Essence* also learn about Black history and culture with reviews of books such as Angela Davis' *Women, Race & Class* and Barbara Christian's *Black Women Novelists* as well as excerpts from the fiction and poetry of other Black writers. A December 1983 article entitled "Celebrating Kwanza" encourages readers to renew their African cultural heritage by developing Black traditions for Christmas. In August 1983 "Travel tale" describes a family train vacation that traces Black-American historical sites. "Stokely Carmichael: Ready for the revolution" in November 1983 teaches readers about the more recent Black history of the 1960s and provides information on the current political activities of Carmichael and his organization.

The abundance of such articles shows that, in contrast to most women's magazines, *Essence* tries to educate readers about political and cultural issues in addition to teaching them to be good consumers. The magazine's dependence on advertising (ad revenues constituted $10 million of its $17 million total earnings in 1982) is the material base of the contradictory constellation of images in the magazine each month. The numerous messages of Black liberation, education and politicization often come into conflict with the magazine's attractive images of consumerism.

Haircare products, for instance, are an important advertising category in *Essence*. In December 1982 20.8 per cent of its ad pages were for hair products; in December 1983 13.6 per cent were. These ads include hair dyes, relaxers, permanents, activators, shampoos, wigs, and gels, often encouraging readers to pursue white ideals of beauty. Although the Black community purchases these products, such ads often conflict with *Essence*'s progressive editorial material which encourages Black liberation and self-confidence. This contradiction is especially striking in the August 1983 issue when a poem by June Jordan critical of excessive treatment of hair appears above an ad for "Just So Curl Activator." Two pages before the poem, "Sir Hair Food" is advertised and two pages after is an ad for "Class Curl." Reading Jordan's poem[6] in close proximity to these ads immerses readers in a confusing constellation of opposing messages.

Paralleling the Black nationalism developed in the editorial sections, almost every ad in *Essence* uses black models. These images offer readers both positive and negative self-reflection.

Here Black nationalism serves consumerism rather than political liberation; the ads encourage Black pride so that readers will buy more. These images of Black consumerism frequently echo the stereotypical and degrading portrayals of women in other women's magazines. The fragmented image of a woman and an explicit male surveyor, for example, are repeated in an ad for Aviance Night Musk (July 1983, p. 53) as they appear in the white version of the ad (see Chapter 4). The "Gentlemen prefer Hanes" ad (December 1983, p. 66) uses black models to encourage competition between women and their visual reification as does its white counterpart.

Occasionally an ad offers readers a positive self-image. The Black Owned Communications Alliance ran an ad in March 1982 showing a Black child dressed as Superman, looking in a mirror only to see the image of a white Superman. "What's wrong with this picture?" the ad asks. "Plenty, if the child is Black and can't even *imagine* a hero the same color he or she is" (p. 159). The text of the ad urges support for black media so that children can see Black people "doing positive things besides playing basketball and singing songs." One wishes that *Essence* itself would take this advice and portray the Black women in its ads more positively. Like *Ms.*, *Essence* is a magazine that has set higher standards for itself than do other publications and has much to live up to.

The front cover, as we have seen, the most important ad in a magazine, positions readers with respect to what will follow inside. *Essence* shows more variety than other fashion and beauty magazines by picturing families and men in addition to the usual image of a glamorous woman's face. Like other women's magazines, however, *Essence* presents fictional images on its covers rather than photos of the important historical and political figures, writers and leaders who appear in the articles inside. This choice of fantasy figures establishes a context in which the positive articles will be read. As the first images readers come into contact with, these fictive motifs of glamor set the agenda for the magazine's presentation of Black ideals. Were *Essence* also to publish on the cover appealing photos of the black intellectuals and leaders it discusses inside, it would help to shape readers' tastes and values. Documentary cover images would also help to reduce the constellation of contradictions *Essence* presents.

The model Iman has appeared several times on *Essence*'s cover as a symbol of ideal beauty. A September 1983 article "Spotlight: Iman!" reifies the Somalian model as a "million dollar face." We are told that her first thought as she saw that her taxi was about to be involved in a collision was "God – my face" (p. 65). The article recounts Iman's rapid recovery and is accompanied by a large photo of the model in a seductive pose by Francesco Scavullo, who often photographs *Cosmopolitan*'s cover models. Behind such a glamorous image of Iman, are the material conditions revealed in a different publication, when another of Iman's photographers, Norman Parkinson, offers a sense of what Iman is subjected to in a photo session:

> "I have a passion for the opposite sex. One knows the way their *muscles* work. I suppose you could say that's how I came to get involved as I did, with breeding race horses."
>
> Parkinson stood behind his camera and talked Iman into position. Her back was against the sculpture, with its curls and axelike blades of rusting steel. "Knee up, darling . . . Fingers like spikes. Very *spiky* chicken . . . Shoulders back. Head down. We don't want to lose an inch of that neck.[7]

Both the glamorous cover images of Iman and the article that presents the model as a woman whose first concern in a possibly life-threatening accident is her face serve to distract readers from the reification Iman undergoes in photo sessions like the one described here.

The images of glamor based on white standards of beauty that predominate in the ads in *Essence*, along with cover photos that valorize fictive models of the future self, overwhelm the progressive political articles in *Essence*. The result is a constellation of contradictions within which the readers are asked to vacillate. *Essence* has developed this system of contradictions because of both its roots in the heightened Black consciousness of the 1960s and the necessary ties of a profit-making magazine venture to consumerism. While *Essence* offers women many more important political messages than most other women's magazines, the contradictory system it creates with these negative images of Black women misdirects readers.

LATINA: THE FINANCIAL CONSTRAINTS OF LAUNCHING A NEW MAGAZINE

In early 1982 two Chicanas in Los Angeles undertook a monumental project. Without the backing of a major publishing corporation, Grace Soto and Virginia Maese decided to start on their own a magazine for English-speaking Latina women in the US, a neglected yet monied market in Soto and Maese's view and one severely underrepresented in the mainstream media. The glossy magazine was to be patterned on the success of publications aimed at Blacks, such as *Essence* and *Ebony*, and was subtitled "the bilingual bicultural magazine for the changing American woman." Operating on a skeleton budget of $20,000, the women released the premiere issue in fall 1982; the press-run of 25,000 was distributed only in California, primarily in East Los Angeles, an area with a large Mexican-American population. The second issue appeared in February 1983 and had a broader national distribution throughout the southwest and in other areas with large Latino populations such as New York, Chicago, and Florida. The magazine's only chance for success was to become a "women's advertising magazine," capable of attracting sufficient advertising revenue to pay the bills. Ironically, however, the difficulty *Latina* has had in securing advertisers allowed it to publish a greater amount and wider variety of editorial material than do most other women's magazines.

Latina's ad volume in the first two issues was extremely low. The Fall issue had 9.2 ad pages and 64 editorial pages and the February/March issue had 12.6 ad pages and 94 editorial pages – the reverse of the usual ratio of two-thirds advertising to one-third editorial material of most women's magazines. Among the few four-color advertisers *Latina* attracted were Max Factor, Pacific Telephone, McDonald's, and Coors. *Latina*'s editors blamed the low $10,000 in advertising revenue in the first issue on advertisers' lack of knowledge of the Latino market. In fact, they argued, "the bilingual bicultural segment, not the Spanish-speaking only segment, accounts for more than 50% of the $18 billion in consumer goods purchased by Mexican Americans."[8]

The rich editorial mixture that the lack of advertisers facilitates addresses various cultural interests of Latina women. Far from a homogeneous group, the audience must be reached through features as varied as a regular column on psychic palm reading and critical exposés of stereotypical portrayals of Latinos in the media. Articles on family concerns such as "Parenting: Four families' stories" appear along with such features as "Bachelor of the Month" and the tear-out centerfold of a fully-clothed male celebrity. A number of progressive political and feminist pieces are published, but the magazine also includes sexist portrayals of women. Overall, however, *Latina*, in the words of Grace Soto, tries to portray "Latinas and Latinos . . . in a positive and truly reflective light" (Fall 1982).

Several features inform readers about their political rights and the advances Latinos have made. In the column "And Justice For All," a Chicano lawyer answers readers' questions about problems such as sexual harassment on the job, non-payment of alimony, and tenant eviction. In a lengthy exposé, Jesús Hernández reports on the police killing of a Latino at a baseball game in a Pasadena park in August 1982. "Red light district," a hardhitting piece in the Fall 1982 issue, recounts the story of a 17-year-old prostitute in San Salvador, encouraging readers' solidarity with women in Latin America. Another of *Latina*'s political concerns surfaces in its regular articles about the media's stereotypical portrayal of Latinos and the effects of the media on children.

Along with these political articles appear a number of literary pieces and reviews intended to keep readers informed of current Latino issues and culture. One poem, "Our Lady of the Angels has no papers" (Fall 1982), protests the INS raids against undocumented workers in Los Angeles under the program "Operation Jobs." A review by Martha P. Cotera of Richard Rodríguez's *Hunger of Memory* (Fall 1982) criticizes the media's excess attention to the book: "By rejecting his Latino cultural values, [Rodríguez] deprived himself of the tools that would have helped overcome the alienation he suffered in the natural clash between home and school" (p. 27).

The magazine also publishes articles on more popular forms of Latino culture. Several features give instructions for preparing traditional meals. Religious beliefs surface when the editors print on page one of the first issue, the single headline, "Thank you God for this miracle." In the February/March issue another message reads "Thanks again Lord!" this time accompanying the picture of a home altar, common in some Latino households, in which elements of everyday life such as a trophy, a jar of Vicks

VapoRub, a cassette tape, and a religious statue stand before a portrait of Christ (p. 75). These examples of traditional Latino culture appear along with modern cultural concerns – reviews of Latino music, a "Bachelor of the Month" feature and a centerfold on single Latino men. In the Fall 1982 issue the bachelor encourages readers to be concerned about their physical appearance: "You can tell a lot about the way a woman is by the way she dresses. For example, if she is imaginative in the way she puts 'her look' together, she will be imaginative with me" (p. 13).

A palmreader's column prints answers to readers' questions and analyzes xeroxed copies of their palms. To a reader whose mother is against his/her enlisting in the military, the columnist responds: "I perceive from your photograph that any association with the armed forces would surely put your life in jeopardy. The reason being that you are prone to accidents with firearms and you are in imminent danger of losing your life by a firearm." Listing the columnist as Bertha Benedict, PhD, the magazine imparts an aura of authority to the psychic's prognostications, encouraging readers to cultivate a belief in the supernatural and the scientifically unverifiable. Benedict also wrote the horoscope for the first issue of *Latina*, in which she promotes travel and offers readers financial advice. Much of this advice consists of euphemisms for spending, which, as occurs in other women's magazines, will make *Latina*'s readers more attractive to potential advertisers.

In addition to these elements of popular culture that appeal particularly to Latinos, the magazine publishes several features with a more mass cultural base. Topics such as weight reduction, fashion, haircare, and eye make-up, which the media have helped to develop into traditional women's concerns, are given some editorial space in *Latina*. These features often have a Latino slant: "A Vidal Sassoon Salon make-over for La Rubia and La Morenita" (February/March 1983), for example, recounts the beauty makeovers of a blonde mother and her dark-haired daughter. "Esteban Luna sweater line" (Fall 1982, pp. 17ff) features the fashion of Mexican designer Luna and encourages women to be sex-objects with phrases such as "This sexy two piece knit plunges . . . simply starting a casual affair"; "This little number . . . is just plain sassy and sexy" and "This khaki, almost see-through knit sweater shows just enough to. . . ."

Most of the beauty and fashion features in *Latina*, however, while similar to those in traditional women's magazines, present a Latino perspective in order to appeal to the specific audience the Editors seek.

Although the founders of *Latina* have not yet published a women's magazine in which the editorial content is strongly shaped by advertising, their ultimate goal is, in fact, to publish a "women's advertising magazine." The Editors are aware of the contradiction between their desire to offer Latina women a rich, diverse editorial mixture that will appeal to the specific cultural needs of the Latino community and their own need to shape editorial content so that it attracts advertisers.[9] Already, in the second issue, Soto and Maese urge readers to complete a marketing survey and offer a subscription discount to those who do. Noting that "this information is very important to us and our potential advertisers" (February/March 1983, p. 6), the Editors argue that completing the survey will mean that Latinas "refuse to remain invisible any longer" (p. 92). Here, however, visibility only means that women are defined once again as consumers. Readers are asked about their income, education, credit cards and the brand names of the products they buy. *Latina*'s expressed goal of fighting against the invisibility of Latina women in the media is conflated with the magazine's need to obtain advertising revenue to survive. Under the guise of making Latinas visible, the magazine in fact asks them to become more visible as consumers. This is the dilemma of the women's advertising magazine today: messages about women's liberation and advancement are ultimately subordinated to financial exigencies.

SPANISH-LANGUAGE MAGAZINES AND LATINA WOMEN IN THE UNITED STATES

Although Spanish-speaking women are not as large a minority in the US as are Black women, a greater number of magazines exist for Latinas. Because of the continued immigration from Latin America, a growing number of women in the US are more comfortable with Spanish than English. While many Black women read the mainstream English-language women's publications because of the paucity of Black-oriented magazines,[10] women more at home in Spanish than English have available a large number of glossy magazines in their own language. The principal corporation behind these publications, the Miami-based De Armas Group, currently markets eleven magazines for Spanish-speaking women.

In comparison to other magazine audiences, however, the Spanish-speaking population is relatively small. According to the 1980 census, men and women who speak Spanish at home comprise only 5 per cent of the US population, or 11 million people, of whom only about one-fourth do not speak English well.[11] Most of the 76 per cent of Latinos in the US fluent in English buy English-language magazines. In addition, although the potential audience of women in the US who prefer Spanish is over one million, in fact not all of these women are attracted to the Spanish-language publications. De Armas' own figures show that the US circulations of its three main women's magazines range from 16,000 to 36,000.[12] How is it, then, that such a large number of magazines can be profitably published for this relatively small audience?

While it is true that this is the era of specialized publications aimed at "class" rather than "mass" audiences, the success of the De Armas Group is instead due to the company marketing numerous editions of these women's magazines throughout Latin America. The editorial material for each of the eleven magazines is prepared in Florida and sent to Latin American countries on film negatives, with vacant space for each country to add its own advertisements. A magazine such as *Vanidades* (Vanities), for example, has ten separate advertising editions for Mexico, Venezuela, Puerto Rico, the Dominican Republic, Colombia, Central America, Ecuador, Peru, Chile, and the US.[13] The relatively small US Spanish-speaking readership is in fact an extra source of revenue earned from an editorial product that has already been prepared for use throughout Latin America. While only sustaining the cost of a single editorial preparation, De Armas sells space to a greater number of advertisers than would normally fill one issue of a magazine. The company can afford to market eleven magazines for the relatively small group of Spanish-speaking women in the US because the main expenses of editorial preparation have already been met.

The Miami-based Editorial América and its parent corporation De Armas Publications, one of the largest Spanish-language publishing empires in the world, dates from shortly after the 1959 Cuban Revolution. Establishing a small distribution company in Miami with other Cuban exiles, Armando De Armas soon thereafter purchased the well-known women's magazine *Vanidades* which had been left without a base of operations after the Cuban Revolution. With licenses from the Hearst Corporation, De Armas then launched *Buenhogar*, a spin-off of *Good Housekeeping*, in 1966 and *Cosmopolitan en español* in 1973. Today the company publishes fifteen magazines, the majority of which are addressed to women. Among them are *Tu* (You) and *Coqueta* (Coquette) for young girls and teens, *Fascinación* (Fascination) and *Activa* (Active Woman) addressed to working women, a Spanish-language version of *Bazaar*, and *Ideas para su hogar* (Ideas for Your Home), a service magazine.[14]

Besides these publications from Miami, Latina women in the US read *Claudia* and *Vogue*, two magazines published in Mexico and exported here. First published in 1965, *Claudia* is now owned by Editorial Mex-Ameris, publisher of other mass circulation magazines in Mexico such as *Rutas de pasión* (Ways of Passion), *Ultima moda* (The Latest Fashion), and *Novelas de amor* (Love Stories). Maintaining a controlling interest in both Mex-Ameris and *Claudia* is the O'Farrill family, also a principal stockholder of the Mexican television monopoly Televisa and owner of the newspaper *Novedades* and several radio stations.[15] Under license from Conde Nast, the Spanish version of *Vogue* is edited in the Mex-Ameris building in Mexico City. Earlier, Rómulo O'Farrill was connected as well with *Tu* and *Activa*, magazines now owned by De Armas; Provenemex, the company that launched these publications is also owned by Televisa. In 1977 Provenemex started a third glossy women's magazine, *Buena vida* (Good Living), also exported to the US.[16]

Spanish-language women's magazines in the US, then, belong to two principal media monopolies. Most are published by the Miami-based De Armas Group, while three belong to the O'Farrill family. The lack of diverse ownership of these publications has profound effects on their content. Two Latin American sociologists, Viviana Erazo and Adriana Santa Cruz have argued that De Armas' publications in Latin America are prime examples of "transnational women's magazines," publications edited outside the countries in which they are distributed, and owned along with several other magazines by a single group. Further, much of the advertising and editorial content in these magazines transcends national borders. In their study of twenty-seven women's magazines in Latin America, Santa Cruz and Erazo found that an average of 60 per cent of the ads promoted transnational products; Mexican women's magazines had even higher percentages; *Buenhogar* averaged 82 per cent of its ads for foreign products, *Claudia* 78 per cent and *Vanidades* and *Cosmopolitan de México* each had 75 per cent. This transnational ownership and content, the two critics contend, results in the promotion of a transnational feminine ideal.[17]

When these magazines are then distributed to Spanish-speaking women in the US, the transnational cultural models address still another audience. Beneath the guise of national culture – Latin American language, customs, and tastes – the US editions of these magazines in fact promote transnational products, helping to integrate Latina women into the US consumer society. One study, conducted by Russell Marketing Research for De Armas found that only between 1 and 5 per cent of respondents read other English-language women's magazines including the seven sisters and the fashion and beauty publications.[18] Spanish-language women's magazines, then, play an important role in socializing this group of women to become good consumers. Whether urged to buy transnational products in Mexican magazines exported to this country or in special US advertising editions of the De Armas publications, Spanish-speaking women are offered models of an ideal female consumer beneath the thin veneer of their own language and culture.

Claudia, the principal Mexican-owned magazine that Spanish-speaking women in the US read, is a good example of these ideal models of consumption. First published in Mexico in 1965 with Mexican and Argentinian capital, *Claudia* was also distributed in Brazil and Argentina. As we have seen, Santa Cruz and Erazo's findings show that 78 per cent of the ads in the Mexican edition of *Claudia* are for transnational products and, in addition, the magazine has a very high advertising-to-editorial ratio: with 54 per cent of its pages containing purchased ads and 18 per cent covert advertising, only 28 per cent of the magazine is free of advertising.[19]

Claudia promotes consumption of transnational products

through an especially frequent use of covert advertising, in spite of the following notice on the table of contents page in each issue: "*Claudia* does not permit editorial advertising. The mention of prices, products, brands or well-known firms is to provide a service for readers and implies no responsibility." On cover two of the August 1982 issue, for example, an ad for Miss Clairol hair dye pictures the Mexican star María Félix and uses her signed testimony to endorse the product which is also promoted on page 74 of the issue by a "publireportaje" (advertorial) that likewise features Félix and her testimony for the product. Often *Claudia* publishes articles about television stars and programs broadcast by the Mexican TV monopoly Televisa, whose principal stockholders include the O'Farrill family.[20]

Claudia's editorial sections further support elitist ideals of consumption. Along with the usual consumerism that most women's magazines encourage in their fashion, beauty, decorating, and food features, *Claudia* promotes what might be termed a fashionable consumption of culture. Through monthly features on general-interest topics such as history, art, dance and occasionally world events, the publication encourages a sense of cultural elitism in readers. (The magazine's relatively small circulation in Mexico of 101,350 adds to this aura of cultural privilege). *Claudia* suggests to readers that consumption of the latest poetry and art ideally occurs together with purchases of the latest fashion and beauty aids. Latinos in the US who read this imported publication can also partake in its sense of cultural privilege, at the same time that they learn to consume the numerous transnational products advertised both covertly and overtly inside.

Let us examine more closely now several of the eleven De Armas women's publications – magazines whose editorial material is prepared first with Latin American audiences in mind and then distributed as separate advertising editions in the US. The three principal De Armas women's magazines, *Vanidades*, *Buenhogar*, and *Cosmopolitan en espanõl*, are indirectly supported by a publication for the teenage audience, *Tu*, which not only sells products to Spanish-speaking teenage girls but prepares them to become faithful readers of the other De Armas publications later.

TU: THE DEVELOPMENT OF YOUNG CONSUMERS AND FUTURE MAGAZINE READERS

The De Armas Group began its search for Spanish-speaking teenage spenders in the US in July 1981 with the first issue of *Tu*. The magazine had been successfully launched in Mexico a year and a half earlier by Provenemex, a Mexican publisher of magazines and comic books, owned, as we have seen, by the consortium that controls Mexico's television monopoly. Now De Armas would distribute *Tu* in the US offering advertisers access to the Spanish-speaking equivalent of the teenage girls who read *Young Miss*, *'Teen*, and *Seventeen*.

In its first two years in the US, however, *Tu* attracted few advertisers. While the October 1982 edition in Mexico sold 35 ad pages, for example, the US edition that month sold only one page, although it ran six ad pages for other publications De Armas distributes. Only a handful of advertisers purchased space in the US *Tu* in its first two years here, among them Maybelline, Max Factor, and Myrugia. Nonetheless, unlike most new magazine ventures which fail because of such limited advertising volume, *Tu* offers De Armas advantages in spite of its early inability to secure ads. With the Mexican edition paying for most of the costs of editorial production, the unsold ad pages in the US *Tu* are used to advertise other De Armas publications. In addition, the editorial features help to develop consumerist tastes in young readers who will then be more attractive to advertisers in the future.

The magazine's bright colors, childish graphics and design, numerous exclamation points, and overall editorial tone are a first indication of the young audience it addresses. Another is the monthly column, "Direct Line" in which teenage readers, some as young as 12, solicit pen pals. Among the finalists of a contest for readers to be the magazine's cover girl (February 1982), are a childish-looking 11-year-old from Colombia and a 13-year-old from Chile. Like *Young Miss* and *'Teen*, *Tu* reaches girls at an early age with messages of consumerism and proper socialization.

As do the English-language magazines for teenage girls, *Tu* publishes advice columns to answer questions about beauty, physical appearance, appropriate products, and correct female behavior: "My waist is a horror! Help me to reduce it, please"

(October 1982, p. 7); "What kind of purse should I buy to go with a very elegant bone-colored evening dress?" (September 1982, p. 7); "My boyfriend loves lamb, and I'd like to make him a prize-winning dish. Can you help me?" (March 1983, p. 9); "A group of girls from school wants to organize a fundraising activity to help a charity organization. What ideas can you suggest?" (May 1983, p. 6). The advice in this column educates girls about their expected social roles, from concern with physical appearance and commodity consumption, to meal preparation and charity work.

The beauty articles each month induce insecurities and guilt and promote products to remedy these. Like their English-language counterparts, they use an upbeat tone in prose and graphics to create a sense of excitement. We see this pattern of blame, the commodity solution, and upbeat language in the title of one beauty feature in the September 1982 issue, "Did you abandon your face? Rescue it! Super face-saving techniques." The fashion features, like those in *Young Miss* and *'Teen*, portray models in childish, playful poses. Also like *Young Miss*, *Tu* publishes a monthly advice column written by a man, "Between You and Me." The appearance of intimacy between the columnist and readers implicit in the title adds a sugarcoating to the voice of male authority that shapes young girls' socialization here. In December 1981 the column began, "Girls who know how to recognize their errors fascinate me" (p. 50) linking self-deprecation to male affection.

The young readers of *Tu* receive contradictory messages from the magazine: they are to remain childish yet learn to be properly socialized adults at the same time. In fact, however, beneath the childish format and style, *Tu* intensifies the insecurities of young adolescents instead of encouraging readers to strive for the self-acceptance of mature, assured women. The March 1983 cover asks prospective readers, "[Do you have a] pale face, frog's skin and witch's hair? Protect your beauty!"

Self-criticism serves as a bridge between childhood and adulthood, two poles between which *Tu* continuously asks readers to vacillate. Self-scrutiny teaches traditional female sex-roles in a February 1982 feature, "What kind of a girl friend are you? How will you be as a wife?". In order to be happily married later, the article tells readers, they must begin to remedy their defects now. Conflicting messages of adulthood and childhood continuously interact in *Tu*. One headline on the front cover of the December 1981 issue uses childish phrasing to direct readers to act adult-like: "Leave the baby bottle behind! You're not such a little girl any more!" Directly above it, however, is the childish line, "Dolls for New Year's Eve! Sam Jones, Sly Stone, Mark Hamill, Guauu!" As we have seen, magazines for adult women continue to urge women contradictorily to be childish and adult at the same time. Readers of a magazine such as *Tu* are not only learning proper female sex roles through these opposing poles but to develop a taste for images that portray women childishly – a taste that will help to attract them in the future to other women's magazines.

Unlike its English-language counterparts, however, *Tu* devotes numerous pages each month to celebrities and stars. Many of them are young male entertainers, about whom readers are encouraged to cultivate romantic fantasies. Other celebrity features present female role models such as Brooke Shields, Priscilla Presley, and Princess Caroline, and claim to reveal the personal secrets of famous people. In addition to these full-color articles, *Tu* publishes a newsprint section about celebrities and jet-setters called "Gossip"; here the magazine develops young readers' taste, helping to prepare them to enjoy in the future a similar feature entitled "Faces" in *Vanidades*. The primary content of both features consists of photos and sensationalistic tidbits of information about international (usually non-Latin American) celebrities. As García Calderón has noted in her study of Mexican women's magazines, such features on the jet set present the "beautiful people" as imitable. Readers are told that by acquiring objects, they can temporarily possess the enchantment of the jet set. However, the lifestyle of celebrities is also unattainable for most readers, García notes, so magazines often portray the famous as unhappy and suffering.[21] *Tu*, for example, frequently presents Princess Caroline of Monaco and her sister Stephanie as difficult children who create problems for their parents. We read of Jon Voight's gambling losses and Lynda Carter's sense of being a prisoner in her marriage. The articles allow us to dream, yet ultimately remind us to be content with our own social position.

Tu places itself within the Latin American tradition of women's magazines with its features on travel and food. Colorful photographs entice readers to expensive tourist spots such as

Jamaica, Acapulco, Hawaii, Austria, and Greece. Although these vacations are out of the financial reach of most teenage readers, the travel features align readers' fantasies with mainstream tourist locations – resorts that are also the subject of travel articles in De Armas' other Spanish-language magazines. The food features are similar in format to those in *Vanidades* and *Buenhogar*, yet offer less complicated recipes and often suggest that correctly prepared food will win male affection. Headlines such as "Catch him with this little dish" and "The way to conquer him!" attract readers' attention to a recipe feature in May 1983 (p. 7). One February 1983 feature, "Love is . . . pleasing him always," begins: "Invite him to dinner – or breakfast – and be eager to wait on him. Strive for excellence in decorating your table. Take care of every detail. Show him your love by pleasing him. Serve him your favorite meal. . . . Give him a prince's treatment!" (p. 73). Like *Seventeen*, *Tu* schools young girls in expected wifely skills such as cooking, home decoration, and crafts. In style and format, however, these features utilize the traditions of Latin American women's magazines.

The "complete mini-novel" in *Tu* prepares readers to be future consumers of similar romance fiction in Spanish-language women's magazines. "The other woman returned" in November 1982 encourages competitive feelings between women with its preview line: "An interesting encounter. A rapid wedding. And barely newlyweds, the intrusion of an ex-girlfriend tarnished the happiness of the couple. It was up to him to prevent his marriage from failing" (p. 92). The accompanying drawing shows a distraught woman biting her nails, pulling her hair, and yelling "grrr!" presumably because of the other woman's return. "Fleeting marriage" in the October 1982 issue begins with a preview line typical of much romance fiction. "They accused Monica Reizola of wanting to marry a wealthy aristocrat who could be her father. Her worst enemy is his son. In an atmosphere heavy with adverse criticism, the climax rapidly approaches. How could Monica rebuild her life after being a victim of misfortune?" (p. 92). Ultimately marriage triumphs in this story, allowing readers to cultivate dreams that conflate upward social mobility and love. These mini-novels are an easily read introduction to the genre for young Spanish-speaking girls. The taste for romance fiction developed here will lead them to buy other magazines later, as well as the Spanish-language Harlequin-type romance books advertised in *Tu* and sometimes given away free with the magazine as a promotion at newsstands.

Besides the exclusive use of Spanish throughout the magazine, then, features such as the gossip columns, travel pieces, food articles and romance fiction add the appearance of Latin American culture to this publication. The ostensible Latin American characteristics of *Tu* perhaps remind young Latina women in the US of the countries from which they or their families have migrated. This outward use of Latin American culture, however, only thinly masks the deeply rooted transnational culture of consumerism that pervades the magazine. Although the extensive features on stars and celebrities, for example, follow the cultural model of Latin American women's magazines rather than North American ones, these features emphasize US and European figures.

Even though it sells so few ads, the US edition of *Tu* promotes transnational consumerism because the magazine is modeled on the editorial formulas that De Armas developed early on in *Vanidades*. With a few minor exceptions, the editorial pages of *Tu* remain the same whether they appear in the Mexican edition which sells many ad pages or the US edition which sells only a few. De Armas' cultural model for women's magazines continues intact, although Spanish-speaking women here are likely to interpret it differently by virtue of their distinct cultural surroundings. However, while the mixture of Latin American and US cultural traditions in *Tu* is attractive to many young girls in Latin America, it may be unenticing to Spanish-speaking teens in the US. It remains to be seen whether the De Armas US edition of *Tu* will succeed in gaining a large enough group of readers to attract more advertisers. Without this advertising revenue to make the US venture profitable, the De Armas Group will have to be content with the magazine's current, more indirect role in profit-making: developing consumerist desires in young Spanish-speaking women in the US and influencing their cultural taste toward the company's other Spanish-language publications.

VANIDADES: TRANSNATIONAL CELEBRITIES AND ELITE IMAGES OF CONSUMPTION

For years *Vanidades* has presented itself as a general-interest magazine for women. Promoting the image that it is not merely a homemakers' or a fashion magazine, *Vanidades* includes features on "Psychology," "The Arts," and "Celebrities." A special section in each issue called "The Newspaper" claims to present "what's behind the news . . ." (12 July 1981, p. 67). But *Vanidades'* general-interest topics in fact reproduce many of the trivial themes that have traditionally distracted women from important political issues and critical thinking. One article under the "Psychology" heading, for example, "The truth about lying," tells readers that actors, painters, writers, musicians and others in creative professions have an innate tendency to lie (20 January 1981). Under the heading "Reports" (21 July 1981) another piece claims to study the existence of life after death. "The Newspaper" usually includes only a few international news items and these present "soft news"; most of the section focuses on such topics as medicine, women in the news, and celebrities, which appear along with quizzes such as "Are you sensual?" and romance fiction by the popular writer Corín Tellado.

The trivial nature of most of these so-called news items became especially apparent in 1982 when the section was renamed "Faces." The retitled feature is the logical extension of its predecessor: where the previous section contained a variety of soft news, the new version focuses only on entertainment stars and members of the "jet set." Stories about figures such as Princess Caroline, Brooke Shields, and Jaclyn Smith now replace the few "news" items that previously appeared on topics such as the Nobel Prize, the wedding of New York Governor Hugh Carey, or the *Washington Post* reporter who won a Pulitzer Prize for an invented news story.

Even when *Vanidades* claimed to broaden its readers' interests, it in fact limited readers by presenting trivial themes as if they were international news. When *Vanidades* premiered its "new 1982 image" in January of that year, many of the magazine's traditional features were merely given a new appearance. One section, "Women on the Front Page" was moved to the front of each issue so that readers, in the Editor's words, could "rapidly discover what the dynamic, contemporary woman is doing in different parts of the world" (p. 4). Directly following a feature about movie stars and using similar graphics and design, "Women on the Front Page" appears to be a continuation of the feature on the stars. And like most of the features on celebrities, it emphasizes US and European figures instead of Latin American ones. When Latin American cultural figures do appear, they are members of the elite rather than popular classes. A letter from a Colombian reader (3 March 1982) asks that more interviews with Latin American celebrities be published, pointing to a serious contradiction in *Vanidades*; although transnational commercial messages appear to be presented through Latin American cultural images, these messages in fact often use European and US cultural models. Latin American language, customs and tastes are only a thin veneer covering transnational models of success, stardom, and beauty. A figure such as Princess Caroline of Monaco, for example, who appears frequently in *Vanidades* while only rarely in US women's magazines, has virtually come to be considered a part of Latin American culture, so frequently is she represented in Latin American women's magazines.

Both in its previous and updated forms, *Vanidades* presents elite culture and consumer goods as if they were within the reach of all its readers. The arts section opening each issue focuses on expensive cultural forms such as the opera, ballet, theatre, hardcover books, and valuable art collections. Another regular feature, "The Decorator's Workshop" presupposes the comfortable economic position of an ideal reader with such titles as "The Importance of the second floor," "Adapt the terrace to your lifestyle" (20 January 1981), and "A house with a tropical air" (24 November 1981). This last feature pictures an elaborate house with a swimming pool, beyond the reach of many Latin American and US minority women. Recipes for elaborate, costly drinks often appear, giving editorial support to liquor advertising.[22] Both the fashion features and advertising in *Vanidades* often portray expensive designer clothing which few readers can afford; in contrast to some US fashion magazines, clothing in a medium- or low-price range is rarely shown. Travel features further uphold this sense of elitism, encouraging expensive tourism accessible only to a few.

As Michele Mattelart has shown, many of the cultural images in Latin American women's magazines present one class's experience as the norm, while failing to depict the lives of poorer classes.[23] *Vanidades'* editorial pages address an ideal reader, privileged with upper- or upper-middle-class spending power, thereby encouraging less-monied readers to feel inadequate because they are unable to consume so ostentatiously. Similar to images in US magazines such as *Bazaar* and *Vogue*, these elite messages in *Vanidades* overlay the feelings of inadequacy they invoke with the utopian pleasure of an upper-class fantasy. "Vanities," the magazine's title, has come to signify not only women's pride in personal appearance but the ostentatious display of the fashion, wealth, culture, and attainments of the upper classes. Readers from all classes are to identify with the exaggerated self-love of the elite women portrayed in *Vanidades*, vicariously defining themselves through these ideal tropes. The dream is pleasurable, allowing temporary escape from everyday work, boredom, or feelings of inadequacy.

The food features in each issue, however, offer a somewhat more attainable elite culture. Here, ordinary food is transformed into baroque displays of successful womanhood. As Roland Barthes pointed out in his essay "Ornamental cookery,"[24] such glamorous portrayals of food are intended to appear both well-designed yet casually prepared. What one knows to be precisely arranged lemon slices or watercress garnish in the lifesize pictures in *Vanidades* must look as if they were randomly strewn over the food. Yet the food is always to look elegant, carrying the aura of upper-class consumption. An "accordion cantelope" is filled with wine-soaked fruit and served on a bowl of ice (21 July 1981); stuffed peppers are named "Florentine peppers" and served with ornately garnished "Florida-style grapefruit" (3 March 1982). Unlike most of the other elite images in *Vanidades*, however, this appearance of upscale consumption is relatively attainable for some US minority women because the recipes require ordinary, average-priced ingredients. Although the elaborate meals require free time that many women who work the double day do not have, these features afford readers a relatively attainable mode of participation in elite culture in contrast to most of the other images in *Vanidades*.

THE LATIN AMERICAN *GOOD HOUSEKEEPING*: WOMEN'S SYMBOLIC ATOMIZATION INTO FACES, PSYCHES, AND KITCHENS

Adorning the covers of most issues of *Buenhogar* are two visual tropes of ideal femininity. In addition to the usual large photo of a glamorous young woman, a second, smaller photo is inset in the lower right corner showing food or handiwork that the reader can learn to make inside. Together these images present a capsule version of *Buenhogar*'s ideal Latina homemaker. Readers are to achieve the "good home" not only by decorating their residences and preparing visually pleasing meals but also by decorating themselves according to the magazine's instructions. These two cover photos are visual abbreviations that direct readers to see themselves and their households in the same terms – objects to be beautified.

Buenhogar emphasizes its role in teaching women to beautify themselves, in parallel fashion to their households, in one of its ads designed to attract new subscribers: "*Buenhogar* is more than a magazine for the homemaker. It's fashion! It's beauty! It's up-to-date!" (15 December 1981, p. 80). The magazine's interest in beautifying readers' physical appearance stems, of course, from its desire to attract cosmetics and fashion advertisers. In ideological terms, however, the magazine attempts to attain discursive closure by linking in readers' minds personal and household beauty as parts of a single cultural continuum. On the pages of *Buenhogar* the two become extensions of one another; the housewife can forego neither.

Begun in 1966 as a Spanish translation of Hearst's *Good Housekeeping*, *Buenhogar* today more closely resembles Latin American women's magazines than its US counterpart. While including some translated material such as the advice columns of Ann Landers and Dr. Joyce Brothers, the De Armas publication emphasizes such Latin American mass cultural staples as romance fiction, movie star interviews, and recipes for Latino food. Although the US cultural influence is often visible in the numerous blonde, fair-skinned models and the products and lifestyles promoted, the magazine's numerous Latin American cultural trappings provide readers with the appearance of their national cultures. Because the magazine circulates in many Latin American countries and the US where varieties of Spanish are spoken, for example, *Buenhogar*'s recipes often provide alternative terms in parentheses: "tomates (jitomates)" to indicate tomatoes, "carne de res (vacuno)" for beef or "hongos (setas, champiñones)" for mushrooms (22 September 1982, pp. 67ff). Thus, readers in different parts of Latin America and the US have a sense of a personalized mass culture designed expressly to take into account regional differences.

De Armas Publications argues to advertisers that *Buenhogar* is "conceived and edited for the modern, well-educated affluent married woman."[25] A study conducted by Russell Marketing Research, however, shows that only 6 per cent of *Buenhogar*'s US readers have graduated from college and 78 per cent have a weekly family income of under $300.[26] Of the three principal De Armas magazines, *Buenhogar* has been the least successful in amassing advertising volume. Although published bi-weekly, it sold only 92 ad pages in the US in all of 1982 and 134 in 1983. It charges only $765 for a four-color ad page and $1035 for the back cover.[27] While not as affluent as De Armas projects in its ads to advertisers, most of *Buenhogar*'s readers are married and have children. Much in the magazine directs these readers to a traditional view of marriage and a self-scrutiny that will facilitate consumerism.

A cluster of articles in one issue, for example, links love, marriage and children: "How to know if you're really in love," "How to conquer (and keep) a man through his [astrological] sign," "What men expect from marriage," "My husband wouldn't believe our daughter was his," and "Divorce and children" (15 December 1981). Framing this cluster are two regular features – a column on pregnancy and another featuring pictures that readers have sent in of their children. This group of articles and its frame encourage women to see their love relations as a continuum that includes "conquering" men, pleasing them in marriage, having children with them, proving paternity to them, and even eventual divorce from them. The arrangement of the cluster implicitly urges readers to fear the negative effects of divorce; by following the instructions in the feature on pleasing their husbands, they will avoid needing the advice given in "Divorce and children."

According to *Buenhogar*'s editorial profile, the magazine teaches the young married woman "how to improve herself, her marriage, her children and her household."[28] Again emphasizing a continuum composed of personal beauty, marriage, children, and the home, the magazine introduces a process of self-scrutiny designed to facilitate consumerism. Improvement becomes the code word to encourage this scrutiny; the status quo must always be improved upon, whether it be one's appearance, one's marriage or one's home: "No one's perfect" (18 May 1983) recommends name-brand cosmetics to remedy face flaws; and "10 Ways to improve your kitchen" (15 December 1981) advises readers to make cosmetic changes in their kitchens rather than suggesting more substantial changes in the household division of labor. Within the trope of self-scrutiny, such distinct entities as one's face, psyche and kitchen are similar objects – personal shortcomings that need improvement.

Like other forms of mass culture, *Buenhogar* has many attractive elements that entice women to read it and purchase commodities. Readers appropriate the magazine for popular ends in the "Letters" column in which they solicit help in finding lost relatives, old friends, and new pen pals. In one issue, for example, a reader from the Dominican Republic asks the magazine to publish her home address so that she can begin friendships and recipe exchanges with other readers. A Mexican woman writes with the request that readers help her to locate her uncles and grandfather who have migrated to the US and now live, she believes, somewhere in Arizona. A reader from Peru seeks someone who will offer her a job as a maid in Spain so that she and her children can return there to care for her father (27 January 1983). Through letters such as these readers have encouraged *Buenhogar* to serve their popular needs, helping to transform the magazine into a mass medium that Latinos can use to communicate with one another across continents.

In addition to the attractive features on celebrities, readers can enjoy a more mundane voyeurism in the monthly column "A Real-Life Case," a feature often translated from the American *Good Housekeeping*. Melodramatic titles such as "I was adopted by my own father" (2 June 1982), "My mother-in-law was destroying my marriage" (28 July 1982), and "My husband wouldn't believe our daughter was his" (15 December 1981) highlight these features which read like fiction yet are ostensibly true accounts. The conflation of the bizarre and the everyday in these narratives allows readers both the excitement of voyeurism and a type of self-recognition. The dual pleasure of this mundane voyeurism serves as the counterpart of the stellar voyeurism in which one participates when reading the features on celebrities.

Buenhogar's food and decorating features also link the glamorous to the everyday as a means of attracting readers. The enticing displays of perfectly prepared food are idealistic yet down-to-earth because they offer assistance in the everyday task of meal preparation: following the glossy photos of food in each issue is a newsprint section with the corresponding recipes that can be torn out and used in the kitchen. These food features offer readers a way of fulfilling everyday needs glamorously, sometimes playing on readers' psychological needs as well with titles such as "Conquer him with these delights" (27 January 1983). The sections on home decorating similarly link the everyday to the glamorous, but this time with images that are beyond the financial reach of most readers. While many readers might wish to decorate their homes attractively, few can afford the expensive New York furniture promoted here. Nonetheless, they can at least imitate these glamorous room arrangements in their own residences and achieve a minimal participation in these ideal visions of domesticity by making the crafts and handiwork for which the magazine provides instructions.

Throughout the magazine, then, the two visions of ideal womanhood pictured on the cover – the perfectly prepared meal and the perfectly adorned woman – are expanded to include a more encompassing spectrum of self-improvement. Ideal visions of personal beauty, marriage, children, household and celebrities appear together with the common everyday concerns of women who have work to do at home. This coupling of the ideal with the everyday offers readers pleasurable dreams that relate directly to real-life problems. That these ideal yet down-to-earth dreams are presented using Latin American language and culture makes them all the more attractive to Spanish-speaking women in the US.

A LATINIZED *COSMOPOLITAN* FOR THE UNITED STATES MARKET: MELDING THE TRADITIONAL WITH THE MODERN TO ATTRACT A DIVERSE AUDIENCE

Witnessing the popularity of Helen Gurley Brown's revamped *Cosmopolitan* since 1965 in the US and the success of its own

Vanidades and *Buenhogar* throughout Latin America, the De Armas Group launched a third women's magazine in 1973, a Spanish-language version of *Cosmopolitan.* The publishers gambled that certain Latin American women would be as receptive to Gurley Brown's messages of sexual liberation as women in the US had been. The premiere issue announced: "*Cosmopolitan en español* is edited for the new Latin American woman . . . [who is] capable of dealing with all types of subjects (yes, even sexual questions) without the embarrassment that has confined [her] within suffocating boundaries."[29] The mythical "Cosmo girl" thus spawned a Latin American sister, the "Chica Cosmo," who would help to integrate Latina women into transnational consumerism and at the same time encourage sales of the new De Armas publication.

The editorial material of the Spanish-language *Cosmo* suggests that the publishers primarily seek an audience of Latin American working women, readers with enough spending power to be attractive to advertisers. One monthly column, "The Cosmo Girl at Work" offers advice about getting ahead on the job. Other articles such as "Don't let them step on you in the office" (February 1981), "Learn to manipulate your boss" (October 1982), "Change jobs like a professional" (September 1982) and "Work until 6 . . . Serve dinner at 8" (April 1983) establish unrealistic expectations for working readers and are testimony to the magazine's attempt to reach employed women to increase ad volume. Often these pieces employ an idealistic optimism, suggesting that alienation and job tensions can be surmounted. Articles such as "Accelerate your promotions: How to get along well with your boss" (March 1983) encourage fantasies of upward mobility in readers who, were they indeed to attain such job promotions, would be even more attractive to *Cosmo*'s advertisers.

There is a difference, however, between the audience *Cosmopolitan* seeks in Latin America and the one it actually reaches. A Russell Marketing Research study showed that although 71 per cent of the magazine's readers work, only 43 per cent are employed full time. Most readers are single, between the ages of 18 and 34, although 11 per cent are under 18.[30] Letters to the editor published in the magazine also reveal several very young readers: an 11-year-old wrote in March 1983, 12-year-olds in September and November 1982, a 13-year-old in May 1983 and

15 to 17-year-olds in several other issues. Although *Cosmopolitan*'s Editor, Cristina Saralegui, argues that the majority of the readers "work all day outside the home . . . cook, maintain [their] home[s] beautifully and raise children" (May 1983, p. 7), the figures from Russell Marketing Research which De Armas distributed to advertisers in the early 1980s show that most readers work only part time, are single, and have no children. The discrepancies between the Editor's projections and the market surveys represent the differences between the readers the magazine desires to reach and the actual audience. The editorial pages reflect the continual interplay between the projected and actual audiences.

I have first examined the Latin American audience of the Spanish-language version of *Cosmopolitan* because the US audience is not the primary one for which the magazine is designed. The combined circulation of the seven editions in Latin America is 293,124 while the US edition has a circulation of only 32,454. Like their Latin American counterparts, the US Spanish-speaking readers are primarily between 18 and 34, but in contrast, only 3 per cent have graduated from a university. Sixty per cent work outside the home and the family income of the majority is under $200 per week. Unlike the Latin American readers, 67 per cent of US readers have children in their household and 54 per cent are married. Less affluent and educated than the readers of *Cosmopolitan* within Latin America, the US Spanish-speaking readers are not as desirable a target for advertisers. Indeed, De Armas has succeeded in selling many more advertising pages for its Mexican and Colombian editions of *Cosmopolitan* than for its US edition.[31]

Consequently, when Spanish-speaking women here open *Cosmopolitan en español*, they find an editorial product designed primarily to attract women in Latin America – not the US. The original English-language *Cosmopolitan* was modified substantially in 1973 to address women in Latin America. In a comparative study of the original English-language *Cosmopolitan* and the Mexican edition, Anna Lucía Zornosa found that although retaining several sexually explicit aspects such as the front cover, the Spanish-language version published fewer articles on sex and contraceptives, non-stereotyped jobs for women, and beauty, diet and fashion. Instead, there were many more articles in the Spanish-language edition on celebrities and stars, male and female relations, self-knowledge and self-improvement. Zornosa argues that because the average US reader has more sexual and personal freedom than the Latin American readers of *Cosmopolitan*, the magazine must modify its message for Latin American consumption. The Spanish-language edition allows women partial vicarious participation in US sexual liberation while at the same time adhering to the more traditional norms of their countries.[32]

Readers of the Spanish-language *Cosmopolitan* in the US encounter several similarities to Helen Gurley Brown's original publication. Women are reified and encouraged to view themselves as fragments in such Latin-edition articles as "How to make your mouth more kissable" (May 1983) and "Make your 'derrière' the target of all the looks" (March 1983). This last piece recommends exercises, sensual underwear, and extremely tight-fitting jeans to "show off a shapely derrière" and generalizes: "It's the physical attribute that the Latin man most admires in a woman" (p. 47).

Like the Helen Gurley Brown magazine, the Spanish-language *Cosmopolitan* both distorts and co-opts feminism. Editor Cristina Saralegui attempts to contest the criticisms of what she terms "rabid feminists" that her magazine is frivolous, places too much emphasis on women's physical appearance, and presents a superficial, foolish "Cosmo girl" as a role model. She proposes an alternative to this allegedly "rabid" feminism: women should take care of their houses and children and work outside the home "with a smile . . . without misunderstood aggressiveness, hysterical shouting or bra burning" (September 1981, p. 7). Saralegui offers an alternative definition of women's liberation: "One can be *very* feminine, a wife, a mother, work at home or outside the home, be faithful in love . . . and be liberated at the same time! To be 'liberated' means nothing more than being a *modern* woman" (January 1981, p. 7). Besides distorting feminism, the magazine co-opts it with a piece such as the August 1982 "How to be aggressive in love (without frightening men!)." Saralegui promises readers that this feature will show them "a new way to be aggressive, the *feminine* way" because men have become afraid of liberated women. This redefined feminism will pacify the fears of some Latina readers that the magazine represents a break with their traditions. At the same time, the co-optation and use of certain feminist ideas reassures readers that the magazine is modern and up-to-date.

As Chapter 5 demonstrated, the concept of the "Cosmo girl" that Hearst develops each month to promote the original magazine often attempts to link spurious cultural sophistication to consumerism. The Latin American counterpart, the "Chica Cosmo," also takes on different characteristics to suit the corresponding editorial or advertising purpose. In the April 1981 *Cosmopolitan en español*, a full-page ad uses the "Chica Cosmo" to deflect women's concern from liberation. The text, accompanying a picture of a woman dressed for a white-collar job, reads:

> I'm the *new* Cosmo Girl. . . . More than liberating myself, I seek to IMPROVE MYSELF. . . . Because I know that in this highly competitive world, only by improving myself will I achieve all my goals . . . and succeed in being treated as I deserve: an intelligent and very up-to-date woman.
>
> My magazine is *Cosmopolitan*. It's the only one that speaks my language. Cosmo helps me to be more attractive . . . to triumph on the job . . . with men . . . and above all, to know myself better every day.
>
> In every woman there's a Cosmo Girl. Don't you think it's time to awaken Yours? (p. 19).

Here, the "Cosmo girl" becomes the Latin American white-collar working woman, less concerned with liberation than with self-improvement. Aware that a number of Latina women look with disfavor on the stereotypical images of women's liberation that media such as Helen Gurley Brown's *Cosmopolitan* have helped to foster, the Spanish edition hopes to substitute the more acceptable goals of succeeding at work and with men, becoming more attractive, and improving the self. These modified goals articulate in more diverse ways with consumer purchases than do feminist goals.

In an editorial column in May 1985, Saralegui expands the concept of the "Cosmo girl" to include motherhood, again to attract Latin American women who might find the standard Cosmo girl offensive. Readers of the English-language *Cosmopolitan* might indeed be surprised to read Saralegui's remarks here: "I consider that it is *precisely* the young woman, full of hopes and the desire to struggle in life, who is most preoccupied with maintaining her beautiful 'nest' and *also* the one who has the most children (considering that after 35, doctors consider it *dangerous* to bring a baby into the world because of the accompanying risks)" (p. 7). The Editors of the De Armas publication expect this modified Cosmo girl to succeed as well with Spanish-speaking readers in the US as it does in Latin America.

While a figure such as the "Chica Cosmo" retains some characteristics of the US model and modifies others, several features in the Spanish-language magazine represent more clearly a Latinization of *Cosmopolitan*. The Editor frequently promotes travel to Latin American locales such as Cancún, Caracas, and San Juan. The monthly "Cosmo Tells All," a gossip column with photos of the international jet set, also includes news about Latin American celebrities. Often, entire articles appear on Latin American entertainment stars such as Charytin and Leonor Benedetto. The "Bachelor of the Month" column features a glamorous Latino man selected from readers' submissions.

One of the most noticeable examples of Latin American culture in the magazine is the monthly column "Letters to the Sorceress" in which readers request instructions for supernatural rites to remedy their social and emotional problems. In May 1983, for example, in response to the 46-year-old reader who asks for a spell to make her 50-year-old boyfriend come back to her, the columnist prescribes the following:

> Beneath the light of a full moon write your man's name in honey on your arms, top and bottom. Then, undulate toward the moon as if your fingers were rose petals that repeatedly open from the stems of your wrists. Finish the ritual by eating the honey from your arms, licking all the sweetness, your saliva dominating and dissolving the name. With the letters entering your body one by one, he will feel irresistibly attracted to you . . . forever (p. 98).

Another reader writes with the confused vague complaint that her sisters have given a bad reputation to their home and have turned her mother against her. The columnist offers a ritual called "The Prince of Rice: A spell to fight a bad reputation." Again, under a full moon the reader is to throw three handfuls of rice on the eldest sister, then gather the grains from the floor and place them on the belly of the figure of a man she has made from dark, fertile earth. When the rice grows and flowers, her sister will marry and this will change the reader's life. To assure that the other sisters marry she must repeat the ritual on them. The columnist then promises a fairy-tale ending: "After these weddings, you will marry. Your mother will accept your good intentions and will change, embracing you with gratitude and loving you eternally" (August 1982, p. 98).

Each month hundreds of readers write letters to this column,[33] and from those selected for publication, one senses that many of the correspondents are troubled. In each case, the columnist, Gay-Darlene Bidart, author of *La Bruja Desnuda* (The Naked Sorceress), published in Mexico, offers a few lines of amateur psychological advice before suggesting the ritual. Sometimes this advice is sound, but it is usually undercut by the accompanying ritual. Performance of the ritual, or at least the knowledge that it can be performed with little difficulty if one so chooses, disguises rather than remedies the powerlessness that many who seek advice here feel in the face of their problems. When a reader from Honduras writes that her new boss is about to fire her and her fellow workers in a personnel reorganization, the column recommends "The spell of knots for freeing oneself from a boss without losing one's job." Instead of counselling the women to organize to protect their rights, the sorceress notes: "The following spell will help you to lose the fear of being without a job, and to get this boss off your back forever!" (July 1982, p. 98). While offering only spurious solutions to readers' problems, the column is a prime example of the Latinization of *Cosmopolitan* to attract readers who have a different cultural heritage.

Like its English-language counterpart, *Cosmopolitan en español* contains several contradictions. The Spanish version, too, offers readers vicarious participation in a pseudo-sexual liberation, but one much less daring and transgressive of established sexual mores than the original US version. Adapted primarily for women in Latin America, not the US, *Cosmopolitan en español* can only employ certain less-daring symbols of sexual liberation in order to respect local traditions. At the same time, the magazine promotes images of modernity to attract readers and encourage consumption of up-to-date goods and services. The result is a publication that is both traditional and modern. It co-opts and redefines the idea of women's liberation to include the lifestyles of the varied groups of women that its publishers wish to attract: both women with children and those without, unpaid homemakers and salaried employees, the single and married, and the affluent and less monied. Although using the vocabulary of a spurious women's liberation, the magazine presents very traditional messages. While Spanish-speaking readers in the US might not find the publication as daring and innovative as other magazines in English readily available on news-stands here, its use of Latin American culture gives them the sense that it is published especially for them.

The producers of mass culture have known for decades that television programs, films, radio entertainment, and magazine features must contain seeds of popular sentiment to attract audiences. Readers of romance fiction, like viewers of daily soap operas, for example, find vicarious male valorization of their own constantly wavering sense of sexual attractiveness through the fictive images of female desirability they read about and see in these forms of mass culture.[34] The magazines for minority women frequently employ this technique and other commonly used elements of popular sentiment; in addition, however, these publications utilize special linguistic, cultural and political elements to entice women. But while reading the "Letters to the Sorceress" feature in the Spanish-language *Cosmopolitan* or a progressive article on Black history in *Essence*, minority women also receive messages that they, too, may participate in the American Dream through consumerism. The purchase of products advertised in *Essence* and *Latina*, for example, such as a relatively inexpensive hair straightener or the beer of a large brewery which is notorious for unfair labor practices toward its Chicano workers, is linked within the cultural system of these magazines to achieving upward mobility while remaining loyal to one's ethnic and racial heritage. Language, culture, and politics combine in these magazines with other seeds of popular sentiment used traditionally in mass culture, to encourage minority women to buy products.

9 Class Not Mass: Special-Interest Publications and Pseudo-Individualized Consumption

Contemporary magazines reach "class" audiences both by limiting their readerships and by focusing on special-interest topics; the concentrated groups of readers that attract advertisers can be constituted both economically and thematically. The redesigned *House & Garden*, for example, focuses on monied consumers, while a magazine such as *Weight Watchers* concentrates its audience thematically, addressing women interested in losing weight. Magazines such as *Bride's* and *Parents* seek different classes but limit their audiences thematically and temporally, in conjunction with key life events. Some magazines concentrate their readers both economically and by topic: *Cuisine* and *Gourmet* focus on expensive food preparation, *House & Garden* on upscale home decoration, and *Ms.* on feminist topics viewed primarily from a white, middle-class perspective.

The special-interest magazines often encourage readers to conceive of themselves as members of a distinct group linked to certain modes of consumption. *Big Beautiful Woman* and *It's Me*, for example, address large-size women as an oppressed sector that can liberate itself by purchasing special products. The wedding preparation and childcare magazines encourage women to perceive themselves as brides and mothers and as those primarily responsible for weddings and parenting. Because of their commercial goals, the special-interest publications address readers with messages of pseudo-individualized consumption linked to the ideological roles expected of members of such groups. The large-size reader of *Big Beautiful Woman*, the ostensibly sexually liberated reader of *Playgirl*, and the body-conscious reader of *Shape* all receive normative messages from the magazines about the roles expected of them as members of these unique groups and the special consumer needs that the advertisers' products will meet. Thus, these magazines' specific commercial goals shape the ideological messages of their editorial material. The special-interest publications create "class" audiences for advertisers by persuading readers to engage in the pseudo-individualized consumption allegedly appropriate to the special roles and obligations of membership in a unique group.

BIG BEAUTIFUL WOMAN AND *IT'S ME*: COMMERCIALIZED LIBERATION FOR LARGE WOMEN

The widely publicized struggles of the 1960s and 1970s against oppression based on class, race and gender heightened awareness of the harmful effects of prejudice and stereotyping. Several oppressed groups assumed active confrontational stances rather than merely focusing on their victimization. By the 1970s these political movements had also affected other sectors of society which, although not victims of class or racial oppression as groups, nonetheless frequently encountered prejudice and stereotyping. An organization such as the Grey Panthers fought against ageism and promoted the rights of older people; the gay pride movement fostered positive self-images among gays to counter the long-held stereotypes of a large part of the population.

Less attention has been paid, however, to another strong set of prejudices – the negative attitudes many hold toward those who do not fit the ideal image of beauty fostered in the media. Large-size women, for example, have begun in recent years to complain about their second-class citizenship and their exclusion from commonly held ideal models of beauty. Arguing that common prejudices exaggerate the importance of outward appearance, newly formed groups of large-size women insist that they are valuable people whatever their size. Two special-interest magazines, *Big Beautiful Woman* and *It's Me*, aim to encourage a sense of pride in large-size women and to earn a share of the financial benefits of large women's greater integration into consumerism.

BBW or *Big Beautiful Woman*, subtitled "Fashions for the Large-Size Woman" began publication in 1979 with a confrontational attitude toward prejudices against large women. Each month the magazine opens with a "Statement of Policy" that reminds readers, "your dress size has nothing to do with your success or failure as a person." Urging readers to stop feeling guilty about being large, Editor Carole Shaw asks: "Are you any smarter if you wear a size 8 dress? Is your basic character any more worth while if you're 120 lbs. than at 220-plus? Will the world applaud you in 100 years if you forgo that piece of cake and settle for black coffee?" (see, for example, October 1983, p. 4). Shaw argues that once large women, who make up 25 per cent of the population, stop apologizing for their size, they will be able to exercise political and economic clout.

In each issue, *BBW* encourages a critical revision of common stereotypes about large women and instills in readers a strong sense of pride. Numerous letters to the editor attest to the magazine's role in teaching self-acceptance, recounting touching stories of readers' previous suffering because of society's negative view of their size. Men also write to congratulate the magazine and express not only their approval of large women but their strong attraction to them. The numerous fashion features in each issue employ large-size models, jarring readers from their normal expectations about beauty and fashion ideals and offering large women different role models from those the media traditionally present.

Somewhat contradictorily, however, *BBW* channels into consumerism the large-size woman's quest for acceptance and nonstereotypical treatment. Freedom from second-class citizenship, according to *BBW*, entails readers' full integration into fashion and beauty consumerism. While the "Statement of Policy" protests the superficiality of focusing on the external to judge people's worth, the magazine as a whole in fact strongly emphasizes external appearance to promote fashion and beauty products. The Editor argues in the May/June 1983 issue, for example: "Hopefully [*sic*], the decade of the 1980s will be the age of Human Liberation. An age that will look past all the transient things of life such as size, age, wrinkles, degree of physical beauty, and will focus on the lasting and ultimately most valuable assets: character, proficiency in your chosen endeavors, and enjoyment of life, given and received" (p. 5). Directly beneath these remarks, however, Shaw herself emphasizes physical appearance by promoting six fashion features that follow in the issue and a J. C. Penney fashion show in Atlanta in which she will participate.

Frequently, the magazine suggests that large women will begin to achieve liberation by purchasing fashionable clothes and cosmetics. Even a short story, "The second spring of Harriet Spencer" (May–June 1983) recounts the rejuvenation of a middle-aged woman through the purchase of new clothes. One reader herself links large women's liberation to commercialism, writing in April 1981: "Once BBW's [big, beautiful women] feel attractive they will be encouraged to buy more fashionable clothes which will, in turn, become an incentive for the manufacturers to produce more creative and fashionable styles. I love the letters from your readers who say they bought their first belt in years, first pair of jeans, bought makeup, etc. This is a wonderful beginning for these women" (p. 11). In effect, *BBW* helps to guide the discontent of large-size women into a concept of liberation that posits consumerism as a remedy.

In its project of attaining the right to attractive fashion for its large-size readers, *BBW* reproduces some of the trivialized portrayals of women of the mainstream fashion and beauty magazines. Models in *BBW*'s fashion features often pose as sex objects for an implied or explicit male viewer. "Shapely standouts," for example, a feature on pantihose in the April 1981 issue showed three pairs of large-size women's legs straddling a reclining male who gazed approvingly at these fragments of their bodies. In "A+ Classics" (August 1982) models exhibit several trivialized poses that Goffman delineated, such as "coy knee bends" and "flooding out."[1]

Through poses such as these which are encoded as glamorous, successful and even liberational, the models are reduced to the products they exhibit. Readers are invited to become transformed as well into these desirable clothes, to allow their identities and the products to become one. "Fat offends Western ideals of female beauty and, as such, every 'overweight' woman creates a crack in the popular culture's ability to make us mere products," one critic has argued.[2] *BBW*, however, like its competitor *It's Me*, performs the reverse function by integrating large-size women into consumerism. In the process, these magazines inadvertently reduce large women to mere products – pantihose or other apparel that promises to make readers as attractive as their slender counterparts.

BBW prints complaint and praise forms at the end of each issue for readers to send to stores to encourage them to make available stylish and quality merchandise for large women. In early 1981 the magazine announced that the greatest number of complaint slips returned were addressed to Lane Bryant, the largest retailer for special-size clothing. According to *BBW*, readers complained that the company used small models in its ads, sold poor quality clothing at high prices, and failed to stock certain sizes.

BBW made public its readers' dissatisfaction with Lane Bryant, however, shortly after this retailer of large-size clothing began to test-market a competing magazine for big women. *It's Me*, financed by Lane Bryant and distributed in its stores, claims an editorial purpose of telling the size-16 woman, "if you are heavy, don't say you aren't going to get a new hairdo or go to the dentist or buy any new clothes until you lose weight. Don't deny yourself. Accept yourself as you are."[3] The magazine assumes a less confrontational attitude than *BBW*, recognizing that many of its readers want to lose weight rather than remain large; however, it encourages them to feel good about themselves regardless of their size. With articles on health, exercise, and low-calorie recipes, *It's Me* advises readers on the dangers of sugar, diuretics and food additives, and the causes of diabetes. Where *BBW* publishes recipe features such as "Chocolate cream roll: Devilishly delicious" (July–August 1981) and "Goodies galore" (May–June 1983), *It's Me* offers recipes for low-sugar desserts and nourishing egg dishes. Although it encourages readers to exercise, and eat non-fattening foods, *It's Me* does not accept ads for diet pills and similar weight-reduction aids.

Sometimes, however, visuals in the magazine contradict the nutrition and diet articles; in the Winter 1981 issue, for example, a fashion feature pictures models consuming fattening sundaes, sodas, and sandwiches in a coffeeshop setting. While aware that a number of readers are concerned about losing weight, Lane Bryant's vested interest is in selling large-size clothing. In keeping with this material interest of the magazine's backer, Editor Bruce Clerke argues that medical research now shows that it is not healthy for all people to be thin. About 35 per cent of the clothes featured in the magazine are from Lane Bryant stores.[4]

Where *BBW*, like the adolescent girls' magazine *'Teen*, offers readers the opportunity to purchase a transparency of the magazine's cover so that they can pretend to be "cover girls," *It's Me* has a contest in each issue entitled "You Could Be an *It's Me*

Model." Readers in fact model in the magazine and appear on the cover. Thus, the possibility of transforming oneself into the magazine's images of ideal beauty is more concretely real here than in *BBW*. Even if readers choose not to participate in the contests, they witness the success of ordinary women like themselves in attaining the magazine's images of ideal beauty.

BBW, in contrast to *It's Me*, frequently emphasizes male acceptance as the reward large women deserve. Admiring men are pictured in features and write letters to the editor about their fondness for large women. A popular feature "BBW Friendship Page" prints want-ads from women and men who wish to meet others. In August 1982, for example, the feature published 250 such ads over five pages.[5] Frequently, the magazine publishes features about weddings that resulted from people having met through the "Friendship Page." These success stories not only encourage readers to purchase ads themselves but to participate in the consumption the magazine recommends in order to attain male love and approval.

BBW and *It's Me* are important publications because they attempt to reverse some of the stereotypes of ideal beauty that pervade other women's magazines.[6] They increase communication between women who have suffered prejudice because of their size, revealing problems and solutions that large women share. Both magazines, however, urge readers to transcend their second-class citizenship by purchasing products. Although *It's Me* has a more direct connection to the large-size clothing marketer Lane Bryant, *BBW* is also a commercial venture and has a vested interest in encouraging consumerism to increase its own advertising volume. While this consumption-based idea of liberation may advance the financial ends of these two magazines, it cannot provide readers with long-lasting liberation.

FITNESS, HEALTH, DIET, AND ATHLETICS: FROM *SHAPE* TO *WOMEN'S SPORTS*

In contrast to *BBW* and *It's Me* which celebrate large women and encourage them to be proud of their size, another group of magazines focuses on people's new interest in health, sports, fitness and diet. *Shape*, *Fit*, and *Slimmer*, published in California, promote ideal body images for women that are to be attained through exercise, dieting, grooming, and the purchase of products. *Weight Watchers* encourages weight reduction through planned food consumption based on the organization's nutritional program and purchase of the parent company's products. *Spring*, published by Rodale Press from 1982 to 1983 addressed a new generation of health-conscious women and promoted exercise, health food, and natural healing, along with beauty and grooming. *Women's Sports*, another California publication, emphasizes sports, fitness, and health for the "active American woman."[7]

As the titles indicate, *Shape*, *Fit*, and *Slimmer* focus readers' attention on their bodies. *Shape*'s Publisher Joe Weider attempts to naturalize a masculinist vision by comparing women to cars: "Would you rather be seen in a body that has sagging headlights and a bulging, oversize trunk, or one with the sleekness and power that makes it a classic?" (September 1981, p. 10). Later in the issue, Betty Weider extends her husband's metaphor in her article, "How to turn a 5-horsepower body into a '10'" (p. 96). Besides reifying women as inanimate objects that are traditionally part of male culture, these two sentences ask readers to view themselves through the eyes of a scrutinizing male surveyor; readers are first to look at themselves negatively as "sagging," "bulging," and "only 5-horsepower," and then to imagine themselves transformed into "sleekness," "power," and, ultimately, the grade "10," following through on the male surveyor's rating system made popular by the movie of the same title.

The means of transformation that Weider and his wife advocate here and throughout the magazine is weight training. In the February 1982 issue we learn of the Weiders' business connection to this activity: "Meet the Weiders – the First Family of body building. Ben Weider [Vice-Chairman of *Shape*'s Board] is president of . . . the group that controls body-building competition world wide. Betty Weider has spent over thirty years as both a model and an advocate for women's body building. Joe Weider, *Shape*'s publisher, created the Weider System of Fitness" (p. 6). Besides promoting his weight training interest throughout the magazine, Weider uses his publication to urge readers to buy products from Weider-owned enterprises. Ads for related Weider products such as Dynamic Cell Toner Tablets appear on twenty pages of the September 1981 issue, for example. While *Shape* promises readers in its premiere issue that it will function as "the last word on how to be your healthiest and most gorgeous" (p. 8), these physical characteristics are to be attained by consuming Weider products and participating in the family's exercise enterprise – weight-lifting.

Fit and *Slimmer* also emphasize physical appearance to the exclusion of other important human values. *Fit* tells readers that the magazine's primary concern is "the physical you" (October 1982, p. 7) and, while *Slimmer*'s subtitle is "Health and Beauty for the Total Woman," the magazine in fact focuses on weight reduction, diets, and attaining slimness. An offshoot publication of *Runner's World* magazine, *Fit* nonetheless trivializes women's participation in exercise and athletics by including sexual innuendos in the editorial material and focusing women readers' attention on superficial concerns. Models frequently appear in seductive poses and the titles of articles are often sexually suggestive: "Sexercise for couples," "Bedding down: Sleep habits of the American female," and "Bicyclists who are a '10'" (October 1982 and March 1983). *Fit* urges readers to complete questionnaires about their attitudes toward such topics as breast size, scars, blemishes, and high heels. In both *Fit* and *Slimmer* articles on entertainment stars encourage readers to identify with celebrity role models in order to achieve an ideal body image.

Slimmer, with the explicit comparative adjective that serves as its title, and *Fit*, with its implicit comparison to the "unfit," both urge readers to view themselves moving between two poles based on physical appearance: a negative present state and a positive future one. *Slimmer*'s numerous articles on diet and exercise push readers toward the pole of slimness, although not without contradiction: the book review feature in the September 1981 issue, for example, discusses several diet and exercise books but ends by promoting two fattening dessert cookbooks, noting "we all deserve a little sweetness in our lives" (p. 14). Such contradictory editorial material encourages readers to oscillate between the poles of the non-slim and the slim, a wavering that is likely to inhibit weight reduction and extend readers' perceived need to purchase the magazine in order to attain the ideal body image implied in the title.

Shape, *Fit*, and *Slimmer* also channel readers' desires to attain ideal body types into the purchase of consumer goods. *Shape* includes features on "fashions for fitness," aerobic shoes, exercise videotapes, bicycles, vitamins, shampoos, dance and exercise classes, and health clubs; ads for many of these products also appear in the magazine. Similarly, *Fit* and *Slimmer* include features on fashion, cosmetics, haircare, swimwear, toiletries, and diet books which correlate either with current advertising in these magazines or the publishers' hopes for expanded areas of ad revenue. While *Shape* and *Fit* include much advertising for their respective owners' products (Weider's health aids and *Runner's World* magazine), the advertising revenues that make the magazines profitable enterprises are earned by channeling readers' desire to attain fitness and ideal bodies into the purchase of these other consumer goods.

Weight Watchers, like *Slimmer*, emphasizes weight reduction and like *Shape* and *Fit*, heavily promotes its parent corporation's goods and services. A subsidiary of H. J. Heinz Inc., Weight Watchers International owns a worldwide classroom program for weight reduction, a large line of controlled calorie food products, weight-loss camps, and publishing ventures. Among the latter is *Weight Watchers* magazine which serves as a showcase for many Weight Watchers and H. J. Heinz products. In the July 1982 issue, for example, ads for these products appeared on ten pages, including an ad for Heinz's Star Kist tuna on cover two.

Somewhat surprisingly, however, beginning on the front cover, many of the visual and verbal images in *Weight Watchers* encourage women to eat. The magazine's connection to these two giant food product manufacturers, H. J. Heinz and Weight Watchers International, explains the logic of the emphasis on eating in a weight-reduction magazine. The front covers often depict smiling, slender women raising an attractive piece of food to their mouths. In August 1982, for example, all of the photographs on the table of contents page also relate to food consumption: pictures of enticing, apparently fattening food and of a woman's parted lips form a semiotic collage that, in conjunction with the front cover, urges readers to consume food. One feature's title, "For Your Information" was changed to "Tidbits," another subtle food image. Each month the magazine publishes a notice alerting readers that the designation "Legal" or "Maintenance" appears on food ads to show readers how the advertising products are acceptable to the Weight Watchers diet plan. While the label is not a guarantee, it is similar to the *Good*

Housekeeping Seal of Approval since it constitutes an additional recommendation of the advertiser's product; these labels function as one more incentive for food consumption and thus form part of the magazine's overall constellation of food promotion.

At the same time, the magazine also encourages dieting, through participation in the Weight Watchers Program along with consumption of the company's products. Advice columns from the founder of Weight Watchers and the Psychological Director of the organization appear, as do testimonies from formerly overweight women such as "I used to sneak into the closet and eat a few hamburgers" (August 1982) and the closing feature each month, "Before and After." Like *Shape*, *Fit*, and *Slimmer*, *Weight Watchers* publishes articles on haircare, fashion, toiletries, cosmetics, and kitchen appliances, many of which are covert advertising features. Unlike *BBW* and *It's Me*, slender models predominate in *Weight Watchers*, visually signifying that by purchasing Weight Watchers' services and products and the other low-calorie food advertised in the magazine, readers can continue to consume yet become slim. These correct purchases will, in a sense, allow readers to have it both ways.

While *Spring* and *Women's Sports* sometimes publish diet articles, these magazines are not primarily focused on weight reduction. Launched by the Rodale Press in April 1982, *Spring* emphasizes "lifestyle, natural health, self-care and fitness."[8] The magazine's content suggests that the audience Rodale Press seeks here is the adult baby-boom generation, many of whom now have children of their own; it is an audience that came of age in the 1960s and has retained several aspects of the sixties counter-culture such as consumption of health food and an interest in natural healing and healthy lifestyles. Besides its health orientation, *Spring* publishes a good deal of fashion and beauty editorial material; one section, "Good Health, Good Looks," merges the areas of health and beauty and includes articles on haircare, face creams, and workout clothes. Much covert advertising appears in these sections and such linking of health to beauty in the editorial sections reflects the magazine's need to attract additional advertisers besides the marketers of health food products.

Women's Sports can be understood as a fitness magazine only in the sense that it promotes nutrition and exercise as a means of attaining overall health and proficiency in sports. Its aim, in

Publisher Doug Latimer's words, is to "encourage more and more women to discover for themselves the added dimensions that participation in active sports can bring to their lives."[9] Along with news articles on women sports figures and sports in which women now excel, the magazine publishes a number of well-researched informational pieces on nutrition, health, sports psychology, and training. Its 125,000 readers are 97 per cent women, most of whom participate in athletic activities.[10]

Unlike the diet articles in many women's magazines, *Women's Sports*' occasional weight-reduction features emphasize exercise and sound nutrition. Editor Amy Rennert reminds readers in the June 1982 issue, "Let's get strong, not just thin" (p. 4). The weight-loss feature that month "Waving good-bye to fat city" advocates exercise with a sensible diet, one low in calories but high in carbohydrates. Similar to the informational food articles in *Spring*, a small piece in *Women's Sports*, "Active Woman's Almanac" (December, 1981), informs readers that most commercially prepared yogurts contain additives and are homogenized, a process which kills the bacteria that make yogurt nutritious; an easy home recipe for yogurt is offered as an alternative. Unlike *Spring* and most other women's magazines, *Women's Sports* sometimes takes an explicit progressive political stand; in the August 1982 Editor's column, Rennert urges readers and well-known sports figures to involve themselves publicly in the peace movement, describing her own participation in the massive June 1982 peace rally in New York City.

While all six of these magazines claim to be presenting positive, wholesome images of women, *Women's Sports* does so most authentically. *Spring* mixes its health orientation with traditional women's consumerism and images of consumption predominate in the other four exercise and diet magazines. Urging women to consume, however, is less important to the publishers of *Women's Sports*. The magazine maintains its advertising volume at one-third of each issue's pages and does not reduce the editorial pages or the size of the magazine in months when less is sold.[11] *Spring*'s experiment with linking natural health and fitness to consumerism proved financially unprofitable; Rodale Press suspended publication of the magazine in 1983.

BRIDE'S, *MODERN BRIDE*, AND *PARENTS*: KEY LIFE EVENTS AS MAJOR PERIODS OF CONSUMPTION

Another group of special-interest magazines focuses on initiating women into married life and the duties of childraising. Large corporations such as Conde Nast, publisher of *Bride's*, Ziff-Davis and CBS Publications which successively owned *Modern Bride* in the early 1980s,[12] and Gruner & Jahr, publisher of *Parents*, have found that major life events such as weddings and the birth of children are especially lucrative times to bring advertisers' messages to female consumers. These events signal women's increased responsibilities to buy consumer goods for others in addition to themselves.

Bride's, for example, was founded during the Depression when advertisers were reducing their expenditures even in the affluent magazines. Wells Drorbaugh, then Advertising Manager at *House & Garden* realized that in spite of the economic hard times, millions of women were getting married and therefore could be convinced to buy products for their new households. Drorbaugh launched *Bride's* in the New York–New Jersey area in September 1934 and in 1939 began national publication. In spite of record low levels of national consumer spending, advertisers had faith in the ability of a new magazine such as *Bride's* to convince women to purchase products. The publication continued to sell large numbers of ad pages after the Depression and was purchased by Conde Nast in 1959.[13]

Both *Bride's* and *Modern Bride* sell remarkable numbers of ad pages in their six issues each year. In 1983 *Bride's* averaged 307 ad pages per issue with only 154 editorial pages, while *Modern Bride*'s average was 257 ad pages to 131 editorial pages. Both magazines realize the bulk of their revenues from ad sales rather than circulation. In 1983 *Bride's* earned $19.4 million of its $25.8 million total revenues from ad sales; *Modern Bride* made $16.1 million of its $22.1 million from ads that year. When *Bride's* March 1983 issue sold 495 ad pages, it was recorded as the largest consumer magazine ever published in the United States.[14]

Bride's and *Modern Bride* achieve these high ad revenues in part by structuring their editorial material to respond to certain real needs of people about to be married. In addition, however, they instill a large array of pseudo-needs in women which also greatly augments advertising volume and revenue. A couple setting up a new household, for example, might indeed need dishes, utensils, and cookware; "Essentials for your first kitchen" (*Modern Bride*, February/March 1983), however, tells readers that a food processor, a convection oven, bundt pans, souffle dishes, electric woks, and a "sporkit" for testing whether pasta is properly cooked are "indispensable" for new brides (p. 402).

Both magazines encourage readers to complete the "Gift Registry Checklist" printed in each issue as a means of structuring gift-giving to conform to what the magazines contend are the bride's needs. Under the category "Needs," for example, the printed form lists five kinds of silver spoons, three different forks, three knives, and eleven serving utensils. In the blanks adjacent to these and the some 160 other items on the list, readers are to write how many of each item they "need" (see, for example, *Bride's*, June/July 1981, p. 47). The products highlighted on these Registry Lists correspond closely to those that appear on the ad pages in both magazines. Recognizing this, Howard Friedberg, Advertising Director at *Modern Bride* terms bridal magazines "thing-oriented rather than people-oriented" and notes, "it's often difficult to tell the editorial and the advertising apart."[15] One result of the close homology between advertising and editorial material in these magazines is their continuous record of growth in ad volume and revenue; even during the economic recession of the early 1980s when other magazines were suffering ad declines, both *Bride's* and *Modern Bride* posted increases in ad volume and revenue.[16]

Besides addressing readers' real and imagined needs for goods and services such as wedding apparel and accessories, home furnishings and equipment, honeymoon travel, liquor, tobacco, toiletries, cosmetics, and financial services, *Bride's* and *Modern Bride* offer some advice features that do not directly promote commodities. Articles such as "Illness in the family" and "Weddings and the disabled" (*Bride's*, October/November 1983 and June/July 1981) give useful information on planning wedding ceremonies around disabled participants or a family illness. However, these advice pieces not related to consumer goods sometimes present stereotypical models for women, and attempt to anchor certain dominant social mores; the feature "Becoming a Wife," for example, advises readers how to assume the new role that will be expected of them (*Bride's*, October/November 1983). Thus, the two wedding preparation magazines uphold the traditional status quo ideologically at the same time that they teach readers to purchase numerous commodities. The mystique of the ideal bride presented visually and verbally in both magazines is extremely attractive, and readers are drawn to the magazines as well by the practical needs addressed in some of the features.

Just as *Bride's* and *Modern Bride* imply that the primary responsibility for organizing a wedding and establishing a new household lies with the woman, *Parents* assumes that the duties of childraising are primarily women's domain. In all three magazines advice-giving is the principal mode of address; the major life events on which these magazines focus require women to follow a set of correct customs and procedures, according to the magazines, and a related set of proper consumption patterns.

The advice-giving structure underlying each issue of *Parents* begins with the Editor's column, "Inside *Parents*" which highlights one article in the issue. Frequently the Editor recounts an episode from her personal experience of raising children to teach readers a lesson relating indirectly to the article that the column promotes. Throughout, the magazine advises on health, family life, love, marriage, money management, beauty, grooming, food, crafts, pet care, jobs, and, most frequently, raising children. Each month a chronological series of eight features appears with advice on raising children from the time of the mother's pregnancy to the children's early teen years. Unlike readers of the bridal publications who purchase the magazines only for an average of ten months,[17] women are drawn to *Parents* through advice articles such as these for a longer period of time – from early pregnancy until their children enter adolescence.

Anxious to attract some of the advertisers who buy space in the seven sisters, *Parents* categorizes itself as a service magazine.[18] Its recipe features are surrounded by food ads as occurs in the seven sisters and, like these magazines, *Parents* has updated itself for current times. A monthly feature "Women at Work" offers advice to mothers employed outside the home while raising children. Occasionally, articles present feminist viewpoints, distinguishing the magazine from traditional service publications. "Is your job hazardous to your pregnancy?" (August 1983), for example, notes that businesses employ a double standard for men and women with regard to workplace health and safety. "Childbirth through the ages" (November

1983) argues that the common practice of women lying down to deliver babies has replaced the upright position practiced throughout history because the prone position is more convenient for doctors, not mothers.

Like the bridal magazines, *Parents* attracts readers by addressing practical, special-interest needs that women experience at certain periods of their lives. In the process, however, all three magazines uphold ideologically the pervasive notion that women have the primary responsibility for weddings and childraising. This notion has commercial advantages for both the magazines and their advertisers. It is easier to market products to "a unique concentration of young mothers," as *Parents* terms its readership,[19] than to a more diverse, changing group of both mothers and fathers who are experimenting with new models for the household division of labor. Ideological effects and commercial goals coincide uniquely in these magazines. The useful advice in many of the editorial features attracts readers at the same time that it teaches stereotypical conceptions of the self; by encouraging women to view themselves primarily as brides and mothers, each of these magazines helps to create a concentrated, like-minded audience of women that advertisers can more easily and profitably address.

THE ELITE PUBLICATIONS: IDEALS OF DOMESTIC, CULINARY, AND SOCIAL AFFLUENCE

Besides aiming magazines at readers' special interests, publishers also attempt to limit their audiences by attracting only affluent women. Magazines such as *House Beautiful* and *House & Garden* (even before its upscale redesign in January 1983) focus on home decoration in a more concentrated fashion than do the seven sisters and also seek more affluent readers. *Bon Appetit*, *Cuisine*, and *Gourmet* emphasize gourmet cooking, distancing themselves from the standard, inexpensive recipes featured in the seven sisters and limiting their audiences by the high-priced ingredients required for the gourmet recipes. *Town & Country*, although classifying itself as a general editorial magazine, is a special-interest publication in the sense that it is "a service publication for the affluent,"[20] focusing on the homes, lifestyle patterns, and consumer habits of the rich. Some of these publications are more elitist than others; *Town & Country*, *Cuisine*, *Gourmet*, and the revamped *House & Garden* present more affluent images than do *Bon Appetit* and *House Beautiful*. However, all use the formula of special-interest editorial material directed to a limited, upscale audience as a means of securing high advertising revenues.

House Beautiful and the *House & Garden* of 1981 and 1982 are the competing shelter publications from Heart and Conde Nast respectively. The implicit ideal reader of each beautifies herself, her home, and the meals she prepares as if all were objects of equal value. The August 1981 cover of *House & Garden*, for example, pictures an elaborately decorated dressing table, the purchase of which will enable women to beautify both themselves and their homes. Beneath the picture of the table appears the cover line: "The new sensuality: How your bathroom affects your sex life" and inside the issue, readers are encouraged to transfer their sexuality to the objects the magazine promotes. Features such as "Feel-great decorating – A love affair with flowers," "Food for the senses," "The new sensuality – The dressing table: The bedroom's most intimate ornament," and "The bathroom: Your house's erogenous zone" urge women to express their sexuality by preparing meals and decorating their homes. Although it appears that the ideal homemaker is actively to create her environment here, in fact she is to adorn herself and her home as parallel passive sex objects; the glance of the approving male surveyor is implicit in each of these scenarios.

Both *House Beautiful* and *House & Garden* grew in circulation and revenue along with the post-World War II boom in housing construction and home ownership.[21] When recession and high interest rates slowed housing sales in the early 1980s, and more women entered the paid workforce, the two magazines adapted to the times. JoAnn Barwick, Editor of *House Beautiful* attributes emotional value to homes as she indirectly urges readers to buy the furnishings and decorations advertised in the magazine: "What else can we spend money on that gives back to us the serenity, the warmth, the sense of well-being a home can offer?" (February 1983, p. 13). In the August 1982 issue, she addresses working women readers, suggesting that one way to cope with the fast pace of one's career, family, and personal life is to have a comfortable, well-designed house to come home to. Both columns uphold the concept of the "house beautiful" that will provide deserved emotional rewards to readers who invest in its purchase and decoration.

House & Garden also adapts to the difficulties of the housing market and the new demographic status of women in the early 1980s with articles such as "Housing and the single woman" (August 1981); the piece has limited applicability to the vast number of single working women in the country, however, since all of the examples it cites are of women who were able to purchase a house because of financial help from their parents or an inheritance. Later in the issue, "New ways to finance a house" tells readers: "Despite the widespread report of its death, the American dream of owning a home is still alive and well" (p. 66). Both *House & Garden* and *House Beautiful* must encourage readers to purchase homes and decorate them properly even in times of economic recession so that advertisers will continue to buy space in the magazines. "Women discover new credit options" (*House Beautiful*, August 1982) subtly implies that a woman can continue to create a "house beautiful" even during a recession by "using plastic money to enhance purchasing power" (p. 22).

In 1982 Conde Nast spent $8 million to redesign *House & Garden* and reposition it for a select, affluent readership. Circulation and advertising revenue had fallen in 1981 and 1982 and Conde Nast believed it could boost advertising by seeking affluent members of the baby-boom generation as readers. The new *House & Garden* appeared in January 1983 with heavier paper stock, more editorial pages, new graphics and layout, and a focus on elite homes and lifestyles. In its trade ads the magazine told prospective advertisers that they would surround themselves with excellence by purchasing space in the new *House & Garden*. During the following months the magazine cut its circulation in half to 500,000 and doubled its subscription price; although it lost half of its previous advertisers, it attracted others. Nonetheless, according to *Folio 400* figures, the magazine lost nearly $10 million in ad revenue in 1983, down 44 per cent from 1982.[22]

House & Garden's new editorial material and format give it more similarity to *Town & Country* than to its previous principal competitor *House Beautiful*. An ad in the new *House & Garden* promises readers "Life made more civilized by renowned tastemakers" (November 1982, p. 146). A monthly feature follows through on this theme, highlighting important "tastemakers" in whom readers are to cultivate a voyeuristic interest. In February 1983, for example, the feature focuses on England's George IV; it appears across from ads for an expensive chandelier made from "the same handmade Waterford crystal that now hangs in such famous places as Westminster Abbey" (p. 17) and a $21,392 set of Aynsly china: "Even in the palaces of kings, this is the dinner service usually reserved for occasions of state" (p. 19). The montage between this ad and feature implicitly invites readers to imitate the taste of England's royalty through purchases.

Town & Country also focuses a number of its features on the activities of the rich. Like a society page, the opening feature in each issue presents news and photographs of the upper class under such headings as "Weddings" and "Parties." The magazine's "Annual Racing Guide" includes such articles as "The 115th running of the Saratoga Season," with photos of the rich who attend the races. Primarily focusing on the East Coast, articles offer readers glimpses into exclusive clubs, affluent homes, expensive resorts, and the private lives of the rich. "At Home" (July 1983), for example, depicts "nine lovely ladies in their individually unique summer gardens in New York, New Jersey, and Connecticut" (p. 127).

Like *House & Garden*, *Town & Country* has articles on art, antiques, home decoration, beauty, and fashion. As occurs in other women's magazines, articles often lend direct and indirect support to the advertisements. "The shape of summer" (July 1982), for example, not only urges women to buy swimwear, toiletries, and cosmetics but also expensive accessories and jewelry from the exclusive establishments that frequently advertise in the magazine. In December 1983 features such as "The bravura of Bijan" and "Master parfumeurs: The Guerlains" also coordinate with purchased advertising.

The redesigned *House & Garden* highlights the exclusive homes of the rich in the US and Europe, in contrast to the less expensive models it previously presented along with its competitor *House Beautiful*. Remodeling and "how-to" features no longer appear. This deliberate attempt to focus the magazine away from the practical needs of the majority of the population does not mean that the less-monied sectors no longer read the magazine. While non-affluent people also read *House & Garden*, vicariously participating in the lives of the rich and learning about the so-called "tastemakers," Hearst still can assure advertisers that an elite, monied group constitutes the core of the readership.

Like *Town & Country* and the revamped *House & Garden*, *Cuisine* and *Gourmet*, published by CBS Publications and Conde Nast respectively, seek especially affluent audiences. *Cuisine* tells advertisers: "Think rich. Think *Cuisine* . . . They live rich lives . . . They entertain richly . . . How'd you like to talk to 2,500,000 of them? And know they'll hear you. Think rich. To get rich."[23] *Gourmet* terms itself "the magazine of good living," a concept which it defines for readers through articles on architectural wonders, foreign travel, dining out, and gourmet recipes.[24] Figures for 1983 show that *Cuisine*'s average circulation was 775,818 and *Gourmet*'s 626,527, while their somewhat less elitist competitor *Bon Appetit* had a circulation of 1.3 million.[25] Even the wider, total readership figure that *Cuisine* cites above represents a small enough part of the US population to back the magazine's claim that it is read primarily by an upscale audience.

Gourmet adds to its aura of affluence by using expensive photography and printing.[26] The magazine's ideal reader has a well-to-do lifestyle, implicit in such regular features as "Paris Journal," which in July 1983, for example, tells readers where they can find good restaurants open in Paris even in August, "Specialites de la Maison" with monthly reviews of expensive restaurants in New York and California, and "Gourmet Holidays" which urges international travel to indulge in gourmet eating. Readers are encouraged to travel to Tokyo to eat and to visit such places as Indonesia, Parma, and Scotland both for cultural and gastronomic enrichment. Travel ads invite readers to South Africa to see "a city built on gold . . . favorite restaurants, fashionable shops and boutiques, extraordinary museums, [and] nightlife" (November 1983, pp. 153 and 206). In the same issue the social upheaval occurring in another part of the world is also masked by a romanticized view of the third world, "Guatemala country cooking," which offers to teach readers to prepare traditional peasant and Indian foods from this Central American country.

Cuisine, which also publishes ads for travel to South Africa, invites readers in its October 1983 issue to view the breads of India as "A connoisseur's collection," and to participate vicariously in the affluent lifestyle of William F. and Pat Buckley in their "Connecticut country house" (pp. 80 and 67). Like *Gourmet*, it has a Wine Editor who apprises readers of the correct expensive wines to purchase. *Cuisine* publishes ads for less affluent products than does *Gourmet*, and like *Bon Appetit*, includes a number of advertisements for ordinary food products.

More California-oriented than *Cuisine* and *Gourmet*, *Bon Appetit* is published in Los Angeles by Knapp Communications and its largest group of readers resides in California. Women comprise 75 per cent of its audience[27] and it is primarily women's letters that appear in the "RSVP" column each month. *Bon Appetit*'s gourmet recipes include illustrations and step-by-step instructions, explaining skills that *Gourmet* and *Cuisine* presume readers already possess. While some of *Bon Appetit*'s ads are for expensive products, a number are for more widely used food items. Recognizing that gourmet cooking can have prohibitive time and monetary constraints for many, *Bon Appetit* publishes regular features such as "Too Busy to Cook?". *Cuisine*'s "Dinner parties for fall: Three timesaving strategies" (October 1983) and *Gourmet*'s monthly feature "Gastronomie Sans Argent" show similar concerns.

The shelter and gourmet publications along with *Town & Country* consciously limit their audiences both by the subject matter addressed and the affluence of the implied reader. With varying degrees of elitism, most of these publications intentionally aim to exclude non-monied readers, as in the case of *Newsweek Woman* which is only distributed to women subscribers in upscale zip-code areas. Although non-affluent women also read these magazines, the "class not mass" approach underlies the investments that large conglomerates such as Conde Nast, Hearst, CBS and Knapp have made in these publications. Attributing an even more glamorous face to consumerism than do the traditional home service magazines, these publications help to reinforce class divisions while at the same time offering non-affluent readers the chance to transcend these divisions in fantasy through the purchase of consumer goods.

PLAYGIRL: THE COMMODIFICATION OF SEX

The purported sexual liberation movement of the 1960s and 1970s emphasized changes in the outward form of sexual practices while leaving intact many of the underlying relations of gender inequality. Sexual freedom was frequently confused with women's liberation so that the former became a substitute for the latter. According to this position, a magazine such as *Playgirl* is liberational because it accords women opportunities for overt sexual fantasy that were previously available only to men in magazines such as *Playboy*.

In fact, however, *Playgirl* promotes sexual commodification rather than liberation. In marketing highly pleasurable spaces for women to enjoy the transgressive and forbidden, *Playgirl* at the same time commodifies the erotic. The magazine encourages women to view both men and themselves as sex objects, a reifying process linked to the sale of advertised products. While there is apparent equality of the sexes in the opportunities for fantasy that *Playboy* and *Playgirl* offer,[28] in reality women experience greater trivialization in the publication intended for them than do the male readers of *Playboy*. From the subtle connotations of the respective titles to the sex roles developed in each magazine's verbal and photographic sexual fantasies, there exists an encouragement of subordination for women and power and strength for men.

Playgirl is the logical extension of both the fashion and beauty magazines and the health and fitness publications which sexually reify women to a lesser degree in order to sell products.[29] The subtle and strong sexual pitches in magazines such as *Vogue*, *Cosmopolitan*, *Fit*, and *Slimmer* become explicit sexual fantasies in *Playgirl*. One of *Playgirl*'s monthly features. "Erotica," for example publishes "erotic adventures" readers have submitted; written in the first person, these fantasies present detailed accounts of sexual liaisons with strangers in public or semi-public places, the sexualization of professional work situations, as well as unique encounters with one's boyfriend or husband. In August 1982 another feature entitled "Couples: An intimate look at erotically memorable moments" tells in photo-novel form the story of a hairdresser seducing her customer while she cuts his hair. Directly following is an ad for an "elegantly seductive nightgown" with the imperative headline: "Make your fantasies come true." Where other women's magazines use attenuated sexual fantasies to sell products, *Playgirl* presents detailed, developed fantasies and uses them overtly to sell products.

Like *Cosmopolitan*, however, *Playgirl* sometimes links its sexual fantasies to traditional values that some readers simultaneously hold. One short story, "The best money can buy" (August 1982) recounts the adventures of a young working woman who, overwhelmed by bills, agrees to weekend prostitution with her boss; the story's open ending, however, hints that he falls in love with her instead. "Playgirl Funnies," a comic strip appearing later in the issue, tells a similar story in which a man informs his lover that he would like the freedom to sleep with other women; by the end of the episode, however, he asks her to marry him. *Playgirl* allows readers the chance to transgress dominant moral values imaginatively while at the same time retaining the security of these values.

In the decade since its initial publication in 1973, *Playgirl* has attained only a small monthly readership of about 700,000.[30] It remains a special-interest publication with a limited rather than a mass audience largely because it chooses to transgress prevailing moral values openly. By tapping into the legacy of the purported sexual liberation movement of the 1960s and 1970s *Playgirl* tries to sell products under the guise of allowing women to enjoy sexual freedom and pleasure. In fact, the magazine offers neither authentic sexual liberation nor a more all-encompassing freedom for women; instead, women and the experience of pleasure are once again commodified, this time overtly and unsubtly, as *Playgirl* extends the process of sexual reification begun in other women's magazines.

MS. AND THE MYTH OF LIBERATIONAL CONSUMERISM: THE IDEOLOGICAL CONSTRAINTS OF MIDDLE-CLASS FEMINISM

In early 1971 a group of writers and editors, disenchanted with the publishing industry's neglect of women's issues, began to plan a new magazine that women would own and control. With the help of only one large financial backer and volunteer labor, the group published an immensely successful preview issue in January 1972 as an insert in *New York* magazine. After the 300,000 copies sold out in eight days and the new magazine received over 20,000 letters from readers, the group obtained financial backing from Warner Communications while retaining for the staff majority control of the stock. The new *Ms.* magazine was on its way to overcoming the high odds against women founding and continuing to control their own publication. Although its staff envisioned a publication that would reach millions of women across race, class, and economic divisions, *Ms.* became a special-interest publication read primarily by relatively privileged women who are nonetheless second-class citizens by virtue of their sex.[31]

Categorizing itself as "a national news magazine written for women, about women, by women," *Ms.* claims that it strives editorially for the elimination of subordination based on sex and race.[32] But the magazine is also a business venture and, even though its founders gave some of the profits to the women's movement, the laws of free enterprise affect the magazine's content. Of its $9.3 million total revenues in 1983, *Ms.* earned $5.1 million from advertising.[33] Besides enabling the magazine to continue publication and providing money for women's causes, the advertisements in *Ms.* promote a consumption-based model of women's liberation and sometimes undercut the magazine's positive editorial messages.

Early on, the staff of *Ms.* publicized its view that increased opportunities for women to consume are liberational. When announcing the magazine's premiere issue the founders noted: "Women are looking for products of quality advertised in a way that respects women's judgment and intelligence."[34] One of the magazine's initial goals, as Publisher Patricia Carbine stated it in 1974, was to convince advertisers to begin to see women as a target market: "it was time for the automotive community, the financial services community, the insurance community, the credit card community, the airlines, the travel world, the corporate world to begin to direct their advertising messages to women. We felt women wanted information about the full range of products." Carbine added that the first subscriber study *Ms.* conducted showed the magazine to be "almost a dream for quality product marketers."[35]

These statements reveal the magazine's reformist goal of changing sexist marketing patterns. Such a project, however, focuses on the symptoms rather than the causes of sexism and is characteristic of liberal, non-radical feminism. *Ms.* collaborates in the selling of its readers in reified form as upscale consumers to advertisers. With the magazine's cooperation, advertisers learn to see feminists and those who subscribe to the mass culture of feminism as potential spenders, a "target market" in

Carbine's words. The staff's argument that the wide variety of advertising the magazine solicits more correctly reflects its readers' broad purchasing patterns than does advertising in traditional women's magazines[36] is an ideological screen which masks the fundamental contradiction of viewing increased consumerism as liberational. The reification of readers that most advertising fosters in fact leads to a constellation of contradictory messages in *Ms*.

The conflict between the magazine's commercial goals and its feminist ones surfaces in the interplay between the ads and editorial material. The reinforcement between ads and editorial features at work in most women's magazines also functions in *Ms*.[37] but this relation additionally becomes one of conflict and opposition in *Ms*. In April 1983, for example, readers immersed in the article "Three generations of Naranjo women" are interrupted by trivialized visual and verbal images of women in a Maybelline ad with the headline, "Polished lips have shine appeal" (p. 61). Turning the page, readers encounter an ad for Dexatrim appetite control capsules with twelve photos of women before and after use of the product. The headline, "If you can't lose weight, do what these people did," contrasts strongly with the positive image of women on the facing page where the photo and headline communicate women's strength: "Hannah Senesh: Poet, parachutist, freedom fighter," the title of this month's "Stories for Free Children" feature (p. 63).

Chapter 4 examined several ads in *Ms*. that denigrate women. By heightening insecurities about trivial aspects of physical appearance, reducing women to fragments of themselves through metonymic visual portrayals, and presenting male visual consumption as the best measure of self-approval, many ads in *Ms*. contradict the positive feminist messages on the editorial pages. The ideological constraints of liberal feminism are revealed in this contradictory structure which asks readers to oscillate between the opposing poles of liberation and subjugation. While a number of positive images of women in *Ms*. inspire continued struggle to change sexism, they are sometimes overwhelmed by the attractively presented negative images which join forces with other pervasive mass cultural images to convince women that their subjugation is desirable.

In another important sense, however, these contradictions are only apparent. While much of the editorial material in *Ms*. is progressive, it represents a middle-class feminism which, in fact, correlates closely to the middle-class consumer goods promoted in the advertisements. The same worldview that romanticizes minority women in the editorial feature "Three generations of Naranjo women," for example, metonymically reifies women in the adjacent ad as "polished lips." While the readers of *Ms.* – a group of relatively privileged women – oscillate between the contradictory messages of liberation and subjugation on the magazine's pages, they are at the same time shielded from the class contradictions of society.

Unlike other women's magazines, however, a number of editorial features in *Ms.* focus readers' attention on a wide range of important issues. Many lengthy letters from readers are published each month, showing intelligent, thoughtful responses to the articles. Here readers argue and disagree with one another and evaluate the magazine's content. There is a sense of real communication between the women who write letters and those who read them, and an opportunity for serious thought about some feminist issues. Overall, the articles in *Ms.* presuppose a more rather than less intelligent reader instead of addressing what many magazines assume to be the lowest common denominator of the mass audience. By including articles on a wide variety of topics rather than only those traditionally presumed to be of interest to women, *Ms.* help to broaden, develop, and further educate its readers. Unlike many other women's magazines *Ms.* is a publication designed to be read rather than merely thumbed through. The intelligently written informational articles are surrounded by attractive consumerist visuals, however, which, as we have seen, sometimes undercut the features and distract readers from the learning at hand.

To a large degree, the readers of *Ms.* constitute a "class" audience. *Folio 400* lists *Ms.* in its "Women in Business" category and, as we have seen, Carbine termed the magazine's audience "almost a dream for quality product marketers."[38] A travel article in May 1983, "Spas worth going abroad for" (p. 34), for example, focuses on elite European resorts, listing only one relatively inexpensive spa in Mexico. Although the staff claims to desire to reach a wide audience that includes the underprivileged, many advertisers seek upscale readers; consequently, a good deal of the magazine's editorial material must address this sector.

There is a further explanation for the elitism of *Ms.*, beyond this material one. Although there are many progressive elements in the editorial features which contribute to women's politicization, the magazine is limited by the liberal feminist consciousness of its staff. Just as the staff members fail to see the denigration of women in some of the ads they publish, so, too, do they understand feminism in elitist terms. Mariana Valverde has argued that both the ads and editorial material in *Ms.* show womanhood and feminism to be primarily white, middle-class, and heterosexual: "The unemployed woman, the Indian woman, the lesbian, the immigrant woman . . . are relegated to cameo appearances. Their 'lifestyles' (as opposed to their oppression) are described as being those of "minorities." The average reader may find these lifestyles interesting to read about, but the accounts [do] not directly challenge the class and race privileges of the supposedly average middle- or upper-class reader."[39] This liberal feminist consciousness, then, although progressive, works as well with the magazine's material goals to limit the audience to privileged women.

In 1983 *Ms.* lost 11,500 readers and was down 26 per cent in news-stand circulation.[40] Nearly three-quarters of the students in a course I teach on women's magazines had never read *Ms.* before studying it in my class. In spite of special issues which the magazine publishes such as "The young feminists: A new generation speaks out" (April 1983), *Ms.* suffers from a generation gap because many of today's young women are unfamiliar with the preoccupations of women who came of age in the 1960s and 1970s. Like other magazines that have changed with the times, *Ms.* must also adapt itself to the 1980s and 1990s if it wishes to communicate feminist values to young women and sell them upscale consumer goods.

While the commercial goals of many of these special-interest publications often mesh closely with the ideological messages they endeavor to secure, in some cases serious contradictions result from the attempted union of a liberal political ideology to a commercial venture. The progressive but non-radical ideologies of a *BBW* or a *Ms.*, for instance, are ripe for co-optation by commercial exigencies. Both magazines could insist that advertisers portray women in non-sexist poses, for example – just as *Essence* insists that advertisers use only Black models – but neither magazine believes its advertising to be offensive. Whcther the normative messages these magazines give readers about their membership in special groups mesh closely with the publications' commercial goals or produce contradictions, advertisers can be assured that elite groups of readers have been constituted to purchase their products.

10 Acquisitions, New Launches, and Adaptations: Women's Magazines Enter the 1990s

By the end of the 1980s, several changes had occurred in the women's magazine industry, but the structural continuity of these publications, with one exception, persisted. Transfers of ownership, new launches, demises, and changes in advertising practices occurred; video magazines appeared on cable television. But all except one of the modifications were rooted in the same cycle of publishing profit, advertising, and women's role as primary purchasers that structures the women's magazines studied here from the early 1980s.

CHANGES IN OWNERSHIP

In 1984 Rupert Murdoch purchased *New Woman* for $20 million, Conde Nast bought *Gourmet* for $24 million, and CBS took ownership of twelve Ziff-Davis consumer magazines for $362.5 million, among them *Modern Bride*. A number of media analysts called this last figure exorbitant and it was believed to be the highest sum ever paid for a group of magazines. By mid-1985, CBS accused Ziff of overstating the magazines' earnings by as much as $3.9 million and later brought suit over the matter. In July 1987, the litigation still unsettled, CBS announced the sale of its entire magazine division to a group of the division's senior management.[1]

Peter Diamandis, former CBS executive and Publisher of *Woman's Day*, led the new magazine group, paying $650 million for the CBS division and renaming it Diamandis Communications Inc. He quickly sold seven of the magazines to help pay off the debt, among them *Modern Bride* which Cahners bought for $50 million. Diamandis had earned nearly $243 million for the company. In a surprise move in April 1988, however, only twenty-six weeks after buying the group from CBS, Diamandis sold the entire corporation to the French publisher Hachette for $712 million, making a profit of nearly $303 million in the six-month lifespan of the company.[2]

This extremely lucrative sale caused much notice within the publishing industry and business circles. Prudential Insurance of America, which had financed Diamandis, made about $200 million on its brief investment and Diamandis' management group, $95 million. Diamandis' own pretax profit was estimated to be between $18 and $25 million. Hachette, which had offered CBS $600 million in 1987 for the twenty-two titles CBS then owned, now, less than a year later, paid $712 million for seven fewer magazines. Analysts argued that *Woman's Day* was the biggest reason Hachette was willing to invest so much. The magazine had increased ad volume 36 per cent since 1984 and in 1987 had a $4 million increase in ad revenue.[3]

An even larger sale eclipsed the Diamandis–Hachette deal in August 1988 when Walter Annenberg announced that Rupert Murdoch would acquire Triangle Publications for $3 billion. For this unprecedented price Murdoch added to his media empire only three publications – *TV Guide*, *Seventeen*, and the *Daily Racing Form*, but *TV Guide* with a circulation of 17.2 million was the largest magazine in the country at the time of the sale.[4] Given the competition from *Sassy*, the new slick magazine for teenage girls, Murdoch may experiment with more daring changes than Annenberg made in *Seventeen*; Murdoch's newly acquired teenage publication may begin to resemble *New Woman* which Murdoch modified after purchasing it in 1984.

Family Media, which had acquired *Ladies' Home Journal* from Charter in 1982, bought *Savvy* for an estimated $6–$9 million in February 1985. Under Family Media, *Savvy*'s ad volume increased 10 per cent and its ad volume 35 per cent from 1986 to 1987. The company spent $2 million to relaunch *Savvy* in April 1987. In November 1985 Family Media sold *Ladies' Home Journal* to Meredith, publisher of *Better Homes and Gardens* for $96 million, having raised the *Journal*'s ad volume 8 per cent and its ad revenue 16 per cent over the previous year. Although the *Journal*'s circulation rate base was five million – one of the lowest of the home service magazines, Robert A. Burnett, President of Meredith pointed to the positive aspects of one company's owning two of the seven sisters magazines: "With *Better Homes* at eight million and the *Journal* at five million, we have a very strong pair of flagship products." By 1988, Meredith had raised the *Journal*'s circulation by 125,000.[5]

Repositioning itself away from the women's service magazines, Family Media in early 1988 purchased and reissued *Taxi*, a women's fashion title which an Italian firm had published in the US from August 1986 to November 1987. Family Media also agreed to manage a joint venture with Times Mirror Magazines – the July 1988 launch of *Model*, aimed at women 16–22. *Savvy*, *Taxi*, and *Model*, along with the company's *Health* and *1001 Home Ideas*, are marketed as a group with a potential 3.4 million circulation and establish Family Media as a strong force in the women's magazine market. In June 1988 the company announced plans to reposition *Health* as a fashion and beauty title and the recruitment to the magazine of Dianne Partie Lange, Managing Editor of *Self*.[6] Because of declining ad pages, however, *Savvy* ceased publication with the February 1991 issue.

In one of the biggest changes of ownership in the late 1980s, Time Inc. entered the women's magazine field in November 1986, announcing the purchase of a 50 per cent interest in *McCall's*, *Working Mother* and *Working Woman*. The three magazines formed the basis of a new company, the Working Woman McCall's Group, jointly owned with Dale Lang, Publisher of *Working Woman* since 1978. Time Inc. and Lang each contributed $44 million to the venture; Lang and his staff took charge of advertising and Time focused on circulation, using its enormous leverage at the news-stand and its subscriber base of 14.5 million names to increase the circulations of the three titles. Lang and Time sold *McCall's* to the New York Times Magazine Group in May 1989 for $80 million and Lang then bought full ownership in *Working Woman* and *Working Mother*.[7]

In another major change of ownership, John Fairfax Ltd, the giant Australian publisher of eighty magazines and fifty-three newspapers, bought *Ms.* magazine in September 1987. Patricia Carbine and Gloria Steinem, founders of *Ms.*, relinquished their positions but agreed to remain as consultants for five years; Sandra Yates, president of Fairfax Publications, US, replaced Carbine, as Publisher and Anne Summers, former head of the Australian Office of the Status of Women, became Editor-in-Chief. *Ms.* had been suffering from a lack of capital and a decline in readership for much of the 1980s. Down in ad volume, it made a profit of only $400,000–$500,000 for the year ending July 1987. Fairfax, which had invested tens of millions in its new teenage publication *Sassy*, agreed to provide the capital to expand the circulation of *Ms.* and thereby attract more advertisers.[8]

Among the changes initiated were a higher rate of $1 per word to freelance writers and timely payment, an enlarged, nine-inch format, a news magazine section that imitates the graphics of the major US news weeklies, and the endorsement of political candidates, previously illegal because of the magazine's tax-exempt status. Fairfax's ads in trade publications reified the readers of *Ms.* as monied consumers: one ad pictures a woman with $10 bills covering her as a dress, with the heading: "What do you call a woman with serious money to invest? *Ms.*"[9] The new owners expanded upon the magazine's previous attempt to link feminism to consumerism.

In June 1988, a mere seven months after its purchase of *Ms.*, Fairfax divested both this publication and its newly launched *Sassy*. Yates and Summers bought the two magazines for an estimated $30 million and formed a new company, Matilda Publications.[10] While appearing to be different, the cultural messages of the new *Ms.* and *Sassy* form a single continuum in which elements of both authentic and spurious liberation for women are linked to signs that urge reification of the self through commodities.

In October 1989, Lang Communications bought *Ms.* and *Sassy*, and three months later Chairman Dale Lang suspended publication of *Ms.*, announcing a daring gamble he would undertake. *Ms.* was to reappear in mid-1990 entirely devoid of advertising, attempting to sustain itself by readers' subscriptions of $40 per year. Robin Morgan, the new Editor, and Gloria Steinem, who had suggested the daring move to Lang, were immensely optimistic that *Ms.* could now return to its original feminist goals, free from pressures from advertisers. Steinem noted that *Ms.* lost certain cosmetics and haircare product accounts when it published editorial material that ran counter to these advertisers' goals. Although *Ms.* never sold enough ads to make a profit, it had to compromise its editorial goals merely to remain solvent in its seventeen years as an advertising magazine.[11]

Lang's radical experiment with *Ms.* met with skepticism among media analysts. Although he still hoped to make some profit,[12] by removing the magazine from the standard profit-making strategies of the industry, Lang helped to recast the publication as a new communications medium. The cynical greed evidenced in one analyst's remarks no longer applied to *Ms.*: the new magazine would probably fail, James Kobak noted, because by offering readers 100 pages of editorial material per issue, "they're ignoring the first law of publishing – the less you give 'em the more you can charge."[13] Many found it difficult to understand that a corporate head would willingly withdraw a publication from the standard profit-making cycle. But by doing so, Lang offered women an historic opportunity to create a radically new mass medium.

DEMISES AND LAUNCHES

Several women's magazines ceased publication in the mid-1980s, often because they were directed to an extremely narrow audience, were founded by individuals or small groups with minimal capital, or, when backed by large corporations, failed to attain enough ad revenue and circulation to turn a profit. *Latina*, for example, started by two Chicanas in Los Angeles with little financial backing, had difficulty finding advertisers and readers; after appearing irregularly for a few years, it ceased publication in 1985. Rodale's *Spring* also proved unprofitable and, although backed by a large publishing concern, was discontinued in its second year. *Cuisine* lost the battle for advertising dollars and readers to its competitor *Bon Appetit*; *It's Me* ceased publication, while its rival *BBW* survived.

Slimmer and *Fit* were victims of the proliferation of fitness magazines in the 1980s. As one writer noted, "there sometimes seem to be more magazines on newsstands designed to keep [women] fit than there are aerobics classes in Manhattan."[14] Advertisers perceived many of these publications as duplicating one another and as being incompatible editorially with certain products. Leo Scullin, a senior Vice-President at Young and Rubicam ad agency highlighted this last problem by asking, "How do you tie in Jell-O to triathlon sports?"[15] Although *Slimmer*, published by the owners of *Playgirl*, and *Fit* were unable to survive the competition in the category, *Shape* attracted several national advertisers by 1985, its circulation having risen to 550,000. *New Body*, another fitness title founded in 1982, had attained a circulation of 275,000 as a bi-monthly and by 1988, had not only survived but increased its frequency to nine times per year.[16]

Whether undercapitalized or unsuccessful in spite of strong financial backing, many new publications fail because they are unable to transform themselves into profitable advertising magazines. If the editorial philosophies of the founders are incompatible with the products and images advertisers currently market, a magazine is not likely to survive. Sometimes a large publishing corporation, convinced of a new venture's ultimate ability to succeed, will subsidize a magazine for five or more years, as occurred with *Self* or *Vanity Fair*, for example. In other cases, companies decide to cut their losses early on because there is little expectation of the publication's financial success. In spite of the enormous difficulties in launching new advertising magazines for women in the 1980s, there are several success stories.

The fashion and beauty category has proven one of the safest areas for magazine starts. In 1988, *Folio* called it "the hottest magazine category" because it surpassed all others – up 13 per cent in ad volume in 1987 after a similar 8 per cent rise in 1986.[17] Leading the category and fourth in the country in 1987 ad growth was the recent entry, *Elle*, launched in 1985 as a joint venture of Murdoch Magazines and the French publishing giant Hachette. With 2080 ad pages, *Elle* showed a 47 per cent increase in 1987 and its monthly paid circulation in 1988 was 851,152. Similar in format to *Vogue*, *Elle* markets itself as "an international style magazine . . . for the sophisticated, affluent, well-traveled woman."[18] While *Vogue* has maintained its own position with a 1.2 million paid circulation and high ad volume, *Bazaar* has lost ground to *Elle*. In spite of changing to heavier paper, using more color on its opening pages, and even experimenting with younger models – a modification to which readers objected – *Bazaar*'s circulation remained at 760,759 in 1988.[19]

Another fashion publication, *Details*, although not in strict terms a new magazine, entered a different league after its purchase in January 1988 by the S. I. Newhouse subsidiary, Advance Publications, now also publisher of *Vogue*. Newhouse paid over $2 million for *Details*, in spite of the magazine's very low circulation of 100,000. Established as an avant-garde publication in 1982, *Details* now uses heavier paper stock, and enjoys the benefits of an association with Newhouse.[20]

Taxi, launched in the US by an Italian publisher in August 1986, focuses on international fashion and upscale consumption. After ceasing publication in November 1987, it was purchased by Family Media in January 1988 and relaunched in May that year. *Taxi*'s circulation of 250,000 is primarily news-stand purchases.[21] Like *Elle*, *Taxi* represents the attempt of a European publishing concern to attain a share of the US readers of fashion magazines; initially unsuccessful in that goal, *Taxi* now competes with titles such as *Vogue*, *Bazaar*, and *Elle* as a US publication that retains much of its original European flavor.

In February 1988, the Australian publisher John Fairfax Ltd launched *Sassy*, aimed at girls 14–19 and modeled on the successful Australian magazine for teenage girls, *Dolly*. With large-size format, high-quality paper, and an emphasis on sophisticated fashion, *Sassy* hoped to lure readers from *Seventeen*, *'Teen*, and *YM* (formerly *Young Miss*) and attract the other teenagers who read magazines such as *Elle*, *Vogue*, and *Cosmopolitan*.[22] Indeed, *Sassy* appears to be a version of *Elle* for girls under 20, mixing photographs of avant-garde fashion with verbal editorial texts that attempt to mimic current teenage speech patterns. Frequently, postmodernist, self-reflexive phrases interrupt sentences, and editorial comments and rejoinders appear in the text in brackets. Referring to Jane Pratt, Editor-in-Chief, for example, one feature notes: "Jane agrees on Johnny Depp and R. E. M. but is visibly bummed that Barbara hasn't heard of Keanu Reeves. [Not yet anyway – Jane]" (June 1988, p. 45).

The mixture of the mature and the childish on the formal level is matched in the magazine's content. A primer for one's first sexual encounter, answering questions such as "Should I talk during sex?" and "How long will it take?", and articles on the physiology of sexual arousal, boys' bodies, condoms, AIDS, gay couples, and abortion have been criticized as provocative and sensationalist by editors of the competing *'Teen* and *Seventeen* and defended by *Sassy* as information teenagers want to know.[23] In fact, *Sassy*'s features often combine certain elements of sensationalism and forbidden knowledge with moral lessons that uphold predominant moral values. Because of its appearance as transgressive and sophisticated, its readership is growing faster than predicted. It doubled its initial estimates of ad volume with 240 paid pages in its first six issues and in September 1988, its guaranteed circulation rose to 400,000. Nonetheless, only seven months after *Sassy*'s launch, Fairfax sold the magazine along with *Ms.* to the two women who headed *Ms.*, who formed the new corporation, Matilda Publications. In October 1989, Dale W. Lang, owner of *Working Woman*, *Working Mother*, and *Success* bought *Ms.* and *Sassy*.[24]

At the opposite end of women's lifespan, another new publication seeks affluent women over 40. *Lear's*, which made its debut in February 1988, has an editorial philosophy that life is better after 40 and that women re-entering the workforce after raising families are tired of seeing young models in magazines. Founded by Frances Lear with funds from her large divorce settlement, the magazine promises to avoid articles on diets, children, recipes, and decorating.[25] As a women's advertising magazine, however, it promotes costly, exclusive consumer goods and a number of its articles encourage a commodity-based self-indulgence. The cover credit in the second issue (May/June 1988), for example, notes that the woman on the cover is a 52-year-old film-maker but promotes the brand-name clothes, accessories, and make-up she wears; while several articles focus on noteworthy women, a number of others promote a preoccupation with the self, especially the body and physical appearance, advising special baths, visits to spas, beauty aids for the skin, and expensive fashion and jewelry. Letters from readers printed in the second issue complain about this focus. Although *Lear's* includes a number of older women as models and subjects of articles, quite young-looking women also often appear in ads and features. *Lear's* is partially reformist but not revolutionary in this respect.

Lear's first issue carried 76 ad pages but its second dropped to 46, followed by a third "soft month" for advertising. The magazine's largest ad category is automobiles, rather than fragrances and apparel. Although its rate base is only 200,000, *Lear's* distributed 475,000 copies of its first issue and sends 25,000 copies of each issue free to selected "upscale households."[26] While the ad volume in its first issues is healthy for a new magazine, to become financially viable, *Lear's* will have to increase ad pages, ad categories, and paid circulation.

Children and parenting are the focus of a cluster of new magazines which, by the mid-1980s, was already dubbed a "baby-boomlet" group. *Folio* noted that a more accurate term would be "mother boomlet" since it was not the birth rate that had risen but the number of baby-boomer women in their child-bearing years. Meredith launched *Motherhood* and McCall's *Baby!* in late 1985; two years later Time Inc. invested over $5 million for a 49 per cent interest in *Parenting*, and the New York Times Magazine Group bought *Child*, a large-size, heavy-paper publication originally owned by Taxi Inc., featuring expensive clothing and toys for upscale parents to buy for their children. Rodale's *Children*, subtitled "Happy, healthy, and fit," went from quarterly to monthly in 1988. The publishers of the new parenting titles hoped to capitalize on the ability of "Yuppies" to spend large sums on their children. Even magazines such as *Fathers*, called by its publisher "a delayed reaction to the women's movement of the 1960s"[27] and Meredith's *Grandparents* tried to link people's affection for children to consumerism.

All of the magazines in this new genre will not survive, analysts predict; too many publishers have attempted to enter this "window of opportunity" created by the large number of first children being born and the presumed affluence of their two-income parents. The new publications compete with the well established *Parents* on the news-stand as well as with the more than ten, controlled circulation publications sent to expecting women and new mothers such as *American Baby* and *Baby Talk*. The magazines also face competition from the numerous books, video cassettes, and cable television programs on babies now available.[28] The titles that survive will be those that succeed in establishing a commodified version of the child as a viable sign of ideal womanhood, linking affection for one's children and grandchildren to consumer goods. The magazines that continue to attract readers through such signs will thereby attract large advertising volume and revenue.

Among other magazines launched in the mid- and late-1980s are Hearst's *Victoria* (March 1987), an offshoot of *Good Housekeeping*, focusing on romantic furnishings, food, and entertaining; *Black Elegance* (*BE*), a fashion and beauty title published since 1986 by Go-Stylish Publishing Inc.; Rupert Murdoch's *In Fashion*, less avant-garde than *Details* or *Vogue*; Bauer Publishing's *First for Women* which spent an estimated $10 million to acquire supermarket checkout counter space and sold its premier issue in 1989 for 25 cents; *Mirabella*, edited by Grace Mirabella for Murdoch Magazines, launched in 1989 as a fashion magazine seeking older readers than *Vogue*; *Cooking Light*, launched in February 1987 by Time Inc.; and *Good Food*, first published in 1974 by Triangle and relaunched by the company in 1985. By 1987 *Good Food* was second in the country in ad page growth, up 80 per cent from 1986.[29]

VIDEO ADAPTATIONS OF MAGAZINES

With the advent of cable television, a number of magazine publishers saw an opportunity to increase audiences, enhance revenues and widen the visibility of their publications. Television programs based on their magazines might also attract new subscribers, as well as offer a foothold in the electronic media. Not surprisingly, the largest magazine category – the women's publications, whose female audiences are also the primary viewers of daytime network television – dominated the new cable magazine ventures of the early 1980s.[30]

Often, advertising agencies helped to develop cable magazines, as Dancer Fitzgerald Sample did in 1983 with McCall's *Working Mother* to enable clients such as General Mills to advertise to working women. Similarly, Young and Rubicam, General Foods and *Woman's Day* joined forces that year to produce "Woman's Day USA" for the USA Cable Network. Benton and Bowles, Procter & Gamble, and Hearst/ABC produced two series for cable based on editorial material from *Good Housekeeping* which appeared on the Hearst/ABC Daytime Cable Network along with versions of *Cosmopolitan* and *Newsweek Woman*. Noxell sponsored an edition of *Co-Ed* magazine for teenage girls on the USA cable channel as did Kraft a program based on *Redbook* for the Christian Broadcasting Network, which also broadcast the video version of *American Baby* magazine. *Essence* produced its own show for national syndication.[31] While some of the video magazines offered programming relatively free of product promotion, most were structured around the marketing concerns of their sponsors.

The two *Good Housekeeping* spinoffs, "A Better Way" and "The Good Housekeeper," inaugurated in July 1983, were transparently tied to commercialism. Hosted by John Mack Carter, Editor-in-Chief of *Good Housekeeping*, the half-hour interview program "A Better Way" invited as guests women who had found improved ways to live.[32] Commercials promoted Procter

& Gamble products such as Crisco shortening, Downey fabric softener, Mr. Clean liquid, Crest toothpaste, Tide detergent, and High Point coffee. On one 1983 program, Carter interviewed Reverend Jane Shields of Delaware, a Lutheran minister, and showed a film clip of her at work. Carter abruptly changed the subject at the end of the interview, however, by asking Shields if she was concerned about her family's nutrition; in an awkward attempt at transition, he then remarked that the creators of the program understood that concern and had invited a registered dietician as the next guest. Shields remained to ask the dietician a series of pre-rehearsed questions whose answers included advice that one keep spaghetti and dry milk on hand and the promotion of microwave ovens. Carter than summarized for the viewers "what we have learned" in a patronizing, elementary-school fashion.

Even more childish was *Good Housekeeping*'s other cable spinoff, a one-minute ad segment in the trappings of an animated feature, "The Good Housekeeper." Here, one Procter & Gamble product "sponsored" a short cartoon which instructed women how to perform household tasks such as washing windows or hanging pictures. While a voiceover gave viewers instructions in childish rhymes, the cartoon figure of a woman danced around, visually demonstrating how to do the jobs. A regular ad for the sponsoring product followed, such as Lilt home permanent or Duncan Hines Cookie Mix.

"The Good Housekeeper" appeared as advertising on Hearst/ABC Daytime Cable Network, often during another of Hearst's cable magazines, "A View from Cosmo." Here, Helen Gurley Brown interviewed such figures as a professional male escort and the author of a book on dying, and discussed topics the magazine avoided such as child abuse and rape. By 1984, "A View from Cosmo" had moved to the Lifetime Cable Network, also partly owned by Hearst, and had expanded to include segments on food, decorating, relationships and celebrities.

Like the two spinoffs of *Good Housekeeping*, the electronic version of *Redbook* and *Woman's Day* openly promoted their sponsors' products. "*Redbook*'s Family Chef" which appeared on the Christian Broadcasting Network in 1983 was hosted by two members of *Redbook*'s staff. With Kraft as the program's sponsor, ads included products such as Le Creme whipped topping, Miracle Whip sandwich spread, Parkay margarine, and the company's salad dressing, barbecue sauce, and cheeses. The hosts reminded the audience in one program on new breakfast recipes, that the March issue of *Redbook* contained a feature on the subject. In another segment, "Cornelius Corner," a man representing Corning Glass demonstrated microwave breakfasts, promoting by name the Pyrex measuring cup and microwave cookware his company manufactures. Credits at the end of the program included *Redbook* advertisers such as Congoleum flooring and Jenn-Air Ranges.

Young and Rubicam's copyright appeared at the end of "Woman's Day USA" broadcast on the USA cable network in 1983. The show's subtitle, heard in a voiceover, underscored the key role of the audience as purchasers: "Your weekly menu planner – what to buy and how to buy it." Expanding on a regular *Woman's Day* magazine feature, "Month of Menus," a calendar with meal plans which readers are to tear out and follow at home, the cable program began by visually displaying seven meals. Later, nutritional information and the calorie count of each meal was presented, and the following week, shorter segments entitled "Today's Meal" demonstrated the recipes individually. Meanwhile, the sponsors hoped, viewers would follow the advice of "George," who, standing in front of shelves containing General Foods products, recommended a shopping list of items to buy in order to prepare the meals.

Other segments of the program included "How to Buy," "Major Cooking Methods," "Making Do," and "The *Woman's Day* Silver Spoon Award." In programs aired on 21 February and 25 August 1983, the General Foods products advertised in commercials included Minute Rice, Dream Whip, Jell-O, Tang, Gravy Train, Gaines Burgers, Grape Nuts, Fruit & Fibre cereal, Master Blend coffee, Stove Top Stuffing, Kool-Aid, GF International coffees, Good Seasons salad dressing, and Sanka. The demonstrated recipes required items such as pudding mix, whipped topping, packaged dough mix, mayonnaise, and evaporated milk. When George offered shopping advice in his 21 February segment, on the grocery shelves behind him were several packages of Minute Rice, which two commercials on the program advertised that day. Besides highlighting products, the program promoted *Woman's Day* itself with numerous shots of the magazine in grocery bags and on kitchen counter tops. The reciprocal advertising between the magazine and the program paralleled the support that General Foods products on the program gave to those advertised on the pages of the magazine.

A most refreshing departure from the transparently commercial structure of many of the cable magazines for women was the program "Newsweek Woman" which appeared on the Daytime network. Without commercial interruption, several news segments reported on special issues relating to women. Topics included the unequal treatment of women prisoners in job training programs, women and pornography, legislation to force men to pay child support, pay equity, mothers organizing to prevent gang violence, and computers trapping women in dead-end jobs. Both the reporters and anchors who introduced the new segments were primarily women, so that the show stood in sharp contrast to the standard national news programs both in content and in the gender of the people presenting the news. Copyrighted by Post-Newsweek Video Inc., the program bore little resemblance to the special edition magazine *Newsweek Woman* discussed in Chapter 7.

In general, the experiment with video magazines was not financially successful. Where a magazine could survive with an audience of 100,000 or 200,000, television audiences had to be much larger to meet expenses. While some publishers could not sustain the high cost of television production, others were unhappy with the results of their investments. *Better Homes and Gardens* cancelled its USA Network program in 1982 after only one season, dissatisfied with the quality of the production. In early 1983, Hearst/ABC was only able to charge advertisers $325–$600 for a 30-second commercial, where the daytime rate on network TV for that time ran to $15,000. In the first quarter of 1983, advertisers bought only 40 per cent of Hearst/ABC's daytime spots and a number of public service ads filled the unsold space. While *Essence*'s syndicated program ran for four years, in July 1988 it was cancelled because advertising revenues barely met production costs. In contrast, "The American Baby TV Show" on the Christian Broadcasting Network was one of the few long-running success stories. In its seventh year in 1988, it ran twenty-six different shows per season, each with six minutes of advertising. Production costs for each show were between $20,000 and $25,000 that year, while the ad revenue approached $131,500, making the show extremely profitable.[33]

MODIFICATIONS IN ADVERTISING TECHNIQUES

While some changes in magazine advertising practices occurred in the mid- and late-1980s, there were no radical modifications in the signs used to address women. *Elle* published a mini-catalogue in August 1988, *Working Mother* included a wall poster for daycare centers, and *McCall's* announced a 32-page pullout section for its September and December 1988 issues, an advertorial awarded to K-Mart for being one of its top five advertisers.[34]

Magazines placed more emphasis on merchandising opportunities for advertisers, sometimes helping to pay for promotions such as fashion shows, sporting events, and contests. *Family Circle*, for example, offers advertisers national TV spots during the Women's Professional Tennis Tournament and free vacations at the tournament. *Essence* gives a merchandising allowance of 1 per cent of net advertising expenditures to companies purchasing at least three ad pages in the magazine. *Sassy* gives a 0.5 per cent such allowance and offers advertorial posters, editorial sampling ("You [the advertiser] provide the product/item; we write about it"), Sassy Club sampling, contests and retail promotions.[35]

While there were numerous rumors in the early and mid-1980s that magazines, especially the seven sisters, were selling space to advertisers below the rate-card prices, Dale Lang, Publisher of *McCall's* made news in May 1987 by announcing that *McCall's* would officially abandon its rate card. Unofficially, the other seven sisters were also rumored to negotiate rates. Ad agency teams began the practice of rate negotiation sessions with publishers. Despite such rate cutting, five of the seven sisters had ad volume losses in 1987, with *Good Housekeeping* down 13.3 per cent; *McCall's* was down in ad pages in 1988, in spite of its striking move, but up 23 per cent in 1989. And Lang sold the magazine for $80 million that year, twice what he had paid for it.[36]

Several magazines modified the way they marketed themselves as cultural commodities. *Seventeen* changed its subtitle to: "It's where the girl ends and the woman begins"; its trade ads termed the magazine's reader "The Seventeen woman," "The other woman" and "The other female head of the household," emphasizing that the reader's consuming and spending power was that of a woman rather than a girl's, and more openly using sexual innuendos to attract advertisers. *New Woman*, after its purchase by Rupert Murdoch, became more openly imitative of *Cosmopolitan*. *Playgirl* in 1987 eliminated complete male nudity and began to advertise that it had a new editorial mix with more lifestyle coverage; its aim was to be sold next to *Cosmopolitan* on the news-stand rather than isolated with the other adult magazines. *House & Garden* changed its name to *HG* in March 1988, widened to a nine-inch format as did many women's magazines seeking upscale audiences in the late 1980s, and began to use simple, bold lettering on its cover like *Vogue*; its editorial material was broadened to include the lifestyles of beautiful people in addition to beautiful homes, and a former Editor of the British *Vogue* was appointed as Editor-in-Chief.[37]

In spite of the immense sums of money that changed hands as magazines were bought and sold, launched and relaunched in the 1980s, their cultural messages changed only superficially. While the reports in news media and trade publication, often follow the magazine publishers' emphasis on the significance of even minor changes in their business practices, radical changes have not occurred in the industry and its cultural products. Even when versions of magazines appeared on so different a medium as television, quite similar messages resulted. As long as enormous profits continue to be made from directing this constellation of signs to women, the magazines' encoding strategies will remain structurally constant.

Conclusion: The Articulation of Desire and Consumerism in the Master Text

The negative hermeneutic project that underlies the information and analysis in this book has sought to foreground as well the positive pole of desire that structures this pervasive form of gendered mass culture. Jameson's insistence that the ideological and the utopian in cultural texts cannot be understood apart from one another is key to analyzing the cultural leadership that women's magazines exercise. Compelling, but necessarily transitory pleasures work to win credibility for these master narratives, thereby securing the publishers' and advertisers' commercial goals.

Indeed, commodified desire is an important semiotic tool whereby the encoders of magazine texts strive to anchor a preferred social accenting in the grand tale that they construct about reality. The commodity base of the pleasure must be so pervasive that it appears to be an essential characteristic of contemporary feminine desire. The smaller narrative segments – from individual ads and parts thereof, to fashion features, advice columns, and voyeuristic documentary fiction – combine to build a master tale that aims to win readers to this consensual view about reality.

But the ostensibly agreed-upon values that underlie this "common-sense" articulation of pleasure to commodities at the same time constitute a pseudo-consensus that, precisely because of its commercial base, turns on a spurious sense of solidarity and conformity with the values of one's peers. If women, at the magazines' urging, experience a sometimes real and sometimes utopian sense of community while reading these texts, confident of participating in normal, expected feminine culture, they are at the same time learning consumerist competitiveness and reified individualism. Magazines figuratively assimilate an idealized individual consciousness to a similarly idealized group consciousness as one of their primary narrative strategies.

In individual ads and features as well as in the intergeneric clusters formed between the two, initial narrative disequilibria such as "undesirable panty lines" or "facial wrinkles" move toward a commodity solution along both rapid and gradual narrative paths. The absence of or threat to the desirable which structures the opening state of narrative instability implies both an initial pre-lapsarian moment either in the past or present and a homologous moment – the commodified regeneration of the desirable in the future. As Todorov has argued, the new equilibrium, although similar to the first state is never identical to it.[1] In the fictional narrative resolutions within the magazine texts, readers experience one important level of pleasure; but to secure the desirable, they must re-enact the narrative in the public sphere by purchasing goods and services. This double narrative strategy regenerates itself continually because the commodity resolutions can only offer temporary pleasures.

As we have seen, the framing function of the representations in women's magazines is necessarily what Hall would term a "leaky system." The narrative strategies can only attain relative closure, and contradictions continue to obtain even while readers experience pleasure. Thus, certain narrative interpellations are repeatedly foregrounded in the struggle to secure consensus because women's everyday experience interacts dialogically and often contradictorily with the representations in magazines. And sometimes, as Jameson has theorized, magazines deliberately invoke such contradictions as a means of controlling oppositional impulses.

A woman reading *Weight Watchers*, for example, might experience the magazine as a "leaky system" when, at one moment in her enjoyment of the text, she questions the strong emphasis on eating in a weight-loss publication; her everyday experience, in contrast, shows her that increased eating causes weight gain. And she might enjoy utopian pleasure in engaging with these representations of attractive eating, even while the contradictions function. As Hall notes, however, negotiated readings of texts do not necessarily constitute counter-hegemonic visions. In Jameson's formulation, *Weight Watchers* might deliberately awaken these transgressive impulses of forbidden eating precisely to control them, channeling these desires into H. J. Heinz food products. Walkerdine's analysis of the role of fantasy in establishing various "regimes of meaning" similarly suggests that the very "unreality" of the representations in a magazine such as *Weight Watchers* is an important element of the strength of the discursive regimes it foregrounds.

This book has emphasized a "text-centric" analysis of women's magazines, while by no means assuming the audience to be passive or unified.[2] The immense circulations and profits of these publications suggest that the master narratives they construct succeed quite well in channeling women's desire into consumerism. Despite (and because of) the "leakiness" of the semiotic systems at work, and the negotiated and oppositional meanings that readers often develop, a structural continuity persists in the textual strategies of women's magazine. Readers' individual and sometimes shared modes of resistance to representations in magazines have not affected radical changes in the structure of capitalist society nor even in the magazines themselves. The senders and receivers of these cultural texts participate in an immensely unequal power relation; readers have little input into the monthly representations that claim to be about their lives, notwithstanding publishers' acute awareness of the demographics of readers and the target audience's probable receptivity to various representations.

Despite the struggles that occur in discourse, the disarticulation and rearticulation of received signs, the oppositional and negotiated decodings of the necessarily "leaky" messages, women's magazines repeatedly succeed in linking desire to consumerism. The critical decoding of these texts offered here is intended as one such oppositional reading, a negative hermeneutic process that estranges and calls into question the textual strategies that conflate commodities and desire, at the same time recognizing the immense power and attractiveness of this linkage.

Appendix

Table A1 Advertising Volume in US Women's Magazines, 1981–83
(Total pages per year)

Magazine	*1981*	*1982*	*1983*
Bazaar	1,331	1,382	1,558
Better Homes and Gardens	1,464	1,334	1,353
Bon Appetit	1,128	1,018	995
Bride's	1,593	1,675	1,819
Buenhogar (US)	93	81	127
Cosmopolitan	2,361	2,289	2,464
Cosmopolitan en español (US)	171	203	206
Cuisine	557	459	523
Essence	970	935	967
Family Circle	1,669	1,694	1,790
Glamour	2,086	1,886	2,032
Good Housekeeping	2,062	2,015	2,096
Gourmet	830	843	932
House Beautiful	1,097	956	1,082
House & Garden	1,260	965	826
Ladies' Home Journal	1,028	930	1,177
Mademoiselle	1,527	1,525	1,574
McCall's	1,158	1,053	1,121
Modern Bride	1,303	1,440	1,519
Ms.	497	580	n.a.
New Woman	289	486	564
Parents	825	869	921
Playgirl	528	483	461
Redbook	1,145	1,049	1,102
Self	801	833	928
Seventeen	1,329	1,307	1,312
'Teen	547	556	650
Town & Country	1,183	1,716	1,814
Vanidades Continental (US)	464	594	507
Vogue	2,718	2,796	3,104
Weight Watchers	282	343	334
Woman's Day	1,477	1,465	1,604
Working Mother	625	848	855
Working Woman	763	1,017	1,185

Source: "Ad Linage," *Advertising Age*, 20 December 1982, pp. 33–4 and 19 December 1983, pp. 35–6.

Table A2 Advertising Rates for US Women's Magazines, 1982, 1983 (in dollars)

Magazine	*1982*		*1983*	
	1 page, 4-color	*Cover 4*	*1 page, 4-color*	*Cover 4*
Bazaar	16,200	19,970	17,980	22,170
Better Homes and Gardens	73,820	103,470	78,985	110,715
Bon Appetit	17,660	20,225	20,660	23,665
Bride's	13,800	15,160	15,450	16,980
Buenhogar (US)	765	1,035	840	1,135
Cosmopolitan	32,170	41,730	32,170	41,730
Cosmopolitan en español (US)	1,030	1,390	1,030	1,390
Cuisine	15,750	20,475	16,510	21,500
Essence	11,320	15,000	13,000	17,250
Family Circle	71,350	106,100	67,350	103,500
Glamour	24,340	28,900	28,370	33,690
Good Housekeeping	58,020	78,180	63,820	86,000
Gourmet	13,600	15,600	13,600	15,600
House Beautiful	19,775	24,100	21,750	27,190
House & Garden	25,430	31,555	16,575	20,500
It's Me	3,800	4,300	3,800	4,300
Ladies' Home Journal	48,000	67,200	50,400	70,600
Mademoiselle	16,280	18,800	18,720	21,710
McCall's	59,830	84,630	59,830	84,630
Modern Bride	13,875	14,990	15,540	16,790
Ms.	8,720	11,765	9,800	13,300
New Woman	14,812	18,613	11,400	14,325
Newsweek Woman	10,965	none	12,980	none
Parents	28,475	34,100	31,680	38,000
Playgirl	7,220	13,020	7,220	10,155
Redbook	42,675	55,935	42,675	55,935
Savvy	6,950	8,690	10,240	12,285
Self	15,500	17,200	17,900	19,850
Seventeen	19,250	23,100	20,900	25,075
Shape	2,754	3,672	6,307	8,408
Slimmer	2,360	3,675	2,360	3,675
Spring	4,760	5,710	7,595	9,115
'Teen	12,750	14,350	13,455	15,700
Town & Country	10,900	14,900	13,070	17,865
Vanidades Continental (US)	1,200	1,615	1,320	1,780
Vogue	18,000	21,000	20,000	23,300
Weight Watchers	12,845	13,380	13,660	16,090
Woman's Day	64,310	100,120	67,600	105,210
Women's Sports	2,892	3,620	2,892	3,620
Working Mother	7,760	10,960	9,400	13,280
Working Woman	10,875	13,600	13,100	16,500
Young Miss	9,115	9,960	11,620	12,695

Source: SRDS, 27 May 1982 and 27 April 1983.

Table A3 Average Advertising Revenue per Issue of Top US Women's Magazines, 1982

Rank among US Consumer Magazines	*Magazine*	*Average Revenue Per Issue*
1	*Good Housekeeping*	$9,205,417
3	*Better Homes and Gardens*	$8,357,417
5	*Family Circle*	$6,246,882
6	*Woman's Day*	$5,927,267
7	*Cosmopolitan*	$5,634,583
8	*McCall's*	$5,166,750
11	*Glamour*	$3,909,750
12	*Vogue*	$3,762,833
13	*Redbook*	$3,757,917
15	*Ladies' Home Journal*	$3,615,417

Source: *The Folio: 400/1983*, p. 82.

Notes

INTRODUCTION

1. Fredric Jameson, "Reification and Utopia in Mass Culture," *Social Text* 1 (1979), 134.
2. See Roland Barthes, "Ornamental Cookery," in *Mythologies*, trans. Annette Lavers (New York: Hill & Wang, 1972), pp. 78–80 and Roland Barthes, *The Fashion System*, trans. Matthew Ward and Richard Howard (New York: Hill & Wang, 1983).
3. For a discussion of several of these methodologies, see my "Demystifying *Cosmopolitan*: Five Critical Methods," *Journal of Popular Culture* 16 (1982), 30–42.
4. Roland Marchand discovered a similar continuity in the themes and motifs of advertising in the United States from 1929 to the mid-1930s. See his *Advertising the American Dream: Making Way for Modernity, 1920–1940* (Berkeley: University of California Press, 1985), pp. xv–xvi.
5. See Michel de Certeau, *The Practice of Everyday Life* (Berkeley: University of California Press, 1984), pp. 165–76.
6. See Stuart Hall, "The Rediscovery of 'Ideology': Return of the Repressed in Media Studies," in *Culture, Society, and the Media*, eds Michael Gurevitch, *et al.* (London: Routledge, 1982), pp. 56–90.
7. In the September 1981 issue of *Vogue*, for example, purchased advertisements accounted for 463 of the magazine's 610 pages, or 76 per cent; the November 1981 *Better Homes and Gardens* broke records with the most advertising revenue in a single magazine issue – $12,315,582 for 177 pages of ads of the issue's 246 total pages.
8. See Adriana Santa Cruz and Viviana Erazo, *Compropolitan: El orden transnacional y su modelo femenino* (Mexico City: Editorial Nueva Imagen, 1980), p. 22.
9. See advertisements, *Advertising Age*, 17 May 1982, p. 13, 6 December 1982, cover 3, and 17 January 1983, p. M-55. For information on the largest advertising categories in women's magazines, see William Abbott, "Ten Years Back, Ten Years Ahead," *Folio* (September 1982), 216ff.
10. Michele Mattelart, "Women and the Cultural Industries," *Media, Culture and Society* 4 (1982), 133–51; Fredric Jameson, *The Political Unconscious: Narrative as a Socially Symbolic Act* (Ithaca, New York: Cornell University Press, 1981), especially p. 287; Tania Modleski, *Loving with a Vengeance: Mass Produced Fantasies for Women* (New York: Methuen, 1984), pp. 14–15; and Janice Radway, *Reading the Romance: Women, Patriarchy, and Popular Literature* (Chapel Hill: The University of North Carolina Press, 1984), p. 106. For other important studies of audiences, see David Morley, *Family Television: Cultural Power and Domestic Leisure* (London: Comedia, 1986); Ien Ang, *Watching Dallas: Soap Opera and the Melodramatic Imagination* (London: Methuen, 1985); Dorothy Hobson, *Crossroads: The Drama of a Soap Opera* (London: Methuen, 1981); and Laurie Schulze, "On the Muscle," in

Fabrications: Costume and the Female Body, eds Jane Gaines and Charlotte Herzog (New York and London: Routledge, 1990), pp. 59–78.

11. Responses of thirty-four undergraduate students at the University of Massachusetts, Amherst enrolled in Fall 1980 in a comparative literature course, "Mass Culture: Literary and Ideological Structures."
12. Dennis Porter, *The Pursuit of Crime: Art and Ideology in Detective Fiction* (New Haven: Yale University Press, 1981).
13. Letter from Levine to McCracken, 23 November 1983.
14. Letter from Mueller to McCracken, 21 May 1982. For similar statements by a number of other editors of women's magazines see "Donahue Transcript #01287," Multimedia Entertainment Inc., Cincinnati, 1987.

1 THE COVER: WINDOW TO THE FUTURE SELF

1. See John Berger, *Ways of Seeing* (London: Penguin, 1972), p. 132.
2. *Ibid.*, p. 10. Film theory has developed important reformulations of the notion of the implicit male spectator. Laura Mulvey's classic analysis of patriarchal scopophilia, "Visual Pleasure and Narrative Cinema" (*Screen*, 16, No. 3 (1975), 6–18) and her "Afterthoughts on 'Visual Pleasure and Narrative Cinema' inspired by King Vidor's *Duel in the Sun* (1946)," in Laura Mulvey, *Visual and Other Pleasures* (Bloomington: Indiana University Press, 1989), pp. 29–38, are part of an intensely developed debate about the filmic positionalities of male and female spectators which has primarily utilized feminist adaptations of psychoanalytic theory. See Annette Kuhn, *Women's Pictures: Feminism and Cinema* and *The Power of the Image: Essays on Representation and Sexuality* (London: Routledge & Kegan Paul, 1982 and 1985), Teresa de Lauretis, *Alice Doesn't: Feminism, Semiotics, Cinema* (Bloomington: Indiana University Press, 1984), and Mary Ann Doane, *The Desire to Desire: The Woman's Film of the 1940s* (Bloomington: Indiana University Press, 1987). For a critical overview of the contending issues in the debate, see Tania Modleski, *The Women Who Knew Too Much: Hitchcock and Feminist Theory* (New York: Methuen, 1988), pp. 1–15. Recently, Jane Gaines has argued that emphasis on the notion of the male spectatorial position can occlude and ultimately reinforce the other important ideological codes in a given image. Edward Snow suggests that there are non-patriarchal elements as well within the male gaze. See Jane Gaines, "White Privilege and Looking Relations: Race and Gender in Feminist Film Theory," *Screen* 29 (Winter 1988), 12–27 and Edward Snow, "Theorizing the Male Gaze: Some Problems," *Representations*, No. 25 (1989), 31–41. Nonetheless, the concept of the implicit male surveyor is an important tool with which to begin an analysis of cover photographs because it estranges the widely held conception that these are simply reproductions of reality. Analysis of the point of view that underlies a photographic image, that it is "a record of how x [has] seen y," is an essential first step in decoding a sign system such as the magazine cover.
3. George Gerbner, "The Social Anatomy of the Romance-Confession Cover Girl," *Journalism Quarterly* 35 (1958), 299.
4. Christy Marshall, "Why Women's Books Sag," *Advertising Age*, 6 April 1981, pp. 3ff. *Redbook*, for example, sold only 86.2 pages of ads for its

December 1981 issue compared to 101 the previous December. Annual figures for 1981 showed the magazine down 222 pages from 1980 totals when it had ranked the lowest of the seven sisters in ad revenues. See "Advertising Pages in December Consumer Publications," *Advertising Age*, 21 December 1981, pp. 39–40 and Cecelia Lentini, "Balancing Act in Women's Magazines," *Advertising Age*, 19 October 1981, p. S-64.

5. Peter Lawrence, late Editor of *Woman*, quoted in Marjorie Ferguson, "Imagery and Ideology: The Cover Photographs of Traditional Women's Magazines," in *Hearth and Home*, eds Gaye Tuchman *et al.* (New York: Oxford, 1978), p. 100.
6. "Last Minute News," *Advertising Age*, 3 May 1982, p. 1; "Ad Linage," *Advertising Age*, 20 December 1982, pp. 33–4; Charlene Canape, "The New Money Makers at Hearst," *New York Times*, 6 March 1983, p. F-8.
7. See Hearst's ads in *Advertising Age*, 29 November 1982, p. 29 and 6 December 1982, pp. 38–9.
8. See Philip H. Dougherty, "Redbook Rejuggles its Image," *New York Times*, 11 February 1983, p. D-15; *Redbook*'s ad in *Advertising Age*, 21 February 1983, pp. 34–5; "Last Minute News," *Advertising Age*, 25 October 1982, p. 1 and 17 January 1983, p. 8.
9. Paul Rosenfield, "Anatomy of a Cover Girl," *Los Angeles Times*, 5 December 1982, Calendar, pp. 1, 36.
10. See Angela McRobbie, "Working Class Girls and the Culture of Femininity," in Women's Studies Group, *Women Take Issue: Aspects of Women's Subordination* (London: Hutchinson, 1978), p. 99.
11. Louis Gropp, Editor-in-Chief of *House & Garden* explained his magazine's desire to increase single-copy sales: "Newsstand sales show you're in touch with where people are. It's the constant decision-making aspect of publishing. People have to decide to buy you on the newsstand." See Eric Pace, "Magazine Renovation Success," *New York Times*, natl. ed., 3 September 1981, p. 40.
12. See, for example, the ad for *Woman's Day* in *Advertising Age*, 2 March 1981, p. 24, in which potential advertisers are told: "we devote more editorial pages to beauty and fashion combined than to any other category."
13. Standard Rate and Data Service, *Consumer and Farm Publications* 63, No. 10 (27 October 1981), 515. (Hereafter referred to as SRDS.)
14. See Erving Goffman, *Gender Advertisements* (New York: Harper & Row, 1976). The covers of *Self* in April, May, June, and July, 1981 are good examples of body clowning and licensed withdrawal. (Permission to reprint denied.)
15. Roland Barthes, "Le Message photographique," *Communications* 1 (1961) 127–38. Trans. as "The Photographic Message," in *Image – Music – Text*, ed. and trans. Stephen Heath (New York: Hill & Wang, 1977), pp. 15–31.
16. Sergei Eisenstein, *Film Form: Essays in Film Theory*, ed. and trans. Jay Leyda (New York: Harcourt, Brace & World, 1949), pp. 30, 37.
17. Roland Barthes, "Rhétorique de l'image," *Communications* 4 (1964), 40–51. Trans. as "Rhetoric of the Image," in *Image – Music – Text*, pp. 32–51.
18. See Judith Williamson, *Decoding Advertisements: Ideology and Meaning in Advertising* (London: Marion Boyars, 1978), pp. 20–4. For further observations on the chromatic code in advertising, see Georges Péninou,

"Physique et métaphysique de l'image publicitaire," *Communications* 15 (1970), 96–109.

19. See Chantal Henry, "Discours d'escorte et promotion publicitaire," *Revue des Sciences Humaines* 63, No. 192 (October–December 1983), 118 (my translation).
20. Edward Said, *Beginnings: Intention and Method* (New York: Basic Books, 1975), pp. 5–6.
21. Stuart Hall, "The 'Structured Communication' of Events," Media Series: SP No. 5 (Birmingham: Centre for Contemporary Cultural Studies, University of Birmingham, 1973), pp. 13, 24.
22. Advertisement, *Advertising Age*, 26 April 1982, p. 37. See also *Better Homes and Gardens'* heavy-paper, four-page ad series in *Advertising Age*, 22 March 1984, pp. 25–8 and 12 November 1984, pp. 33–6, which link reader action to product purchases.
23. Berger, pp. 132–3.

2 COVERT ADVERTISEMENTS

1. Raymond Williams, *Television: Technology and Cultural Form* (New York: Schocken Books, 1975).
2. See Williams, *Television*, pp. 91–3 and "Natural Breaks," *The Listener*, 24 August 1972 in *Raymond Williams on Television: Selected Writings*, ed. Alan O'Conner (New York: Routledge, 1989), pp. 184–7. Although Williams noted in 1984, "I have always argued [that commercials] don't interrupt the programs, they help constitute them" (Stephen Heath and Gillian Skirrow, "An Interview with Raymond Williams," in *Studies in Entertainment*, ed. Tania Modleski (Bloomington: Indiana University Press, 1986), p. 15), his work as a whole shows an understanding of commercials as *both* interruptions and parts of television's overall flow.
3. See Williams, *Television*, p. 70. Williams began to see television as flow, rather than interrupted viewing, after a week-long cross-Atlantic journey to Miami where, somewhat disoriented, he watched US television with the eyes of an outsider. To his surprise, the evening movie was not only interwoven with ads for products, but with preview ads for two movies to be broadcast later in the week. "I can still not be sure what I took from that whole flow. I believe I registered some incidents as happening in the wrong film, and some characters in the commercials as involved in the film episodes" (Williams, *Television*, p. 92). I would argue that Williams' view here is that of the outsider; most habitual viewers of US television have learned to recognize these distinctions. Nonetheless, Williams' fatigue and different television background functioned as estrangement devices that allow us to see the double existence of ads as both interruptions and parts of the larger flow. For an opposing view to Williams' with respect to daytime soap operas, see Modleski, *Loving with a Vengeance*, pp. 100–1.
4. Cited in Carola García Calderón, *Revistas femeninas: La mujer como objeto de consumo* (Mexico City: Ediciones El Caballito, 1980), p. 164 (my translation). For a discussion of covert advertising in British magazines, see Kathy Myers, "Understanding Advertisers," in *Language, Image, Media*, eds

Howard Davis and Paul Walton (New York: St. Martin's Press, pp. 205–23.

5. Advertisement for the *New York Times Magazine, Advertising Age*, 9 August 1982, p. 37.
6. See *Cosmopolitan Research*, January 1982, p. E-3. For *Vogue*'s argument see its advertisement in *Advertising Age*, 14 September 1981, p. 16.
7. Dennis Harvey, Vice-President and Editor of the *Toronto Star*, quoted in Anna Sobczynski, "Editorials vs. Advertorials," *Advertising Age*, 10 May 1982, p. M-26.
8. See *Cosmopolitan Research*, January 1982, p. R-15.
9. For studies of mean reading time, see *Cosmopolitan Research*, November 1980, p. R-21 and Simmons Market Research Bureau studies; *Seventeen*'s argument appears in its advertisement in *Advertising Age*, 2 November 1981, p. 13.
10. See, for example, Jameson, *The Political Unconscious*.
11. Bill Blass and Karen Fisher, "Designing the Right Image," *Advertising Age*, 14 September 1981, p. S-4.
12. See the ads for *Mademoiselle*, *Self*, *House Beautiful*, *Cuisine*, *'Teen* and *Modern Bride* in the following issues of *Advertising Age*: 7 March 1983, p. 9; 16 May 1983, p. 21; 9 May 1983, p. 40; 25 April 1983, p. M-2; 17 January 1983, p. 6; and 6 December 1982, cover 3, respectively.
13. See the ad for *Modern Bride* in *Advertising Age*, 6 December 1982, cover 3; the *Seventeen* ads in *Advertising Age*, 17 May 1982, p. 13 and 22 February 1982, p. 12; and the *Bride's* ad in *Advertising Age*, 28 March 1983, p. M-27.
14. *Cosmopolitan* Advertising Rate Card, No. 51, September 1981; *House & Garden* advertisement in *Advertising Age*, 10 May 1982, pp. 26–7; *Woman's Day* advertisement in *Advertising Age*, 2 March 1981, p. 24; and *Vogue* advertisement in *Advertising Age*, 14 September 1981, p. 16.
15. *Advertising Age Yearbook* (Chicago: Crain Communications, 1982), p. 235 (my emphasis).
16. See Cecelia Lentini, " . . . to the New," *Advertising Age*, 26 July 1982, p. M-32.
17. Marilyn Abbey, "Haute Couture Big But Social Chic Sells Better," *Advertising Age*, 19 October 1981, p. S-68.
18. See "Adbeat," *Advertising Age*, 14 June 1982, p. 63.
19. Cited in Garcia Calderón, *Revistas femeninas*, p. 165 (my translation).
20. Patterning its editorial content on the promotional schedule of the cosmetics industry, *Cosmopolitan en español* endorses several "new collections" in a similar article in its October 1981 issue, "Everything new in Cosmo make-up" (pp. 40–5, my translation): Germaine Monteil, Elizabeth Arden, Lancôme, Ralph Lauren, Estee Lauder, Max Factor, Mary Quant, L'Oréal, and Revlon.
21. Schering-Plough's purchased ads in this issue of *'Teen* are for the following products: Coppertone, p. 15; For Faces Only, pp. 34–5; Scholl's sandals, pp. 37–8; and Maybelline cosmetics, pp. 27–8, 104, and cover 3. The corporation's covert ads are for Tropical Blend, pp. 68–9 and 82–3 and Maybelline, p. 6.
22. *Self*, another Conde Nast magazine also promoted Gignac's book in its January 1981 issue.

23. Stuart Ewen, *Captains of Consciousness: Advertising and the Social Roots of the Consumer Culture* (New York: McGraw-Hill, 1976), pp. 41–8.
24. Anna Sobczynski, "Everything's Not All Rosy," *Advertising Age*, 2 March 1981, p. S-20; "Products – Some Winners, Some Losers," *Advertising Age*, 11 January 1982, p. 36. By early 1982, however, Oil of Olay had fallen three percentage points to a 30 per cent unit share and from a 40 per cent dollar share to a 38 per cent. See Pat Sloan, "Cosmetics Marketers Promise Face-lifts," *Advertising Age*, 7 March 1983, p. 12.
25. Anna Sobczynski, "Editorials vs. Advertorials: It's a Separate Piece," *Advertising Age*, 10 May 1982, p. M-24.
26. *Ibid.*, p. M-25.
27. Advertisement, *Advertising Age*, 25 January 1982, p. 21.
28. Johnson & Johnson, Coca-Cola, Warner Lambert, American Home Products, Hormel, and General Foods Corporation. Several companies have also purchased ads in this issue of *Woman's Day*: Johnson & Johnson (pp. 31 and 43), American Home Products (pp. 114 and 157), Warner Lambert (p. 66), and Hormel (p. 140).
29. For a discussion of these and other concerns of publishers and advertisers about advertorials, see Sobczynski, pp. M-24ff.
30. Advertisement, *Advertising Age*, 10 May 1982, p. 15.
31. Advertisement, *Advertising Age*, 2 March 1981, p. 24.
32. Kidder, Peabody and Company Inc. of New York is the investment company named in Geri Jefferson's "Consumer Savvy: Budgeting Your Economic Survival," *Elan*, April 1982, p. 8.
33. Jaclyn Fierman, "An Industry Faces Recovery," *Advertising Age*, 2 March 1981, p. S-6.
34. *Claudia*, March 1982, masthead.

3 CRITICAL APPROACHES TO PURCHASED ADVERTISING

1. See Erik Barnouw, *The Sponsor: Notes on a Modern Potentate* (New York: Oxford University Press, 1978); Frank Luther Mott, *A History of American Magazines 1741–1850*, Vol. 1 (New York: D. Appleton and Co., 1930), pp. 337, 340; and John Tebbel, *The American Magazine: A Compact History* (New York: Hawthorn Books, 1969), p. 48.
2. Tebbel, pp. 107–8; Mott, *A History of American Magazines 1865–1885*, Vol. 3 (Cambridge, Massachusetts: Harvard University Press, 1938), p. 11; and Vol. 4 (Cambridge, Massachusetts: Harvard University Press, 1957), pp. 21–9.
3. Tebbel, pp. 196–7; Mott, Vol. 4, p. 32.
4. Santa Cruz and Erazo, *Compropolitan*, p. 22.
5. Mott, Vol. 4, pp. 580–8.
6. *Cosmopolitan Research*, March 1982, p. AS-12.
7. See Ewen, *Captains of Consciousness*, pp. 23–30.
8. *Ibid.*, pp. 35–6.
9. *Ibid.*, p. 38.
10. *Ibid.*, pp. 25 and 167.
11. Raymond Williams, "Advertising: The Magic System," in *Problems in*

Materialism and Culture (London: Verso Editions and New Left Books, 1980), p. 185.

12. *Ibid.*, p. 189.
13. See Fredric Jameson, "Cognitive Mapping," in *Marxism and the Interpretation of Culture*, eds Cary Nelson and Lawrence Grossberg (Urbana: University of Illinois Press, 1988), p. 353.
14. This understanding of ideology as false consciousness surfaces in Althusser's discussion of the Ideological State Apparatuses (ISAs), one of which is the communications industry. In contrast to the more violent Repressive State Apparatuses (the army, the police, and prisons, for example), ISAs are specialized institutions such as the family, schools, churches, trade unions, culture, and the mass media, which maintain the dominant order through ideology. See "Ideology and Ideological State Apparatuses," in *Lenin and Philosophy and Other Essays* (London: New Left Books, 1971), pp. 162–70.
15. See Stuart Hall, "The Rediscovery of Ideology: Return of the Repressed in Media Studies," in *Culture, Society and the Media*, eds Michael Gurevitch *et al.* (London and New York: Routledge, 1982), pp. 56–90; "Culture, the Media and the Ideological Effect," in *Mass Communication and Society*, eds J. Curran *et al.* (London: Edward Arnold, 1977), pp. 315–48; and "Encoding/Decoding," in *Culture, Media, Language: Working Papers in Cultural Studies (1972–1979)*, eds S. Hall *et al.* (London: Hutchinson, 1980), pp. 128–38.
16. Michel de Certeau, *The Practice of Everyday Life*, trans. Steven Rendall (Berkeley: University of California Press, 1984), pp. xix, 40.
17. See Stuart Hall, Ian Connell, and Lidia Curti, "The 'Unity' of Current Affairs Television," in *Popular Television and Film*, eds Tony Bennett *et al.* (London: BFI Publishing, 1981), p. 116.
18. Jameson, *The Political Unconscious*, p. 47. For an application of the semiotic rectangle to advertising, see Chapter 4.
19. *Ibid.* p. 287.
20. *Ibid.*, p. 142.
21. See Christine Gledhill, "Pleasurable Negotiations," in *Female Spectators: Looking at Film and Television*, ed. E. Deidre Pribram (London: Verso, 1988), p. 75.
22. Angela McRobbie, "*Jackie*: An Ideology of Adolescent Femininity," in *Popular Culture: Past and Present*, eds Bernard Waites *et al.* (London: Croom Helm and Open University Press, 1982), p. 264.
23. Tony Bennett, "Media, 'Reality,' Signification," in *Culture, Society and the Media*, p. 307.
24. Valerie Walkerdine, "Some Day My Prince Will Come: Young Girls and the Preparation for Adolescent Sexuality," in *Gender and Generation*, eds Angela McRobbie and Mica Nava (London: Macmillan, 1984), pp. 162–84.
25. Herbert Schiller, *Culture, Inc.* (New York: Oxford University Press, 1989), p. 156.
26. See David Morley, *Family Television: Cultural Power and Domestic Leisure* (London: Comedia, 1986); *The Nationwide Audience* (London: British Film Institute, 1980); and "'The Nationwide Audience' – A Critical Postscript," *Screen Education*, No. 39 (1981), 3–14.

27. Terry Lovell and Simon Frith, "'How Do You Get Pleasure?' – Another Look at *Klute*," *Screen Education*, No. 40 (1981), 17.
28. Interview with Stuart Hall conducted at the University of Massachusetts, Amherst, 1 March 1989 by the Audience/Culture Group.
29. See, for example, the National Advertising Review Board, "Advertising and Women: A Report on Advertising Portraying or Directed to Women," March 1975; and Matilda Butler and William Paisley, *Women and the Mass Media: Sourcebook for Research and Action* (New York: Human Sciences Press, 1980), pp. 95–114. Exceptions to this pattern include: "Black Group Rips Five Campaigns," *Advertising Age*, 4 April 1983, p. 71; Denise Warren, "Commercial Liberation," *Journal of Communication* 28 (1978), 169–73; and Judith Williamson, "Woman Is an Island: Femininity and Colonization," in *Studies in Entertainment: Critical Approaches to Mass Culture*, ed. Tania Modleski (Bloomington: Indiana University Press, 1986), pp. 99–118. For an excellent critique of the various approaches to feminist media analysis see H. Leslie Steeves, "Feminist Theories and Media Studies," *Critical Studies in Mass Communication* 4:2 (1987), 95–135.
30. See Gaye Tuchman, "Women's Depiction by the Mass Media," *Signs* 4 (1979), 528–42.
31. Janice Winship, "Handling Sex," *Media, Culture and Society* 3 (1981), 26.
32. Noreene Janus, "Research on Sex-Roles in the Mass Media: Toward a Critical Approach," *The Insurgent Sociologist* 7, No. 3 (1977), 19–31.
33. Preben Sepstrup, "Methodological Developments in Content Analysis," in *Advances in Content Analysis*, ed. Karl Eric Rosengren (Beverly Hills: Sage Publications, 1980), pp. 133–58.
34. Dorothy Hobson, "Housewives and the Mass Media," in *Culture, Media, Language*, eds. Hall *et al.*, p. 112. For other feminist studies that emphasize the active reader/viewer see, *The Female Gaze: Women as Viewers of Popular Culture*, eds Lorraine Gamman and Margaret Marshment (Seattle: The Real Comet Press, 1989) and *Gender and Generation*, eds Angela McRobbie and Mica Nava (London: Macmillan, 1984).
35. See Roland Barthes, *Elements of Semiology*, trans. Annette Lavers and Colin Smith (Boston: Beacon Press, 1967), pp. 9–12.
36. Barthes, *Mythologies*, p. 110.
37. Williamson, *Decoding Advertisements*, p. 12.
38. *Ibid.*, p. 44.
39. Lawrence Bardin, *Les Mécanismes idéologiques de la publicité* (Paris: Editions Universitaires, 1975), p. 30.
40. See Hall, "The Rediscovery of Ideology," p. 84.
41. See also Judith Williamson, "The Problems of Being Popular," *New Socialist*, September 1986, pp. 14–15 for important arguments against simply celebrating popular culture rather than critically evaluating it.
42. Conde Nast discontinued this package in January 1983, replacing it with two others: (1) "Conde Nast Ltd." which offers special rates for advertisers who run three, six, nine, or twelve pages a year in three or four of its upscale publications: *House & Garden*, *Vogue*, *GQ*, and *Vanity Fair*; (2) "Conde Nast Package of Women" for advertisers who buy six, nine, or twelve pages in each of four or five magazines: *Vogue*, *Glamour*, *Mademoiselle*, *Bride's* and *Self*. See *New York Times*, 10 August 1982, natl. ed., p. 41.

43. "100 Leading Media Companies," *Advertising Age*, 27 June 1983, pp. M-64 – M-65.
44. *Ibid.*, pp. M-50 – M-51; advertisements, *Advertising Age*, 28 February 1983, p. 47 and 28 March 1983, pp. 32–3; and *The Folio: 400/1983*, p. 84.
45. *The Folio: 400/1983*, p. 114.
46. *Ibid.*, p. 112 and "And Furthermore . . .," *Advertising Age*, 7 December 1981, p. S-75. Compared to the average advertising revenue per issue of the top women's magazines in 1982, this *Better Homes and Gardens* record is impressive (see Appendix, Table A3).
47. See *Cosmopolitan Research*, March 1982, p. C-6.
48. Already in 1974–5, *McCall's* cut its circulation 10 per cent and raised its CPM 7 per cent. Through higher cover and subscription prices, *McCall's* readers began for the first time to provide more income than the advertisers. The higher prices were also intended to prove that circulation reached audiences who actually read the magazine, having paid more for it. In February 1982 *McCall's* advertised that December 1981 news-stand sales were up 30 per cent from the previous December and that "At a time when every purchase a woman . . . makes is carefully considered, more women are *choosing – and using McCall's*." See "*McCall's* to Trim Base, Raise Cover, Sub Prices," *Advertising Age*, 16 December 1974, p. 81 and advertisement, *Advertising Age*, 15 February 1982, pp. 52–3.
49. See "Last Minute News," *Advertising Age*, 24 May 1982, p. 1; SRDS, 27 July 1983, pp. 568–9, 249, and 251; and "Ad Linage," *Advertising Age*, 19 December 1983, p. 35.
50. See Bob Donath, "Magazines Hang Hats on Special Interests," *Advertising Age*, 18 November 1974, p. 38. Other magazines with higher news-stand than subscription sales are *Cosmopolitan* (96 per cent), *New Woman* (69 per cent), *Mademoiselle* (67 per cent), *Bazaar* (63 per cent), *Glamour* (61 per cent), and *Vogue* (60 per cent). See *Cosmopolitan Research*, March 1982, p. C-4.
51. See *Cosmopolitan Research*, October 1981, p. R-12. *Cosmopolitan* extends this logic to its survey of readers' diverse interests, specifically, sports and leisure activities: "She's important to advertisers because her diverse interests mean she has many consumer needs." See *Cosmopolitan Research*, January 1982, p. R-15.
52. *Mademoiselle Beauty/Health Reader Survey*, Research Report No. 5409, November 1979, pp. 3b–10b.
53. *The Folio: 400/1983*, pp. 136–46.
54. *Ibid.*, pp. 480–7.
55. See SRDS, 27 October 1981, p. 519 and advertisement, *Advertising Age*, 11 January 1982, p. 27.
56. See *Cosmopolitan Research*, October 1981, p. AS-7 and "*Newsweek Woman* 1982," (brochure).
57. SRDS, 27 July 1983, pp. 249, 545, 546, 571, 574, and 619.
58. See SRDS, 27 July 1983, pp. 557 and 540; 27 October 1981, p. 530. Some of the large-circulation women's magazines have elaborate discount structures. *Family Circle*, for example, offers numerous special rates: (1) the Dollar Volume and Renewal Discounts which reward three or more full-run, four-color ad purchases and those renewed for the following year; (2)

the Maximum Plus Discount, up to 32 per cent for advertisers who buy more than sixty pages per year; (3) the Spread Discount, a 5 per cent reduction for a full-run page spread in a single issue; (4) the Consecutive Page Discount, a 20–35 per cent reduction for four or more consecutive full-run, four-color pages in a single issue; (5) the Special Advertising Section Discount through which advertisers receive a 20 per cent reduction for appearing in the section of ads that are run ahead of the main editorial section; (6) the Fractional Page Discount, a frequency discount for full-runs of ads of at least one-third page; (7) the Winter Season Discount, a mechanism to increase the ads in January, the lowest circulation season; here advertisers who buy full-run display ads in the popular November or December issues earn a discount on a comparable-size ad in the succeeding January issue; (8) the Brand Discount through which a half-page color ad for a single brand or product in four or more consecutive issues receives a 2–4 per cent discount; and (9) the Roll-Out Discount through which advertisers who expand regional test-market ads into full-run ads within one year receive a rebate. In addition to these standard discounts for display ads, *Family Circle* offers discounts for classified ads and reading notices: the dollar volume discount, the frequency discount, the book publishers, records, schools, and gardens 15 per cent discount, and the supermarket-home kitchen product circle 20 per cent discount. Ads appearing in the "Gail Burke Better Living Ideas" section cost between $10,175 and $11,800 for which advertisers are given a four-color illustration, approximately 100 words of copy, the page space, finished copy, four-color art, production, and positives. (Usually advertisers must pay these production costs themselves.) See SRDS, 27 July 1983, pp. 544–5.

59. SRDS, 27 July 1983, pp. 545 and 554.
60. *Ibid.*, pp. 550, 545, 552, and 540–1.
61. Bristol Myers began a $7 million campaign in December 1981 to introduce Clairol Kindness Body Wave. Gillette began a $17.4 million ad and promotion campaign for Aapri facial scrub in June 1981; the Gillette Co. promotion budget for 1980 was $340.7 million, up 21 per cent from the previous year. In late 1981 Beecham budgeted $40 million to introduce triple protection red-stripe Aqua Fresh toothpaste, while General Foods began a $10 million campaign for Gravy Train Dry Dog Food (see *Advertising Age*, 2 November 1981, p. 18; 6 April 1981, pp. 88 and 72; and 2 November 1981, pp. 18 and 8). These figures include other media advertising and promotion besides that in magazines but they remind us of the large sums spent for advertising which the consumer ultimately subsidizes in the price paid for advertised products.
62. "For the Record," *Advertising Age*, 15 February 1982, p. 87.
63. See SRDS, 27 April 1983, pp. 554, 555, and 571 and 27 July 1983, pp. 59 and 619.
64. See *Mademoiselle Beauty/Health Reader Survey*, p. 18a and *Vogue Beauty/Health Subscriber Study*, Research Report 10127, February 1980, p. 2A; for the CPM figures see *Cosmopolitan Research*, March 1982, p. C-6.
65. SMRB, *1982 Study of Media and Markets*, Vol. P-28, pp. 0108–0121.

4 THE CODES OF OVERT ADVERTISEMENTS

1. See Figure 4.2. Occasionally, a foldout attached to the cover presents a series of four ad pages about a company or product as the reader begins the magazine. Or, an advertiser obtains the four-page effect by purchasing the first three pages along with cover two.
2. Althusser's theory of interpellation has been criticized as a deterministic doctrine that assumes people offer no resistance and are inevitably shaped to be what they are called (see, for example, Liliane Jaddou and Jon Williams, "A Theoretical Contribution to the Struggle against the Dominant Representations of Women," *Media, Culture and Society* 3, No. 2 (1981), 105–24). At least, however, study of the process of interpellation can help to make people conscious of how ads address them, thus encouraging a critical resistance. Just as a child who has been addressed for many years with a diminutive form of her or his name, at a certain point of development decides that it is no longer appropriate, so, too, semiotic analysis can show women and men that some of the stereotypes with which ads often address them are inappropriate and should be resisted. The theory of interpellation does not imply that one cannot unlearn what one has been taught for many years.
3. An interesting variation of these ads for cosmetics that offer to teach us a language occurs when an ad and the facing editorial page create this meaning jointly. The large image of a container of Chanel eyeshadow in an ad in the February 1983 *Cosmopolitan* works in montage with the headline of an article on the facing page, "Language of eyes" (pp. 124–5). The Chanel ad does not have to promise explicitly that the product will speak for us because the article on the facing page makes this meaning clear. Where a magazine such as *New Woman* tries to increase an ad's effectiveness through subliminal synergism – a color tint block behind an editorial headline that matches the predominant color of the ad on the facing page – *Cosmopolitan* expands an ad's message by an article and headline that make explicit a subtle implication of the ad. In this case, the article in combination with the ad promise that a product will do the talking for us. It does not matter whether or not the editors have intentionally placed this Chanel ad next to the feature entitled "Language of eyes." What is of significance is that a new text created by the montage of these two images is present for readers to assemble.
4. Janice Winship, "Handling Sex," *Media, Culture and Society* 3, No. 2 (1981), 25–41.
5. Creamer Advertising Agency which developed the long-running series lost the $5 million account to Wyse Advertising in early 1983 after much protest from women. "For the Record," *Advertising Age*, 4 April 1983, p. 69.
6. Goffman, *Gender Advertisements*, pp. 41, 57–83.
7. Williamson, *Decoding Advertisements*, p. 70.
8. See Fredric Jameson, "The Great American Hunter, or, Ideological Content in the Novel," *College English* 34 (1972), 182.
9. Goffman, *Gender Advertisements*, pp. 45–70.
10. See Valerie Walkerdine, "Some Day My Prince Will Come," in *Gender and Generation*, eds Angela McRobbie and Mica Nava (London: Macmillan,

1984), p. 176 and Rosalind Coward, "Sexual Violence and Sexuality," *Feminist Review*, no. 11 (1982).
11. Williamson, *Decoding Advertisements*, p. 68.
12. Jameson, *The Political Unconscious*, p. 287.

5 FASHION AND BEAUTY: TRANSGRESSION, UTOPIA, AND CONTAINMENT

1. *'Teen* claims that it is "devoured" by 5.7 million girls between the ages of 12 and 19, and reaches one out of three girls in this age group every month (advertisement, *Advertising Age*, 1 November 1982, p. 67). One reader notes in a letter to the editor that she has subscribed to *'Teen* since she was 10 (March 1982, p. 6). Many of the magazine's fictional protagonists are 15. The principal editorial themes suggest that readers are frequently in their early teens.
2. Robert Stein, Editor of *McCall's*, quoted in Tamar Levin, "Women's Magazines: A Mix for Everyone," *New York Times*, natl. ed., 9 August 1982, p. 13.
3. Angela McRobbie and Jenny Garber, "Girls and Subcultures," *Working Papers in Cultural Studies*, 7/8 (1975), 208–22.
4. *Young Miss* Editorial Profile, SRDS, 27 May 1982, p. 536.
5. Advertisement, *Advertising Age*, 2 August 1982, p. M-9; "For the Record," *Advertising Age*, 28 March 1983; SRDS, 17 October 1983, p. 592.
6. Advertisement, *Advertising Age*, 17 January 1983, p. 6.
7. Mary McCabe English, "How to Stay *Seventeen* – and Keep Growing," *Advertising Age*, 2 August 1982, pp. M-27 – M-28 and "*Seventeen* Reader Profile," 4 March 1982.
8. See "100 Leading Media Companies," *Advertising Age*, 27 June 1983, p. M-80 and the following advertisements *Seventeen* published in *Advertising Age*: 29 November 1982, p. 12; 7 February 1983, p. 27; 14 March 1983, p. 9; 28 February 1983, p. 23; 7 June 1982, p. 66; 19 April 1982, p. 13; and 17 January 1983, p. 9.
9. In December 1982, for example, a mother's letter in the magazine expresses her approval of the "Sex and Your Body" column.
10. "Media Moves," *Advertising Age*, 7 June 1982, p. 66.
11. Advertisement, *Advertising Age*, 28 February 1983, p. 21.
12. Advertisement, *Advertising Age*, 7 March 1983, p. 9.
13. Philip H. Dougherty, "*Glamour* Magazine's Relevance," *New York Times*, natl. ed., 18 July 1983, p. 21.
14. Begun in 1937, *Glamour* claims to have "grown with the consumer market" it reaches, with 5 per cent of its editorial material on travel, and 6 per cent on each of the categories of health, furnishings, food, culture, and general interest. It tells electronics advertisers in *Glamour* that it publishes more editorial material about electronics than any other women's magazine and is the only one with an Electronics Editor. In search of car advertisers, the magazine argues that it has more articles about automobiles than other women's magazines as well as a special column "Car Buyer's Guide." See *Cosmopolitan Research*, January 1982, p. E-1; *Glamour* Advertising Rate Card,

No. 33, February 1982, p. 1; *Glamour Facts*, 1982; and advertisements, *Advertising Age*, 7 June 1982, pp. M-22 – M-23 and 12 April 1982, pp. M-34 – M-35.

15. Advertisement, *Advertising Age*, 11 October 1982, pp. M-52 – M-53.
16. "1983 Women's Views Study," *Glamour*, January 1983, pp. 138–9ff. See also Ira Ellenthal, "Ruth Whitney: Editor-in-chief of *Glamour*," *Folio*, December 1982, pp. 52–3.
17. *Advertising Age*, 8 November 1982, pp. M-48 – M-49.
18. Sixteen per cent of its editorial material is about beauty and grooming, 14 per cent about health, and 9 per cent about apparel. In 1981, of a total of 800.7 ad pages, 339.8 were for toiletries and cosmetics and 102.6 for apparel, footwear and accessories. See *Cosmopolitan Research*, January 1982, p. E-1 and March 1982, p. AS-1.
19. Verne Westerberg, publisher of *Self*, has argued that *Self* did not begin as a beauty magazine but broadened its content to include beauty topics because "people who feel good want to look good." In fact, however, the magazine has linked health and beauty consistently since its inception. For Westerberg's comments, see Stuart J. Elliott, "*Self* Near Five Still Fights Skeptics," *Advertising Age*, 26 September 1983, p. 41.
20. Advertisement, *Advertising Age*, 5 September 1983, p. 5.
21. See ABC figures cited in *Cosmopolitan Research*, February and March 1982; advertisement, *Advertising Age*, 16 August 1982; and "Helen Gurley Brown's Mix: Sex and the Bottom Line," *New York Times*, 6 March 1983, p. F-8.
22. Advertisement, *Advertising Age*, 26 July 1982; underscoring and ellipses in original.
23. *Cosmopolitan* subscription order card.
24. *Cosmopolitan* Advertising Rate Card, No. 51, September 1981.
25. Allan J. Moore, "The Cosmo Girl: A Playboy Inversion," in *Dialogue on Women*, ed. Robert Theobald (New York: The Bobbs-Merrill Company, 1967), p. 86.
26. See Charlene Canape, "The New Moneymakers at Hearst," *New York Times*, 6 March 1983, p. F-9; *Cosmopolitan Research*, March 1982, p. C-6. In contrast, *Cosmopolitan*'s CPM was $10.17, *Glamour*'s $11.86, *Mademoiselle*'s $13.72 and *Vogue*'s $14.78. The only other women's magazine with a higher CPM than *Bazaar*'s in 1982 was *Savvy*, at $29.51.
27. N. R. Kleinfield, "Major Magazines Losing Ad Pages," *New York Times*, 5 May 1981, pp. D-1 and D-12; advertisement, *Advertising Age*, 22 November 1982, p. 11.
28. Income figures from *Bazaar* advertisement in SRDS, 27 October 1981, p. 507. SMRB studies (1981) show slightly lower figures than these which *Bazaar* quoted from Starch INRA Hooper Primary Audience Study, 1981.
29. Quoted in Bernadine Clark, "The Women's Magazine Rack," *Writer's Digest*, June 1983, p. 25.
30. Advertisements, *New York Times*, 13 November 1979, p. D-24; 14 March 1980, p. D-14; 27 February 1981, p. D-16; and 16 March 1981, p. C-24.
31. Barthes, *The Fashion System*, p. 244.
32. *Ibid.*, p. 243.
33. *Ibid.*, pp. 250–2.

34. Advertisement, *Advertising Age*, 22 November 1982, cover 3.
35. Letter from reader, *Vogue*, February 1981, p. 22.
36. Interview with *Vogue* reader, 15 July 1983.
37. Advertisement, *New York Times*, 14 December 1979, p. D-24.
38. Publishers Information Bureau, December 1981, cited in "The Leadership of *Vogue*: A Matter of Facts," *Vogue Research*, 1982, and *Cosmopolitan Research*, January 1982, p. E-3.
39. 1981 SMRB figures cited in *Vogue Research Report*, No. 10185, October 1981, pp. 2–4.
40. Barthes, *The Fashion System*, p. 249.
41. Advertisements, *New York Times*, 14 December 1979, p. D-24; 9 October 1980, p. D-20; and 4 March 1981, p. D-24.

6 SERVICE AND HOME: THE SEVEN SISTERS ADAPT TO THE 1980s

1. Nancy Yoshihara, "Women's Magazine Dilemma," *Los Angeles Times*, 23 December 1979, IV, pp. 1 and 5; and *The Folio: 400/1981*, p. 188.
2. Christy Marshall, "Why Women's Books Sag," *Advertising Age*, 6 April 1981, pp. 3 and 83; N. R. Kleinfield, "Major Magazines Losing Ad Pages," *New York Times*, 5 May 1981, pp. D1 and D12; and Colby Coates and Stuart Emmrich, "Outlook Mixed for Media," *Advertising Age*, 15 February 1982, pp. 1 and 84.
3. See Jan Jaben, "A Fire Sale Ahead? WD May Prove a Tough Sell," *Publishing News*, June 1990, 1ff.
4. Diamandis quoted in Ira Ellenthal, "Behind the Lines," *Folio*, February 1984, pp. 47–8.
5. See Coates and Emmrich, "Outlook Mixed for Media" and the advertisement for *Woman's Day*, *Advertising Age*, 2 March 1981, p. 24.
6. Publisher Robert F. Young quoted in "Women's Magazines Lose Pep," *Business Week*, 30 August 1982, p. 72. For information on ad rate changes see "For the Record," *Advertising Age*, 27 December 1982, p. 17; "Last Minute News," *Advertising Age*, 15 March 1982, p. 8; SRDS, 27 October 1981, p. 519; and advertisement, *Advertising Age*, 23 May 1983, p. 7.
7. See "Women's Magazines Lose Pep," p. 72; *The Folio: 400/1983*, p. 484; and *The Folio: 400/1984*, p. 333.
8. In 1937 *Woman's Day* was enlarged into a magazine and still distributed free in A & P stores, with a circulation of 775,000. When demand soared for both magazines, the publishers began to charge 5 cents a copy. By 1952 *Woman's Day* claimed a circulation of 3.8 million and over $6 million in annual advertising revenue even though it was still distributed only in A & P supermarkets. In 1956, however, two Chicago wholesalers and twenty-three food retailers sued A & P and several food companies, charging antitrust violations because A & P published the magazine as a competitive device to increase sales in its stores. The suit was initially dismissed but that decision was later overturned. With its ad revenues declining, A & P sold the magazine to Fawcett Publications in 1958. That year *Family Circle* bought out one of its other supermarket competitors,

Everywoman's magazine and claimed a new circulation for the combined publication of five million. In 1962 Cowles Magazines and Broadcasting bought *Family Circle* for $4.3 million in stock. See Stuart J. Emmrich, "*Family Circle* Marks 50th," *Advertising Age*, 6 September 1982, p. 10; James Playstead Wood, *Magazines in the United States*, 3rd edn (New York: The Ronald Press, 1971), pp. 293–303; Theodore Peterson, *Magazines in the Twentieth Century* (Urbana: University of Illinois Press, 1964), pp. 283–4, 288–90; and William H. Taft, *American Magazines for the 1980s* (New York: Hastings House Publishers, 1982.)

9. See Wood, p. 295.
10. E. Barbara Phillips has argued that in order to reassure readers, magazines like *Family Circle* continue to glorify traditional values when women's roles are in fact changing. (See "Magazines' Heroines: Is *Ms.* Just Another Member of the *Family Circle*?" in *Hearth and Home*, eds Tuchman *et al.* (New York: Oxford University Press, 1978), p. 124.) Certainly this is part of their ideological function. *Woman's Day*, for example, prints a quotation from the Bible at the top of the table of contents page each month. One article, "How Strong is Your Family Life?" asks readers to complete a quiz to see if their family "measures up" to a certain ideal. The opening paragraph notes: "The American family has seen a dizzying succession of changes in recent years – alternative lifestyles, unconventional relationships. . . Yet, even in today's technological world, the family reigns supreme. It still does some things better than any other institution of society" (3 March 1983, p. 66). Another feature in the issue, "Back from the Brink of Divorce," upholds marriage and the family; it tells the stories of four couples who got back together after separating and reassures readers, "Yes, you can recover from a close call with divorce" (p. 92). However, it is important to add to Phillips' thesis. Magazines such as *Woman's Day* and *Family Circle* also try to integrate modernity in a balance with the traditional in order to attract a wide range of readers.
11. See Ira Ellenthal, "Profile: Ellen Levine," *Folio*, April 1983, pp. 68–70.
12. See "*Woman's Day* Gets New Look," *Advertising Age*, 7 February 1983, p. 60.
13. See *Woman's Day* advertisement, *Advertising Age*, 15 November 1982, pp. 46–7. Other ads in this series include one that pictures a young woman sitting in a jeep outside a country store reading *Woman's Day* and another with a slender, tanned woman sunbathing beneath palm trees with a copy of *Woman's Day* at her side. See ads in *Advertising Age*, 18 October 1982, pp. 26–7 and 28 February 1983, pp. 33–4.
14. Berger, *Ways of Seeing*, p. 132.
15. Thorstein Veblen, *The Theory of the Leisure Class* (New York: New American Library, 1953; originally published 1899), p. 126.
16. *The Folio: 400/1984*, p. 49.
17. Frequently *Family Circle*'s ads in *Advertising Age* present the testimony of satisfied advertisers whose sales increased beyond expectations because of an ad or editorial promotion in *Family Circle*. See, for example, the testimony of Saco Foods, 21 June 1982, pp. 22–3 and 8 November 1982, pp. 25–6; and Maytag, 26 April 1982, pp. 22–3.
18. George W. Bryan, first publisher, cited in Peterson, *Magazines in the Twentieth Century*, p. 215.

19. Norton Simon sold *McCall's* in 1973. McCall's Publishing Company, privately held by the Pritcher family of Chicago (owner of Hyatt Corporation) earned 90 per cent of its $110 million in revenue in 1982 from its flagship publication *McCall's* magazine. In 1982 Time Inc. in partnership with Lang Communications bought *McCall's*, selling the magazine three years later to the New York Times Magazine Group. (See *Los Angeles Times*, 24 September 1973, I, p. 16; "100 Leading Media Companies," *Advertising Age*, 27 June 1983, p. M-58; Geraldine Fabrikant, "Time Takes a New Approach," *New York Times*, 20 November 1986, pp. D-1 and D-5; and "1989: The Year in Review," *Publishing News*, January 1990, p. 38.)
20. In 1980, for example, the other seven sisters magazines each sold between 160 and 193 ads for smoking materials which *Good Housekeeping* was forced to replace with other advertising (see *Cosmopolitan Research*, March 1982, p. AS-12).
21. See Frank Luther Mott, *A History of American Magazines*, Vol. 5 (Cambridge, MA: Harvard University Press, 1968), pp. 137–42.
22. Advertisement, *Advertising Age*, 8 November 1982, p. 7. See also ads in *Advertising Age*, 14 June 1982, pp. 22–3 and 24 May 1982, p. 7, and Bernice Kanner, "Women's Magazines Learn new Ways to Store's Heart," *Advertising Age*, 30 October 1978, pp. 60ff which reports that the seal boosted the sale of Stove Top Stuffing 56.7 per cent, Lucky Charms Cereal 70.8 per cent and Morton Salt 3 per cent.
23. *The Folio: 400/1984*, p. 329; see also advertisement, *New York Times*, 9 February 1984, p. D24.
24. *Women and Advertising: A Motivational Study of the Attitudes of Women Toward Eight Magazines* (New York: *Good Housekeeping* Magazine, 1954) cited in C. H. Sandage and Vernon Fryburger, *Advertising Theory and Practice*, 6th edn (Homewood, Illinois: Richard D. Irwin Inc., 1963), p. 438.
25. *McCall's* told readers that it instituted the feature as a challenge to see if it could successfully apply the information and ideas from its service pages to the life of one reader (September 1982, p. 76). The magazine's story to advertisers, however, was different. In a trade journal *McCall's* called the feature the "Reader of the Year publicity campaign," listed sponsors by name, and enjoined potential advertisers: "Picture your products in *McCall's* next Reader of the Year issue. Insure your participation now." See, advertisement, *Advertising Age*, 16 August 1982, pp. 25–8.
26. Advertisement, *Advertising Age*, 16 August 1982, p. 26.
27. See, for example, Camilla R. Bittle, "Precious Moment," *Good Housekeeping*, October 1983, pp. 166–7; Isobel Stewart, "In the Arms of Love," *Good Housekeeping*, May 1981, pp. 154–5; Marsha Portnoy, "Loving Strangers," *McCall's*, February 1983, pp. 88ff; and Jessie Schell, "Two Against One," *McCall's*, October 1983, pp. 154ff.
28. See Cecelia Reed, "*McCall's* Works to Keep Dialog Going," *Advertising Age*, 18 October 1984, p. 43.
29. See *The Folio: 400/1983*, pp. 480–7; "No *Redbook* Changes Foreseen by New Owner," *Advertising Age*, 9 June 1975, p. 8; "Charter's Dim Hopes for a Second Empire," *Business Week*, 23 November 1981, p. 46; Leah Rozen, "Blyth Leaving 'FC' for Top Post at 'LJH'," *Advertising Age*, 27 April 1981, p. 14; "For the Record," *Advertising Age*, 5 April 1982, p. 67; "Last Minute

News," *Advertising Age*, 3 May 1982, p. 1; and "Charter Sells 'LJII', Others," *Advertising Age*, 12 July 1982, p. 3.

30. Advertisement, *Advertising Age*, 14 February 1983, pp. 24–5.
31. See "Last Minute News," *Advertising Age*, 25 October 1982, p. 1 and 17 January 1983, p. 8; advertisement, *Advertising Age*, 22 November 1982, cover 3; "Last Minute News," *Advertising Age*, 20 September 1982, p. 8; "For the Record," *Advertising Age*, 23 August 1982, p. 49, and 20 December 1982, p. 37; "Last Minute News," *Advertising Age*, 28 February 1983, p. 8; "Ad beat," *Advertising Age*, 23 May 1983, p. 88; and advertisement, *New York Times*, 5 December 1983, p. A20.
32. *The Folio: 400/1984*, pp. 329, 339, and advertisement, p. 339. After the first half of 1984, however, *Redbook* claimed that its news-stand sales were up 10 per cent. In 1985 it told advertisers that its circulation was 404,000 over the published rate base and that the median age of its readers, 36.8, made it the only major women's service magazine with a median age under 40. See *Redbook*'s advertisement, *New York Times*, 27 September 1985, p. 50.
33. So termed by Sandra Forsyth Enos, Articles Editor, *Ladies' Home Journal*, quoted in Bernadine Clark, "The Women's Magazine Rack," *Writer's Digest*, June 1983, p. 25.
34. *The Folio: 400/1983*, p. 492.
35. *The Folio: 400/1984*, p. 333.
36. See Peterson, *Magazines in the Twentieth Century*, p. 384; Wood, *Magazines in the United States*, pp. 387–8; *The Folio: 400/1984*, pp. 329–36; and SMRB, *The 1982 Study of Media and Markets*, Vol. M-7, p. 0004.
37. Offering between 130 and 150 separate advertising editions each month, *Better Homes and Gardens* targets separate regions of the country, specific states, and even parts of states, along with fifty-six individual cities known as "top markets." Several advertising editions reach only upscale readers. Discounts are given to food advertisers purchasing space in special recipe sections and to companies buying ads in the "Family Health" sections. These multiple options attract many advertisers: the magazine's 1983 ad revenue totalled $109,038,000, the second largest in the country of all monthlies, surpassed only by *Good Housekeeping*. See SRDS, 27 July 1983, pp. 249–51; Jack Hafferkamp, "Magazines: Prognosis Bodes Well for a Steady Recovery," *Advertising Age*, 17 October 1983, pp. M-9ff, and *The Folio: 400/1984*, p. 87.
38. *Cosmopolitan Research*, March 1982, p. AS-12.
39. See advertisements in *Advertising Age*, 9 August 1982, p. 35; 26 April 1982, pp. 36–7; 12 April 1982, pp. 57–8; and 13 September 1982, p. 21.

7 NEW WORKERS AND CAREER WOMEN: TAPPING A NEW GENERATION OF SPENDERS

1. Robert Stein, Editor of *McCall's*, noted, "In the 1960s *McCall's*, like other women's service magazines, pushed for large circulation with the mistaken idea that was the way to compete with TV." Quoted in Nancy Yoshihara, "Women's Magazine Dilemma: Who Are They For?" *Los Angeles Times*, 23 December 1979, IV, p. 5.

2. Bob Donath, "Magazines Hang Hats on Special Interests," *Advertising Age*, 18 November 1974, p. 1.
3. Lynn T. Weiner, *From Working Girl to Working Mother* (Chapel Hill: University of North Carolina Press, 1985), p. 4.
4. *The Folio: 400/1981*, p. 188.
5. See N. R. Kleinfield, "Major Magazines Losing Ad Pages," *New York Times*, 5 May 1981, pp. D-1 and D-12.
6. Cited in Yoshihara, "Women's Magazine Dilemma," p. 5.
7. See Norma Green, "*Woman News* Victim of Tight Economy; Earlier Feminist Books Thrive," *Advertising Age*, 28 October 1974, p. 53.
8. Yoshihara, "Women's Magazine Dilemma," p. 5.
9. Constantine Kazanas of Knapp Communications, quoted in Tom Ashbrook, "Does Your Magazine Want You?" *The Boston Globe*, 15 February 1983, pp. 35 and 40.
10. *Newsweek Woman 1982* (brochure).
11. 1983 rates. See SRDS, 27 July 1983, pp. 347 and 545. In addition to *Newsweek Woman*'s standard low rate, several discounts are available. Advertisers who place an ad in a regular *Newsweek* edition receive a 10 per cent discount on their *Newsweek Woman* ad, and the standard frequency discounts are available.
12. According to the publicity brochure, for example, 94 per cent of the readers of *Newsweek Woman* do not read *Working Woman*, 88 per cent do not read *Mademoiselle*, and 74 per cent do not read *Woman's Day*.
13. *Newsweek Woman* is published once a month; to find the dates for a given calendar year, see the magazine's entry in SRDS.
14. Letter from Mueller to McCracken, 21 May 1982.
15. Laura Green, "Hard to Get Start-Up Money," *Los Angeles Times*, 18 December 1981, IV, p. 27 and *Cosmopolitan Research*, March 1982, p. C-6.
16. Advertisement, *Advertising Age*, 14 December 1981, p. 75 and *The Folio: 400/1984*, p. 311.
17. See Philip H. Dougherty, "Savvy Is as *Savvy* Does," *New York Times* 19 December 1980, p. D-13; Laura Green, "Hard to Get Start-Up Money," p. 27; advertisement, *Advertising Age*, 14 December 1981, p. 75; and *The Folio: 400/1983*, p. 311. In a June 1982 interview, founding Editor Daniels noted that the Savvy Company would welcome a takeover by Playboy Enterprises, which was considering the purchase. One month later it was announced that Daniels had resigned, was filing a suit to settle her contract, and that the magazine might be sold to American Express. Alan Bennett, Daniel's original partner, remained as Publisher and Wendy Reid Crisp succeeded Daniels as Editor in late 1982. In early 1985 *Savvy* was acquired by *Family Media* which appointed a new Publisher, Talia Carner, Cosmetics Marketing Manager at *Redbook* since 1981. See "*Savvy* Goes a Long Way," *Advertising Age*, 28 June 1982, p. M-16; "Press Time," *Advertising Age*, 2 August 1982, p. 8; and "Publisher for *Savvy*," *New York Times*, 27 March 1985, p. 47.
18. A notable exception is an instructive piece by Elaine Showalter printed in the column in May 1981. Showalter explains that the immense productivity of Victorian men such as Charles Dickens was only possible because of

a large network of servants, wives, mothers, daughters, and sisters who carried out routine tasks for the men, constituting an "invisible domestic machinery" (p. 79).

19. Philip Dougherty's term. See "Reaching Working Women," *New York Times*, 10 November 1978, p. D-15.
20. Advertisement, *Advertising Age*, 21 June 1976, p. 53.
21. Philip H. Dougherty, "*Working Woman* to Be Published," *New York Times*, 18 June 1976, p. D-11; Dougherty, "Reaching Working Women," p. D-15; and Bob Donath, "Rebuilt *Working Woman* Set to Lure Advertisers," *Advertising Age*, 6 June 1977, p. 6.
22. Philip H. Dougherty, "Tic-Tac Toe in the Confection Trade," *New York Times*, 3 June 1977, p. D-7; *Who's Who in American Women*, 1984–85, p. 484; Philip Dougherty, "Dale Lang Acquires Women's Magazine," *New York Times*, 31 January 1978, p. 40; "Magazines that Mirror Women's Success," *Business Week*, 11 January 1982, pp. 39–40. For a detailed account of the struggle between Frankel and Buckler for control of *Working Woman*, see Donath, p. 6.
23. Advertisement, *Advertising Age*, 26 April 1982, p. M-45; see also "Magazines that Mirror Women's Success," p. 39; Dougherty, "Reaching Working Women," p. D-13; and *Who's Who in American Women*, 1984–1985, p. 786.
24. *The Folio: 400/1984*, p. 311.
25. Horton cited in Nancy Josephson, "As Romance Cools, Computer Magazines Heat Up," *Advertising Age*, 17 October 1983, pp. M-42 – M-43; Kate Rand Lloyd, "Stereotypes Don't Pay Today," *Advertising Age*, 26 July 1982, pp. M-14ff; and Dougherty, "Reaching Working Women," p. D-13. Horton was the former Group Vice-President of Playboy Enterprises; when he came to *Working Woman* in 1978, the claimed rate base of 200,000 actually represented 90,000 subscribers. Under Horton the fiction and articles on needlecraft were dropped; by the first quarter of 1982, *Working Woman*'s ad volume surpassed that of *Ladies' Home Journal* and *McCall's* during that period and moved close to *Redbook*'s and that of *Woman's Day*. See Stuart Emmrich, "*Working Woman* Enters 7 Sisters' Turf," *Advertising Age*, 19 April 1982, p. 24. With the June 1983 issue Kate Rand Lloyd became Editor-at-Large and Gay Bryant succeeded her as Editor. Bryant was succeeded in 1985 by Anne Mollegen-Smith.
26. SMRB, *The 1982 Study of Media and Markets*, Vol. M-7, pp. 0047, 0059, 0065, and 0269.
27. Laurie Ashcraft, "Ads Start to Roll with the Social Punches," *Advertising Age*, 26 July 1982, pp. M-24 – M-26.
28. See Stuart J. Elliot, "*Working Mother* Likes Niche," *Advertising Age*, 17 October 1983, p. 58 and advertisement, *Advertising Age*, 9 May 1983, p. 29.
29. Frank Luther Mott, *A History of American Magazines 1885–1905*, Vol. IV, p. 580; *The Folio: 400/1984*, p. 329; and SRDS, 27 July 1983, p. 575.
30. March 1982 figures show that almost half of married women in the US with pre-school-aged children were employed as were over half of unmarried mothers with pre-school children. See Weiner, p. 141.
31. In the May 1983 issue, for example, there were 27 ad pages for food plus 7

for household products, 17 for childcare aids, toys and children's clothing, 10 for beauty products and toiletries, $6\frac{1}{2}$ for cigarettes, 3 for women's apparel, and 1 for cars.

32. SMRB, *The 1982 Study of Media and Markets*, Vol. P-28, pp. 0096–0097.
33. Cecelia Lentini, ". . . To the New," *Advertising Age*, 26 July 1982, p. M-32.
34. See "Editorial Description," *The Folio: 400/1984*, p. 340.
35. The Bureau of Labor Statistics forecasts that two-thirds of the women between 25 and 54 will be in the workforce by 1990. See Weiner, p. 141.
36. The official circulation figure that *New Woman* guarantees to advertisers is in fact much lower: 1,029,735 in 1983, for example. Nonetheless, this number was double that of *Working Woman*, *Ms.*, and *Working Mother* that year, triple that of *Savvy*, and nearly equal to that of *Self*, *Vogue*, and *Mademoiselle*. See *The Folio: 400/1984*, pp. 311 and 319.
37. Quoted in "*New Woman* to Aim at 'Exciting Females,'" *Advertising Age*, 30 November 1970, p. 12.
38. *Ibid.*, p. 12.
39. "Women's Magazines: One Up, One Down," *New York Times*, 20 June 1972, p. 60 and "*New Woman* Suspends Publication until February 1973," *Advertising Age*, 26 June 1972, p. 98.
40. See "Murdoch Buys Magazine," *New York Times*, 26 May 1984, p. 34; "Murdoch Organization Acquires *New Woman* Plans Move to NYC," *Folio*, August 1984, p. 55; and Philip H. Dougherty, "Publisher for One of 7 Sisters," *New York Times*, 30 January 1985, p. D-19. Despite the remarkable comeback after its rough start, *New Woman*'s revenue and circulation declined somewhat before it was put up for sale in January 1984. While its ad volume rose 16.5 per cent in 1983, its ad revenue was down 9.7 per cent from 1982 and total revenue declined 4.6 per cent. Subscription revenue was also down 4.6 per cent and news-stand circulation, although extremely high compared to other magazines, was down 10 per cent from the previous year. Sensing the magazine's potential, however, publishing giants such as CBS and Gruner & Jahr competed against Murdoch in the bid to buy *New Woman*. See *The Folio: 400/1984*, p. 315 and "Murdoch Organization Acquires *New Woman*," p. 55.
41. For an excellent study of the use of modernity to disguise traditional messages in Latin American women's magazines, see Michele Mattelart, "Notes on 'Modernity': A Way of Reading Women's Magazines," *Communication and Class Struggle*, Vol. I, trans. Mary C. Axtmann, eds Armand Mattelart and Seth Siegelaub (New York: International General, 1979).

8 REACHING MINORITY WOMEN: LANGUAGE, CULTURE, AND POLITICS IN THE SERVICE OF CONSUMERISM

1. Cited in Philip H. Dougherty, "Advertising: A Magazine for Negro Women," *New York Times*, 11 February 1970, p. 71.
2. Philip Dougherty, "Advertising: ANA Forms Unit to Study Agency-Client Problem," *New York Times*, 31 July 1970, p. 44; Dougherty, "Advertising: New Black Magazines Planned," *New York Times*, 8 December 1971, p. 108; and Dougherty, "Advertising: Marketing Ecology," *New York*

Times, 5 October 1972, p. 77.

3. Cited in C. Gerald Fraser, "Ousted *Essence* Magazine Chief Accuses *Playboy*," *New York Times*, 6 May 1971, p. 31.
4. See Fraser, p. 31 and "Statement of Ownership," *Essence*, December 1983, p. 134.
5. *The Folio: 400/1984*, p. 133 and *Folio*, September 1984, p. 100.
6. To end my pestering my friend
   said okay I'll come over and show you how you dred
   your hair. She came by and told me I
   should take a shower and apply a little bit
   of plain shampoo then rinse.
   I did and when I asked her, "Well, now what!"
   She said, "That's it!"
   And I been dredding ever since.
   (*Essence*, August 1983, p. 124)
7. Ad, *New York Times*, 6 December 1984, p. A-19.
8. Soto and Maese quoted in Juana E. Duty, "Creating a Magazine for Latino Women," *Los Angeles Times*, 3 January 1983, V, pp. 1, 4.
9. Conversation with Grace Soto, LULAC Convention, Anaheim, CA, 30 June 1985.
10. Magazines such as *Ebony* and *Jet* have long attracted male and female Black readers; in the early 1980s *Black Family* and *Travis* were launched for general Black audiences; *Elan* and *Flair* were shortlived magazines for Black women also founded in the early 1980s. *Essence* remains the only magazine for Black women that has survived.
11. US Department of Commerce, Bureau of the Census, "Conditions of Hispanics in America Today" (Washington, D.C.: US Government Printing Office, 1983), p. 8.
12. SRDS, 27 May 1982, pp. 577–9.
13. See SRDS, 27 October 1983, p. 646. It is important to note, however, that according to Armando De Armas, head of the publishing conglomerate, 85–95 per cent of the foreign advertising in the separate Latin American editions of his magazines is purchased by United States companies. See Anne B. Freedman, "Upscale Latin Magazines Prospering," *Advertising Age*, 2 June 1980, p. 51.
14. For an explanation of licensing agreements for international editions of such magazines as *Good Housekeeping*, *Cosmopolitan*, and *Bazaar*, see Lee Boaz Hall, "International Licensing for Special Interest Magazines," *Folio*, October 1984, pp. 90–5ff. Paralleling De Armas' immense influence on Latin American women through his company's numerous publications, is his successful venture into Venezuelan politics through the purchase of two important Caracas newspapers – *2001*, a tabloid widely read by blue-collar workers, and *Meridiano*, a sports newspaper. Since the purchase of these two mass-market publications in 1970, De Armas' interests in Venezuela have gained four national congressional seats. See Freedman, p. 51.
15. *Claudia*'s masthead lists Rómulo O'Farrill, Jr. as President of Mex-Ameris, Hilda O'Farrill Avila de Compean as Editor-in-Chief (also the Editor of the society page of *Novedades*), and L. Janine Jarero de O'Farrill as

Executive Assistant. *Vogue*'s masthead also lists Hilda O'Farrill de Compean as President and Rómulo O'Farrill, Jr. as President of the Administrative Council.

16. See Santa Cruz and Erazo, *Compropolitan*, pp. 44–5; García Calderón, *Revistas femeninas*, pp. 22, 34–35; and Jesús M. Aguirre, "Un Hearst Latino americano: El bloque De Armas," *Comunicación: Estudios venozolanos de comunicación*, 1981, pp. 30–1. In November 1982 Editorial América bought seven magazines from Mexico's TV monopoly Televisa, including Mexico's leading *TV-Guide*-type magazine, *Teleguia*; see "World News Roundup," *Advertising Age*, 29 November 1982, p. 3.
17. See Santa Cruz and Erazo, *Compropolitan*, pp. 42 and 86.
18. "*Vanidades, Buenhogar, Cosmopolitan en español* Readership Survey, U.S. Edition" (pamphlet), (New York: Saral Publications, 1978), p. 6.
19. Santa Cruz and Erazo, *Compropolitan*, pp. 86 and 56.
20. See, for example, "Timbiriche Sings and Laughs," August 1982, pp. 122–3; "A New Program: Treasure of Knowledge," September 1982, p. 40; and "Another's Love: The Vicissitudes of a Soap Opera," April 1983, pp. 48ff. Frequently, too, regular ads for other media to which the O'Farrill family is connected appear in *Claudia*, including the newspaper *Novedades* (May and June 1982 and March and July 1983), the Mexican *Vogue* (February, March and June 1982 and April and July 1983), and Televisa (January, August, and July 1982 and March and July 1983).
21. See García Calderón, *Revistas femeninas*, pp. 106–9.
22. See, for example, the 24 November 1981 issue in which "Festival of cocktails" gives instructions for preparing fancy drinks from the Dominican Republic and "Refreshing drinks," presents further recipes for elaborate cocktails. "Your bar" in the 21 July 1981 issue tells readers how to prepare "exquisite and original" cocktails with expensive liqueurs and flavorings (pp. 56–7). The 8 December 1981 special Christmas issue contains four features on preparing fancy drinks.
23. See "Notes on 'Modernity': A Way of Reading Women's Magazines," pp. 160–1.
24. See Barthes, *Mythologies*, pp. 78–80.
25. Advertisement, *Advertising Age*, 25 May 1981, p. S-20.
26. See "*Vanidades, Buenhogar, Cosmopolitan en español*: Readership Survey, U.S. Edition," pp. 8–9.
27. "Ad Linage," *Advertising Age*, 23 January 1984, p. 68 and SRDS, 27 May 1982, p. 577.
28. SRDS, 27 May 1982, p. 576.
29. *Cosmopolitan de Mexico* April 1973, quoted in García Calderón, *Revistas femeninas*, p. 77.
30. "Cosmopolitan Readership Profile 1979–80," De Armas Publications.
31. See SRDS, 27 May 1982, pp. 577–8 and "*Vanidades, Buenhogar, Cosmopolitan en español*: Readership Survey, U.S. Edition," pp. 7–9. The total ad page figures for the Mexican, Colombian, and US editions are as follows:

	1982	1983
Mexico	789.5	605.2
Colombia	569.0	456.0
United States	193.0	176.0

See "Ad Linage," *Advertising Age*, 23 January 1984, p. 68.

32. See Anna Lucía Zornosa, "Collaboration and Modernization: Case-Study of a Transnational Magazine," *Studies in Latin American Popular Culture* 2 (1983), 24–35.
33. See "Querido Cosmo," *Cosmopolitan en español*, January 1981, p. 6.
34. For excellent studies of the roots of women's attraction to such forms as the romance novel and the soap opera see Radway, *Reading the Romance*, especially pp. 85–109 and Modleski, *Loving with a Vengeance*.

9 CLASS NOT MASS: SPECIAL-INTEREST PUBLICATIONS AND PSEUDO-INDIVIDUALIZED CONSUMPTION

1. See Goffman, *Gender Advertisements*, pp. 46 and 57.
2. Susie Orbach, *Fat is a Feminist Issue* (New York: Berkley Publishing Corporation, 1978), p. 21.
3. Editor Bruce Clerke, cited in Christy Marshall, "New Women's Magazine Aims Big," *Advertising Age*, 2 March 1981, p. 40.
4. See Sharon Barrett, "*It's Me*: Making a Size 14 Fashionable," *Los Angeles Times*, 15 May 1981, V, p. 18 and Carl Gannon, "*It's Me*: Fashions for Over Size 16," *Los Angeles Times*, 23 March 1982, IV, p. 5.
5. The feature was so successful that in the June 1983 issue the Editor announced that the want-ads would appear from then on as a separate publication available by subscription, instead of in *BBW*.
6. See Brett Silverstein *et al.*, "The Role of the Mass Media in Promoting a Thin Standard of Bodily Attractiveness for Women," *Sex Roles* 14 (1986), 519–32. The authors show, for example, that in four popular women's service magazines, readers are encouraged to stay in shape and be slim while at the same time thinking about food and cooking; women receive many more such messages than do men in popular men's magazines.
7. *Women's Sports* Rate Card, No. 4, October 1981.
8. Senior Editor Cathy Perlmutter, cited in Bernadine Clark, "The Women's Magazine Rack," *Writer's Digest*, June 1983, p. 45.
9. *Women's Sports 1980–81 Subscriber Study* (brochure), p. i.
10. *Women's Sports Magazine Audience Profile* (brochure).
11. Telephone interview with *Women's Sports'* Editor Amy Rennert, 29 June 1982.
12. CBS purchased *Modern Bride* from Ziff-Davis in late 1984; in 1987, however, CBS put its entire magazine division up for sale.
13. Theodore Peterson, *Magazines in the Twentieth Century* (Urbana: University of Illinois Press, 1964), pp. 262–3 and 272.
14. See *The Folio: 400/1983*, p. 136 and "Ad Linage," *Advertising Age*, 21 February 1983, p. 56.

15. Quoted in Anna Sobczynski, "Bridal Books' Success Wed Traditional Values," *Advertising Age*, 18 October 1984, p. 44.
16. See, for example, *The Folio: 400/1981*, p. 96.
17. See Sobczynski, "Bridal Books' Success," p. 44.
18. See Anna Sobczynski, "Answering Parents' Cries for Help, Advice," *Advertising Age*, 18 October 1984, p. 42.
19. Advertisement, *New York Times Magazine*, 16 September 1984, p. 109.
20. SRDS, 27 July 1983, p. 237.
21. Peterson, *Magazines in the Twentieth Century*, pp. 217 and 269.
22. See "*House & Garden*'s New Focus," *New York Times*, 7 July 1984, pp. 33ff; advertisement, *Advertising Age*, 28 February 1983, pp. 25–6; and *The Folio: 400/1984*, p. 210.
23. Advertisement, SRDS, 27 July 1983, p. 162.
24. SRDS, 27 July 1983, p. 164.
25. *The Folio: 400/1984*, p. 188.
26. For details of the magazine's quality control, see Karlene Lukovitz, "Color for Connoisseurs: Four Studies in Quality Printing," *Folio*, August 1982, pp. 68ff. In fact, *Gourmet*'s standards of acceptibility are partially responsible for the small amount of food and soft drink advertising in the magazine – only 6.6 per cent of total ad space. In contrast, travel advertising is *Gourmet*'s top ad category, correlating to the magazine's high level of travel editorial – 48 per cent. See Stuart J. Elliot, "Conde Nast Has *Gourmet* Cooking," *Advertising Age*, 24 September 1984, p. 104.
27. See "ABC Magazine Publisher's Statement," 31 December 1981, p. 46 and "*Bon Appetit* Research Report, MRI," Spring 1982.
28. See, for example, readers' letters to *Playgirl* which express this belief: "Operating Equipment," April 1982, p. 6 and "Raised Ire," August 1983, p. 6.
29. In fact, *Playgirl*'s owner, Ritter-Geller Communications, also publishes *Slimmer* which, as we have seen, also commodifies women sexually by presenting them through an implicit male optic.
30. SRDS lists *Playgirl*'s total paid circulation as 674,381; see 27 July 1983, p. 562.
31. For further details about the founding of *Ms.*, see "A Personal Report from *Ms.*," *Ms.*, July 1972, pp. 4–7; "Now Feminists Have Their Own Magazine – *Ms.*," *Advertising Age*, 1 November 1971, p. 8; "*Ms.* Gains Financial Help from Warner," *Advertising Age*, 22 May 1972, p. 96; and "How to Sell Magazines Today: As the Sellers See It," *Advertising Age*, 18 November 1974, pp. 54ff.
32. *The Folio: 400/1984*, p. 311 and "A Personal Report from *Ms.*," p. 7.
33. *The Folio: 400/1984*, p. 311.
34. See "Now Feminists Have Their Own Magazine – *Ms.*," p. 8.
35. Quoted in "How to Sell Magazines Today: As the Sellers See It," pp. 136, 137.
36. See "A Personal Report from *Ms.*," p. 7.
37. A column entitled "A henna head trip," for example, appears across from a shampoo ad featuring Victoria Principal with voluminous red-tinted hair and another feature, "A salad for your face," offers indirect support to the Maybelline make-up ad on the facing page (May 1983, pp. 44–5 and

116–17). In 1984 *Ms.*, announced a special advertorial insert on travel; purchase of ads entitled travel advertisers to mention in the advertorial section (see Philip H. Dougherty, "Advertising," *New York Times* 27 November 1984, p. D-29.) Although *Ms.* uses a number of the techniques of covert advertising discussed in Chapter 2, it does so less frequently than do most women's magazines. Coexisting with this editorial support for ads, however, are contradictions between advertising and editorial messages.

38. "How to Sell Magazines Today," p. 137.
39. See Mariana Valverde, "The Class Struggles of the *Cosmo* Girl and the *Ms.* Woman," *Heresies* 5, No. 2 (1985), p. 81.
40. See *The Folio: 400/1984*, p. 311.

10 ACQUISITIONS, NEW LAUNCHES, AND ADAPTATIONS: WOMEN'S MAGAZINES ENTER THE 1990s

1. See James B. Kobak, "1984: A Billion Dollar Year for Acquisitions," *Folio*, April 1985, pp. 82–95; "On Deadline," *Folio*, January 1985, p. 7; N. R. Kleinfield, "CBS to Buy 12 of Ziff's Magazines," *New York Times*, 21 November 1984, pp. D-1 and D-5; "Briefings," *Folio*, June 1985, pp. 11–12; and "CBS Set to Sell Magazine Division," *Santa Barbara News Press*, 14 July 1987, p. B-4.
2. "Ten Newsmakers of 1987," *Advertising Age*, 28 December 1987, p. 15 and Patrick Reilly, "Diamandis Hits Goal," *Advertising Age*, 19 October 1987, p. 1.
3. See Karlene Lukovitz, "Peter Diamandis: The Making of the $25 Million Man," *Publishing News*, Pilot Issue (1988), pp. 67–72; Patrick Reilly, "A Gold Rush for U.S. Titles," *Advertising Age*, 18 April 1988, pp. 1 and 90; Patrick Reilly, "Second Time's the Charm in Hachette Pursuit of DCI," *Advertising Age*, 18 April 1988, p. 90 and "Hachette's Blueprints for Growth," *Folio*, June 1988, p. 34.
4. See Kurt Eichenwald, "Murdoch Agrees to Buy *TV Guide* in a $3 Billion Sale by Annenberg," and James Hirsch, "Murdoch's Odd Trio: TV, Teens, and Track," *New York Times*, 8 August 1988, pp. 1 and C-6.
5. Burnett cited in "Meredith Won't Tinker with Added Magazines," *New York Times*, 25 November 1985, p. D-2; see also "Family Media Turns to Chic," *Folio*, April 1988, pp. 57–8; "Family Media, Inc." *New York Times*, 8 February 1985, p. D-3; Philip H. Dougherty, "Advertising" and "Global Marketing Debated," *New York Times*, 27 March 1985, p. D-21 and 13 November 1985, p. D-21; *The Folio: 400/1986*, pp. 65, 158, 159 and 185; "Rising Above the Crowd: Magazines with the Most," *Advertising Age*, 14 April 1988, p. S-13 and Jennet Conant *et al.*, "What Women Want to Read," *Newsweek*, 23 February 1987, p. 67.
6. "Family Media Turns to Chic," p. 57 and "Briefings," *Folio*, June 1988, p. 7.
7. Geraldine Fabrikant, "Time Takes a New Approach," *New York Times*, 21 November 1986, pp. D-1 and D-5; Stuart J. Elliot, "Time Inc. Shows Ardor for Women," *Advertising Age*, 24 November 1986, pp. 2 and 81; and "1989: The Year in Review," *Publishing News*, January 1990, p. 38.

8. See Leslie Wayne, "Australia Concern to Buy *Ms*.," *New York Times*, 24 September 1987, pp. D-1 and D-4 and Bruce Horovitz, "Media Group Buys Struggling *Ms*. Magazine, Promises Funds," *Los Angeles Times*, 24 September 1987, IV, pp. 1 and 4.
9. See advertisement, *Advertising Age*, 18 April 1988, p. S-15; John Gabree, "New *Ms*. Has a Few New Twists," *Los Angeles Times*, 5 February 1988, V, pp. 1 and 8; and "The *Ms*. Reporter," *Ms*., February 1988, pp. 17–33.
10. See "Briefings," *Folio*, June 1988, pp. 7–8 and Garry Abrams, "A New Duo Seizes the Reins at *Ms*.," *Los Angeles Times*, 4 August 1988, V, pp. 1 and 7.
11. See Diedre Carmody, "*Ms*. Magazine Prepares for a Life Without Ads," *New York Times*, 5 March 1990, p. D-9; Paul Farhi, "*Ms*. Magazine: The Sequel," *Washington Post*, 5 March 1990, pp. D-1ff; Pat Guy, "*Ms*. Divorces Ads," *USA Today*, 5 March 1990, p. 2B; Susan Hovey, "A Radical Vows to Take *Ms*. Back to Its Roots," *Folio*, March 1990, pp. 41–2; and Jan Jaben, "Can *Ms*. Survive?" *Publishing News*, December 1989, pp. 1 and 61.
12. See Lang Communications' press release of 13 October 1989, "*Ms*. and *Sassy* Deal Completed by Dale W. Lang." Lang noted: "We are seeking a profitable, alternative way to publish *Ms*."
13. Quoted in "*Ms*. Magazine: The Sequel," p. D-1.
14. Richard W. Stevenson, "Fitness Magazine Explosion," *New York Times*, natl. ed., 15 June 1985, p. 19. Bob Anderson, Publisher of *Fit*, after selling his *Runner's World* to Rodale Press in 1985, launched *Swimwear Illustrated*, a catalogue in magazine form to market his mail-order swimsuits, Ujena of California. By 1987 it had attained a news-stand circulation of 225,000, and Anderson followed up with a large-size publication, *Bikini*. See John Gabree, "A Monthly That Speaks Teentalk," *Los Angeles Times*, 18 February 1988, V, p. 8.
15. Cited in Stevenson, p. 22.
16. See Stevenson, pp. 19 and 22 and SRDS, 27 May 1988, p. 629.
17. "1987: Turnaround Year for Consumer Titles," *Folio*, April 1988, p. 44.
18. SRDS, 27 May 1988, pp. 607–8; "1987: Turnaround Year," p. 44; and "Didier Guerin: French Connections," *Folio*, March 1988, p. 56.
19. See Geraldine Fabrikant, "Wooing the Wealthy Reader," *New York Times*, natl. ed., 14 October 1987, pp. 29 and 33; "1987: Turnaround Year for Consumer Titles," p. 44; and SRDS, 27 May 1988, pp. 633 and 615. In July 1988, Hachette announced that *Elle* would begin publication in the People's Republic of China and be supported by an *Elle* brand of clothing which Hachette will manufacture there. See "*Elle* Looks to the East," *Folio*, August 1988, pp. 51–2.
20. See Patrick Reilly, "*Details*-Oriented: Newhouse Clout Helps Hip Book," *Advertising Age*, 14 March 1988, p. 55 and John Gabree, "*Details*, a Trendy Comer Among Fashion-Conscious Periodicals," *Los Angeles Times*, 24 March 1988, IV, pp. 1 and 7.
21. See "Family Media Turns to Chic," p. 57.
22. See Gabree, "A Monthly That Speaks Teentalk," pp. 1 and 8 and Jan Jaben, "*Sassy* Doubles Ad Projections Yet Competitors Feel 'No Effect,'" *Publishing News*, Pilot Issue (1988), p. 25.
23. See Skip Wollenberg, "*Sassy* Too Sexy for Teen Market?" *Santa Barbara*

News Press, 6 March 1988, p. D-1. For a serious critique of the style and content of the premiere issue of *Sassy*, see Gabree, "A Monthly That Speaks Teentalk."

24. See "*Sassy* Doubles Ad Projections" and *Sassy* Rate Card, Matilda Publications, June 1988, and Lang Communications Press Release, 13 October 1989.
25. For further information on the founding of *Lear's*, see Elizabeth Mehren, "In Her Own Image," *Los Angeles Times*, 21 February 1988, IV, pp. 1 and 12.
26. Patrick Reilly, "*Lear's* Second Issue Off and Running," *Advertising Age*, 18 April 1988, p. S-28 and "In Her Own Image," p. 12.
27. Cited in Bruce Horovitz, "Family's the 'In' Thing – And Publishers Know It," *Los Angeles Times*, 26 May 1987, IV, p. 9; see also "Briefings," *Folio*, July 1985, p. 11.
28. See Horovitz, "Family's the 'In' Thing"; John Peter, "Those Baby Magazines," *Folio*, October 1987, pp. 205–7 and J. Scot Finnie, "*American Baby*: Hungry for Growth," *Folio*, July 1988, pp. 63–4.
29. See Sue Hoover Epstein, "Triangle's Recipe for *Good Food*'s Relaunch," *Folio*, July 1985, pp. 41–2; "1987: Turnaround Year for Consumer Titles," p. 44; and "1989: The Year in Review," pp. 37–8.
30. See Sandra Salmans, "Video Is Drawing Publishers," *New York Times*, 18 April 1983, pp. D-1 and D-5 and "Magazines Find Video an Attractive Medium," *New York Times*, natl. ed., 11 July 1988, p. 30.
31. Steve Knoll, "Translating Magazines into Programs," *New York Times*, 29 July 1984, p. H-22; "P & G Backs Two Series for Daytime," *Advertising Age*, 28 March 1983, p. 12; Salmans, "Video Is Drawing Publishers"; and "Magazines Find Video an Attractive Medium."
32. See "P & G Backs Two Series for Daytime."
33. See "'Unwary Publishers May Get Burned by Cable': Levine," *Folio*, April 1983, pp. 12–13; Salmans, "Video Is Drawing Publishers," p. D-5 and "Magazines Find Video an Attractive Medium."
34. See "New Approach In Advertising," *New York Times*, natl. ed., 13 July 1988, p. 46; Patrick Reilly, "Rolling Out Posters," *Advertising Age*, 14 March 1988, p. 78 and Philip H. Dougherty, "*Outside*'s Publishers in New Venture," *New York Times*, natl. ed., 22 July 1988, p. 41.
35. "*Sassy* Merchandising Opportunities," *Sassy Media Kit*. For more information on new merchandising practices see Julie A. Laitin, "Merchandising '88: The Competitive Edge," *Folio*, June 1988, pp. 104–10.
36. "Ten Newsmakers of 1987," *Advertising Age*, 28 December 1987, p. 15; "Negotiating Teams Step Up Rate Pressure," *Folio*, April 1988, pp. 22–3; "1987: Turnaround Year for Consumer Titles," p. 44; and Warren Berger, "Trashing the Rate Card: Did It Work?" *Publishing News*, October 1989, pp. 35–7.
37. See advertisement for *Seventeen*, *Advertising Age*, 1 February 1988, p. 5; "Magazine Watch: Publishers of Adult Titles Diversify," *Folio*, October 1987, pp. 93–4 and Patrick Reilly, "*HG* Puts on New Face – Again," *Advertising Age*, 1 February 1988, p. 4.

CONCLUSION

1. Todorov, *The Poetics of Prose*, trans. Richard Howard (Ithaca, New York: Cornell University Press), p. 111.
2. For a critique of "text-centricity," see Laurie Schulze, "On the Muscle," in *Fabrications: Costume and the Female Body*, eds Jane Gaines and Charlotte Herzog (New York and London: Routledge, 1990), pp. 59–78.

Index